SO-AAZ-593

ALSO BY MELISSA FAY GREENE

Praying for Sheetrock

THE TEMPLE BOMBING

Melissa Fay Greene

FAWCETT COLUMBINE • NEW YORK

Many of the designations used by manufacturers and sellers to distinguish their products are claimed as trademarks. Where those designations appear in this book and the publisher was aware of a trademark claim, the designations have been printed in initial capital letters (i.e., Coca-Cola).

Sale of this book without a front cover may be unauthorized. If this book is coverless, it may have been reported to the publisher as "unsold or destroyed" and neither the author nor the publisher may have received payment for it.

A Fawcett Columbine Book
Published by Ballantine Books

Copyright © 1996 by Melissa Fay Greene

All rights reserved under International and Pan-American Copyright Conventions. Published in the United States by Ballantine Books, a division of Random House, Inc., New York, and distributed in Canada by Random House of Canada Limited, Toronto.

Unless otherwise noted, photographs are provided courtesy of the Jacob M. Rothschild Papers, Special Collections Department, Robert W. Woodruff Library, Emory University, Atlanta.

Permission granted by KTAV Publishing House, Inc., to quote from *Gates of Heaven* by Rabbi Chaim Stern. Copyright © 1970, 1979, and 1992.

http://www.randomhouse.com

Library of Congress Catalog Card Number: 97-90025

ISBN: 0-449-90809-7

This edition published by arrangement with Addison-Wesley Publishing, Inc.

Text design by Karen Savary
Cover design by Barbara Leff
Cover photo courtesy of The Temple, Atlanta

Manufactured in the United States of America

First Ballantine Books Edition: May 1997

10   9   8   7   6   5   4   3   2   1

CONTENTS

In loving memory of
my grandmother,
Mary Pollock

And with love to
my husband,
Don Samuel

The Gods we worship write their names on our faces, be sure of that. And a person will worship something, have no doubt of that either. One may think that tribute is paid in secret, in the dark recesses of his or her heart, but it is not. That which dominates imagination and thoughts will determine life and character. Therefore it behooves us to be careful what we are worshiping, for what we are worshiping we are becoming.

From GATES OF HEAVEN

PROLOGUE

OCTOBER 12, 1958
3:37 A.M.

Fifty sticks of dynamite in the middle of the night blew apart the side wall of the Temple, Atlanta's oldest and richest synagogue, which stood in pillared, domed majesty on a grassy hill above Peachtree Street.

The brick walls flapped upward like sheets on a line. Offices and Sunday school classrooms burst out of the building; the stairwell came unmoored and hung like a rope ladder; bronze plaques commemorating the war dead from the two world wars spun out like saucers; the stained-glass windows snapped outward, like tablecloths shaken after dinner; and all was momentarily red-hot, white-lit, and moving like lava. Then the strangely animate flying rooms and objects stood still—as in the childrens' game of musical chairs, the children freeze when the music stops—leaving erratic silhouettes and capricious statues of rubble, burst pipes, ashes, and mud, the whole of it colorfully twinkling in the quiet night from the bright bits of stained glass sprinkled over the scene.

The sound of the blast traveled heavily for miles, a locomotive of sound tearing through the city. Hundreds were startled awake by it, including Governor Marvin Griffin. Some fell out of their beds at the reverberation; windows in a nearby apartment building shattered; and one old lady, reared on Confederate lore, momentarily mistook the boom for renewed Union bombardment in the Battle of Atlanta.

Telephones at police headquarters and at the newspapers bottlenecked with inquiries and with reports of a "loud explosion." At 2:00 A.M. a United Press International (UPI) staff member had logged the receipt of a phone call warning that the bombing would be coming, but the call had been considered the work of "a crackpot" and the information had not been relayed to police. At 3:45 A.M. the UPI staff took another call, this one from "General Gordon of the Confederate Underground": "We bombed a temple in Atlanta. This is the last empty building in Atlanta that we will bomb. All nightclubs refusing to fire their Negro employees will also be blown up. We are going to blow up all Communist organizations. Negroes and Jews are hereby declared aliens." Meanwhile, police cruisers roamed up and down Peachtree, searching in vain for the cause of the thunderclap.

In the four hours between the registering of the sound of an explosion within the city limits and the discovery by a custodian that the historic Reform Jewish temple had been attacked, there were those in Atlanta who permitted themselves to hope that the noise had not come from a bomb. There were civic leaders who fell to imagining the demise of a gas furnace, an industrial mishap, or a backfiring road-maintenance vehicle. For though they lived in the Deep South in its era of mayhem, of violent white backlash to the federal government's proposed course on racial integration, the Atlanta civic leaders believed they had kept terrorism and race hate at bay.

The mayor, William Berry Hartsfield, was an old-fashioned, fair-minded white man. At the start of his political career, he had looked like Woodrow Wilson with his thin, sideways-combed hair and metal-rimmed spectacles; now, toward the end of twenty-five years in office, cheery and balding, he looked like Dwight Eisenhower. He had determined that Atlanta ought to move through the twentieth century without racial violence; he coined the phrase "The City Too Busy to Hate" and he sat down, when necessary, with black leaders. The chief of police, Herbert Jenkins, was a serious and decent man who, quite unlike his peers in other southern cities, conferred confidentially with the black elite in periods of racial friction. At the helm of the *Atlanta Constitution* stood Ralph McGill, the famous rumpled, broad-beamed, free-thinking, liberal-leaning, loved and hated southern editor, who stood up for the Supreme Court when it came to be despised below the Mason-Dixon line. "They used to say there are two types of people in the South," said the journalist George Goodwin: "Those that couldn't eat breakfast until they'd read Ralph McGill, and those that couldn't eat breakfast *after* they read Ralph McGill." And at the head of the board of directors of the Coca-Cola Corporation sat Robert W. Woodruff, an oil portrait of whom hung alone in the mayor's office, a man with an instinct for what was good for Atlanta in terms of business and in terms of human decency, whose quiet behind-the-scenes remarks steered millions of dollars and man-hours into constructive channels.

Atlanta thus, in the age of demagogues, with the rise of southern leaders like Herman Talmadge, Lester Maddox, Strom Thurmond, Ross Barnett, Harry Byrd, and George Wallace, was governed locally by fairly enlightened white authorities and inhabited by a population generally moderate in outlook. The young city stood on a rocky shelf of land overlooking the moist black-earthed cotton kingdom. Cotton, and human chattel, had passed through early Atlanta, and changed hands for cash in early Atlanta, without ever becoming the city's mainstays. So the burdens and tasks of the twentieth century had been taken up a bit easier here; the adaptations to modern life had not required, initially, so complete a social revolution as was required in the slave belt.

Atlanta's white citizens were largely apolitical, optimistic, taught by their business leaders to be concerned with modern business affairs, prepared to enter the mainstream of American progress and enterprise. They cheerfully had forgotten the brutish incidents that had taken place on their own soil a few decades earlier: in 1906 the Atlanta Race Riot had been front-page news all over the world, when enraged white mobs roamed through the city on a rumor, destroying black people's houses and murdering dozens of black citizens. In 1915 a Jewish cotton-mill manager was accused of murder and lynched by a jeering mob. The midcentury Atlanta citizens drew their collective skirts away from their own mixed history and from the ugliness of racial warfare now erupting in other southern cities. They gave themselves leeway to hope, on that October morning before dawn, that the noisy explosion had not been a bomb, that it was not the opening volley in a modern Battle of Atlanta, that it did not mean that the racial violence bloodying the rest of the South had now stained their city. They saw Atlanta as unique. They thought, simply, "It can't happen here."

From May 17, 1954—the day the Supreme Court ruled in *Brown v. Board of Education of Topeka* that states could not lawfully segregate schoolchildren by race—until the end of the 1950s, hundreds of homes, schools, and houses of worship across the South exploded. Homemade bombs, bunches of dynamite, and suitcases filled with gunpowder killed and injured scores of people and demolished millions of dollars of property.

These days the science of terrorism is so far advanced that a middle-of-the-night bomb blowing out the side of a building would be called a dud. Bombs these days drop jumbo jets out of the sky and splatter chunks of commuter buses, and the commuters inside, into trees and telephone wires and onto the sides of buildings. Bombs shear off the fronts of public buildings, killing the adults at work and the children at play inside them. The late-twentieth-century homemade bombs leave craters, fill cemeteries with body parts, and push their makers into prominence and seats at negotiation tables. The bombs of the 1950s, by comparison, look like child's play. But the bombs of the 1950s were the beginning: not since the Civil War had Americans bombed other Americans. At noon or midnight, while inhabitants worked, prayed, or slept and while children did school lessons, their homes, churches, or schools suddenly leapt into the air.

It was a chaotic, violent, drunken era in which the rules that had always applied were being erased. Social anarchy arose. Angry white men broke with the laws of the land and made new, covert covenants with one another, where ties of race and blood superseded ties of nation and citizenship. Their associations took shape under the aegis of the Ku Klux Klan or of new entities, such as "states' rights" parties and "White Citizens Councils," founded to defy the Supreme Court and combat integration. At their most civilized, the club members gathered for evenings of discussion, prayer, and potluck supper, and subscribed to newsletters like the *Thunderbolt* with its lightning-bolt letterhead, columns of racist diatribe, and caricatures of Jews and blacks. At their least civilized, the white race units and states' rights parties opened their meetings with Nazi salutes, held cross burnings and firelit marches, terrorized families, and planted bombs.

Once indicted, arrested, and examined in court, the accused bombers—white men in their twenties and thirties—hinted darkly of vast networks of support behind their actions, of secret brotherhoods reaching into the highest echelons of society, of out-of-town fat cats bankrolling their maneuvers. In the same period, the acknowledged and nationally known leaders of these prosegregation forces publicly denied all knowledge of the terrorism. "That's one great trouble with our movement," sighed George Lincoln Rockwell, the infamous Virginia-based segregationist and anti-Semite, when questioned about some bombings. "Ninety percent of the people in the movement are lunatics."

The bombs were the lunatics' reply to the *Brown* decision.

By the mid-1950s the homemade bombs of segregationists were going off practically on a biweekly basis in the neighboring states of Alabama, Florida, Tennessee, South Carolina, and North Carolina. In 1957 and 1958, bombing incidents included two black churches and two black ministers' homes in Montgomery, Alabama; a suitcase exploding in the black business district of Clinton, Tennessee, at rush hour; the municipal auditorium in Knoxville, Tennessee, bombed during a concert by Louis Armstrong; and a bomb misfiring at the house of Martin Luther King Jr. in Montgomery. A black YWCA in Chattanooga, Tennessee, was bombed, as were, in North Carolina, a black drive-in theater in Charlotte and the home of the chairman of the human relations committee in Durham. In the twelve months before the Temple bombing, there were forty-seven bombings or attempted bombings around the South.

Yet Atlanta, until October 1958, was an oasis, a city of flowering trees and wide avenues, of soda fountains and air-cooled movie houses into which people thronged on sweltering summer nights, regardless of the feature. Until the fall of 1958, buildings stayed on their cornerstones, schoolchildren returned home happily from school, and black ministers arose in the morning unscathed from their beds. Still, the clock was ticking for this southern city, for the peaceful old way of life was founded on premises increasingly untenable: that a city may consist of religiously distinct and racially segregated communities with little commerce between them, in which a clearly defined white business elite—however well intentioned—holds all the reins of power, with no plan for relinquishing them.

It was a tumultuous and half-lawless time across the South after *Brown*. Racial groups jockeyed for position like schoolkids shoving in a cafeteria line: which groups would attain middle rank and which would be abandoned to the rear were crucial issues in our racist, suspicious midcentury. Across Dixie, some of the fights over racial prominence involved not only white against black and black against white, but Christian-born white against Jew. Where Jewish people were available, and sometimes where they were not, whites aimed at blacks *through* the Jews.

Ten percent of the bombs from 1954 to 1959 were cast at Jewish targets—synagogues, rabbis' houses, and community centers. In the twelve months before the bombing of the Temple in Atlanta, eleven sticks of dynamite were found at a temple in Charlotte; a synagogue in Miami and the Nashville Jewish Center were bombed on the same day; undetonated dynamite was found at a temple in Gastonia, North Carolina; a Jacksonville, Florida, synagogue was dynamited, and dynamite with a burnt-out fuse was found at Temple Beth-El in Birmingham, Alabama, on the same day. The simultaneity of some of the bombings hinted at southwide organization of the terrorism.

Meanwhile, in Atlanta, the Temple served as the hub of the religious, social, and philanthropic operations of an old and august Jewish community, whose earliest members had set up shop in the city shortly after Appomatox. The modern congregation of businessmen and retailers, pharmacists and doctors, represented the elite of Atlanta Jewry; the financial successes of a few families were second to none; still, they were not members of the best clubs, nor part of the white power structure that governed the city, for they were ethnic outsiders. They occupied a hard-earned and respectable middle-rung position in the social hierarchy, clearly below that of the wealthiest white Protestants, and far above that of the African Americans (who possessed, not unlike the Jews, their own business success stories, their own governing elites). The Temple Jews did not kid themselves that there was anything invulnerable or permanent about their social status. Unlike the self-confident Protestant white majority, the Jewish citizens of Atlanta had not forgotten the lynching of the Jewish mill manager forty-three years earlier. And they were conscious that a vicious new strain of anti-Semitism was flowing into the poisonous cant of the South's latest demagogues. Nevertheless, in the 1950s, the upwardly mobile Jewish families of the Temple—with reason to fear for their own security—placed their delicate social status and physical safety at risk by timorously, even unhappily, taking the side of the African Americans in what was then known as "the Negro question."

By 1958, Atlanta was ringed by smoke. The bombs were like the sound of an approaching enemy front. The explosions—which, in a perverse way, heralded the beginning of social change—were coming closer. The bombs were like flares sent up from the last forces within besieged cities: It's happening here! And these flares had been seen and heard now in every southern capital except Atlanta. McGill wrote in those years that Atlanta's white power structure was on guard "like citizens of medieval walled cities who heard that the great plague was coming."

The chief target of the Atlanta bombing—a Pittsburgh-born Reform rabbi, Jacob M. Rothschild—was at home asleep when the bomb exploded. He had returned late the night before from a speaking engagement in St. Paul, Minnesota, and had gone to bed exhausted. The phone woke him up around 7:45 A.M.

"Always able to shake off sleep more quickly than I," recalled his widow, Janice Rothschild (the rabbi died in 1973), "he scurried around to my side of the bed to answer." It was a weeping Robert Benton, the Temple custodian, who had just arrived to open up the building for Sunday school.

"I heard Jack groan, a long horrified, 'OH NO,' " said Janice. "Then, in fast staccato, 'I'll be right there. You'd better call Mrs. Shurgin' [the Temple administrator]. He hung up and told me, 'The Temple's been bombed.' " The rabbi hastily dressed and drove to the bomb site, where he identified himself and consulted with the Atlanta police detectives already roping off the area.

In his sports coat and tie, head bowed as he listened to police, he looked administrative, authoritative—a bit like Mayor Hartsfield, then in his Eisenhower period. Rothschild was a smooth-skinned, balding man in black-topped eyeglasses. His small eyes, curved nose, and round, plump lips were grouped closely together on a white oval face. Rabbi Rothschild had long been seen by the local media, elected officials, and Christian clergy as standing on the front lines of race. And he did, in fact. He stood on the front lines of race by choice, however, and not (as he suspected they believed) because to be Jewish was to be racially compromised and therefore closer to the Negro.

Rothschild, a paragon of the Reform rabbinate, was cloaked by decency and seriousness the way his Orthodox colleagues literally were draped by black clothing. He was the sort of man who, in a public forum, would clear his throat and then raise the ethical question, the very question he had turned over and over in his mind for many weeks, while slumped in front of TV baseball in his den or seated alone in his study, snapping down cards in solitaire. This he would stunningly and eloquently say, and heaven help those who were not ready for it.

He had arrived in Atlanta in 1946. In 1947 he had begun to speak on the Negro question, and by 1952 the Negro question occupied so great a portion of his time and thoughts that—near the end of his life—he would say it had been his greatest cause, that without it his pulpit would not have been worth as much. Rabbi Rothschild, in short, supported integration and said so publicly and repeatedly in sermon and speech and editorial.

And he had invited black speakers onto his pulpit and black dinner guests into his house.

And what stood behind it all, one felt, was not muscle or rugged good looks, the kinds of things that would do you some good in a crowd. Among the tall, handsome, silver-templed Atlanta ministers, Rothschild looked somewhat the four-eyes, the egghead, the bookworm. But he had seen bloodshed on Guadalcanal and had sat with dying boys, Jewish and Christian, in hospital tents as bombs fell, the first Jewish chaplain to come under fire in World War II. What stood behind the eloquence and the quietly revolutionary actions was a clarity of mind and a history of having not flinched under fire.

At the Temple, by daylight, detectives in business suits kicked through the debris and masonry and waded through the water pouring from broken pipes. They stooped to examine displaced articles: a shred of a child's choir robe, a single page from a Hebrew prayerbook, a broken candelabra. A sliver of wood had been driven through a brick wall by the explosive force. The detectives pulled at the brims of their hats in misgiving and talked among themselves in low tones. In fact, the technology had not been invented yet that would have enabled them to read in the rubble who had dropped and left a suitcase after midnight—the DNA typing, the retrieval of clues the size of molecules. Still, they continued for most of the day to poke their long-toed brown Florsheim shoes into the mess. They would conclude, from the evidence, only that the bomber was skilled with dynamite, for all fifty sticks had blown up; that with the dynamite and the "Confederate Underground" phone calls, the crime resembled the anti-integration bombings, the segregationist backlash, in other southern cities; and that two hundred thousand dollars' worth of damage had been inflicted. (*Confederate Underground* was the catch-all term, the half-imaginary alliance among any number of disgruntled right-wing groups, seeming chiefly to consist, on any given day, of some individual with a grievance and a telephone.) Vague reports surfaced in the neighborhood of the Temple of a "scar-faced Negro" and of "two white men in an old-model black car," but these led nowhere.

Today, with modern forensics, the bombs that amputate the front of public buildings and rip apart commuter buses generate crates of information. In the 1950s, the explanation was that "the bomb blew up the evidence."

In short, the crime scene, as relayed by newspaper and television photography to all Americans, yielded no physical clues to police about the identity of the perpetrators or their motives.

Rabbi Rothschild was no hysteric. At the bomb site early that Sunday morning, his demeanor was flat. He crossed his arms and took it in. He had been psychologically flirting with the bomb throwers for nearly a year now, ever since other southern synagogues had begun to explode. "Maybe if we talk about it, we'll be bombed, too," he had said in a sermon in May. He consciously had thrown the switches and turned the wheels known to excite the South's violent extremists: he had spoken in favor of racial integration.

He was aware that he lived in strange times, when the pronouncement of elemental moral observations stirred political havoc. A man with the power of speech in the Deep South in the 1950s was like a magician: political careers rose and fell, citizens quailed in horror or reached for their whips and pistols when certain formulas were recited. White men covered their faces with sheets, and their car tires pitched gravel when they tore down country roads with bound victims in their backseats. And the terrible secret, known only to the magicians, was that the incantations consisted of everyday words: "All men are created equal." "The white race is superior." "The Negroes are our brothers." "The Negroes want our daughters." Earlier in the century, George Orwell wrote: "We have now sunk to a depth at which the restatement of the obvious is the first duty of civilized men." Rothschild had the power of speech, so he spoke.

But he commented only tersely from the middle of the rubble. The wreckage spoke eloquently for itself. When asked by a reporter how he felt, Rothschild said only: "Horror." Later that day he and William Schwartz, the Temple president, prepared a statement for the press: "We are shocked and sick at heart at the wanton damage to our House of Worship. We thank God that the explosion took place before our children and teachers arrived for Sunday School this morning. Our shattered religious school building and the broken windows of our sanctuary bear mute evidence to the contrast between the ideals of religious faiths and the practices of Godless men." But the day of the bombing, he was unusually still, the eye of the storm. He seemed, to some, inscrutable. Barraged by questions, he paused, thought, and gave subdued answers, one at a time. He was like the toy fortune-telling eight ball once popular: children asked questions of the black plastic globe—like "Will I ace the test?"—then turned it over and waited while a reply in small white letters— "The outlook is positive"—came swimming to the surface from an inky depth. So Rothschild quietly gave out only measured statements in response to specific questions.

But inwardly, he was processing the disaster, which seemed unmistakably to be saying to him, in deep tones: "We have heard you. Now there is no turning back." He had crossed a great divide. Whether it would divide him from his fellow Jews and fellow whites, he did not know yet. Whether his congregation, which already had endured a decade of his increasingly public pro-integration stance, could stand *this*, he also did not know.

He had before him a long, long day and night, and then weeks of fielding questions and of receiving the heavy, sympathetic handshakes and the sad, furrowed gazes of journalists, officials, detectives, congregants, Christian clergymen—some friends, some strangers. For the moment, when they probed for his inmost thoughts, he modestly directed their attention to the blown-out wall and the broken stained-glass windows. "You see, there really *is* a war on," he meant by this. "We've been trying to draft you on our side for a long time now."

The bombs of the segregationists did not stop progress, but they dogged it. Their message was not lost on anyone inside the South. The bombs reminded people that their actions were being watched, and by whom. Integration, said the bombs, if y'all are planning to go ahead with it, is going to take place in a minefield.

PART I

1

A Cracker Camelot

1

Rabbi Jacob M. Rothschild was brusque; "he was *army*," some said. He had a blunt sense of humor that shot out of his mouth like a fist from a sleeve to sock you on the arm. Some hated it. Among gentiles he was an "ambassador," compelled to make a sweet impression on behalf of a distrusted race. But among his congregants, especially those on the same golf-playing and dinner-party circuit as he and Janice, his lovely wife, he was a smart aleck.

"He could be cutting," admitted Jean Levinson, Rothschild's younger sister, who adored him nonetheless and displays a large, handsome portrait of him on a wall of her Pittsburgh apartment. "I'll give you an example," she said. "When Jack left for the army, Rabbi Chuck Lesser came to our temple to take his place as assistant rabbi, and Jack took him around to introduce him to the staff. And he came to his secretary, who was a very attractive, heavyset redhead, and he said to Chuck Lesser, 'This is Ruth So-and-so.'

"And Chuck says, 'Oh, I guess I'll be seeing a lot of her.'

15

"To which Jack replied, '*Whenever* you see Ruth, you see a lot of her.'

"That was very typical of Jack. He wasn't a sweet thing. That was his sense of humor."

"We were sitting at Jack's mother's funeral," recalled Janice Rothschild. "It was a more Orthodox funeral than we were accustomed to. The attendants had these bowler hats, and Jack looked at me and whispered in my ear (and this was his mother's funeral), 'If Mother could look up and see this, she'd drop dead!'"

"There was a member of the congregation named Barney Kaufmann," remembered their son, Bill Rothschild, an ordained rabbi and a respected attorney. "And Barney hated his sermons. He was a wonderful guy, but he told me the one thing he couldn't take was every time he went to services, all he heard was civil rights and he was tired of it. So he and Dad had a talk one time, and thereafter at 8:35 every Friday night Barney Kaufmann would take a nap. Dad would look down from the pulpit and see that Barney Kaufmann was asleep and all was right with the world. At 8:55 Barney Kaufmann would wake up as Dad was saying 'Amen.' That's what Dad suggested he do since he didn't approve of the sermons: just sleep through them."

Most took Rothschild in stride, especially those who saw him only in a buffet line or at a bridge party, those for whom it was practically a rule of etiquette *not* to appear in temple on Friday nights (as if you didn't have symphony tickets or invitations to a dinner party!). Women greeted his wisecracks with light, musical laughter—"Oh, Jack!"—and fixed him another drink.

"Jack was probably one of the *last* people you'd think should be a rabbi," said Nancy Thal, a Temple member. "You could see him sitting in a *board* meeting. But in a *temple*? It's like that tired old story, 'What kind of business is this for a nice Jewish boy?' I'd have fun with Jack when we played golf, and I'd see him at parties and he had a drink, you know? He was just like one of the guys. I just sort of stopped going to temple because it seemed kind of silly. I mean, I couldn't sit there with a straight face."

Rothschild's sarcasm was taken, by and large, as his way of acting like a regular guy among Americanized Jews for whom a rabbi—no matter how sincere a bridge player and golfer—still was a rabbi and not a retailer, manufacturer, or dentist. About some rabbis, it is told, there is a radiance, an aura of God knowledge, a hint of racial memory of higher spheres. But Rothschild need not have worried about setting this aside by acting the wise guy at parties, because no one ever suggested he possessed it. He was not, by all accounts, a spiritual man. "He was a very *bright* person, in my estimation," said tiny, curly-haired, bright-eyed Aline Uhry, the mother of the prize-winning playwright Alfred Uhry. "He was a most interesting dinner companion; he was wonderful company. He'd tell good stories and good jokes that keep the conversation interesting. But spiritual? No. He was an intellectual man. I think he would have made a marvelous professor."

"I don't think he believed in a personal God," said Emanuel Feldman, rabbi emeritus of Atlanta's Orthodox Congregation Beth Jacob, the editor-in-chief of the scholarly quarterly *Tradition*, a former adjunct professor at Emory University Law School, and a senior lecturer at Israel's Bar Ilan University. Soft-spoken, gray-bearded, literate, and eloquent, Feldman continued: "He had a typical Reform view of God: from my viewpoint—muddled. I asked him once, 'When you say "Blessed art Thou," who's the Thou?' He reflected what he'd been taught in the seminary he studied in, which was basically without religious passion. He was the first to admit he was no Jewish scholar, although, relative to his congregation, on Jewish matters he was an Einstein. His views of God, Torah, and religion were totally opposed to my own views. I mean there were things that he did that I would never do. But we managed to forget about those things and just enjoy each other's company. Listen, we're all Jews. I'm no more; others are no less. He was a very down-to-earth person, a fair-minded person."

Both were amused at the notoriety stirred by a friendship between an Orthodox rabbi and a Reform rabbi. They composed together a cantata for the annual Hanukkah dinner of the Board of Jewish Education, and the community was amazed. They took afternoons off to go horseback riding. One evening, seated on the dais at a Jewish function, the then-young rabbis leaned forward to chat across a man between them. Frank Garson, an older member of the community, occupied the middle seat and was flabbergasted at what he heard. When he could no longer contain himself, he turned to Feldman: "*You* ride horseback?"

"Sure I do," replied the young man. "You think only Reform rabbis can ride horseback?"

"No," Garson replied thoughtfully. "But when a Reform rabbi falls off a horse and you say, 'The rabbi fell off a horse,' the people will say, 'The rabbi fell off his horse? Oh my God! Was he hurt?!' But when an Orthodox rabbi falls off a horse and you say, 'The rabbi fell off a horse,' the people will say, 'The rabbi fell off a *horse*? What was the rabbi doing on a horse?' "

At Rothschild's invitation, Rabbi Feldman occasionally attended Temple functions. Because he could not partake of the nonkosher food served at the Temple, at his seat he always found awaiting him, regardless of how lavish the dinner, a fruit plate—cold and disappointing, but certifiably kosher. One night Rothschild, who did not observe food restrictions, showed up at an affair at Beth Jacob. "We had a sumptuous meal that night," recalls Feldman, "but I'd spoken ahead of time to the caterer. As plates heaped with food were placed before each of the dinner guests, a fruit plate was set down in front of Jack Rothschild, with a note certifying that it was kosher."

Rothschild's wisecracking was not needed to bridge a heavenly distance between himself and others, but apparently it was needed to close some other gap, to maintain the impression that he was just like those with whom he stood in conversation, dabbling on the light surface of things. It was as if he were preoccupied much of the time, the full force of his personality held in check, like a team of horses waylaid on the far side of a river. When he crossed the inner distance and surfaced, and you found yourself suddenly eye-to-eye with the man, out he came with a smart remark. The rabbi's unexpected zingers announced, like the ding of a bell above a just-arriving elevator, that he had surfaced, that he was *back*.

2

Born in 1911, Jacob Rothschild had grown up without money in Pittsburgh, in a succession of dreary brick apartments and duplexes on nearly bald, sloping yards in the urban neighborhood of Squirrel Hill. Steel clotheslines, with limbs like rooftop TV antennas, clustered in the tiny backyards instead of trees. A middling public school student, Jack was talented in sports and cards, and his mother and younger sister doted on him. His father, Meyer Rothschild, from an Orthodox background in Cleveland, faded from family life, diminished by a stroke; Lillie Rothschild went to work as a dress-buyer; teenage Jack worked in Kaufmann's Department Store in boys' clothing, and nine-year-old Jean tended to her father after school.

As he neared high school graduation at the age of fifteen, Jack popped the question of becoming a rabbi. "I don't know how long he had had this idea," said Jean. He called on Dr. Samuel Goldenson, the senior rabbi of Temple Rodef Shalom, but the older man cautioned him: "Jack, you're very young. I'm sure you'll change your mind." So Rothschild enrolled at the University of Pittsburgh. It occurred to him then that he knew no Hebrew. His mother, at his request, hired a tutor. "The Hebrew teacher was a little guy with a hat," said Jean, "the type who carried an umbrella whether it rained or not. He would meet Jack after school, and all of Jack's friends would wait outside and laugh. And Mother said, 'I can't afford to pay this tutor if you're going to laugh at him.' So she stopped the lessons. And the following year he went to Hebrew Union College on scholarship. And he excelled with no basis, no background for it or anything. So that's the profession he chose. I honestly don't know what prompted him to think of that field."

In fact, Rothschild, with his Reform background and mere hint of Hebrew, made a rocky start. Most of the students at the Reform seminary actually came from religious homes. "I made adequate grades, enough to keep up my scholarships," he later said. "I was not scholarly, not interested in being a Talmudic scholar or anything like that." To support himself, he waited tables in a nightclub, sold boys' clothing in a department store, worked in the school gym, and taught Sunday School. Meyer Rothschild died in 1934, and Jack offered to leave seminary to go to work full-time; his mother would not hear of it.

Fellow students called him "Racky." Rabbi Sidney Berkowitz later recalled: "Racky and I sought mutual consolation in the fact that we were both 'Jewishly sterile': the only two members of our class who had come from Reform homes, had attended Reform religious schools, and—to the horror of our classmates—had been confirmed and not bar mitzvahed. I was drawn to Racky for his self-assurance, his friendly outgoing manner, his leadership ability. But there were other more important bonds that inspired my admiration. . . . He not only knew baseball and basketball, but he played them. There was no athletic skill in which he failed to demonstrate some prowess. . . . He may not have known some obscure Hebrew paradigm, but he certainly knew the batting averages of the top major league players. He gave me a new concept of the rabbinical student."

Rothschild felt generally smiled upon in life, a feeling not uncommon in a natural athlete. When he received the highest grade in Talmud, a difficult course taught by a German-born professor, he happily turned his sharp wit upon himself when speaking of his achievement. His high marks, it seems, had prompted a more learned classmate from an Orthodox home to protest to the teacher: "How can you *do* this when you know that I know more Talmud than Rothschild?"

"Silly boy," replied the professor, his thick German accent preserved in Jack's mimicry, "I am a teacher, yes? Vat *you* know you knew ven you came here. Vat Rothschild knows, *I* taught him!"

As a student rabbi, Rothschild served tiny congregations in Henderson, Kentucky, and in Jonesboro, Arkansas; after being ordained in 1936, he served a congregation in Davenport, Iowa. Within a year he was invited by Temple Rodef Shalom in Pittsburgh—his home congregation—to return as the assistant rabbi. "AM RABBI FREEHOF'S ASSISTANT," Jack telegraphed his mother and sister in excitement. "MY LUCK STILL HOLDS."

Meanwhile, the question of *why* he became a rabbi was one that Rothschild deflected, all his life, with a jest: "Because I wasn't born rich and I like to sleep late," meaning he had to work for a living and he believed (wrongly, it turned out) that rabbis clocked short hours.

In 1941, as America entered World War II, Rothschild enlisted in the chaplaincy. He left Pittsburgh in March 1942 for basic training at Fort Bragg. In the photo he sent home, his crisp, brimmed officer's hat looks too big on him, giving him a Barney Fife air, earnest and scrawny. "My duties are extremely arduous," he wrote from San Francisco. "I must report to the office every morning between eight and nine. I am then free until the next morning."

As Second Lieutenant Rothschild, he was shipped out of San Francisco with the Americal Division in September 1942. Three months later his division was in combat, backing up the marines on Guadalcanal.

IDLE GOSSIP SINKS SHIPS is stamped across every letter home from the front, while censors have snipped and burnt dozens of words and sentences from each page, shaping each letter into something like a row of onionskin paper dolls. Rothschild did not try to write home of being under bombardment; of hurrying through services to finish by sundown because, with darkness, air raids began; of interrupting prayers to dive into foxholes; of building makeshift chapels in clearings near the front, with coconut stumps as lecterns and fallen logs as pews for Jewish and non-Jewish soldiers; of visiting rows of boys on bloody cots. None of this did he report until after the war when he was interviewed by Pittsburgh and Jewish papers. In his letters home from the front, he focused with intensity instead on the myopic, neighborly, newsy chit-chat arriving in the mail from Pittsburgh. He seized upon the innocent, gossipy, motherly prattle like a starving man devouring doughnuts.

"Sorry to hear about Rose," he wrote to his mother in October 1942. "Can't imagine what could be the matter with her from your description. Which is not surprising, considering my limited knowledge of medicine—and your handwriting."

"Question: Who the devil is Sonny Fleishman?" he wrote in early November, "or *is* that his name—it's the best I could do with Mother's writing. . . . The fact that you found his address in a Phi Ep directory only further confuses me. 'He only had 10 minutes to catch his train'—What train? Where was he going? What telephone call did you want to thank him for making? No kidding, I'm completely bewildered."

"Went horsebackriding on cavalry horse," he wrote a week later. "I visited a family in town—sort of a date, only around here the family stays up and has a date, too."

He sent home a joke that was making the rounds; a few

years hence, he would be appalled that he had written it: "There's a story about a colored boy from Georgia writing home from the war: 'Dear Boss, I is now in Jerusalem where Christ was born. I wish to Christ I was in Georgia where I was born.' "

"I finally remembered who Sonny Fleishman was," he wrote in mid-November. "And now that I know, I agree with you that it was darn nice of him to call and I'm glad you wrote to thank him."

In December, Jewish soldiers, grateful for his services, built a menorah for him out of twenty-millimeter shells.

"I have a hunch that I'm the only Jewish chaplain on foreign duty with an outfit in actual combat conditions," he said in December.

In January: " . . . 3rd funeral today . . . "

"Conducted a service yesterday for an outfit outside our division and celebrated old home week," he wrote in March, meaning he had found Jews. "It is encouraging to get among my own kind again. At any rate, it assures me that there still are some around somewhere."

"So far my war career has disillusioned me on two fronts," he wrote before being shipped out with his division to Fiji: "to wit: Spam, and South Sea Island Paradises."

Seven months after his arrival in Fiji, Rothschild fell ill with malaria, so he was shipped back to the States for hospitalization. After his recovery, he was assigned to speak to parents of servicemen about the war effort: "Out of cruelty they have learned compassion," he said of his fellow enlisted men and women. "From living in hate, they have learned love. From the loss of freedom they have learned the love of freedom. They shall return not only *eager* to create a better world. What is far more important, they shall come back *prepared* to create that world." It was one of the larger autobiographical clues he would leave about his war experience: it was Rothschild himself who would barge back into civilian life eager to create a better world.

On April 7, 1946, Captain Rothschild was honorably discharged from active duty. He had earned the Asiatic-Pacific Campaign Medal with one Bronze Battle Star, the American Theater Campaign Medal, the World War II Victory Medal, and two overseas service bars.

Within the month he was offered the pulpit of Atlanta's Hebrew Benevolent Congregation—Atlanta's oldest, second-largest, and most socially prominent synagogue, colloquially referred to as "the Temple." The senior rabbi, Dr. David Marx, was retiring. Rothschild accepted the position. "The next person that tells me that it gets cool in the evenings in Atlanta," he wrote to Jean and his mother, "I shall gladly hit them with the nearest object."

3

In July 1946, Rothschild, age thirty-five and fresh out of uniform, rode the Southern Railway into Atlanta, the "Heart of Dixie." He disembarked at Terminal Station in the center of old downtown, ran up a flight of steps from the platform, and rambled across a vast tiled room, swinging his bag and tennis racket. He pushed through the station's sun-warmed glass-and-wood doors and, for the first time, stood blinking in the summer glare of Georgia sunshine, which fell straight through the clean air and ricocheted off a hundred chrome bumpers. As he stood shielding his face, he felt the hot wind flowing along the black-topped streets, blown inland across a thousand acres of cotton land from the sizzling Atlantic beyond. The high, pale, hot sky was the color of sun-bleached denim blowing dry on a line.

The residents here began each day before sunrise by slamming shut all the open windows of their houses, to trap indoors a faint woodsy coolness, the damp air of lichen and moss; the night-cooled air then wandered over still rooms as the sun rose, burning white-hot at all the windows. Here men and women got their work done early, in soft, ironed khaki suits, or cotton dresses and beads, for by midday the merest movement of arm through spongy air brought fatigue and perspiration, the clothes wilted and clung, and drawling voices left words hanging in the air, floating on soft currents of heat and humidity. By three o'clock every afternoon, oscillating fans throughout the city paddled the thick air of motionless rooms, while out on the state road, under the sun's meridian, shackled black convicts swung scythes at the roadside weeds. The heat did not break until the middle of each buzzing night, when a green dew veiled the city and the closed windows were heaved open, to invite it in.

Too warmly dressed, Rothschild stood, waiting for his ride. Trim, fair-haired, sun-tanned, wearing gold-rimmed spectacles, he looked tough and bookish at the same time. He looked like photographs of Isaac Babel, the great Russian-Jewish writer from Odessa who had been killed, by Stalin's orders, only half a dozen years earlier. Babel had ridden with the Cossacks (having been at their mercy in his frightened childhood) and had filled his short stories with the bloody exploits of marauding horsemen and with the starlit ruins and crones of ransacked Jewish quarters. If Babel was the yeshiva-boy-turned-cavalryman, Rothschild was the friendlier, ball-playing American version. But they were both military Jews, then a new world type. After warfare, and for the rest of their lives (though neither would enjoy old age), while appearing to be soft, hesitant, owlish chaps, they would surprise everyone who mistook them with their flintiness, savvy, and nerve.

Atlanta in 1946 was fresh out of uniform and poised at the start of a new life itself. Whether or not it would be a more *just* life—whether or not the city would be a site of the "better world" spoken of by Captain Rothschild—was the great, dark question. He was suddenly on hand to watch for the answer given in bass and alto tones by the keepers of history, those men and women placed by their social, religious, and genetic inheritance on top of the human pile—the "white power structure"— who saw it as their holy task to preserve the blessed order of things over which they presided.

A car pulled onto the gravel and honked; an arm waved, and the driver's-side door half-opened. Rothschild grabbed his bag and ran from the tiled vestibule of the building into the glare.

His chief asset, from the viewpoint of the Temple board that had just hired him, was that he was American through and through—a veteran, a practical man, not too otherworldly, not too Jewish, a regular Joe who played poker and football and just happened to be a rabbi. At the top of the agenda of the Temple community was the winning of citywide acceptance of Jewish people as equals. As an American Reform rabbi—the very latest model among the world's rabbis—Rothschild wore neither yarmulke nor beard nor special clothing, and his language was a flat Pittsburghese untinged by Yiddish; he thus appeared to be a man who could merge easily into American public life. It was not intended by the Temple board that he should try to overturn the pyramid of intricate social relations as he found it, but that he should locate a ramp to the upper tiers that would be open to Jews.

In the passenger seat of the car of his old friend, Dr. Marvin Sugarman, Rothschild, oblivious of the mission for which he had been hired, pried off his damp jacket and held it in his lap. The burning-hot seat cushion chafed his back and the undersides of his legs. The car backfired into the streets of a city newly embarked upon peacetime.

4

During the war, tens of thousands of soldiers, sailors, and airmen were stationed in nearby military camps, overcrowding the city's restaurants, boardinghouses, dance halls, and whorehouses. As the soldiers elbowed into packed foyers and lobbies, eager for novel sensations on their twenty-four-hour passes, their necks and ears looked prominent and their eyes seemed almost to protrude because of their newly sheared heads. The locals shivered at the flat accents and at their Yankee manners: whites and blacks on leave together looking for a place to have supper! whites and blacks inquiring together about overnight quarters! whites and blacks trying to sit together at the front of buses! Smartly pressed, brass-buttoned white soldiers stood in grinning, identical groups—khaki triplets and quadruplets—at the sumptuous affairs given in their honor by Atlanta's cultured matrons. Sons of New Jersey, sons of Ohio, who—eighty years earlier—enthusiastically would have set fire to the stately homes, scattering the lovely ladies and shrieking girls like chickens across a farmyard, now were content to be on the same side as the Rebels as they jerked the upper-class daughters onto the dance floor. With noblesse oblige, the Dixie gentility saw to their comfort, and gazed with relief, not liking what they had seen, into one another's eyes after the boys had careened off.

Tens of thousands of Atlanta civilians had worked in the

war industries. At Bell Aircraft twenty thousand workers manufactured B-29s. Due to the desperate shortage of white manpower, white women, black men, and black women were permitted to perform semiskilled and skilled labor. The black workers and soldiers were warned not to make too much of their wartime positions: "Now, don't you niggers think when this war is over you're going to walk around here in uniforms," and "We don't want you killing no white folks while you're in the army," they were told.

At war's end, on V-J Day, August 15, 1945, a hundred thousand people were on hand to push into the streets to dance, give rebel yells, kiss total strangers, hop rides on top of passing streetcars, beat washtubs, form conga lines hundreds of people long, and wave the newspaper headline JAPS SURRENDER! The thousands of wartime citizens then mostly went back to Connecticut or wherever they had come from, leaving the city relieved, but also deflated: the restaurants and nightclubs stood with shining windows and mopped floors, a whiff of ginger or of peach brandy in the air, prepared to host crowds who no longer came. The good jobs for women and blacks evaporated as the decorated white boys came home from overseas, immodestly demanding that Home, Ladies, and Colored People be the same as they had always been, only more so. Automobile traffic and truck convoys diminished. The empty streets, lined by flowering trees, seemed hushed and poised. Then there were pert young white women pushing perambulators, optimistic young white men like Rothschild launching their postwar careers, and sighing black women tying on aprons.

But despite the old-time southern feeling eagerly embraced by the old guard—content with the black yardmen hoeing in the shadow of grand stone houses, and the grown-up white girlfriends riding on the streetcar two-by-two to town—Atlanta was changed by the war. The city had transformed itself, at the request of President Franklin D. Roosevelt and the U.S. War Department, into a major manpower, transportation, production, and distribution center; and the engine of this progress continued to huff and churn long after the last American warplane was grounded. It took business leaders only a moment to catch their breath—that moment of hush as if in expectation of a parade, during which even the birds fall silent in the treetops—

before they lunged ahead full-throttle, exchanging their flat-brimmed straw hats for brown fedoras. By retooling the war industries and taking advantage of the souped-up rail, highway, and air systems, they were determined to put Atlanta on the peacetime map as the key business city of the South.

The white elite had seen, during the federally invigorated war years, a glimpse of what the future might offer: skilled jobs with good wages for ladies and Negroes, racially integrated gatherings, and government contracts with government suggestions about whom to hire. Now they were busily selecting their options from Column A: commerce, and none from Column B: equal opportunity.

Innocent of all of this, Rothschild shook hands with his friend, pulled his suitcase and tennis racket out of the backseat, and entered the warm lobby of the Biltmore Hotel to rent a room by the month.

5

"Of the twenty-five major American cities, nineteen are port cities," said George Goodwin, a public relations executive, Pulitzer Prize–winning journalist, and local history buff, born in 1917. "Of the six others, you've got Washington, D.C., nation's capital; Dallas–Ft. Worth, petroleum and livestock; Kansas City, livestock and grain; Minneapolis–St. Paul, grain; and you've got Denver, mining, foot of a mountain, and because it's the only possible regional city."

"That leaves Atlanta," he said with the ill-concealed pride of a pleased grandfather, "which has no damn reason to be there." A heavyset, white-grizzled man who seemed to find age a little inconvenient and awkward, he stood and looked out from his high corner office upon the glittering and wooded city. "Atlanta was always kind of different. Its wealth doesn't spurt up out of the ground. It wasn't in the plantation belt like Savannah or Charleston or Mobile, or New Orleans or Memphis or Little Rock. It was located on the higher ground of the Piedmont and was never subservient to cotton nor dependent on slavery. Atlanta's success was based on promotion."

It was a city built on PR, on snappy slogans, on catchy ads

in national magazines. Atlanta grew from the optimism of business leaders and the craft of advertising talents (Goodwin among them), who shared the conviction that Atlanta was a hot property—or who at least shared the conviction that they could persuade *other* people that it was. (Spoofing their own PR legacy, Atlantans would propose ridiculous slogans for the 1996 Olympics:

Atlanta: Not Bad for Georgia.

Atlanta: It's Better than Birmingham.

Atlanta: Come Visit. You Probably Won't Get Mugged.

Atlanta: Atnalta Spelled Backwards.)

The selling of Atlanta—and of the idea of Atlanta—had commenced ridiculously soon after the overgrown railroad junction, functioning since the 1830s, was burnt to the ground by General William Tecumseh Sherman and his Union troops, the victors in the Battle of Atlanta. "The city was just about totally destroyed," said Goodwin. "After Lee's surrender, Confederate money had zero value. The government ceased to exist. The wealth in slaves disappeared. People rebuilt the city with their bare hands.

Atlanta after the Civil War was the perfect locale for the mingling of aristocratic southern breeding, taste, and musty old money, with carpetbagger know-how, northern contacts, and new wealth. It was a city with a brick-and-iron heart clanging with trains and fuming with cotton mills, whose far edges softened into miles of green and flowering neighborhoods. "Atlanta *welcomed* the carpetbaggers," said Goodwin. "Morris Rich [a Temple founder whose little dry-goods store became Rich's Department Store, the largest in the Southeast] was a carpetbagger." The postbellum city leaders—thinking Promotion!—hosted three world's fairs, including the great Cotton States and International Exposition of 1895, which featured Buffalo Bill, John Philip Sousa, and Booker T. Washington. Confederate and Union veterans camped out together in a show of reconciliation—a nineteenth-century version of a photo opportunity.

In the 1920s, the city fathers launched the "Forward Atlanta" campaign to convince national businesses to make Atlanta their regional hub. They advertised in *Forbes, Fortune,* and the *Saturday Evening Post;* sent ambassadors to call on major companies; and lured, in 1926 alone, Chevrolet, Nabisco, Southern Railway, and Lay's Potato Chips. One member of a rival chamber of commerce jealously observed: "If Atlanta could suck as hard as it can blow, it would soon be a city on the Atlantic."

"The city was saying, 'Come see how we are—come join us,' " said Goodwin. "Now Charleston never said, 'Come join us' to anybody in the world. Neither did New Orleans. Neither did Memphis. Nor Richmond. Nor Montgomery. They were closed societies."

After World War II, Atlanta again yearned to be included, with its northern sister cities, in American progress and prosperity. Again the city was traversed by freight traffic; this time the carriers were winged. Mayor Hartsfield had laid out a state-of-the-art airport like an elaborate and beautiful snare, designed to attract and catch the air traffic. *Here,* rather than Macon; come *here,* instead of Birmingham; you'll prefer *us* to Montgomery. The radiant black runways on fields of green were like fingers of an open hand, beckoning to pilots. And, with an assist from the city's image makers, the airplanes came: forty-one every day in 1940, making Atlanta's airport the busiest in the nation. The recurrent PR theme—"Atlanta is a good place to live and a good place to do business!"—was infinitely enhanced by the addition of a port to the list of the city's vaunted assets and charms, an airport, a deep harbor on the ocean of the air.

The epic civic goal of the latter part of the twentieth century would be to cast Atlanta as "The World's Next International City." The epic civic goal of the first half of the century was to transform the image of Atlanta in the national imagination from that of a dazed, black-eyed, tragic Confederate beauty into that of a bustling, efficient, modern regional business hub.

That same PR theme would determine the direction the city would take in 1954 when a new era in race relations was trumpeted from Washington and a grim wrestling began in every township and county in the South. The *Brown* decision would be a second Emancipation Proclamation: the people pushed aside by city planning and dismissed by language—

"coloreds," "niggers," "nigras"—to places beyond the rim of modern life, suddenly would appear en masse on everyone's horizon. A question then would form in the minds of Atlanta's white power structure. It would be a different question, a slightly less insane question, than that occurring to white elites elsewhere in the South. In Atlanta the central question was going to be "What will this do to business?"

And at that moment, Rothschild—with very few others— was going to have to say something along the lines of "I don't give a damn *what* it does to business. We will obey the laws because they are *just.*"

6

The white business elite, the keepers of history, lived in exclusively white and Protestant enclaves; they socialized at the exclusively white and Protestant Capital City Club, Ansley Golf Club, or—most exclusively—the Piedmont Driving Club. They frequented private dining establishments with green-and-red wallpapered fox-hunting scenes and touches of brass throughout the subdued rooms. The well-born business leaders were Democrats, Elks, Masons, Rotarians, and Shriners; they were Methodists, Presbyterians, or Episcopalians; they were patrons of the Atlanta Historical Society, the Mozart Society, neighborhood garden clubs, the Atlanta Athletic Club, and the High Museum of Art, and hosts of the annual visit of the Metropolitan Opera. Many paid dues to the Sons of the American Revolution, while their wives organized teas for the Daughters of the American Revolution (DAR) or the United Daughters of the Confederacy (UDC). They observed Confederate Memorial Day: in 1940, five gray-clad, toothless Civil War veterans hobbled for the last time down Peachtree Street and waved in the annual parade. Lincoln's Birthday, on the other hand, they could have done without.

"It was not a particularly colorful group," wrote Ivan Allen Jr., the mayor of Atlanta from 1962 to 1970. "The fetish of Citizens & Southern National Bank President Mills B. Lane for collecting antique cars was about as wild as we got—and there were few escapades, scandals, or divorces within our group. We were white, Anglo-Saxon, Protestant, Atlantan, business-oriented, nonpolitical, moderate, well-bred, well-educated, pragmatic, and dedicated to the betterment of Atlanta as much as a Boy Scout troop is dedicated to fresh milk and clean air."

"The Power Structure Era in Atlanta," according to the historians Tim Crimmins and Dana White, "survives [in legend] as the city's Golden Day—a kind of Cracker Camelot." In their fur collars, in their warm cars rolling down Peachtree Street into downtown, with breakfasts of ham and eggs and grits under their belts, served to them by the black women already at work in their kitchens by the time they came downstairs in the morning, the businessmen rode on top of the world. But their mental blueprint of the world was ill founded. Like the ancient Indian drawing of a universe in which the earth rests on the shell of a turtle, the businessmens' universe rested on the backs of the underpaid, undereducated, inadequately housed blacks. As far as their circles of acquaintances extended, the only black people they knew—and then, by first name only—were white-jacketed waiters and cooks, blue-uniformed janitors and yardmen, and black-and-white-uniformed maids, who commuted long distances by bus or jalopy to work and who occasionally asked for loans or for help with the law. "It was in the nature of our upbringing that we had seldom come into contact with the problems of the Negro in America," wrote Mayor Allen, "except to note that our maids had to come an awfully long way from wherever they lived to get to our homes every day so they could clean our rooms and wash our dishes and mind our children."

The world of the white elite was a Versailles of lawns and fountains, putting greens and tennis courts, linen tablecloths and fine china. They lived far from downtown and from the all-black neighborhoods with streets of clay, but the wealth was connected to the poverty. And the contented sense of being on top of the world should have been connected to the dark knowledge that someone else was pressed to the underside.

In 1946, when an abrasive Yankee army veteran was hired to head its most prominent Jewish congregation, Atlanta was a city on the make, a city with big ideas. The Temple members had high hopes of moving up with their city, of being swept along in the surge toward industrialization and toward making Atlanta a regional business hub. Urban people and descendants of urban people (unlike the majority of Atlantans who were raw arrivals from farms and rural towns), many of the German-Jewish Temple members knew the mercantile world, mortgage brokering, textiles, law, and European languages. Whether Grandpapa had been a peddler or Grandfather had been mercantile genius Morris Rich or one of his brothers, the Temple Jews were acquainted with the American marketplace. But the chief question for them was whether the Atlanta power elite would permit them to abet the city's progress, or whether their religion would cause them to be held at bay, as talented, tainted bystanders.

Rothschild brought with him, for success, a few credentials—some from seminary, some from the army. The Temple board members who hired him envisioned a squadron leader who, echoing the cry "Forward, Atlanta!" from the downtown elites, would lead the charge of the Temple Jews in their assault on the power structure. Their prize: participation as equals in business and civic affairs.

And would the city of Atlanta make good use of the talents of a thirty-five-year-old Jewish army chaplain from Pittsburgh? Perhaps, but not because he was "eager to create a better world"—that was the *last* thing anybody wanted! If the city were to smile on him, it would be out of respect for his most important credential: he was *white*.

Or damn near.

2

The White Man's War

1

On the home front, as World War II veterans returned from overseas, the Jewish war was not quite over. In the summer of 1946, the Columbians, postwar America's first neo-Nazi group, was founded in Atlanta. Brown-shirted rank-and-file Columbians marched and drilled in public streets and parks, preparing for the overthrow of the existing government. "Their central motivation was hatred of the Jews," wrote the *Atlanta Constitution* journalist and historian Harold Martin, "and [their] members wore armbands bearing the drunken thunderbolt design once worn by Hitler's Elite Guard."

By the fall of 1946, two hundred Columbians in Atlanta were greeting one another with Nazi salutes. Sergeants were commanded by lieutenants, who were commanded by captains, who acted on orders from headquarters on Barstow Street. The headquarters consisted of "a dingy three-room suite in which some of the members lived, sleeping on cots and mattresses on the floor so that someone would always be present to answer emergency calls." Atlanta's whites were encouraged to phone in on a sort of racial-911 whenever they spotted a black family trying to move into a white or mixed neighborhood and to report "generally troublesome Negroes." A library of fifty volumes contained *Mein Kampf* and histories of the Nazi movement.

The Columbians had a simple recruitment strategy. They asked three questions of prospective members:

1. Do you hate Negroes?
2. Do you hate Jews?
3. Do you have three dollars?

Apparently, given the eight hundred applications for membership found in their headquarters, the strategy was an effective one.

Ralph McGill at the *Atlanta Constitution* accused the Columbians of "starting a cut-rate war in the hate racket by charging three dollars for membership instead of the ten dollars charged by the Klan." One day he reported in his column that, according to his informants, he himself had been the subject of debate at a recent Columbians' meeting. "Should they lynch McGill or simply waylay him one night and give him a good slugging?" the members had debated. The vote had been in favor of beating him up. McGill publicly thanked them in his column: "Always grateful for small favors."

The group's leaders predicted Columbian control of the Atlanta city government in six months, of the state of Georgia in two years, and of the federal government in ten years. Their overall program called for the voluntary departure—or, if necessary, involuntary deportation—of blacks to Africa and Jews to Madagascar (a distant island, the occupation of which presumably would not distress the Arab world), confiscation of Jewish wealth, and the establishment of an "American nationalist state" as a "one race nation." They opened chapters in Philadelphia, New York City, and Indianapolis and Gary, Indiana.

Against Jews, the organization sponsored speakers, printed a newspaper, and distributed leaflets revealing the Jewish plot for world domination. Against African Americans they unleashed violence rather than propaganda: they beat up black citizens, picketed their neighborhoods, and dynamited their houses. Unlike the Ku Klux Klan, which strove for secrecy and anonymity, the Columbians in Atlanta were rabble-rousing masters of the riot scene and the soapbox speech. Like today's anti-abortion extremists, they screamed themselves hoarse to try and awaken the public to mortal danger. Certain of the urgency and justice of their cause, some lost track of the line between the practice of citizenship and the practice of terrorism; they turned to violence.

"We're going to show white people how to take control of the government," promised Homer L. Loomis, one of the group's three founders. He was a wealthy Manhattanite, the son of a prominent admiralty lawyer with a Park Avenue address and a listing in the *Social Register*. He flunked out of Princeton and was the defendant in a sensational New York divorce during which his wife told the court that Loomis forced her to read aloud "A Mad Man's Manuscript" from the *Pickwick Papers*—the story of a man plotting his wife's murder—and then told her ominously that he had given it much thought. Loomis later remarried and moved to Virginia, but he failed to become a successful gentleman farmer. By the late 1930s, still unable to find his niche, he drifted into contact with right-wing extremist groups. "Hitler has the right idea," he told his neighbors. "He's not going to let the German race get mixed up with a lot of inferior races." Despite these views, he was drafted, served overseas with the Second Armored Division, and was honorably discharged in February 1946. He then moved to Atlanta with the express purpose of launching a fascist movement. "I'm going to be the Hitler of America," he told friends. He asked his Atlanta recruits to greet him with "Heil, Loomis!"

Emory Burke, the Columbians' cofounder, was thirty-one. An Alabama native and a veteran of anti-Semitic hoodlum gangs in New York City, he was a former staff member of the racist newspaper the *Storm* in the 1930s. Georgia's assistant attorney general Dan Duke noted that Burke's name had appeared on the masthead of "nearly every fascist organization in the country prior to World War II." One day, in an angry confrontation in a judge's chambers, Duke punched Burke. Shortly afterward, Duke's name turned up high on the Columbians' "lynch list."

Of the third founder, John H. Zimmerlee, little is known.

Rothschild, arranging his few belongings in his room at the Biltmore Hotel, working out a preliminary map of Atlanta in his mind, was discovering his superior Jim Crow status as a white man. From the neo-Nazis' viewpoint, he need not have anguished over it: in their celebration of mythical pureblood Aryans, the Columbians were not counting Jews as white people.

2

"The JEWS, who do the greatest part of advertising in newspapers, hate us because we had the courage to come out and tell the truth about how the JEWS are taking all the wealth and money in the nation," said a Columbian leaflet in October 1946. "The JEWS and the newspapers are AFRAID of us because we are organizing the white people of the South."

"Everybody in America is free to hate!" Loomis shouted at a meeting in Atlanta in November 1946. "Hate is natural. It's not un-American to hate. Why does the Jew think that he alone is above criticism and being hated?"

Loomis stirred together a hodgepodge of American prejudices: xenophobia, anti-Communism, race bigotry, and anti-Semitism, creating a poisonous stew with explosive potential. He was like a kid in a basement with a chemistry set who ignores the red warnings on the box while pouring volatile substances into a common beaker.

But, in truth, there was no inventiveness in the Columbian ideology. Loomis was traveling a well-worn path, practically a highway: "the age-old inclination," as the historian Deborah Lipstadt has written, "to find a Jewish conspirator behind a country's problems."

The Columbian vision of the Jew as the greedy behind-the-scenes manipulator, hell-bent on wealth and power, had its beginnings, in America, more than fifty years earlier. In the last decades of the 1800s—a time of urbanization, industrialization, and the start of the decline of the farm and country town as centers of American life—displaced and impoverished citizens angrily looked for the authors of their numerous afflictions. "The dispossessed farmers of the American South and Midwest," wrote the historian Jack Wertheimer, "threw their support behind populist demagogues who blamed the economic distress on a cabal of financiers intent on manipulating markets for their own selfish gain."

"The Jew—stereotyped, involved in finance, and mysterious," wrote Oscar Handlin, "stood ready to be assigned the role of arch-conspirator." Archest among arch-conspirators, in the popular imagination, was the most famous of European international banking families, the House of Rothschild.

"Cotton is a speculator's crop," says Jason Compson, in William Faulkner's *The Sound and the Fury*. " . . . Do you think the farmer gets anything out of it except a red neck and a hump in his back? You think the man that sweats to put it into the ground gets a red cent more than a bare living . . . And what for? so a bunch of damn eastern jews, I'm not talking about men of the jewish religion . . ." "That's all right . . .," says Compson later, watching the value of his stock fall, " . . . those rich New York jews have got to live like everybody else."

After the Bolshevik Revolution of 1917, the generalized notion that Jews were somehow profiting from the misery of red-blooded Americans was given a storyline, with clarity and urgency. "Seeking to ferret out subversive elements, defenders of America tended to suspect recent immigrants to America, such as Italians and Russian Jews, of maintaining direct ties with European bomb-throwers," wrote Wertheimer.

In the 1920s, Henry Ford, the great American inventor and industrialist, involved himself. He was a conspiracy-minded paranoic with a fortune to apply to a campaign against the Jews. "Convinced that Jews were up to no good, Ford opened a detective agency in New York to investigate Jewish influence," wrote Wertheimer. The agency forwarded a copy of the infamous forgery, the *Protocols of the Learned Elders of Zion*. This literary hoax first appeared in Russia around the turn of the century. Published by the Imperial Printing Office, the manuscript was the invention of czarist secret police who based their work in part on an 1864 French satire, "Dialogue in Hell between Machiavelli and Montesquieu." The *Protocols* supposedly comprised the minutes of two dozen secret meetings held in Basel, Switzerland, at the time of the first World Zionist Conference there in 1897. Containing the mythical secret Jewish plot to control the world, it portrayed the Jews as having launched the ideas of liberty, equality, and fraternity and of Darwinism, Marxism, and Nietzscheanism. The Jews were also said to have fomented the French Revolution in order to weaken imperial governments; to transform gentiles into herds of "mentally indolent, obedient animals"; and to realize a Jewish plan, dating from 929 B.C., to control the world.

By the time of its translation into German in 1920, the *Protocols* contained indictments of the Jews for all the disasters of recent history, including World War I. Henry Ford, convinced that he had hit upon a secret text brimming with danger for the American way of life, funded the translation and distribution of long excerpts from the *Protocols*, making it available for the first time to the English-speaking world. From 1920 to 1927, Ford's newspaper, the *Independent*, with a circulation of six hundred thousand, expanded on the *Protocols* and described an astonishing range of Jewish crimes and conspiracies, including "The Scope of Jewish Dictatorship in America," "Jew Wires Direct Tammany's Gentile Puppets," "How Jews Gained American Liquor Control," "The Jewish Associates of Benedict Arnold," "Jewish Jazz Becomes Our National Music," "Jewish Gamblers Corrupt American Baseball," and "How the Jewish Song Trust Makes You Sing." A collection of Ford's articles were published as *The International Jew: The World's Foremost Problem*. The book sold over half a million copies in the United States, was translated into sixteen languages, and provided the basis for editorials such as "The Jewish Peril," which appeared in the *Christian Science Monitor* on June 19, 1920.

In the 1930s, the Jewish-peril alarm was sounded by media-savvy demagogues like Father Charles E. Coughlin and William Pelley. Coughlin's Sunday radio broadcasts, which began as religious hours, veered into isolationist politics; by 1938 he was defending the Nazi persecution of European Jews. Coughlin's right-wing party claimed five million members, and his magazine reprinted the *Protocols*. On the air until he was shut down by the government, Coughlin blamed World War II and America's entry into it on the Jews.

The period between the wars was America's peak of discrimination against Jews by universities, banks, manufacturing industries, insurance companies, utilities, publishers, engineering and architectural firms, advertising agencies, hospitals, law firms, social clubs, and resorts. Some colleges, seeking to detect Jewish applicants regardless of their degree of assimilation, not only required students to name their religious affiliation, but asked "mother's full maiden name" and whether the applicant's parents had ever been known by another name.

And then, in the years following World War II, the intensifying storm of anti-Semitism suddenly abated. "Given what apparently had been an escalation of bigotry during the war," wrote the historian Leonard Dinnerstein, "the transformation in public rhetoric and behavior afterwards was so swift that careful observers were at a loss to explain the changes." On every measurement scale—from polls of "Would you live next to a Jew?" "Would you marry a Jew?" "Have you heard any talk against Jews in the last six months?" to surveys of admission and promotion policies in academic settings, government agencies, social clubs, law firms, and industries—Jews increasingly were being accepted into the mainstream of majority white life, increasingly seen as members of one of America's "three major religions." Catholics, Asians, and even African Americans benefited from a booming postwar economy, a national sense of optimism, and—conceivably—from the country's glance at the Nazi horrors. Dinnerstein wrote: "To what extent the knowledge of Hitler's slaughter of six million Jews contributed to the desire to curb bigotry is impossible to state but after 1945 millions of Christian Americans became more cautious in expressing negative reactions to Jews."

In the South, however, anti-Semitism was given a unique twist, a new interpretation, that extended its life and vitality into the 1950s.

⊷ ≖◆≕ ⊷

In the South in the postwar years, the Cold War unfolded concurrently with the civil rights movement. Two mighty themes in public opinion converged: the national fear of Communist subversion and the regional fear of upheaval in the racial status quo. Southern politicians were in the process of making "the preservation of white supremacy" equivalent to "virulent anti-Communism."

In short, in the South, the two outstanding threats to the

status quo blended paranoically into a single nightmare: the Communists were attempting to weaken America from within by stirring up discontent among the otherwise-satisfied blacks! Integrationists were Communists.

And where were the Jews in this scenario?

Suspect, on both counts. Suspect already in the popular imagination of being soft on Communism, if not outright Bolsheviks. Suspect again—as southern extremists settled on their scapegoats—of being not-quite-white, of being nigger-lovers, of being themselves less than white.

If anti-Communism and segregationist extremism can be seen as two mighty rivers that met and flooded the South, then the Jew can be seen as the hapless fisherman on the far bank who has gotten tangled in his line and pulled into the torrent.

Conspiracy theories, myths, and rumors travel into popular culture through many channels, but it just so happened that in 1931 in Alabama an individual appeared who was easily identifiable as the three-headed monster: a Communist nigger-loving Jew. (Without appearing to nitpick, he was not actually a Communist.) Samuel Leibowitz, one of the outstanding criminal defense attorneys of his day, represented the so-called Scottsboro boys, nine black teenagers who were pulled off a freight train on March 25, 1931, and arrested for the rape of two white women. While Alabama national guardsmen warded off lynch mobs surrounding the courthouse, the young men were quickly indicted, tried, and convicted; all were found guilty and all but the youngest, a thirteen-year-old, were sentenced to death.

The hasty trial and conviction so flauted northern liberal notions of American justice that reversal of the young men's sentences became a cause célèbre on the left. Petitioners calling for a new trial included Albert Einstein, Thomas Mann, Theodore Dreiser, Upton Sinclair, John Dos Pasos, and Leopold Stokowski. Leibowitz was hired by the Communist-supported International Labor Defense. He arrived in Alabama with powerful weapons at his disposal, including the retraction of the rape story by one of the alleged victims. But the prosecutor also had a new weapon: the ability to tap into native resentment of Jewish interlopers.

"When Morgan County Solicitor Wade Wright began his summation . . . he gave voice to all the fears and hatreds of the area residents," wrote historian Dan T. Carter in *Scottsboro: A Tragedy of the American South*. Wright filled his closing remarks with anti-Semitic innuendos and slurs, then pointed a finger at the counsel table where Leibowitz and his Jewish co-counsel sat: " 'Show them,' he paused for effect, 'show them that Alabama justice cannot be bought and sold with Jew money from New York.' " Courtroom observers noted that although some jurors seemed unmoved, others looked electrified.

Again there was a verdict of guilty. "Reporters at the trial," wrote Carter, "noted that Wade Wright's anti-Semitic summation was the most effective single statement by the counsel for the prosecution. Until he spoke, most of the newspapermen felt there was an outside chance for a hung jury, but Wright 'registered to perfection the repressed feelings and prejudices of the twelve good men.' "

"The chant of 'Jew money' at Decatur," wrote one court observer, "damaged the standing of Southern Jews even more than the fulminations of the Ku Klux Klan in the 1920s." None of the Scottsboro boys ever was executed, but the last of them was not freed until 1950. Meanwhile, Leibowitz's repeated appearances on their behalf had made an indelible impression. "Obviously," wrote historian Leonard Dinnerstein in *Anti-Semitism in America*, "Leibowitz's appearance in the Scottsboro case was an example of a northern Jew working to undermine southern values."

"The Negro would behave himself if it wasn't for the Jews," cried Homer Loomis from a speaker's platform in Atlanta in 1946, arousing his Columbians to dance to an old tune. "It's the Jews' fault that the Negroes are getting out of place."

3

On an older street of modest brick bungalows not far from downtown lived one of the elite Columbians. George Michael Bright was a postwar Northern transplant to Atlanta like Jacob Rothschild, and—also like the rabbi—he promptly began to circulate his strong opinions on the Negro question. He was at cross-purposes with Rothschild, however, being a fierce believer in the genetic inferiority of the dark races. In 1946, at the age of 22, when George Bright affiliated himself with the Columbian leadership, it was his first active participation in a group pledged to protect the supremacy and purity of the white race.

Over the next few years, Bright grew aware of Rothschild's presence in Atlanta, and Rothschild grew aware of the existence of Bright's "type," and of the Columbians and similar organizations. "We note the rise of hate groups like the Columbians," he said in a High Holy Day sermon. But it would be more than ten years before Rothschild and Bright came face-to-face. Then each would learn more about the other than either of them could stomach.

Today, on Bright's street, boys and girls bump their fat-tired bikes over sidewalks broken by tree roots, and a postman makes his way up and down the miniature walkways like an old-time peddler. Plaid chairs and television sets are visible from the street through square front windows, and peonies spurt up in patches in the little front yards. One house stands at a bitter remove from the rest. Of gray stone, perched on a slight rise of earth, it is cold to all neighborly airs: an abandoned-looking place with a steep, wild yard; tall, cracked-cement steps with no railings; boarded-up windows; a plastic garbage can standing in the middle of the front yard; and a No Soliciting sign on the front door. Gusts of warm Indian summer air pour gold and maroon leaves onto the street, soft and worn, and the trees stand about with their limbs outstretched and empty-handed, having dumped their gallons of bright paint onto the earth below, but the lone gray house on its treeless yard appears colder by many degrees. Against the warm and radiant Georgia November, it wraps itself in blue and black shadows that appear wintry, bleak. It is the house of a man nursing lifelong resentments and harboring vast suspicions, a house whose front-door peephole was used assiduously.

In this condemned-looking house George Bright has lived as if curled in a trench near the front lines of a war, emerging only to hurl a grenade. Here he strategized in the middle of the night, both elbows on the tabletop, head bent before a high-intensity desk lamp. For miles around, the naive citizenry slept. A native of New York State, an engineer and amateur inventor, Bright was, like his name (and like his desk lamp), high intensity, almost permanently alert. At night he rested only fitfully and paranoically, often startling to wakefulness, the thin blood in his veins laced with a natural caffeine.

Most of the small rooms in his stone house were bare and matted with dust. He lived chiefly in his front room, crowded with living-room and bedroom furniture, where he could sit on his bed and reach a hot plate on the coffee table. Papers, magazines, full ashtrays, and dirty plates rose in layers across the horizontal surfaces. A portable Zenith television with rabbit-ear antennae sat on a desk. The half-crammed, half-empty house lacked in every detail what used to be known as "a woman's touch." If a wife ever had crossed the threshold at this address, she probably would have ordered George to cart everything out so she could start fresh. One pictures pine cleansers sinking into the grit of neglected corners. But there had been no such wife. "Unfortunately, it takes two to marry," said Bright. "I wanted an educated woman, with something up here [tapping the side of his forehead], maybe mathematically inclined. Sometimes I found a girl I liked; sometimes a girl liked me. It just never seemed to be the same girl."

The mix of slovenliness and utilitarian order—like a bunker rank with the odors and crammed with the personal effects of a platoon too long confined—contributed to the inhabitant's single-mindedness. In shuttered, bolted, inhospitable rooms, working under artificial light, Bright was able to find focus.

Bright himself, like his house, seemed honed for efficiency. He was a narrow, thin-lipped, gaunt-faced, balding man with fuzzy gray sideburns, a long nose, and a protruding jaw. In profile he looked like the crescent man-in-the-moon. He wore a cheap watch and, in his short-sleeved, button-down green shirt, a plastic pocket protector filled with retractable ballpoint pens and mechanical pencils.

Framed photographs of his childhood in Rochester, New York—he was one of five children of an Eastman-Kodak engineer and his wife—stood on a desktop. Also displayed were the collage-type picture frames sold in drugstores, filled with sunlit shots of happy toddlers and pretty women with windblown hair. These magazinelike prints had come inside the picture frames for display purposes. The forbidding solitude Bright had arranged around himself—the dust-filled rooms, the forbidding exterior—seemed to suit him in all but this one detail. The prints were for those rare moments when he looked up from an electrical diagram or a political text and wished to rest his eyes, however briefly, on a human face. For such moments, these store-bought images suited him. Human contact enough.

Richard Wasser, a Temple member and an engineer with a graduate degree from Georgia Tech, worked with Bright at Fulton Bag & Cotton Mills in the 1950s. "They had this young man, George Bright, who worked in the adjacent office for the industrial engineers," said Wasser. "He was somewhat balding, and he wore glasses. We were all very friendly, all the engineers knew one another, we were all college graduates, all reasonably similar in backgrounds, so there was an undercurrent of friendship. But George was always considered kind of a weird character. He was never part of the group when we all used to eat lunch together. He was very standoffish and strange. He was argumentative. He would take the opposite side of any conversation. We'd be sitting there talking about, 'Well, this looks like it's doing that,' and he would take the opposite side.

"George was assigned a particular operation to check, and he was supposed to do it on the third shift from midnight to 7:00 in the morning. And everybody worked fairly independently, and we'd come back in, make up our reports, and turn them in. And on several occasions we noticed that George was supposed to work during one shift and we would count on his being part of the team, and he wouldn't show up. And then he would show up on another shift where he wasn't needed. And of course there was an undercurrent of conversation that he was not pulling his load, a lot of animosity from his peers. And my recollection is that he was terminated because he did not work as he was directed. There was some argument at the time. He came back in, wanting to be reinstated, but this-this-and-this was a problem, and it's my impression that it was an almost universal thing that nobody would speak in his behalf."

Bright's chief subject was the Soviet peril—the Communist threat to America's democracy through infiltration and subversion. He had been alerted to this danger through the broadcasts of Father Charles Coughlin, the Catholic priest who hosted a right-wing radio program. Bright came within the orbit of the Columbians and appeared at rallies with Burke and Loomis. He later followed, with the rest of America, the trial in 1949 of the State Department high official Alger Hiss, the exposure in 1950 of the physicist Klaus Fuchs as a Soviet agent, the fall of the French in Indochina, and the nationally televised congressional hearings in which Senator Joseph McCarthy denounced powerful citizens as Communists. The risk to America so riveted Bright's attention that he pledged his life to exposing and uprooting America's enemies. In his shuttered house, he reread the already-memorized books from his shelves revealing the Communist menace, including *Toward a Communist America* by William Z. Foster, the Communist Party candidate for president.

"We had a difficult political situation that arose with Karl Marx when he wrote his *Manifesto*," said Bright. "For what reason he wrote it, nobody will ever know. To recruit Communists into their ranks, the Communists would go around and try to recruit the underprivileged and the unemployed, because those people were ripe for picking. And their main objective was to recruit the black population into their Communist ranks to take over this country. In other words, they were using the blacks.

"Of course it wouldn't come true," he said, and laughed a dry chuckle, a voiceless heh-heh, "because as soon as the Communists came into power—they didn't want the blacks anyway—they would kill them, just like Stalin eliminated the people who helped him get into power. The average Americans were not aware and the black people weren't aware. They were just easily led. Martin Luther King's advisors were Communists. They would take him up to Monteagle, Tennessee, wine and dine him; but they were guiding him to recruit the blacks for the Communists. He was too stupid to catch on, didn't know what was happening. The civil rights movement was started and organized by the Communists."

Even in the last decade of the twentieth century, with the Red superpower in disintegration and its global propaganda machine defunct, Bright remains committed, a monk in the service of anti-Communism. As friars did not exit their monasteries when the first astronauts returned to earth and swore they had not seen heaven, so Bright has not denounced his vocation simply because journalists report that the Soviet Union is dead.

So far off the beaten track, so far from the canon of accepted American history, Bright's worldview was nonetheless logical. He knew that he and his like-minded former associates not only had *not* achieved public acclaim and electoral victory but had been relegated to the fringe of mainstream American thought and life, despite their handle on the truth—thus, the bunker mentality, the isolationism, the grim expression on his face. But he clung to his perspective; he had bound himself over, long ago, to McCarthyite enlightenment. He understood the events of modern southern history in a special way—as the collusion of Moscow with Africa to rob white American Christians of their own country.

"Race mixing is the downfall of civilization," he said. "If you don't love your own race, you don't love anything. That's what made the world and that's what will keep the world going—the purity of the races. The way the world developed was that the white race just happened to surpass all the others. Now why? That's another question, but it's a fact that the white race did. After the Chinese civilization rose and fell, and after the South American civilization rose and fell, the white race in Europe kept rising and came to the top of the whole world.

"Things would have evolved racially in this country. Gradually. Eventually. But not into an integrated society. There are two factions in this society that would not integrate with the blacks: the Jews and the Anglo-Saxons. The Jews are extremely segregated—they are not allowed to marry blacks. And the white people have better sense. They don't have a rule, but their common sense tells them not to dilute their race. And it should occur to the blacks to maintain *their* race purity. But the Communists told blacks they would rule the U.S. and marry the white girls. They promised a white wife for every black. But in doing so, the Communists came up against a brick wall among the

Anglo-Saxons. Including me. The Communist effort here was opposed by people like me."

⸻ ⧫ ⸻

Because he believed McCarthy's conspiracy theories, as embellished by southern demagogues and national fascists, because he deeply believed in this perspective, there was little stridency in him. He was first an engineer, a scientist, an amateur mathematician. He had invented not only a reflecting telescope that enabled people to look deep into their own inner eye but also GripRights, a patented hand exerciser. In his mind, he had analyzed the social and political facts and had accepted the theory that explained them most lucidly.

When he spoke of the truths he understood, he spoke dryly and quietly, as if expounding a mathematical theorem. "I'm in favor of truth. Honesty is the best policy. Don't want any lies, just the truth. When the facts are printed, that's good enough for me—and let the chips fall where they may. And sure enough, it turned out that the top Communists in this country was always a Jew. And so what? I mean, facts are facts. The Hollywood Communists, same thing. Facts are facts. You know, who cares? I mean this is true." He was not, in other words, looking for anyone to hate, not out to get the Jews.

But he did not see the facts upon which he relied in the pages of the *Atlanta Constitution*, for the editor "Red Ralph" McGill took orders from Moscow. "In his column, McGill parroted the Communist line every day.... The *Constitution* wouldn't print the truth." Bright tirelessly read other newsletters, leaflets, and books, and he assimilated the facts quickly enough. Though he might be considered "lunatic fringe" these days, he was once—in the 1940s and 1950s—in the inner circle, privy to the inside information of those waging a secret war to take back America from the Communists, the blacks, and the Jews.

"It is well known," he said, "that all the European Communist leaders and dictators were Jews. Communist dictator of Germany after World War I was a Jew: Rosa Luxemburg. The founders of the Communist Party were all Jews. They had the top command in Russia. The chief of the secret police was a Jew, and he had the power, the power over Stalin. Stalin was the figurehead. The head of the KGB was a Jew with the power of life and death over Stalin.

"The Communist Party in the Southeast was run by a Jew, Gus Hall. Or I call him Gus Hall—that's a counterfeit name. Arvo Halberg. He was a Jew. He got his money from Moscow. So there were people trying to figure out why was the Communist Party in the charge of this small group of related people. And in trying to oppose the Communist movement, the opposers had to oppose the Jewish population because all the top Communists it seems like were Jews." He laughed his dry laugh. "And when you print *that*, you get all the Jews coming down on you."

* * *

"This was typical right-wing segregationist lunacy, dosed with small grains of truth," said Harvey Klehr, a professor of politics at Emory University and the author, with John Earl Haynes and Fridrikh Igorevich Firsov, of *The Secret World of American Communism*. "It's the typical anti-Semitic trope, the classic anti-Semitism of ideologues like Houston Stewart Chamberlain, an Anglo-British author who influenced the Nazis, and other precursors of the Nazis with their belief in pure races."

Bright's thought included a few facts: some of Martin Luther King's advisors and associates were Communists, and Jews were disproportionately represented in the worldwide Communist movements. "There were possibly a hundred thousand members of the American Communist Party at its height in 1939," said Klehr, "and maybe 40 percent of them were Jewish. They were highly overrepresented (although the vast majority of American Jews were *not* Communists). When the number of Jews in the party declined, the majority of American Communists were Finnish: Gus Hall's parents emigrated from Finland; he did change his name from Arvo Halberg."

And while it is true that Rosa Luxemburg was Jewish, she was a founder in 1918 of the German Communist Party and died in 1919 in Berlin during a workers' uprising, having never risen to power. No Jew gave orders to Stalin. Meanwhile, in America, the very real attraction of the Communist Party to Jews before the 1940s was multifaceted: some Russian Jews, victims of oppression and discrimination in the old Russian Empire, were radicalized before they immigrated to America; some believed the Russian Revolution had abolished anti-Semitism; many saw Russia as a bulwark against Nazism.

"For some," said Harvey Klehr, "joining the Communist Party may have been, paradoxically, a way of Americanizing themselves. Israel Regenstreif became John Gates, CP organizer and editor of the *Daily Worker*. It was a way of connecting with the American working class." Finally, Communist parties around the world tend to attract each nation's minorities. Thus, out of a few threads of truth and a skein of outright fabrications and sinister fantasies, Bright and his confederates wove their worldview.

"People of a temperate climate have contributed 99.9 percent of all the advancement of mankind," Bright mentioned during a break in conversation, arranging a fresh cigarette for himself. By the time he had leaned back and expelled his first mouthful of smoke, he was returning to an autobiographical narrative, but the aside was a tip-off that professing hatred of the dark-skinned races was a form of talking about one's own noble forebears and superior lineage, and one's favored position with the Almighty.

Who can tell the impact of years of focused solitude on a mind like Bright's? He lived in a house in which the debris was only his own, a house in which the hundreds of inanimate objects—books and papers, mostly—still did not add up to companionship. Even after many years, his lifelong possessions—the tired bedding, the yellowing volumes, the gritty plates—did not send out even a mute signal of concordance; they might as well have been prisoners kept under lock and key. Since he was, after all, a human being, a social animal, he had to find a network that linked him to others in the precomputer age—a psychological Internet. Since he had no descendants, neither biological nor through ties of affection, he naturally had to find a way to place himself on the human family tree, on a genealogical chart, without appearing to himself to be a dead end of evolution. Had he been a Greek American or an Irish

American or the resident of a rural town, he might have passed as simply himself—a bit of a square peg, a bit of a brain, everyone's odd-duck uncle—and still have been invited to all the weddings and christenings. But as a transient, a loner, a generic American white man, a shy man capable of deriving quiet enjoyment from reading books, how was he to connect himself to a world full of mass upheavals and dazzling technology? From what perspective was he to interpret the daily news? To be *white* was a start. He read history from the viewpoint of a *white* person and understood himself to be a child of Europe, of the "Northern Race," of cave painters and discoverers of fire, of whale hunters, of builders of ships and cradles and flutes from ancient hardwoods. He was a modern representative of a long and distinguished line.

Bright, undistracted by marital and child-rearing tasks, put himself at the service of his race. He had the time, the mentality, and the inclination to serve. He became a conveyor of information among men who viewed the civil rights struggle of American blacks as a racial Armageddon. He became an insider. When he met confederates, there were important words and countersigns to exchange; written materials were slid out of briefcases and passed hand to hand. His telephone rang at odd hours; he scribbled cryptic notations on his calendar. After work there might be a key person to meet at a bar, or a lecture to attend. Bright became a vital link in a chain of being.

Motives? There were motives. Bright was keenly aware of the Jews' motives. Living a life at the very border of poverty (his own street of small houses mostly kept up a brave front as it ran south toward the railroad yard), managing without the conveniences of a new car, a blender, or a microwave—out of touch with the rudiments of late-twentieth-century materialism—Bright still spoke knowingly of the schemes of millionaires, of global politics, of all the gold on earth.

"The Jews wanted the blacks and whites to amalgamate while they remained pure. They didn't mix except when it's to their advantage. They will intermarry with a white if it's to the Jews' advantage to marry that white and get them into the Jewish group to pick a brain or do work. They do that once in a while.

"The Jewish heaven on earth will come when the Jews have

all the gold," he said. "That's exactly their words, in their own official bible. When they have all the gold, then they will be in heaven."

The occult wisdom acquired by Bright was heavily freighted with ideas derived not from the Jews' bible but from the *Protocols of the Learned Elders of Zion*. For the cornerstone of Bright's philosophy, and that of the organizations he joined, was the cardinal point in the *Protocols*: Jewish greed and thirst for power. "The GOLD of the Nations is the real LORD OF ISRAEL."

Bright had been granted access to arcane intelligence. He believed he knew what was in the secret books of the Jews. He had been a recruit in the underground war for America's soul and never had betrayed the trust placed in him. Without this covert understanding of dark forces, without the mutual regard of similar men who made themselves known to him by certain signs, his life might have seemed paltry and unfulfilled. But, with his exposure to truths invisible to the masses, his austere life became a facade, a camouflage. In his heart, he was a frontier guardsman, a race hero, and he knew the location in Atlanta of the headquarters of the Jews. It was the House of Rothschild.

3

The Most Beloved Jew Next to Jesus

1

Freshly showered, wet scant hair combed back, a handful of aftershave thrown over his tanned face (the fleeting, pink suntan of a naturally fair-skinned man), Jack Rothschild bounded up the Temple driveway. He had stashed his bags and tennis racket in his rented room as if posted there by army order and had buttoned himself into a new shirt. In a gregarious mood, he was ready to present himself to his new commanding officer: the rabbi emeritus, Dr. David Marx. But Rothschild was no longer an army captain. In truth, in his curiosity and keenness, he was more like a nephew recently advised of a sizable inheritance, who has shown up (on foot, carrying weather-beaten valises, and attempting to look ingenuous) to survey the estate.

Of white marble and red brick, the Romanesque Temple glowed in morning sunlight that poured on it clearly as water. Traffic moved at its feet. At street level were fine old southern houses and a seminary, and wooded residential drives wound down the slope behind it. The Temple rose above its neighborhood with an air of antiquity, like Stonehenge, or like the first Temple, commanding the clouds from its superior perch.

The congregation was modern, Rothschild would learn, ultramodern and chic, but their temple was a strange and ornate place. Pomegranates, griffins, and cherubim had been chiseled in stone. On a raised platform in the sanctuary sat a massive golden Ark of the Covenant, splendid and ancient and holy looking, as if it had been polished personally by the robed holy men attending it in the Temple of Solomon. The Lion of Judah and the Wolf of Benjamin silently roared at each other across a vast domed inner sanctum.

Down a hallway, in a majestic and high-ceilinged room, behind an imposing desk, flanked by tall windows, a small man bitterly awaited Rothschild. The new arrival rapped out shave-and-a-haircut and threw open the door. From behind the desk, Marx (the prime mover behind the marble colossus on the hill-top, to which Rothschild was no doubt going to ask for the keys) grimly extended his hand.

The invasion of flippant good health, nonchalance, and high spirits made a very poor impression on the slight, dignified, Germanic older man. Even their relative statures, as their fingers briefly touched above the desk (Rothschild leaning over, Marx recoiling) looked incompatible. Rothschild, five-feet-eight-inches tall, was a product of his well-fed, optimistic American century. Marx, age seventy-four and five-foot-two, was a nineteenth-century miniature, the perfection of clothing and grooming carried out to the smallest detail, as in a Victorian doll's house. The elegance of his attire and the delicacy of his self-possession tended to make bulkier, sloppier Americans feel oversized, untucked, and excessively loud. He had this impact now on Rothschild, whose headlong, whistling stroll from the Biltmore and happy sprint up the marble stairs had suddenly come to a halt.

Marx, slowly circumnavigating his desk, looked—and bore himself—like Bismarck, done on a smaller scale. He wore a gold pince-nez and a high starched collar. A bushy, frowning mous-tache was the only register of sentiment on a round, stern, pale face. He had been born in New Orleans in 1872, the child of German-Jewish immigrants, and had served as the rabbi of the Temple since 1895, more than half a century. In 1898, he had been invited to the formal dinner party for William McKinley when the president had visited Atlanta; in 1905, he had banqueted with Teddy Roosevelt; and in 1909, he had been part of the official welcoming committee for William H. Taft. He was a Grand Master Mason, elevated to thirty-third degree of the Scottish Rite. He was considered to be a silver-tongued public speaker who skillfully combined the arts of elocution, rhetoric, and drama. "Dr. Marx had a gift of gab, he was a wonderful speaker, and he spoke like a minister," said Harry Epstein, the Orthodox rabbi of Conservative Congregation Ahavath Achim. "He was one of them. The Jewish community desperately needed an ambassador. He was the ambassador. He would have made a marvelous Presbyterian minister. In the Christian community of Atlanta, Dr. Marx was the most beloved Jew next to Jesus." From behind a podium, clutching it with both hands, Marx held forth in ponderous, trembling, operatic declamations: "*Hear . . . O . . . Israel!*" he boomed, leaving people flabbergasted at the volume from such a diminutive source. "I never had any theological problems growing up," said Cecil Alexander, a distinguished Yale- and Harvard-educated architect. "I thought Dr. Marx was God."

Marx had been furious when he was "promoted" to emeritus status in preparation for the hiring of a new rabbi and compelled to sit through a flowery musical program of commemoration and tribute. Without his approval, the Temple board—eager to move into modern times a little less encumbered by their tireless septuagenarian—interviewed and hired Rothschild. As Marx had made perfectly clear for many years, he was not in need of assistance and was not planning to retire.

Smiling in confusion, the rebuffed Rothschild hastily sought a new pose short of affability but not quite craven. He briefly thought to win over Marx with his usual display of wit and charm, but he saw those window dressings quickly scorned by the intruded-upon older man. He hoped then to reach some wellspring of Jewish feeling and kinship—or, at the very least, of rabbinical solidarity—but found these absent in a man who had dedicated his life to the proposition that Jewish people were not distinct from other Americans. There were no winks, no inside jokes with this rabbi; no warm Yiddish expressions (which sounded to Marx more like throat clearings than words) thickened his speech. Marx greeted Jews with perfect, tepid civility, apparently no more and no less than he extended to Episcopalians.

For Marx, the expression and practice of a man's religion properly belonged within the private sphere of the home. As a rabbi, he addressed himself chiefly to a more fitting public question: How may I speed the acceptance of my Temple members by the white Christian majority on terms of absolute equality?

In search of this acceptance, he had steered the Temple farther and farther from its traditional moorings. His reading of the situation had taught him that if strangers and exotics were despised in the South, then Jews must be neither. He would recast these bearded sons of peddlers, these bilingual wholesalers and quick-witted merchants, these book collectors, violinists, and reciters of poetry—these descendants of a priestly caste—into ordinary, down-home folks.

He had been given a most delicate mission in life: to help his congregants adapt to, and thrive in, this strange, unpredictable America; and to shape the terrain into a welcoming host to this strange people, with their unpredictable mix of the ancient and the modern. He sought, for them all, balance: remain Jews— that was paramount—but do so in a neighborly way, in a cheerful American frame of mind. Do not *schlepp* about with your Jewishness borne like heavy, gloomy, dark-hued clothing; doff the anachronisms; stash your Judaism at home, like an heirloom in a fine old chest, to be opened on Friday nights within the circle of your immediate family. "Some of my happiest childhood memories are of Friday night dinners at my grandparents' home," wrote Ellen Marx Rappaport of Baltimore, one of Marx's granddaughters. "We always lit the Sabbath candles and recited the blessings over the bread and wine. My grandfather believed that the center of Jewish life was the home." Outside the house, in all public matters, conduct yourselves like Americans, indistinguishable from the better segments of the population. Marx could not count on Rothschild (raised in Pennsylvania, educated in Ohio) to understand the work or to continue it.

He looked Rothschild up and down, disliked what he saw (a successor), and concluded the meeting. Rothschild, in his pressed shirt and deflated spirits, backed out. He understood immediately that he had been neither welcomed nor ceded to. He was now like an heir who discovers that his version of the will is but one of many—and is being contested.

Rothschild's sensation of rebuff was richly confirmed over the next weeks and months: Marx repudiated the idea of retirement. He continued to conduct weddings and funerals, refused to co-officiate at them with Rothschild, and compelled well-meaning congregants to choose between them. Most chose Marx. "Rothschild was really not considered the whole rabbi, the real rabbi, as long as Marx was around," remembers Richard Wasser.

Toward the end of that first summer under one roof, Rothschild was obliged to approach Marx to plan his upcoming installation. "What installation?" snapped Marx.

A ceremony was scheduled for September. Rothschild needed to know which parts of the service Marx wanted to perform. Marx pulled a sheet of paper from his desk and waved it at Rothschild. "This resolution says I shall be the rabbi of the congregation until my successor has been duly chosen and qualified. Young man, you may have been chosen, but you will *never qualify*."

"Soon after Jack came, the everlasting light in the Temple went out," remembers Aline Uhry. "The story is that Jack called Dr. Marx and said, 'Dr. Marx, what shall I do? The everlasting light has gone out.' And Dr. Marx said: 'Why are you asking me? It never *went* out while *I* was rabbi.'"

From a religious point of view, Rothschild disagreed about the eternal light. Although it had never failed during Marx's tenure, much else that Rothschild saw as quintessentially Jewish had flickered. Simply, quietly, in a world ruled by Anglo-Saxon Protestants, southern Jews had laid aside their yarmulkes; forgotten their Hebrew letters; cultivated a taste for shellfish, baked ham, and pork roast; and celebrated Christmas and Easter with their children. Many of the age-old traditions of Judaism had become virtually indecipherable to them.

Marx was an adherent of the concept that there was such a thing as "too Jewish." His eradication of the "too Jewish" elements from the lives of the Temple Jews meant, in essence: "We all must live in society. We, as Jews of the American South, must make a home for ourselves here, in one of the Diaspora's hinterlands. Let us not, therefore, go out of our way to cling to religious anachronisms, thereby making ourselves strange to our neighbors. Let us release our grip on Judaic antiquities, while preserving in our lives, and for our children, the distilled and relevant core of the Jewish faith. Let us make of religion a private matter, and adapt our public personae to the demands of our region and country."

He himself explained in 1909, reflecting upon the superiority of the Reform service over the traditional one: "Our services are cast on a high plane of sanity, which, while recognizing the importance of sentiment, does not generate into hysteria so prejudicial to the intellectual side of man's religious nature." The title *Rabbi*, for example, was too Jewish: *Reverend* or *Doctor* frequently was preferable. Prayer shawls and head coverings were too Jewish. Bar mitzvahs were eliminated in 1898 as "inexpedient," as were candlelightings, wine, the holy language of Hebrew, and the bris, or religious circumcision ceremony. The Sabbath service was abbreviated, Anglicized, and made generally more efficient. The shofar, or curved ram's horn, sounded in soul-rattling blasts at the conclusion of the holy fast day of Yom Kippur, was replaced by a mellowersounding trumpet; and the fast itself gave way as many people dashed out to a nearby drugstore during a break in the prayer service. Marx himself disregarded the Jewish dietary laws. He also preached virulent anti-Zionism and remained a steadfast anti-Zionist up to and through 1948, out of fear that support of a Jewish state might expose American Jews to charges of dual loyalty.

An organ and choir enhanced the Temple's worship services. In 1906, the Temple became one of eighteen Reform temples in America to offer Sunday morning worship. This particular innovation failed, however, when the choir members protested: all were Christians, and they needed the day off to attend their own church services. "We had beautiful music in the Temple," said Janice Rothschild. "We had the best voices in town. We really had fabulous music. It wasn't particularly *Jewish* music, but it was beautiful."

"At the dedication of the new temple in 1902, Massenet's 'The Last Sleep of the Virgin' was performed," wrote Stephen Hertzberg, a historian of the early Jewish community in Atlanta, about an earlier structure, "and apparently no eyebrows were raised."

2

The nineteenth- and early-twentieth-century German-Jewish Reform rabbis yearned to be modern, to be shorn of the locks of medieval mysticism, to read from left to right, to lose Shylock.

A modern, rational, "Reform" approach to the old religion originated in Germany and caught on most of all in the new American cities—cities without walls! cities without Jewish quarters! An ocean of tossing iron ships lay between the American Jews and the European capitals of ancient Jewry. In America an individual's ties to the new little Jewish communities—most of which lacked rabbis—were purely optional. The Jewish citizens worked side by side with gentile businessmen and lawyers, who wore fluffy sideburns and confessed to having never met a Jew before and who did not mind inviting one home to dinner. Here, the practice of Judaism did not have to occupy all hours from dawn to midnight, with diet, dress, and personal habits dictated by ancient Hebrew texts. Jews did not have to become conspicuous to the non-Jewish citizenry. In America, the practice of Judaism could become, as Yale law professor Stephen Carter has framed it in *The Culture of Disbelief*, a "hobby."

Across the American South, minuscule Jewish communities sprang up at crossroads and whistle-stops. Peddlers set down their sacks, rented a hole-in-the-wall storefront, and opened Hirsch's Dry Goods or Esserman's & Company or Estroffs; immigrant families arrived to assist an already-established uncle or cousin. From long-distance associations, tiny congregations grew. First they founded burial societies.

Then they met several times a year at one another's houses, sometimes traveling a hundred miles to reach another Jew. They chose from among themselves a person who could teach children the Aleph-Bet. If numbers grew, they built synagogues. When Hebrew Union College showed itself heroically willing to dispatch young rabbis and student rabbis to all corners of the country, many southern congregations became Reform in order to be sent a circuit-riding rabbi. And in the tremendous green isolation from other Jewish people, from kosher butchers and ritual baths and Talmud-Torahs (religious schools), the rural Jews could hardly help but become liberal in practice.

A story is told about a Jewish peddler named Schwartz who, in the course of his lonely travels, was invited to supper one night at a farmhouse in Alabama. He saw immediately that the main course was ham, but he gratefully seated himself and ate with a healthy appetite. The farmwife expressed her surprise: "I thought Moses ordered the Jews not to eat any hog meat."

Schwartz cheerfully replied, "Ah, Madam, if Moses had travelled through Perry County, Alabama, he never would have issued such an order."

"Today we accept as binding only the moral laws . . . but reject all such as are not adapted to the views and habits of modern civilization," said the Reform movement's Pittsburgh Platform of 1885, the movement-within-a-movement that came to be known as "Classical Reform" and that swept the southern congregations. In the Pittsburgh Platform, Judaism was a religion, not a people, and ceremonies and rituals were not necessary in the modern era: " . . . their observance in our days is apt rather to obstruct than to further modern spiritual elevation." The Pittsburgh Platform made reference to the "God-idea." Dr. Marx was educated and ordained in, and was one of the outstanding exponents of, the Pittsburgh Platform, "Classical Reform." By 1860, most of the synagogues in the South were Reform, and they became practitioners of Classical Reform Judaism.

A man from Lexington, Mississippi, explained: "Reform Judaism is the only kind of Jewish religion you can have down here and stick to it." Sabbath services in southern Reform temples featured, primarily, decorum. Congregations in Sunday dress faced forward quietly in pews. Rabbis appeared in business suits and did not insist on adherence to arcane rules extending into the privacy of people's everyday lives. The religion offered was somewhat generic: English hymns to a Supreme Being; an organ producing solemn bass notes during moments of private reflection; an English prayerbook containing words like *Thy, Thou, loving kindness,* and *supplication;* a sermon advocating moral reform—and the whole contained within ninety minutes.

In 1937, the official body of Reform rabbis replaced the Pittsburgh Platform with the Columbus Platform: Jews *were* a people, the rabbis now held; rituals and ceremonies *should* be included in the liturgy; Zion was the center of Jewish spiritual life; and the supreme being was "God." Jacob Rothschild was ordained in the principles of the Columbus Platform.

The Columbus revisions were adopted by most Reform congregations in America outside the South. In the South they were largely ignored. Thus, when Rabbi Rothschild arrived from Pittsburgh and met Dr. Marx in Atlanta, it was the Son of the Columbus Platform (Rothschild) meets the Son of the Pittsburgh Platform (Marx). Of his two Pittsburgh imports—the Platform and Rothschild—Marx, and many others of his generation, decidedly fancied the former.

The Temple members followed Marx in order to sail with him upon the western tide of Reform.

"They wanted to be members of the business community without any special tag," said Herbert Elsas, an attorney and descendant of a Jewish cotton-mill-owning family. "They wanted to be Rotarians. They wanted their religious activities to be closely related to those of their Christian neighbors. The longer the German Jews had been here, the more they wanted that kind of identification. They didn't want to say: 'I'm not Jewish,' but: 'I'm Jewish, but it's not so different.' Marx wanted as much conformity as possible with, I guess, Episcopalian. He didn't want Catholic and he didn't know what the Church of England was, but he thought High Church Episcopalian was a pretty good model."

A literate and ambitious man, Cecil Alexander, raised at the Temple, often has been mistaken over the years for a Christian, given his florid complexion, Yale background, non-Jewish business partner, and prominent career. He has taken it good-humoredly. Recently given an *aliyah*—the honor of reciting a blessing over the reading of the Torah—at his godson Jacob Rothschild's (the rabbi's grandson) bar mitzvah, Alexander crammed for the role for weeks. "They told me: 'You've got to read the prayers at Jacob's bar mitzvah from the Torah and from the Hebrew.'

"And I said, 'Oh no I'm not. I don't have a clue in the world how to do that.'

"But they said, 'Oh no, you've got to do it, you're the godfather,' and so forth.

"I said, 'If you want me to do that, you've got to write it out phonetically and tape it so I can understand it.' So I practiced it; I taped it in my own voice, and practiced it some more. The day arrived and I got up and did the Hebrew. *I* thought I got through it fine. When I sat down, a man leaned over and whispered to me, 'You certainly did that well.'

" 'Well! Thank you,' I said.

" 'Yes sir,' he said, 'I don't think you could have done it any better if you were *Jewish*.' "

On another occasion, Cecil and Hermie Alexander attended a convention of architects in Miami. "We were walking along the beach and ran into this couple we knew. 'Cecil! Hermie!' the husband says. 'Are we glad to see you! Do you know we've been here since Friday night and you're the first Christians we've seen?!'

" 'Hey boy, we're glad to see you, too!' I say. 'We've also been here since Friday night and you're the first Christians *we've* seen. But I got to tell you, we're one up on you: *you* haven't seen any yet.' "

"I went to a bar mitzvah Saturday at the Conservative synagogue and felt like a stranger," said Bill Bremen, a jaunty, patrician-looking man with bushy gray eyebrows and bushy gray sideburns, a beloved community leader. "I couldn't recite the prayers everybody was reciting. . . . We had no bar mitzvahs when I was growing up. In Sunday school, we played. It was a joke, really. We'd go, and look forward to the end of the morning when we'd go to somebody's house and have lunch. That was the extent of Sunday school."

"It is not uncommon," wrote the folklorist Carolyn Lipson-Walker, "to hear that until recent years a middle-aged or older Jew who grew up in the South had never attended a *seder*, seen a wedding *chupah* [canopy] or a *bar mitzvah* or tasted traditional American Jewish foods—gefilte fish, bagels and lox, and chopped liver." One of Lipson-Walker's respondents, a woman in Baton Rouge, reported that yarmulkes made her sick.

Across the Reform Jewish South, there were Bootsies and Bubbas and Doreens with last names like Rosenfeld and Lieberman. For those who served a Friday night Sabbath dinner, the menu might involve "pork chops with okra and tomatoes and black-eyed peas" or "oyster stew, steaks, ham, or fried chicken, Mama's homemade biscuits and cornbread too." At the Passover seder—the festive meal ushering in a week during which all bread products are forbidden—many southern Jews served a plate of matzo at one end of the table and a basket of biscuits at the other. "Southern Jews quickly began to eat Southern foods as proof of their participation in Southern culture and tradition," wrote Lipson-Walker. "Most Southern Jews abandoned the two thousand year old laws which governed which animals could be eaten (pork and shellfish were prohibited). . . . Pork and shellfish became so accepted in Southern Jewish diets that it was served at temples and at Jewish organizational functions. . . . 'We're one of those families that have ham on Yom Kippur,' said a Tulane college student. . . . The Brotherhood of Temple Sinai in New Orleans has an annual shrimp boil; in Baton Rouge a Reform synagogue has an annual crawfish boil; and in Brookhaven, Mississippi, they have a 'High Holy Day Shrimp Fry.' "

A great many southern Jews celebrated Christmas to some extent, though not without a sense of humor—in many homes, the crowning angel was replaced by a star of David or a glazed bagel. One well-meaning family, scolded by their rabbi for having a wreath on their door, exchanged it for a few sprigs of holly. "Well, you just didn't want to be different," said a woman from Vidalia, Louisiana. " . . . In fact, I know so little about Judaism that it's embarrassing. . . . We have very few Jewish customs at home. We celebrated Christmas. Had the biggest Christmas in the world and we lit the menorah and may have gotten two presents at Chanukah and fifty presents at Christmas. . . . And all they wanted was to be sure we didn't speak Yiddish, that we didn't act in any way Jewish."

"We knew we were Jewish," said Jane Axelrod in a deep southern accent. "We went to Sunday school, and it was all about Jewish holidays. You were taught about holidays. And everything else was shushed. You didn't speak of your Judaism. I don't know. I can't explain. It was different. You didn't have a real Jewish home. No background. And I wanted more, and I just . . . You couldn't get it there. It just wasn't there. We were not allowed to date non-Jews. But you just didn't go *overboard* with your Judaism. It was *shushkied*." The executive director of Shearith Israel, a traditional congregation, she is a knockout redhead who wears shapely outfits covered with large geometric designs and dramatic, color-coordinated high heels. Her husband, Herb Axelrod, a salesman, is a relaxed, horn-rim-glasses, argyle-sweater type of guy.

The Axelrods live in an older Atlanta suburb of wooded, curving streets in a spacious, modernist, split-level home. "I can remember my mother when we made the house kosher," said Jane. (She pronounced it: "Ah can remember mah muthuh . . . ")

"She was shocked," Herb said.

"When we became kosher, it was *extreme*," said Jane.

"We were married at the Temple," said Herb. "My grandfather was Orthodox. When he saw no wedding canopy, no head coverings, no breaking the glass, he didn't know *what* I was getting!"

"They didn't even think I was Jewish," said Jane.

And Herbert Elsas said: "Marx tried to take the spots off the Jewish leopard."

3

America itself was raw and new and unpolished, lacking the landed aristocracies of France and England and Germany. Elite status appeared available to all those whose business acumen enabled them to make bank deposits, build grand houses, and wear silk top hats. Still, in time, an American upper class established itself, with many fond glances homeward toward Britannia. As class hierarchies froze, even the wealthiest Jews were found in many cases to be not quite comme il faut; by the 1890s, there was a soupçon of the storekeeper about them. An ambivalence about wealth and moneymaking in the young capitalist nation found expression in its popular attitude toward the Jew: the Jew as money-grabbing, godless, commercial.

In Atlanta—a city for many years younger than most of its citizens—the upper crust had included German Jews for several decades in a pioneer atmosphere of hearty acceptance far surpassing that of the eastern seaboard. In 1844, when Atlanta was a frontierlike settlement, German Jews had arrived and opened up shops offering clothing and dry goods, medical and dental supplies, wines and liquor, window glass, and perfumes. "My great-grandparents were pioneers," said Temple member Caroline Haas Kahn. "My grandmother was the first white baby born in Atlanta. Her parents came here in the 1840s. She was born a few months before the charter of the city was given."

Alexander's forebear was a Revolutionary War officer and lay rabbi out of Charleston. His great-great-great uncle opened the first soda fountain in Atlanta and introduced ice to the city in 1848. "I was fifteen," noted Alexander, "before I discovered that other people *had* ancestors."

Aaron Haas was a founding member in 1882 of the Gentlemen's Driving Club—which later became the Piedmont Driving Club and excluded Jews. A third of the membership of the Masonic lodges were Jewish. By 1895, when Marx was hired in Atlanta, a third of the Temple members were native born, and the rest were working diligently to become acceptable to the sea of American gentiles in which they found themselves. There were Jewish-gentile law partnerships, Jewish city councilmen, Jewish officers of the chamber of commerce, and a Jewish state representative.

But around the turn of the twentieth century, as the city was able to afford finer social distinctions and as its native-born citizens became leery of hordes of new immigrants, Atlanta's warm embrace of its Jewish population began to seem a bit stale. Despite their deep American and southern roots, the Haases and the Alexanders and the Riches and their fellow Temple members began to be excluded from the "best" neighborhoods, the important country clubs and social clubs, the debutante balls and the Junior League, and the stylish resorts. "We [a coastal resort] cater to a strictly Christian clientele," read a letter on ivory letterhead stationery, typical of the first half of the twentieth century.

"Long-resident Jews in Atlanta began to worry that the widespread esteem that they had enjoyed was beginning to fade," writes historian Albert Lindemann, "that the fulsome praise heaped upon Jews by prominent Gentiles in the city, the quite explicit philo-Semitism, was somehow less in evidence than it had been in the immediately preceding decades."

By the early 1900s, the Temple Jews found themselves increasingly denied the privileges of status befitting their ancestry, achievements, and self-image. Professional advancement in banking, commerce, academia, and gentile-owned law firms and medical practices was now out of the question. The clubs they had helped found now refused them as members.

As the Jewish population of Atlanta increased—bulked up by immigration from eastern Europe—the Jews became more identifiable as a group. They seemed more exotic, more alien, and somehow more unappetizing than when their numbers had been small and Jewish workers had included a few good-natured salesmen, merchants, and craftsmen in handlebar moustaches. A feeling gnawed at the Temple congregation that they had been just outside a door into Eden, a door into a world of perfect social equality, when the door somehow slammed shut and that world disappeared. Generations would pass as they tried to locate it and reenter.

4

Smarting from deliberate social slights, the German Jews found solace in the loftiness of their pedigrees as compared to those of the new Jewish immigrants—the poor, religious, Yiddish speakers of eastern Europe. The first waves of Russian immigration came in the 1880s; by World War I, the Russians were a majority of Atlanta's small Jewish population. Two million Russian Jews came to America between 1881 and 1914; eventually their numbers would completely swamp the high-toned Germans. The Temple members charitably oversaw the housing, feeding, and clothing of the Russian destitute and orphans. Then they looked on approvingly and with relief as the immigrants—taken aback by the Temple religious services, which they found to be "shockingly impious"—organized their own synagogues.

In the little Russian shuls (two of which—Ahavath Achim and Shearith Israel—grew to become major Atlanta synagogues), full-bearded men—grocers and butchers and manual laborers—wore yarmulkes and prayer shawls, muttered and swayed and sang out and shut their eyes in vigorous prayer, and took turns holding the Torah, the holy writ, in their arms. Long-skirted women sat in segregated balconies crowded with children. "We didn't know the name of their temple," said Aline Uhry. "We just called it 'the Orthodox.' "

"The families whose ancestors came here first were considered aristocratic," she said. "The early Jews huddled together and looked down on each successive group that came over. Now the Portuguese Jews looked down on the German Jews. They were here before the Germans." [Two congregations of Sephardim—of Jews from Rhodes, Constantinople, Bodrum and Izmir, Crete, and the Dardanelles—were founded in Atlanta in the early 1910s. In 1914 they combined to establish Congregation Or Ve Shalom, still a prosperous and thriving Sephardic synagogue today.]

The German Jews in Atlanta (as in other American cities) hastened to erect distinct barriers between themselves and the newcomers, lest the public mistake one for the other. German Jews referred to themselves as "Hebrews" and to the Russians as "Jews." The German Jews established exclusively high standards at their own beautifully landscaped social club, the Standard Club, one of three Jewish clubs. Another German-Jewish country club, the Ingleside, remembers Uhry, "was so exclusive it failed." Intermarriage between the German Jews of the Temple and the Orthodox was extremely rare. "For a German Jew to marry a Russian Jew was a definite step down," said Fred Beerman, a retired captain with the Atlanta Police Department. At any rate, the aversion was mutual: the Russian Jews found the German Jews impious, with daughters like goyim, like Christians.

On how many continents, among how many races, has this drama been performed? The upper class, the social climbers shinny up toward the summit until they feel they are but a hair's breadth from civil equality and social acceptance (the softly modulated voices betraying no trace of foreign accent; the gas-lit, polished ballrooms waiting; the expressed concern—in America—for baseball outcomes)—if only they can shake the masses, the majority, of their own people. And then here come masses—ill-timed, unwashed, tubercular, needy, reeking of the ghetto, raucously shouting in dialect, and eagerly imposing on the hospitality and pocketbooks of their vaunted brethren. The immigrants' religious frame of reference—God, Sinai, Jerusalem—is wide enough to allow for some overlap with that of the fleeing elites, so that the elites are compelled, almost organically, to look back.

It is the multitude that harbors the secrets of the nation, the ceremonies, melodies, circle dances, spices, lullabies, and revelations, the collective memory of the birth of the people. Meanwhile, the Reformers, the westernizers, the distillers of ancient folk customs into a few clear modern truths, are discom-fited by this sight of their own aborigines, their own native danc-ers. In the Russian Jews, the German Jews saw living replicas of their own great-grandparents, those heirloomed elders flatly preserved in sepia, representative of earlier stages of Jewish thought.

From the point of view of the traditionally pious Russian Jews, the liberal German Jews, apparently cut off from their heritage, were at great risk. With nothing to hold onto, no privi-leged information on the movement of the cosmos, the stylish Americanized German Jews seemed to be throwing themselves upon the currents of popular culture, society's whims, and Christian tolerance.

From the point of view of the German-Jewish Reform Jews, it was the presence of the Orthodox Eastern European multi-tudes that *placed* them at risk, jeopardized their exalted posi-tions; in short, blew their cover. The Temple Jews had been presenting themselves, under Marx's leadership, as a sort of Germanic people, cultivated and well-bred (and they *were* Germanic, cultivated, and well-bred). Then there came the masses, wearing knotted kerchiefs like peasant women, long black cloaks like sorcerers, smelling like onions, their fingernails brown from their produce bins, their eyes and eyebrows black as the Dark Ages.

And in 1913 there was a misstep, a misstep of the sort that in the old days used to lead to a lynching. A young girl, a fourteen-year-old laborer in a pencil factory owned and managed by Jews, was murdered. The German-Jewish people of the Temple were caught out, exposed, denounced by their native and adopted city, their traits confused by the gentiles.

Nonetheless, the German Jews never denied their roots, neither when they were disparaged by Orthodox Jews, nor when they were vilified by Christian whites. They persisted in gathering in their temple and conducting themselves as they had been taught: reciting by memory Hebrew prayers even when the Hebrew letters no longer looked familiar and the prayers themselves were foreshortened; fasting on Yom Kippur; contributing great sums of money to Jewish charities—including immigrant aid societies; and acknowledging their Jewish identity and their deep kinship ties with one another. Even when times grew dangerous, the most vulnerable and frightened of the German Jews left the South, or sent their children on extended visits to family in New York, rather than deny that kinship, that identification.

5

Mary Phagan's body was found by a night watchman in the basement of the National Pencil Factory in the early hours of Sunday, April 27, 1913. She had been battered and slashed, then covered with dirt and sawdust, and a noose was around her neck. Police investigators quickly uncovered the fact that twenty-nine-year-old Leo Frank—a Texas-born, New York–raised Jewish engineer, the superintendent and part-owner of the factory—was the last person who admitted having seen Phagan alive. She had come in on Saturday afternoon to pick up her paycheck from him.

The child's people were tenant farmers, driven by rural

poverty into Atlanta, where urban poverty and the cotton-mill slums had come as a terrible shock and disappointment. They endured filthy conditions, enervating labor, subsistence wages for fourteen-hour workdays, and a social standing second to last. Women and children were forced to work, too.

Who was responsible for this misery? The exhausted, illiterate, exploited urban populations did not require a long answer, a social and economic theory, or a political ideology. *Who*? Who, indeed, if not Yankees, capitalists, and Jews? And Frank was all three. He was a short answer to a complex question, the true answer to which lay in antebellum—even colonial—economic and social arrangements. Throughout the South, wealth and status had been concentrated in the hands of powerful whites. It was no accident that poor whites—like blacks—had ended up landless, unskilled, and malnourished. With a high infant mortality rate, poor whites led a hand-to-mouth existence.

But street crowds arousing themselves with graphic details of a murder do not want a history lesson. *Who killed little Mary Phagan?* was the question rippling through the crowds of Atlantans. The discovery of Phagan's body was like the final straw—a burning one, tossed onto dry bales of bitter discontent and xenophobia. There was a massive outcry of grief and outrage. Ten thousand people went to the morgue to view the body. Pinning the murder on a Yankee capitalist Jew unleashed a sort of emotional riot; what was damaged were not stores but the search for truth and the due process of law.

"I was born in 1909, so I don't have much recollection," said Aline Uhry. "When I started school, I remember the girls. You know how girls jump rope and two hold the ends and they sing those little rhymes? Well, I remember them chanting: 'Little Mary Phagan / Went to work one day / Never did she believe / The Jew'd put her away.' I didn't exactly understand it, but I knew something was wrong with it."

Frank, the child of a middle-class German-Jewish family and a graduate of Pratt Institute and Cornell University, had married into a prestigious German-Jewish family, the Seligs. He was a Temple member, a Standard Club member, and the president of the B'nai B'rith Lodge. Reserved and rather humorless, he was pale and slight of build, with bulging eyes and thick lips.

He was described by newspaper reporters as repellent—prim and nervous, a puzzle to ordinary men. Within the Jewish community, he was appraised differently: "He's supposed to have been a very high-class, studious person," said Caroline Haas Kahn, whose father was one of Frank's attorneys. "He was beautifully educated and very musical—you know, everything you can think of that Jewish people love. Cultured."

He quickly became the sole suspect in Phagan's murder. The other obvious suspect, Jim Conley, the black janitor who probably encountered Phagan in the empty factory after she got her paycheck from Frank, managed to snare the role as the state's chief witness against Frank. Modern forensic reconsideration and a deathbed confession in the 1980s from a former office boy all strongly suggest that the crime was Conley's. But he became a most malleable witness, eager to testify to anything the police suggested. Conley's testimony created an image of Frank as a lascivious abuser of young girls, who used his office for perverse sex with helpless young female employees. Conley testified that on the day in question, he heard a scream, was called to Frank's office an hour later, and beheld Frank "shivering and trembling and rubbing his hands," in which he held a rope similar to the one found around Phagan's neck.

The three daily newspapers leapt upon the crime with an indecent, voyeuristic sensationalism of a sort very familiar to late-twentieth-century magazine readers and TV viewers. The public's appetite for lurid details, and for justice, was boundless: newspaper circulation skyrocketed with slanderous reports of this archetypal southern crime. Accounts of the trial referred to the defendant as "the monster" and "the strangler." On slow news days, writers invented fantastic stories: that Frank had another wife in Brooklyn; that Frank had *killed* another wife in Brooklyn; that he had fathered numerous out-of-wedlock children; that he was a sexual pervert given to pulling innocent girls off trams; that he was "built" differently than normal men.

"Does a Jew expect extraordinary favors and immunities *because* of his race?" wrote Tom Watson, the former populist leader and spokesman for rural Georgians, in his newspaper *The Jeffersonian*. "Here we have the typical young libertine Jew who . . . [has] an utter contempt for the law, and a ravenous appetite for the forbidden fruit—a lustful eagerness enhanced by the racial novelty of the girls of the uncircumcised."

"Are we to understand that anybody except a Jew can be punished for crime?" wondered the former governor Joseph M. Brown. "If so, Georgia will soon become the exploiting ground for every Jew who is criminally inclined."

Every day for a month, the jurors traveled to and from the courthouse through the mobbed streets, where people cried out, "Crack that Jew's neck!" and "Hang the damned sheeny!" and the judge and the defense attorneys were threatened.

In jail, Frank was visited frequently by his lawyers and by Marx. "Of course, Dr. Marx was a little bitty guy, but feis-teeeeee!" said Kahn. "He walked through that mob outside the jail. To see this man walk through these mobs and they just didn't *touch* him. They wouldn't touch him. They never roughed him up; they just yelled."

Then in his prime, Marx moved through a landscape of his worst nightmares: newspaper editorials about the "jewpervert"; angry mobs outside the courtroom screaming for a guilty ver-dict; Jewish merchants in rural counties boycotted; Jewish shops in Atlanta boarded up; Jewish children sent away by train to relatives in the North. Forever after, in his impeccable relations with gentiles, Marx would require, on his part, a strong draft of courage.

The defense's case was not airtight. Frank never was able to present a convincing alibi for his actions during the hour—noon to one o'clock—when the murder likely occurred. And he had made unprecedented phone calls to the night watchman on Saturday night, asking if everything was all right at the factory. His explanation for these calls—that just as he had left work that day, a recently discharged employee had shown up and Frank was uneasy about the man's presence there—somehow sounded like a feeble excuse. Still, beneath the mountain of slander, libel, and perjury, behind all the unsubstantiated accusa-tions of voracious sexual appetite and perversity, these were the only elements of suspicion. Meanwhile, evidence pointing to Conley's guilt went unexamined. The exceedingly slim bit of circumstantial evidence against Frank ought not to have sup-ported a verdict of guilty beyond a reasonable doubt.

Nevertheless, after four hours of deliberation, the jury returned a guilty verdict. Three thousand people in the street outside the courthouse went berserk. The *Atlanta Constitution* reported: "Trolley car conductors left their stations and joined the rejoicing throngs; women in fashionable social circles clapped hands; and the local ballpark posted the news on the scoreboard and fans in the grandstands cheered wildly." Thousands of shrieking demonstrators carried the solicitor, Hugh Dorsey, through the streets, while Phagan's stepfather posed for newspaper photographs with each of the jurors.

The day after the verdict, the judge sentenced Frank to hang. The defense attorneys appealed the verdict three times to the state supreme court and twice to the U.S. Supreme Court, without success. The execution was scheduled for June 22, 1915, four days before the end of Governor John M. Slaton's term.

Slaton had been a fine and popular governor, and he hoped to win a seat at the next election to the U.S. Senate. Frank's plea for clemency arrived on his desk as a political hot potato: commutation would end Slaton's public life—if not his biological life. With simple procrastination for four days, he could have abandoned the issue to his successor, but Slaton agreed to hear the case. He listened to arguments by the defense and the prosecution, visited the pencil factory, and secluded himself with volumes of court proceedings and letters. One of the letters he received was from the trial judge, asking the governor to rectify the judge's mistake in delivering the death sentence.

Before announcing his decision, Slaton made provisions for extra security for Frank and had him transferred to the state prison farm in Milledgeville. The governor then presented to the public the evidence in the case as he understood it, articulating problems with the prosecution's case that Frank's own attorneys had handled less expertly. The circumstantial evidence strongly suggested that Phagan's murder had occurred in the basement—incriminating Conley—and not, as Conley had testified, in the office adjoining Frank's.

Privately convinced of Frank's innocence, Slaton commuted the death sentence to life imprisonment. "Two thousand years ago," he said, "another Governor washed his hands of a case and turned over a Jew to a mob. For two thousand years that Governor's name has been accursed. If today another Jew were lying in his grave because I had failed to do my duty I would all through life find his blood on my hands and would consider myself an assassin through cowardice."

Frank's supporters around the country celebrated, and in Georgia most of the major newspapers commended the governor's courage, if not his good sense. But mobs burned him in effigy. In Marietta, the dummy bore a sign: "John M. Slaton, King of the Jews and Georgia's Traitor Forever." In the same town, Jewish shop owners were ordered to abandon their stores. In Canton, Jewish citizens were ordered to leave the city. Tom Watson, among others, warned that commutation would invoke the law of Judge Lynch.

In Atlanta, pandemonium erupted. Crowds armed with guns and dynamite marched on the governor's mansion; Slaton declared martial law at his residence and called out a battalion of the state militia. The woods around the mansion were "full of men trying to get in," said the governor's wife later. The riot lasted a week, until Slaton's successor was inaugurated amidst screams of "Lynch him!" and Slaton and his wife left the state for extended travels.

In the state prison farm, Frank performed chores and wrote scores of letters. His correspondence to his wife—in which he requested pajamas, toothpaste, and Beech Nut gum—read, wrote Leonard Dinnerstein, like a child's letters home from summer camp. Eventually, his throat was slit by a fellow prisoner who explained that God had told him to murder the Jew. In the prison hospital, Frank assured the doctors who doubted his survival: "I am going to live. I must live. I must vindicate myself."

On August 16, 1915, a band of twenty-five men, including a clergyman, two former state supreme court justices, and an ex-sheriff, stormed the prison farm. They overpowered the guards, the superintendent, and the warden and ordered Frank out of his hospital bed. "Frank got out of bed and made a feeble attempt to dress himself," wrote Dinnerstein, "but one of the men commanded: 'Don't bother with the clothes; just come as you are.' The abductors then handcuffed their charge, and led him out of the building. Frank, stoically calm, as was his wont, looked neither terrified nor surprised; nor did he make any attempt to resist."

In the car, Frank refused several appeals by his kidnappers to confess and apparently spoke so sincerely of his innocence that several of the abductors had misgivings about the lynching. One refused to go on with it and urged that Frank be returned to the prison.

"I think more of my wife and my mother than I do of my life," Frank said as he was led to a tree. Before the noose was put on his shoulders, he made a last request that his wedding ring be returned to his wife. He was stood upon a table with a blindfold across his face, the rope was thrown over a limb and secured, and the table was kicked away.

The thin man hung in midair with his hands tied in front of him, his bare feet bound together, and his neck wound bleeding. As news spread, hundreds of people found the spot; they tore shreds from his clothing and from the rope for souvenirs. A Marietta judge, Newton Morris, intervened when the crowd began to attack the body. Marx himself accompanied the corpse and the widow, Lucille Frank, to New York for the burial.

The oak tree in Marietta became, for a time, a kind of shrine. Citizens drew up plans to build a concrete wall around it. This provoked the observation from a newspaper in Wisconsin: "If the prison in which Frank was kept had been so surrounded, the tree would not need to be now imprisoned." Pieces of the rope took on a life of their own, becoming a bizarre sort of hemp Holy Grail. "They sold pieces of the rope at five dollars an inch downtown," said Rabbi Alvin Sugarman, a soft-spoken man with a trim gray beard who is the Temple's current rabbi.

The most awful and lasting legacy of Frank's murder for the Temple Jews of Atlanta was the sense of isolation: they were marginal, they were dispensable, they were still "the other" in the mind of white Christian Atlanta. They'd been, collectively, like a drowning man to whom no one had bothered to toss a line. Upper-crust white Christian Atlanta had looked the other way when mobs and demagogues went after the Jews. It was a civics lesson not easily forgotten.

"It was then that the line was drawn," said Kahn. "It was a terrible thing: Christians here and the Jews here."

Marx did not speak of Frank with his Christian friends, nor did he ever appear to hold a grudge. He forever solicited and enjoyed the company of Christians, but his entire world had been grossly shaken. After 1915, after accompanying Frank's body to New York to guard against its further mutilation, Marx, convinced more than ever that safety lay in invisibility, focused even more intently on assimilation.

"The likelihood of being attacked as a group is reduced if you become part of the wider community," said Temple member and businessman Tony Montag, whose family once owned the pencil factory. "This was David Marx's response to Leo Frank and the congregation took it up with a vengeance. The drive to assimilate became the fine part of the fabric of this community."

"My father worked with the Montags," said Sugarman, "and one of the things the firm sold was pencils, and one of the pencils it sold was National Lead Company, which was the company Leo Frank had managed. It later became Scripto. And my father said his customers would take the pencils, break them in half, throw them on the floor, and say, 'Get that blankety-blank Jew merchandise out of here.' Whether the pencils had the Montag name or National Lead, they knew. Believe me, they knew. The feeling I had growing up was whenever there was a family gathering or any type of adult Jewish gathering and somebody said, 'Leo Frank,' there was a hush—an absolute fear that still cut. A fear and a memory.

"And I was very much aware, as a child, that you're a Jew, so don't do anything to rock the boat. Blend in with the woodwork. One result of the Frank case, I think, is that when you read the newspaper, for example, if there's an article about a bank robbery, you look to see what the name is and you just pray that the bank robber is named Jones or Smith."

"The way I became aware of the Frank case, which certainly says a lot to me about the attitude of the older Jewish people," said Janice Rothschild, "was when I was a freshman at the

University of Georgia and we learned about it in a required course called Contemporary Georgia. I came home and I said to my mother, 'Did y'all *know* about this?' And Mother said to me, 'Well of course, dear. You know Miss Lucille.'

"I said, 'Miss Lucille *Frank*?'

" 'Yes, of course.'

"You know, as if why didn't I know that Lucille, whom I had known all my life, was Leo Frank's widow? She and her sisters were close friends of my mother's best friends. They were card friends. Well, I didn't know about it, obviously, because nobody talked about it. Nobody said a word. Not that I expected them to say it in front of Miss Lucille, but you would have thought I would have heard of it. Not one word."

"The older people would get up and leave the room if it came up," said Jackie Montag, Tony's wife. "When we were first married, I was told you can discuss politics, money, sex, whatever, but you don't discuss *that*."

"Honey?" said Jane Axelrod, "it was shushkied."

———— ⚜ ————

By 1946, the Temple congregation members were ready to swap their tiny, autocratic, mustachioed, nineteenth-century rabbi—despite his courage in unspeakable times—for a modern version. World War II was over, a new generation was growing up, and the Temple board went for a veteran, who showed up for his interview in uniform. The crème de la crème of Atlanta Jewry were delighted with their catch, at least initially.

"The congregation welcomed him warmly when he arrived in Atlanta," said Janice Rothschild. "So many of its four hundred families rushed to extend him dinner invitations that almost immediately his summer calendar was booked solid. The young 'elite' scooped him up as a perfect fourth at bridge and tennis, the perfect dinner partner for their unmarried sisters or friends. One family gave him carte blanche at their stables; another, the use of a car until such time as he could purchase one of his own.

"Despite this show of affection," she adds, "very few of them attended services or in any other way indicated interest in the job he had come to perform."

Jacob Rothschild, meanwhile, was making his own appraisal. What he discovered in Dixie was a congregation that had—to use Western lingo—"gone native." Its protective coloration was so far advanced that few truly Jewish elements remained. In contrast, he advocated, with a gentle assist from the city's Orthodox rabbis, the establishment of a Jewish state. He lit candles. He made a Hebrew blessing over a goblet of grape wine, which he drank.

He asked the mothers of the youth group members not to bring ham sandwiches to the Temple for the teenagers' snacks. "Since when do Reform Jews keep kosher?" demanded one mother. "And how come you didn't complain when I served you baked ham for supper at my house?"

"At the Temple it's different," said Rothschild.

These were modest enough sallies. But they were greeted with universal shock. Had the congregants known any Yiddish, now was the time they could have used it. When they exhaled, "Merciful heavens!" to one another over Rothschild's eccentricities, what they clearly meant and deeply needed to say was a sort of Yiddish version: "Oi vey iz mir!"

If they had known that the Israel-loving, candle-lighting, chicken-preferring Rothschild was about to position them in the firing line of the violent white racists, their utterances would not have been printable in any language.

4

The Invisible Checkerboard

1

The Temple Jews of Atlanta at midcentury were, as Harvard professor Cornel West has said of contemporary American Jews, "middle-dogs—some were even top-dogs—who still felt like underdogs." Close at hand, however, were a people suffering acutely from discrimination and race hatred.

Unlike the Nuremberg Laws—obliterated in a torrent of bombs, flying masonry, bones, and universal horror—the Jim Crow laws and customs of the American South came through World War II intact. Dove-gray Pullman cars, for whites only, swayed through the soft countryside. Inside, as the white businessmen pitched and slept on thin mattresses, the black porters worked quickly in the darkness, their velvet hands preparing breakfast on pots that slid off the fire when the train veered; tiptoeing, they returned polished shoes to numbered berths and patted tablecloths into place over tiny, anchored tables. In the cities, segregated buses stained the air and streets with grease and diesel as they roared through intersections.

At lunch counters, white ladies—done in by Georgia's

summer and their shopping's exertions—ordered egg salad and sweet iced tea to fortify themselves, and touched the corners of their faces with cloth napkins dampened with ice water. Lulled nearly to sleep, as they sat, by the cool hum of ceiling fans, these women closed their eyes in respite from the heat. But similarly fatigued black women—church ladies in drooping flowered dresses who had gone to the trouble of finding matching handbag and shoes—lined up in reeking garbage-can alleys outside a café's kitchen window to purchase sack lunches they could not then sit on park benches under the trees to eat. And if they should need to visit a ladies' room, they could be certain of experiencing a series of public and private humiliations.

Thus, the twentieth-century world of indoor plumbing, fast-food griddles, diesel engines, and sleek national rail service was penetrated by—disfigured by—nineteenth-century custom, law, and belief.

—————

The South into which Rothschild traveled in 1946 was like another country. Across its five-story cities and whistle-stop towns, its pine barrens and cotton fields, its cotton mills and red clay roads lay an invisible checkerboard of alternating white and black squares—landing places for white and landing places for black, forbidden places for white and forbidden places for black—where the citizens hopscotched, careful not to step on the lines nor rub shoulders in passing.

Rothschild sensed his dislocation every time he stepped outside that first summer. He felt it first in the intensity of the heat and light, which increased, rather than diminished, as months passed. And he sensed it when he looked at the signs. He was in this respect like any traveler to a foreign country who is bewildered by the non-English signage—Bienvenue, Wilkommen—and must fall back upon an inner glossary and common sense to make his way. He saw them first at the train station: White Waiting Room. Colored Waiting Room. Men. Women. Colored. As he bumped along through the city, he sighted more; and in the days to come, riding the streetcar to the Temple, he saw more. Thrown off balance by the signs and by other marks of the Jim Crow system five minutes after arrival, he never regained his footing. He never got used to it, and he never accommodated himself to it. He began to lay down a different moral geometry than he had ever lived by. If he had lived his life on two dimensions until then, there opened up to him a third. Neither the feeble joke he had written home in a letter from the front—"I is now in Jerusalem where Christ was born"—nor anything remotely like it, would ever cross his lips again, nor would he tolerate racial humor in his presence. By the time he shook hands with the Temple board members eagerly awaiting his arrival, he was unsettled, a slightly more perturbed man than the one they had hired.

"He was stunned by the signs," said his sister Jean. So were many outsiders. There were refugees in Atlanta who had been denied seating on German park benches labeled Nur Furarier (Aryans only), and who ended by fleeing for their lives. When these Jewish refugees read the White Only signs displayed matter-of-factly in Atlanta at restrooms and drinking fountains, restaurant and theater entrances, park benches and public libraries, they protested to their new American friends: "But this is like Hitler."

"So many of the newcomers could not understand the racial situation in Atlanta," said Josephine Heyman, a grande dame of the Jewish community and an early liberal who assisted with the settlement of Jewish war refugees and arranged for immigrants to attend lectures by the American educator and writer W. E. B. DuBois. "When they got on streetcars and would see the signs, 'Colored people from the back forward,' 'White people from the front backward,' they were so distressed. . . . They couldn't understand it. We did say to them, 'Now look, there's a big difference between sitting in the back of a streetcar and being led to a gas chamber.' And they said, yes, of course they did [understand that], but they thought that was the beginning, that was the way things got started."

"I was horrified to come to Atlanta and get off the train and find that I couldn't drink out of this water fountain that said Colored Only down at the terminal station," said a native of Baltimore, Rabbi Emanuel Feldman of Congregation Beth Jacob. "Shocking? It was ridiculous. We never heard of such a thing."

"I grew up in Pennsylvania on a black college campus near Philadelphia. I'd been in this larger world, and then we moved to Atlanta and all of a sudden my world was squeezed and constrained," said Julian Bond, the still-handsome, still-youthful, jaunty and eloquent, sandy-haired former Georgia state representative and senator, a cofounder of the Student Nonviolent Coordinating Committee (SNCC), and the first black man to see his name placed into nomination for the vice-presidency, now on the history faculty at the University of Virginia. The son of the president of Lincoln University, he had moved to Atlanta in 1957 at age seventeen when his father became a dean at Morehouse College. "I'd been able to go anywhere, do anything, and all of a sudden, I couldn't. It was a great treat to go into Philadelphia on the weekends for movies. I couldn't do that here: the movies were segregated. To go to the Fox Theater, you had to go way upstairs to the Jim Crow gallery. And you did that, but you felt uneasy about it. It felt awful. It was scary. I didn't like going downtown. I didn't like being in situations where there was a potential clash with whites, and I avoided those kinds of things. I never rode buses. I just didn't go. I was terrified. My mother wanted to take me downtown to get a new suit to go to college, and I said very graciously, 'Mama, why don't you go? You know my sizes; you go ahead and buy the stuff, and I'll wait here.' "

"Now we always teased my mother because she was quite fair-skinned," said Alice Carey Holmes Washington, a retired journalist and high school counselor, and a hip grandmother in tight jeans, political sweatshirt, and gray afro. "We would tell my mother that if she would put on a hat and not take it off, she could go anywhere she wanted to go. I expect many of the things she got for us as children, she just went downtown and didn't say Patty Holmes black or Patty Holmes passing [for white] or Patty Holmes anything. She just did."

"Well, I was a 'damn Yankee' and proud of it," said Frances Pauley, born in Ohio in 1905, the descendant of Ohio settlers who had moved to Georgia in 1908. As a middle-aged white woman, Pauley threw herself into the early civil rights movement. She is a stout-hearted, white-haired, slightly bent woman of failing sight who has stayed in the front lines for the poor, for the homeless, for AIDS victims. "I was thinking about Constance Baker Motley, the lawyer. I tell you, that woman—she was exquisite in the courtroom. You just can't imagine how marvelous she was. I was a witness in a case for her. So it came lunchtime and we were going to break for lunch, so I thought, 'I'll run quickly and ask Constance to go to lunch with me.' And all of a sudden I realized there wasn't one place that I *could* take her for lunch."

So Rothschild noticed the Jim Crow signs, and Jewish refugees from the Nazis noticed the signs, and Ohioans who had lived in the South since 1908 noticed the signs, and black intellectuals from Philadelphia noticed the signs. The signs, in fact, were *intended* for these people, who knew nothing.

No native southerner had to be instructed that the clean, locked restroom, the one with an aura of disinfectant rising from under the door, was for Men or Ladies; that the filthy, stinking restroom, with the brown toilet clogged and the door hanging from a single hinge, was for Coloreds. Even young southerners could tell with their eyes closed that when entrances to hotels, theaters, train stations, or movie houses had double doors under a marquis, were carpeted, or were flanked by potted palms or by black doormen in absurd epaulets, they were entrances for whites. Those for blacks were around back, off the alley, or at the top of steep fire-escape stairs screwed precariously to the brick. The signs, in short, were pedagogical in purpose; they were like bright hand-printed labels in a first-grade classroom—DESK, WINDOW, FLOWER. Locals did not rely on the signs; only fools, "uppity niggers," or Yankees needed signs to tell them which was which.

2

In the 1940s and 1950s, Georgia had not yet awakened from the dream and the nightmare of the Confederacy. Black students were barred from attending public schools with white children and were not accepted at a single southern university, graduate school, law school, or medical school. The percentage of the state budget going to the education of black children was infinitesimal. "The Negro child," Governor Hoke Smith had stated, "should be taught to work." Black children and adults were prohibited from enjoying public parks, playgrounds, botanical gardens, golf courses, and swimming pools; and they were excluded from white churches, hotels, barbershops, restaurants, movie theaters, and cemeteries. In clothing stores, they could not try on clothing. On the sidewalk, they were expected to step into the street to allow whites to pass. "In all the buildings downtown," said the physician Homer Nash, "one elevator was for Negroes, freight, and baggage. The others—all of them—were for white people. If you had to go to the courthouse or had an appointment in one of those tall buildings you've got to stay down here and wait till that Negro elevator came down." Blacks could not join their professional associations. Black doctors and nurses could not treat white patients; black patients could not be seen in white hospitals.

"My father was one of the first black doctors of his generation," said Alice Washington, whose parents had moved to East Point, outside Atlanta, in 1910. "His first patient came as a referral from a white pharmacist in East Point and it was a white couple. In those days, it was completely illegal for a black physician to treat white patients. But, as the story goes, the white pharmacist said to this white couple (because of an emergency situation), 'No, we don't have a doctor. There is a black doctor in town. If you want to see what he would do, all right.' So this young white couple came to my daddy, and fortunately for them, he was at home. He said to them, 'It's against the law for me to treat you, but I have just taken the oath that says I will serve as I am needed.' My father always finished telling this story by saying, 'Fortunately for me, the patient lived.' "

"Men with master's degrees, Ph.D.'s took jobs as redcaps," said the attorney Donald Hollowell. "That was quite common— a man with a doctoral degree working as a redcap or train porter."

The Grant Park Zoo in Atlanta provided two hundred different entrances, exits, and pathways, so that white children safely could contemplate an African elephant or monkey without having the view marred by an African American child. Marriages between black and white were illegal and void, and the individual issuing the marriage license was guilty of a misdemeanor. Any person misrepresenting his or her race was guilty of a felony. And every courtroom in Georgia was provided, by state law, with two Bibles: one for white witnesses, the other for black witnesses.

In this era it was far from obvious to most white Americans that the African Americans in their midst had normal human abilities, ambitions, affections, and proclivities. Centuries of abuse and humiliation by whites had left the black masses stupefied and paralyzed in their dealings with the white world. The appearance of black leaders like DuBois—who had a Ph.D. from Harvard, was an outstanding spokesman for racial equality, and taught at Atlanta University from 1897 until 1914, and from 1934 to 1944—and Benjamin E. Mays—who was an internationally respected theologian, a colleague of the theologians Reinhold Niebuhr and Paul Tillich, and the president of Morehouse College in Atlanta from 1949 to 1967—seemed, to most whites, the exception rather than the rule, as if these leaders were flukes of nature, talking donkeys. A majority of white Americans were not convinced that the Negro race was part of the same species as the Caucasian. Depending on whether they preferred Genesis or Darwin, many whites believed either that God had created different kinds of humans (the white to rule, the black to serve) or that parallel evolutions had occurred in Europe and in Africa, resulting in similar but different species of human (the white to rule, the black to serve). The offspring of interracial unions were seen as godlessly misbegotten, the product of flagrantly unnatural acts. The favorite campaign line of Herman Talmadge, who became Georgia's governor in 1948, was "There are two things the good Lord never made. He never made a mule and he never made a mullata'." He was cheered at every stop.

DuBois once wrote: "Thought streaming from the slaveship: 'Are we men?' " It was a real question in the minds of most southern white folk at midcentury.

3

But there were leaks in the dike: the wall of apartheid began to decay. After World War II, as Atlanta's white power structure bid a delighted farewell to the departing troops and the social disarray they had provoked, the black power structure hung on for dear life to the slight alterations in the racial game plan that had occurred during the war. They, too, had seen the future. For them, it worked.

"Nothing looked the same after the Second World War," said Cliff Kuhn, a member of the history faculty at Georgia State University in Atlanta and the director of the Georgia Government Documentation Project and Oral History Archive on Georgia Politics. "The war itself raised the contradictions between fighting for democracy abroad and being second-class citizens at home. You saw an escalation of tactics in black Atlanta during the war years. Here there was an effort to get black production workers hired by the Bell bomber plant; you saw a lot of pushing and pulling until ultimately there was an order for ten welders, and the order came down through the Urban League, which recruited through the local high schools and other places to find black welders to apply for these jobs. You had black soldiers sitting in the front of the bus—black soldiers from the North. That happened here during the war.

"There was a growing restlessness and assertiveness within the black community. You had Mayor Hartsfield reading about the Texas case. . . . [In *Smith v. Allwright*, 1944, the Supreme Court ruled that the white-only primary, in states where these primaries were an integral part of election machinery, violated the U.S. Constitution's Fifteenth Amendment. This was potentially devastating to overwhelmingly Democratic Georgia, where elections virtually were decided in white-only Democratic primaries.] "The mayor threw it on Police Chief Jenkins's desk: 'Have you read it?'

" 'Yeah, I read it.'

" 'Well, what does it mean?'

" 'It means the Negro is going to be able to sit any damned place he wants if he knows how to get organized, and Atlanta Negroes know how.' "

"Negroes weren't in politics, not in politics," said John Calhoun, a black realtor, the president of the National Association for the Advancement of Colored People (NAACP) in the 1950s, and a member of the Atlanta City Council in the 1970s. "They didn't bother too much about politics. They couldn't participate in the Democratic Party, because they had what they called the white primary, you see. And the white primary would not accept Negroes to vote in it. . . . [Before 1946] it was just a matter of being a Republican and going to vote for the president once every four years. You didn't vote in the local elections at all."

Because Georgia was hostile to the landmark Texas decision, a black man in Columbus, Primus King, brought federal action, and in 1945 Judge T. Hoyt Davis in the Macon district held that *Smith v. Allwright* applied to Georgia. The state appealed to the Supreme Court, and in April 1946 *Chapman v. King* was upheld, clearing the way for a massive black voter registration drive.

"Going door to door, sending taxicabs, paying for them, getting buses and everything—that's what we had to do to get people registered," said Warren Cochrane, the YMCA director.

"The effort lasted for fifty-one days," said the Atlanta University historian Clarence A. Bacote. "We were able to increase the registration of blacks in Fulton County from about 7,000 to 24,750. And that's when we were going to be recognized." Despite purges and threats of violence, one hundred thousand black Georgians voted in the 1946 primary.

In the Fifth Congressional District in Atlanta, Helen Douglas Mankin, a liberal white woman, was elected in 1946—the first Georgia congresswoman—from a field of seventeen candidates. The only candidate to woo the new black voters, she clearly won because of black bloc voting, overcoming a nationwide midterm conservative backlash. "The Mankin election," said Kuhn, "signaled the arrival of black political strength in Georgia."

In 1948, the Atlanta Negro Voters League was founded, and it comprised men and women who had been active in earlier black political organizations and who knew precisely what the abolition of the white-only primary meant. "What made Atlanta great was the Atlanta Negro Voters League," said Harmon Perry, a retired *Atlanta Daily World* photographer. "We helped to make Mayor Hartsfield. We organized across political lines: we had a Democratic chairman and a Republican chairman, a Democratic cochairman and a Republican cochairman. We had John Wesley Dobbs, a great extemporaneous speaker, a Pullman porter who could quote history; we had A. T. Walden, the first black graduate of the University of Michigan Law School. At that time, of the registered voters, we were about 20 percent, and between 80 and 85 percent of our registered voters turned out."

"What you see in the 1940s," said Kuhn, "are the first winds of change."

Also appearing in the postwar years: the gales of a violent white backlash. On the home front, as World War II veterans returned from overseas, the war was not quite over. In Georgia in 1946 it was pretty much open season on the African Americans. "An epidemic of random murder and mayhem was sweeping like a fever through the region, fueled by white fears that black veterans might become a revolutionary force, and that blacks in general would no longer stay 'in their place,' " wrote the historian John Egerton in *Speak Now Against the Day*.

The black soldiers who had lived in integrated barracks, fought beside white men, fought against white men, and (according to the scandalmongers) slept with Frenchwomen came home from World War II to a social minefield. They had to relearn how not to misstep. In the South, a miscalculation, a moment of inattention, could be a fatal error. Between 1890 and 1930, 450 lynchings of black men and teenagers were performed amidst crowds and hoopla in Georgia, not including the "legal lynchings" of hasty courtroom verdicts and mob executions. In the postwar years, a new wave of terrorism began.

Reuben A. Garland Sr., a roisterous scene-stealer of a criminal defense attorney (who later would play a leading role in the Temple bombing case), attended law school at the University of Georgia in Athens. "He was standing on the street in Athens around 1920," said his son, Edward T. M. Garland of Atlanta, one of the nation's leading defense attorneys today, "and a long line of cars drove by, filled with men.

"He said, 'Where y'all going?'

"And they said, 'We're going to a barbecue. Come on!'

"They drove out to Watkinsville and out to a field and got out, and there, tied to a tree in the middle of the field, was a black man. And the sheriff in a white hat was there with a lighted pine torch. And they were saying, 'Tell us you did it, Willie! Confess!' And a woman who had allegedly been raped was standing in the field, and the sheriff took the torch and ran it up and down the black man, burning him. Dad said you could smell the searing flesh. He said the man was screaming like a panther. That was the 'barbecue.' He never forgot it."

So the whites stood astride the two centuries. From the nineteenth century they carried forward the cotton plantations, race theories, and power, nigger-words, ropes, and fire; and in the twentieth century, feeling the pride of ownership, they harnessed electricity, radio waves, and nuclear energy. By midcentury, white men in the South stood at the summit of human domination, in the heyday of white and male supremacy.

4

A segregated black world turned on its own axis beyond the boundaries of—virtually beyond the cognizance of—white Atlanta. At its poorest extreme, this world resembled the rural landscape left by black farmworkers, unlettered people arriving in town all but barefoot, without luggage. They crowded into wooden shacks at the backside of downtown, behind white streets, and along the railroad tracks. Standing in rows, the shacks were constructed of gray wood so mealy it was nearly clothlike, bendable as canvas. Dirt roads meandered about the black section, bypassing garbage dumps, warehouses, and vacant lots full of tall weeds that bloomed in the spring. The dirt roads and dust paths in the black areas lacked streetlights and sidewalks, and in the autumn rains they ran like muddy streams—since no car or wagon could navigate them, the people hiked home, carrying newspapers over their heads and tunneling through weeds as tall as corn. No public services infiltrated these urban hamlets of rural wretchedness: outhouses stood behind the shacks, elderly people and children fetched water from distant spigots with tin buckets, and kerosene lanterns hung from hooks over the front steps when people gathered at each others' homes in the evenings. They would be the last to experience electricity, sewer systems, paved roads, and indoor plumbing, decades behind the rest of the city.

In time, a stone's throw from the see-through wooden shacks, a few attractive houses went up, constructed on lots squared off by surveyors, professionally landscaped, and trimmed with picket fences. A Pullman porter, a redcap, and a waiter in a downtown restaurant were the earliest members of the black middle class; within a few years the black Atlantans also included a doctor, a pharmacist, an attorney, a nightclub owner, a minister, a dentist, an optometrist, a professor, and a grocer, all of whom achieved a modicum of success with all-black clienteles and stepped up to the middle class. They bought the latest clothes in New York or New Orleans, and they imported schoolteachers to teach circles of middle-class children. In Atlanta's famous black business district they worshiped in handsome churches, dined in fine restaurants, purchased a black daily newspaper—the first in the country, the *Atlanta Daily World*—and, at night, danced and listened to black music in blues bars and jazz clubs.

5

"The Royal Peacock was the equivalent to the Apollo Club in New York," said Perry. "All the entertainers who wanted to be successful had to come—Duke Ellington, Arthur Prysock, Count Basie, Dinah Washington; Aretha Franklin was still a gospel singer at that time."

"Oh, this was heaven," said Bond, who was entering college when his family moved to Atlanta in 1957 and he discovered the nightlife of Auburn Avenue. "You walked up a long flight of double-wide stairs; you went in and saw *the* popular stars of the day in an intimate setting you would never have today. Today if you see these people, it's in a stadium. You slipped the maître d' a dollar and got up front. And when the [civil rights] movement began, they would put us up front as a measure of saying, 'We're proud of you. Happy to have you here.' We saw Jackie Wilson, we saw the Drifters, we saw Little Stevie Wonder with his mother leading him up on stage and taking him off stage. You'd see the Supremes, the Temptations, and somebody else on the same bill. All of the people big in rhythm and blues, like Jerry Butler. We'd be seated right where I'd put my arm on the stage like this and Jackie Wilson is right there and he's dancing and doing these twists and dropping the mike and pulling it back up and swirling around and so on. Duke Ellington also would appear at the Magnolia Ballroom. Ray Charles would appear at the Magnolia Ballroom. Elijah Muhammad appeared at the Magnolia Ballroom. Muslims came from all over America to see him."

Atlanta—never a slave capital like Charleston, Richmond, Savannah, and New Orleans—had been forced to rebuild and reconceive itself after the Civil War. It had done so, from the start, with the participation of ambitious ex-slaves who had fled the rural counties. Two lively centers of black life sprang up. The first, a consortium of black colleges, a graduate school, and a seminary, became the "intellectual capital of black America." Across town, Auburn Avenue—nicknamed "Sweet Auburn"—became the "main street of black America," and in 1956 *Fortune* dubbed it "the richest Negro street in the world."

During the day, Auburn Avenue, one of five major streets converging at Five Points in downtown Atlanta, was like an American small town, with modest office buildings and medical offices, hardware and shoe stores, barbers and hairdressers, churches and restaurants. After dark it was like a little New Orleans, crackling with snazzy crowds and a brilliant nightlife, its jazz clubs and blues bars releasing such gorgeous music that the performers there became the most famous of their day and daring white people sneaked across town and across the racial line to hear them.

And it was an all-black world, a darker mirror image of an American main street; it was normal, everyday, mainstream American life—dentists drilling, lawyers reading, diners ordering from menus, ladies in white gloves and snug hats leading small children up the steps of the library—performed by black citizens. And the black people who set foot there, from all over the country, never forgot it; some never left. And those lucky enough to grow up in the vicinity kept Auburn Avenue memories as precious sources of pride. It was, for newcomers, like the first sight of Israel for a Jew, the first breathtaking sense of *majority*. Jewish tourists return from Israel to America burbling about Jewish policemen, plumbers, and prostitutes, and what they want to express is an expansive sense of endless possibility, of not being pigeonholed. They—like the black people who beheld Auburn Avenue at its zenith—experienced as utter novelty what is, for most people on earth, normal life. "If you didn't come down Auburn Avenue, you hadn't been to Atlanta if you were black," said Nash. "You had not been to Atlanta."

"Atlanta had the first black-owned radio station in the country, WERD, founded in 1949," said Harmon Perry, the photographer, a slight, tired-seeming man with a lemony expression. He is given to putting in the bitter-voiced aside, because he has long been accustomed to seeing first-rate information about blacks discounted. "We had the first black CPA in the country, J. B. Blayton. We had Dr. H. E. Welton, the first black graduate of Ohio State School of Optometry. In 1928, R. N. Shaw opened the first optician's shop. These young blacks think they're the first; but it didn't even start with my generation, and I came along in 1923. [Alonzo] Herndon was the first black millionaire in Atlanta. All this was before I came along. In the time of separate-but-equal, this neighborhood was nothing but middle-class blacks—more black homeowners than any other southern city. Blacks living in Chicago, L.A., thought they were better off than us, but they were worse."

By the turn of the twentieth century, Auburn Avenue was already a well-established street. "Now, our parents always called it 'The Avenue,' states Kathleen Adams, a schoolteacher born on Auburn in 1890. "And maybe that came because the first homes for Negroes not only in Atlanta but in other places were the streets or alleys, you might say, that ran up behind the Caucasian homes. And to be living on a front street and it being called Auburn Avenue, they simply said, 'The Avenue.' 'Where do you live?' 'I live on The Avenue.' It was the best-appointed street for Negroes in the city of Atlanta at that time."

She recalled the gentlemen shopkeepers: "The first people . . . were those little boys that had been, let's say, eight to ten years old when they came out of slavery, and naturally they had dreams and they wanted everything to be just like they had seen other people have. They were well trained by the American missionaries. They had all the accouterments of any other race. Even to their dress, they were formal. Whatever they did was on the formal side. Their stores were kept meticulously. Their businesses were monitored and run according to sound business principles. They had a certain pride and dignity as they stood in their store doors or they walked the streets."

"In those days, Auburn Avenue really was a black man's pride and joy, I'll put it like that," a black barber said. "You didn't find people coming to Auburn in their shirttails like they do now, and just kind of loosely dressed. They had a lot of pride and they'd come to Auburn Avenue, they would be dressed up."

"That's where we dressed up, because we couldn't dress up during the day," said a housekeeper named Alice Adams. "We'd dress up and put on our good clothes and go to the show on Auburn Avenue. And you were going places. It was like the white folks' Peachtree."

"Oh, beautiful street!" said Alice Carey Holmes Washington, the former journalist and high school counselor, who was born in 1919. "My daddy's office was on Auburn Avenue and I went to work on Auburn Avenue for the *Atlanta Daily World*. We had Ebenezer Baptist Church on one corner; the Catholic school and Church, on the other; the oldest fire station in Atlanta; then you had residential houses on both ends of Auburn. The first library for blacks was at the corner of Auburn and Hilliard. And the lady who named me was the first librarian at that branch, Mrs. Alice Cary. As the first black librarian, she came with a background in classical literature. She taught Greek literature. When the library opened in 1923, it was the pride and joy of the black community because it was such a struggle to get it. In those days, I guess a library was considered a frivolous frill for black folks, although it was one of the necessities. The young men from Carnegie Foundation brought us this library and put it on Auburn Avenue.

"So every Saturday it was a matter of going to Auburn, and this is one of my pleasant memories: to take seven books and get seven books. And I thank Mrs. Cary for my love for reading, because she was not the typical librarian. When I would return seven books, she would just pick any book at random and say, 'Now why do you think so-and-so said this?' She was checking to see that I had read it, but also to let me know that *she* had read it. 'Do you think had she done this instead of that, that this might have happened?' which was my first introduction to character development. Seven books I would take back, and I'd get seven more. And it was not just any seven—she gave titles and choices in our reading. And my daddy was so pleased that I was reading. When I'd hear my daddy coming home, or when it was time for me to stop reading and set the table or do something, I would go and grab a book. And my mother would call, 'Come on, it's time for you to do this,' and I could hear my daddy say over and over again, 'Leave that child alone: she's *reading!*'

"When we would go up and down Auburn Avenue, it was a matter that you knew everybody. I wish today's children had that sort of safe feeling and sort of proximity to history-in-the-making that we had, because as we would go up and down, we knew the ministers at the church; we knew Mr. Jordan who had a clothing shop; we knew the people who operated the service stations. We loved seeing Dr. J. R. Porter, who was one of the first black dentists in the area. You know, 'Hello, Hello, Hello.' And surely you had better speak politely. In those days, if you did anything, then your folks knew it before you could get home. The thing that I remember very pleasantly was going to Yates and Milton Drug Store on the corner for an ice cream cone. A doctor who lived immediately across the street from us would gather us on the corner and ask us riddles. And if you could do the riddle, then he would buy you an ice cream cone. Then the church I attended was one block over on Houston Street. But there are very pleasant memories that I have of Auburn Avenue."

"The first time I saw Atlanta, I was very interested, very interested," said Donald Hollowell, a native of Kansas, a captain of field artillery during World War II, a graduate of Loyola University School of Law, and today one of Atlanta's most venerated attorneys. He is a tall, impeccable man in his late seventies, with thick, curly white hair and a thick triangle of white moustache on a deeply lined dark face. Wearing an expensive navy-blue suit, gold cufflinks, and a gold Rolex watch, he sat beside a skyscraper picture window overlooking the city. Although he had grown up among white children in rural Kansas and had fraternized comfortably with whites in Europe and in undergraduate and law school, they had not been southern whites. He had found that he needed to adjust his demeanor when he moved to Atlanta in the postwar years, fine-tuning it in order not to offend the white lawyers, magistrates, and deputies—or his own sense of perfect equality. He had visited Atlanta before making the decision to relocate and had interviewed Walden, the most successful and visible member of the black bar, to learn whether another black attorney might have a chance to make a living. "Walden, who was the principal one, told me that he felt that a person who could lay it out like a lawyer and who wasn't afraid to work and who had reasonably good judgment could do very well. I had by then, over the years, seen enough of the South to realize a person *could* live in the South and might do all right."

He closed his eyes for long moments, remembering, resting long, tapered fingers upon his eyelids. "I had no problem asking a question of a white person," he said—though one senses, still, forty years later, the emotional preparation required for the most mundane legal task when the practicing attorney was a black person. "I would always try (1) to be polite, (2) to be fair, and (3) to know what I was doing. I was a Christian, a churchman, I expected to be treated civilly. Occasionally I may have found a judge who wasn't quite ready, or a sheriff or a bailiff. I'd been a military man, an enlisted man, an officer; I don't say I was fearless, but I did not find fear dogging me. If someone let me know that a civil answer to my request was beyond their abilities, and I knew that my request was an appropriate one, then I might need to inquire into the possibility of conferring with someone of greater authority.

"I detested the dual water fountains. In court I insisted that my female clients be addressed as 'Miss.' I was neither a smart-ass nor one to be played with. I did not talk back, but I refused to play the fool."

"Auburn Avenue was a revelation to me," said Hollowell in his low, slow voice. "I had no knowledge of the mass of black folk. In some of the Kansas towns in which we were brought up, there weren't but one or two families. So I had had nothing to help me really understand. See, you're getting pretty far out when you get out in Kansas. I'd never seen anything like Auburn Avenue. To see black people in the banking business and the insurance business, the hotel business, the entertainment business. I mean all of this, I hadn't seen in all my years. I had never seen black lawyers. And there were little homes there: black, you know. Drugstores that were black. And it was a thriving community. I learned that the bulk of black culture was in the South."

"When I was growing up, we had to go into Philadelphia to see a dentist," said Bond. "When we came out here, they were everywhere, just everywhere, and it was amazing to see them. There were rooms full of dentists and doctors and lawyers and optometrists. It wasn't something where you swelled with pride; but, you know, I'd just never seen people do this before. I'd never seen anyone who looked like me do it before. It was kind of a secondhand thrill, but a thrill nonetheless."

"Of course, we had lots of restaurants on Auburn," said Washington. "We'd go to Miss James' Cafe. And they always joked about Miss James. Whatever your meal was—and she had a fixed price—her standard expression was, 'Did you have yams?' and if you said you had yams that added ten cents to the cost of your meal. You had the C&H Grill on Auburn where you could get a split. Do you know what a split is? That's the red link sausage that was cut, and you could have it in a bun that was toasted.

"You had, on the corner, just very close to where the Butler Street YMCA is now, a bakery, which was the Silver Moon Bakery. And every afternoon, you could smell the rolls and pies and things, and many people would stop and take the hot potato pie home, or you'd get a slice of pie for lunch. You had on Auburn Avenue a delicatessen operated by Greek brothers. They had excellent sandwiches, and the sandwiches were made with your choice of meat. But they would put potato salad on there or slaw on it, and when you got it, it would be so tall they'd have to cut it so you could pick it up and bite it."

⊷ ⧓ ⊶

At Five Points, in the center of downtown, white ladies with time on their hands met for lunch in the Magnolia Room on the sixth floor of Rich's Department Store. It was a feminine place, with feminine fare: clear soups, and Jello molds containing marshmallows, and airy blends of eggs and cheese and chicken. Sometimes there were henpecked husbands who had been summoned from a nearby office building to approve a china pattern or a daughter's wedding dress or to witness the acquisition of a fur stole; but they appeared excessively tall and pointy and awkward making their way between the glowing white-linen tables, tripping over the shopping bags parked in the aisles, aware that women were pausing, their silver soup spoons in midair, to follow their gangly progress. It was an intimate, high-priced place where exclusive gossip was shared over frosty glasses of sweetened iced tea; it was a bastion of southern white upper-class womanly culture. But back in the hot kitchen were black women, the creators of the ooohed-over recipes and the frothy confections. When these women went home at night, they shared their inventions. If the white diners on the upper floor of Rich's—capturing the last bite of turkey salad from its lettuce leaf, or the last nibble of bacon from between exquisitely thin slices of home-baked white bread, or the last spoonful of sweet whipped cream crowning a sinful dessert—believed they ate cake while the poor ate crusts, they were mistaken, for in restaurants along Auburn Avenue, black people were eating the real thing, the original turkey salad or club sandwich or lavish dessert, and in larger, cheaper portions. Black cooks *adapted* and trimmed-down their heavy-duty Auburn Avenue recipes to the higher altitude of the Magnolia Room.

On the far side of downtown, well beyond Five Points, stood the black institutions of higher learning: Spelman, Morehouse, Morris Brown, and Clark Colleges; Atlanta University; and Gammon Theological Seminary—eventually known, together, as the Atlanta University (AU) Center. Northern white missionary societies and charitable foundations had sent money and maiden-lady schoolteachers to Atlanta after the Civil War to educate the freedmen, and a national black church had done the same. The result was miles of shady, southern, all-black college campuses. In the ivy-covered brick buildings and on the green quadrangles criss-crossed by walkways (a half block from dirt streets crammed with shacks obscured by yards of weeds, corn, and sunflowers) black scientists, mathematicians, historians, musicians, painters, and philosophers lived and taught. A secret black world of high culture and academic distinction subversively flourished. The highly educated, well-spoken men and women would have been at ease in intellectual circles all over the globe, but in Atlanta they were known to the white community, generically, as "more niggers."

"Southern born men who still oppose Negro colleges have repeatedly acknowledged the remarkable character of our graduates," wrote W. E. B. DuBois in 1905. "Our graduates have made good records at Harvard, Dartmouth, and the University of Chicago, University of Michigan, and Northern professional schools. . . . Research work done at our institution has been, in several cases, published by the United States government, and even recognized abroad."

"Atlanta University was an oasis," said Clarence Bacote. "You could live here, at any of these schools, and not suffer the injustices that the person who had to make his living in the city did. You didn't have to face Jim Crow; you had your own group right out here."

"Every year I talked to my students," said the Morehouse president Dr. Benjamin Mays, "and told them that I did not want them to go up in the 'buzzard's roost' [the Jim Crow balcony] to see anybody's show, to see any theatrical performance. And I made it very strong. I said, 'Even if God Almighty came to preach at a white church I wouldn't go to hear Him.' "

"All the cultural activities for blacks were centered on the university center campus," said Alice Washington. "When I was at Booker T. Washington High School [the only black high school in Atlanta], it was common for our teachers to take us there for lectures, for art exhibits, for things that we could not enjoy otherwise. Because we had teachers who were products of the Atlanta University Center and an administration that was determined that black children would not be further subjected to discriminatory practices, we were able to move freely on the university center campuses. And that was my introduction to seeing Du Bois walking back and forth around the campus. He wore his snap-brim hat, and he always had a cane that he would swing on his arm. As you go back and review these things and look at what you try to provide for your own children by design, you see the benefits that you were given by design by someone who wanted you to rise above."

Even intense young Hollowell—who, in later years, would become a famous warrior of a civil rights attorney—relaxed a little among the graduates and faculty of the universities. "I was very interested in what I saw in Atlanta. I had never been any place where you had a consortium of black colleges or had the exposure to ten thousand students. I had never been exposed to the quantity or quality of black people that one was able to find by virtue of the educational institutions that were here and the numbers of people who function in the system by dint of the fact that the schools were segregated. Everything was segregated. And therefore things in the black community, by and large, were operated by black people. I had never seen so many teachers, professors, administrators. And, being a lawyer, I liked the opportunity to mingle with this set, you know. It was a new experience. I was trying to learn something about the South and learn about black people—my own people—in a way that I had never really been exposed.

"When I first came, you know, the guys used to kid me a lot about eating grits with milk. And I knew nothing whatsoever about collard greens. I was acquainted with every kind of wild green you could think of. I knew about mustard and turnips and Swiss chard and kale, but I had simply never heard of collards. . . . I had not heard about rutabaga. They didn't have it in our section.

"And there were grammatical formations. There were things like, 'Yeah, she's my trim girl.' I had never heard of anything like that. And of course you're going to get all kinds of conjugations of the word *be*. They could really mess with *be*! There were many expressions I had to learn. When I say 'learn,' I mean they were not previously part of my vocabulary."

"It was a very insular world, but a very alive world," said Bond. "When I entered Morehouse in the fall of 1957, you had a feeling you were stepping into a place of great intellectual stimulation. There were concerts and plays and speakers. People were thinking about things. I was just talking yesterday to C. Eric Lincoln, who remembers bringing Malcolm X to the Morehouse College campus in 1959. And I remember seeing him walk across the campus. He was just walking on the college campus, and I thought, 'Gee, this is a famous person.' Martin Luther King taught me at Morehouse. I remember seeing Roland Hayes, who was a great tenor—this guy had sung all over Europe, and he sang on my college campus. Just people like that. Everybody in the black world: Langston Hughes, the poet, came, and I sent him poems. I have correspondence from him now. We wrote back and forth. So every light in black America came to the AU Center, and if you were a student, you saw these people, you talked to them, and your own professors were intimates of these people, because our world was still fairly sealed-off and self-contained. It was an exciting place to be."

For illiterate youths just off the farm or emerging from the lopsided, gray urban shacks, for whom no high school existed and even grade school barely functioned, the universities offered remedial and high school work. But for the students like Bond, raised in book-lined homes, the children of professors, teachers, librarians, physicians, college presidents—and of redcaps and Pullman porters with Ph.D.'s—the universities offered the stars. And the atom and the sonnet and the fugue. And the football game and the frat house and the social mixer.

"The white citizens of Atlanta had no idea, no idea," said Bond, recalling the amazement of whites during the sit-in movement at Atlanta lunch counters in 1960. "When we sat-in for the first time, some white woman was quoted in the paper as saying, 'What is this?' and she was told, 'These are Negro college students.' And she said, 'I didn't know they *went* to college.' And I *believe* she didn't know. How *would* she know? She wouldn't have read about it in the paper. How would she know? She lived in a separate world, too.

" 'I didn't *know* they went to college!' It was like: 'Oh! I didn't know they *ate*.' "

All this lay close at hand, within the green rim of the fields basking in the summer haze circling the city, as Rothschild took up his duties as rabbi of the Temple. Beyond the wall of Jim Crow signs, beyond the complex etiquette of white supremacy (the myriad unwritten rules of which he was going to bungle), beyond the white-only eateries and white-only parks, beyond the quick downward glances of Negroes with whom he attempted eye contact, there lay a vast, deep, cultured black world, a business hub, a rhythm-and-blues capital, an intellectual and theological center. It would not seek him out. If he were extremely attentive, he might deduce its existence. If he worked very hard, he might make contact.

First he would have to overcome his sense of dislocation, his outsider status. With regard to black people, he would have to decline the superior position being offered to him by the Jim Crow system. With regard to white people, he might have to reclaim his "white-skin privilege" long enough to denounce it meaningfully. It was going to be complicated.

From across some inner chasm—perhaps it was this distance itself that had driven him into the rabbinate, a career that would institutionalize his feeling of separateness—he meditatively absorbed the sights and mores of his adopted city, Atlanta. When his course was set, he surfaced, powerfully and without his trademark wisecracking. When he chose to surface as a *rabbi*—not as a bridge partner, a tennis player, or a witty dinner guest—he would move his social circle, his congregation, and other people for miles around with his anger and eloquence.

In the interim, sensing already his inchoate rejection of the most fundamental premises of southern life, feeling he might be in for a rocky ride, he contacted a colleague across the state, Rabbi Louis Youngerman at Congregation Mickve Israel in Savannah. "Greetings and Salutations!" wrote Rothschild. "As one transplanted Yankee to another, I really should have more aptly begun: We who are about to die salute you."

5

"Dear Rabbi: My Son Melvin . . ."

1

Suspicious and devious they may have appeared to the anti-Communist underground, but the Temple members, among themselves, spoke not of getting all the gold, nor of world domination, nor even of racial mongrelization. What the Jews discussed on their grassy knoll above Peachtree Street and—on the other side of town—what George Bright and his confederates *imagined* the Jews discussed had no points in common. For the Temple members spoke of bridge games, of dance steps, of theater, of real estate, of politics, of St. Nick.

In September 1948, the public school in the Temple neighborhood, E. Rivers Elementary, accidentally caught fire after hours and burnt down. Several nearby institutions offered space for temporary classrooms, and the board of education chose three: one of the buildings chosen was the Temple. "That choice in itself sent ecstasy throughout the image-sensitive segments of the congregation," remembers Janice Rothschild. "Then the approach of Christmastime titillated these same folk beyond all reason.

101

"Jack . . . had agreed in the name of hospitality to forgo both Jewish sensitivities and separation-of-church-and-state scruples and permit the guests to celebrate the holiday in their usual fashion. Thus it happened that in 1948 Temple halls were decked with holly and Temple schoolrooms with Christmas trees.

"Pleased as Jack had been to be of service to the community, he was not at all pleased by the almost sycophantic reaction he observed among many congregants."

The Temple members' pleasure in the Christmas adornments provoked him. The Temple was not—and was not about to become—a Unitarian church, open to the four winds, respectful of any religious tradition that blew in. There *was* no halfway point, no meeting ground, no compromise—religiously speaking—between the Temple's customs and those of First Methodist. And if the Jews thought the sound of children's voices chanting "O Little Town of Bethlehem" in the Temple was a step in the right direction, even if they merely saw it as a public relations coup, they were wrong.

"Far more important than filling our schoolhouse with strangers," he thundered at them from the pulpit, "is the need for filling our Temple with *Jews!*"

"Why can't we have Christmas?" he rhetorically asked in a sermon entitled "What Can We Tell Our Children?" and quietly, as if to children, he explained: "It is a religious holiday, of *Christians*. We are *Jews*.

" 'I want a Christmas tree.' [But] it is a symbol of the birth of Jesus, and the crowned star of Messiah-ship . . .

" 'What about Santa Claus?' I've never been able to understand the feeling that Jewish parents have to do their part to keep alive the myth of Santa Claus. *Tell our children the truth.*"

And when he finished and looked smilingly down on his congregation, he saw they slouched beneath him glumly, like children just told that Santa Claus is a fake.

A cranky side was being revealed in the new rabbi's jaunty personality, the members thought. He snapped at them unpredictably. But *he* was the new element in the community, not they: he was nipping at the forelegs of a flock trained for half a century to run along certain well-worn paths because he'd gotten it in his head that they ought to be trotting in a different direction. He rebuked them, they felt, when they failed to follow a trail that existed only in *his* mind.

Rothschild did not see himself as brusque or demanding. He was bewildered, and wearied, by their hurt feelings, their taking offense. In fact, he was basically imperturbable, not easily ruffled. His surface flashes of temper were not indicative of inner storm. He heedlessly snapped because he himself was not the type to process and catalogue the little insults and rebuffs of everyday life, because he did not have a clear receiver on that channel. He assumed no one did. If told he had flattened people's feelings, he assumed those feelings would puff up again on their own, without insincere doctoring from him.

Rothschild felt impeded, sidetracked, by the congregation's ceaseless snacklike appetite for the superficial and the inappropriate; whereas within him there yawned a hunger, a starvation, for matters of fundamental importance.

He wanted to think, with them, about ethics, about how a person ought to live who has one eye on his neighbor and the other on the cosmos. He wanted to perfect, with them, a clear new Jewish voice, the timbre of which would be compelling, due in part to a grasp of modern life and in part to the inheritance of ancient wisdom. He wanted what every rabbi since the dawn of the rabbinate has wanted: for his congregation to see the holy Jewish texts as a moral blueprint for their lives.

But he could not get anywhere near any of that. The intervening noise was too great. Talking to them was like trying to talk to one's companions in a crowded bar in which a band is playing. He understood now what he had only glimpsed in seminary: that once the door to modernity was unlocked, secular life with all its dazzling rides, stars, and attractions banged the door wide open and came barging in, rushing to occupy every inch of available space. Jewish rabbis of every denomination were throwing their weight against that door, not—in most cases—to seal and bolt it again, but to close it to some degree, to create—in the room behind it—some sense of moderation, of control, of quiet in which thoughtful and just lives could be built.

Meanwhile, his congregation ooh'ed and ah'ed over the trays of trinkets delivered every hour by the secular world; they pawed and sniffed and stroked and examined absolutely anything that was set out, like fervent shoppers at a Rich's one-day sale. To get them to *desist*, to get their *attention*, was using up all his energy. The deeper questions quietly receded from accessibility. He came home from work, turned on the TV, untied his shoes, and lay on the sofa in his suit in front of a football game, stewing. Janice, working at her desk in a back room, often did not discover he was home for half an hour.

When, in the 1960s, they celebrated Jack Rothschild's twentieth anniversary as rabbi of the Temple, the congregation would lampoon its initial feelings of dismay and panic. They would recall, in a song composed by a congregant and sung by pant-suited, laughing Sisterhood members, what they had been thinking during Rothschild's early years:

> Rothschild! What a lovely name,
> And what a lovely family tree.
> He's probably a nephew of that charming Baron Guy!
> But this Rothschild hit Atlanta like a Jewish General
> > Sherman.
>
> He *wasn't* related to Baron Guy.
> He wasn't even German!
> He's so Yankee! He's so cranky!
> When we're here—twice a year—hear him fuss!
> He's Reform all right, but to him that means
> Reforming us!
>
> Why should he object to a Christmas tree
> When it's such a beautiful sight?
> How mean can he be? Maybe he'll agree
> If we keep the tree BLUE and WHITE!

But in 1946 and for much of the next twenty years, the congregation greeted Rothschild's innovations not with laughter but with, in effect, a collective gasp, followed by the southern admonition of "*Whoa*, boy."

They did not accept his basic premise—so antithetical to the lifework of Dr. Marx—that Judaism ought to be somehow more to them than a religion, that Jews were a "people." Ethnicity was not so in vogue in the 1950s. So thrilled were they to be Americans (in such a century!) they naturally shied from anything that would seem to add an asterisk, a hyphen, a footnote to their full and normal citizenship. They rained personal letters upon Rothschild, as correctives.

One prominent congregant, a pharmacist, wrote in 1952:

> We shall continue to shout from the housetops, "THERE IS NO SUCH THING AS A JEWISH PEOPLE. WE ARE AMERICANS OF THE JEWISH FAITH."
>
> I agree to teaching the children Jewish history. I like the idea of books relating to Jewish stories and plays, but I certainly do not subscribe to the idea of laying stress *only* on One Country, to wit: ISRAEL, and having the children work out puzzles which when pieced together show a map of Israel, the wonders of Israel, or the face of Ben Gurion.
>
> Please understand that I do not rebel at teaching our Youth something about that Wonderful land and the accomplishments of its Wonderful people, but to do it continuously and to the exclusion of other wonderful Countries and other wonderful peoples, this I will fight from every angle. . . .
>
> As for the Hebrew language being the one audible bond that we have, I would like you to line up two or three hundred "old time" members of The Temple, ranging in ages from 40 to 80, and find out just how many Hebrew words these people know.

Another prominent congregant, an insurance agent, had the misfortune in 1951 to read about a convention of Jewish teenagers in which the young people were led in song by young Reform rabbis. "It appears these gentlemen have turned their backs on Reformed Judaism," he bitterly wrote to Rothschild, meanwhile withholding his annual contribution. "I believe the late Isaac M. Wise [the founder of the American Reform movement] would turn over in his grave if he knew that the American youth of Jewish faith were singing songs in Hebrew instead of 'The Star-Spangled Banner.' "

"I think we should continue to have Hebrew on the opposite page from the English text," wrote another. "It makes for good scenery."

"I believe the members of the Congregation, especially those who have children, can recognize that in certain respects the Zionists have turned the clock backward rather that forward," wrote a community leader in 1957. "As I view it, the forward steps taken by our forebears were not taken with the idea of going backward but going forward. Surely the children who go to the Sunday School should not be indoctrinated with the Zionist propaganda—some of it is very subtle."

"Dear Jack," wrote a congregant wishing to challenge the rabbi's suggestion that American Jews on vacation ought to visit synagogues in foreign countries. "Line up all the travelers from Atlanta who have visited Europe or South America or the Caribbean Isles during the past five years, ask them 'DID YOU ATTEND THE FRIDAY NIGHT OR SATURDAY MORNING SERVICE DURING YOUR TRIP?'—more than likely, if good friends of yours, and they would dare speak out frankly, my bet is they would say, 'ARE YOU *NUTS*?' "

Seated at his desk, in what was formerly Dr. Marx's office in the Temple, responding to the letters, Rothschild scribbled away with an ink pen and handed pages out to his assistant, Eloise Shurgin, who then banged away at a manual typewriter whose lowercase *o*'s and *a*'s hit the page loaded with ink and whose uppercase *D*'s, *M*'s, and *R*'s leapt above the line of the other letters, like a line of kindergartners exhorted to stand still in which a few simply can not resist jumping. He wrote, she typed, he signed, she mailed. He had had in mind, albeit abstractly, important work to accomplish, moral leadership to exert, spiritual uplifting to perform. But he found himself, day after day, chest-deep in correspondence as he sweated at his desk, his glasses sliding down his nose and his shirtsleeves rolled up.

It was the last great era of written communication, the end of the modern period preceding universal telephone use. Even a quick reminder of a lunch date, a cross-town confirmation of a speaking engagement, or a notice of a visitor's expected arrival time at the airport came by mail. Rothschild would open a letter on a Monday announcing a rabbinical meeting in New York that Friday, and he would respond by letter that he was coming, to please reserve a room.

There were letters on brittle lavender stationery wrought in the spindly handwriting and finely parsed sentences of the maiden ladies of the congregation. These writers took modest, flustered issue with a turn of phrase from one of his sermons and ended as sweetly evasive as they began, with questions like "Wouldn't it perhaps be more effective if . . . ?" There were terse, manly letters on business stationery—with logos of plumbing-supply or housing-construction companies—in which the writers occasionally offered brusque compliments. But these letters more likely contained barks of unhappiness with the rabbi's Zionism and religiosity; these had been hammered out during a morning coffee break and thrown into the Out box with bills to customers. The writers typically warned Rothschild not to turn religious on them, and they seemed to conceive of God, if at all, as a burly, brass-tacks sort of guy who put in a day's work under heavenly logos of plumbing supplies and lumberyards.

"My father . . . was president of the congregation in 1895 when Dr. Marx was called as its rabbi. At that time, all ceremonials were discontinued," a mortgage broker pelted out on letterhead, working the metal levers of his manual typewriter. The manual typewriter was a machine of cultivated violence: tiny hammers pummelled the page drawn through a polished black box, making a sound much like that of a rotary lawnmower. These days, even a letter writer's fiercest irritation tends to be processed by the muted clicking of a computer keyboard and transformed into distant, back-lit, televised sentences. But in the 1940s and 1950s, a truly annoyed letter writer sent the words smashing almost through the paper, and the recipient held a true artifact, powdered with correction paper and exasperation. If a letter writer were truly agitated, the recipient might see points of light coming through the lifted page. To a blind person, such a letter might be mistaken for Braille. A period—as in, "And that's *final* [period]."—was lobbed like a hand grenade. "I personally think," typed the mortgage broker, "that the lighting of the candles and other ceremonials that *you* have installed should be discontinued." Period.

The venetian blinds were furry with dust; the hot sunlight banged around the rabbi's huge and handsome study, ricocheting off the clock face and chrome desk set. The Temple in the 1950s stood above the tree line in its neighborhood, so no benevolent greenery darkened the air between Rothschild at his desk and the radiant sky. He felt at times like a clerk, or like a pieceworker in a sweatshop. Once every thirty seconds the oscillating fan stanched the perspiration on his face, and the papers on his desk rustled and shivered under his fingers like living things.

He wrote letters to, and opened letters from, other Reform rabbis, no doubt also tethered to desks heaped with requests, compliments, and reproaches. What was their policy on Christian–Jewish intermarriage, he wondered. On congregants hosting Friday night social affairs? On local Christian blue laws? He wrote with wry brevity, his letters the written equivalent of his wisecracking talk.

"We tried to combat the growing tendency of Friday evening social affairs by passing a resolution at the annual meeting of the congregation," he wrote to Rabbi Herbert Waller in Louisville, Kentucky. "The resolution was passed unanimously and it would appear that our members have unanimously maintained the custom of having parties on Friday nights."

"I have organized a youth group at The Temple and have had opposition to allowing them to dance in the social hall on Sunday," he wrote to Rabbi Milton Grafman in Birmingham. "That's the Sabbath around here, Son. What do you do with your youth group?"

The bulk of his correspondence with other rabbis was wonderfully, ridiculously mundane and gossipy. Like other Americans yearning for upward social mobility, American Jews drifted from city to city. They then signed on with the local Reform congregations, and the local Reform rabbis—unsure of whom they had on their hands exactly—wrote to one another for clarification. An Illinois rabbi wrote to Rothschild that he had just loaned forty dollars to a Jewish man with a broken-down car who claimed to be from Atlanta. "Will I ever see my money again?" "Afraid not," Rothschild wrote back. "We don't know anyone here by that name."

"Dear Jack; A young fellow in our Congregation, Marvin Klein, is stationed at a camp at Columbia, about five miles from Atlanta," wrote Rabbi James A. Wax from Memphis. "He is a fine lad, taught in our Religious School, and will appreciate any courtesies shown him."

"Oi! Are you confused!" wrote Rothschild. "The only Columbia I know is Columbia, S.C., where Ft. Jackson is located. We own a Columbus in Georgia, near which Ft. Benning is located. Columbus is 100 miles from Atlanta. Columbia is 165 miles from Atlanta. Your young man may be an excellent product of your Religious School but I ain't going that far to say 'hello' to him."

And there were letters from well-intentioned Christians, invariably sounding a bit misinformed.

"Dear Rabbi: I am a Gentile and for 17 years have been looking for a Christian organization of the Jews, which I understand you are connected with," said one correspondent in 1954. " . . . I am an old man in my eighties and will soon be passing away, and will probably have a small legacy to leave some Christian-Jewish organization. . . . May God bless you in all your labors, that you may be a true light unto the Gentiles, is my prayer for you and all who are laboring for the end that Jesus will soon come and redeem his people (the Jews)."

"I am afraid that your informant has badly misled you," Rothschild wrote politely (probably wishing he could begin, "Oi! Are you confused!") " . . . You may be interested to know that there is no respectable Christian organization of Jews. From time to time we hear of Jews converted to Christianity who then set about to convert other Jews, but I assure you that these are looked upon with something of pity and contempt. . . . I pray that God will grant you many years of vigorous health and that we may each work in our own way and through our own beliefs to bring about that world of peace and brotherhood for which all men strive and pray."

And there were pleas from some anxious parents who

were experiencing a breach in relations with their child; they wished to throw Rothschild into the breach. A Birmingham, Alabama, mother wrote:

> Dear Rabbi,
>
> My son, Melvin, has been residing in Atlanta since he finished his Army Career two years ago. He is a Buyer at Davison-Paxon's. . . . Melvin is 26. He has been dating Jane D——, also a Buyer at Davison's for over a year now, and their relationship, I feel, has reached a serious stage with proposed marriage. Jane D—— is Presbyterian, and my husband and I are against inter-faith marriage. We are very distressed and very unhappy over this situation and feel that this is not for him because she is not a Jewess.
>
> Please contact Melvin and talk with him. My Son, most likely, would not appreciate it if he knew that I wrote you on this matter. . . . I spoke to Rabbi Grafman in Birmingham and he said that he would like to speak to Melvin. I told Melvin to come home and do that but he will not do it.
>
> He has not joined a Temple since he came to Atlanta. I wish that he would do so that he could participate in Jewish activities in the Community. We have heard so many fine reports about you, Rabbi Rothschild, and your Temple. Please ask Melvin to consider joining.

Rothschild met with Melvin. Melvin *was* planning to marry Miss D——. Rothschild urged them to consider Jane's conversion to Judaism and then wrote back to Melvin's mother that Jane seemed to be a very fine person who, if she were to convert, ought to be accepted by the family. "I strongly feel that the marriage should not take place without prior conversion," he wrote, "and I gained the impression that Melvin agrees with me on this point."

The questions of interfaith dating and intermarriage were at the heart of what Rothschild identified, initially, as his greatest task: to staunch the flow of emulating love, admiration, and yearning toward the gentile world. The letters cascading onto his desk were filled with the agitation and hairsplitting of an excitable people trying to break free of their minority status, trying to redefine themselves almost out of existence. "THERE IS NO SUCH THING AS A JEWISH PEOPLE." The Temple congregants appeared to Rothschild to be scurrying to fit into their bright American city without heaving overboard absolutely everything the Jewish millennia had bequeathed them—just most of it.

At times Rothschild appeared to his congregants, and to himself, to be trying to bar their way, like a security guard standing with crossed arms beside the threshold into a society ball. Just over his shoulder, it seemed, they could glimpse fabulous times to be had in the Christian world; but they stood outside, in the dark, in the street, as he tried to load into their arms heavy brass menorahs and awkward Torah scrolls; over their shoulders they felt themselves shadowed by bearded Talmudists in long coats, smelling of pickles and herring. It was as if Rothschild stood beside the entrance into a brilliant mansion glittering with candelabra and told the Jews to turn back, to be pleased with the lesser gifts he handed them—tarnished candlesticks and plastic Purim masks and little cardboard boxes of Hanukkah candles. Of course, it was not actually Rothschild who barred the door to breathtaking social success with the Protestants. The Protestants themselves barred it. But the rabbi, it was felt, was not making things any easier. In this he was a disappointment. And they let him know it.

What to keep? What to toss?

Rothschild would not live to hear the title of the modern Czech novel by Milan Kundera, *The Unbearable Lightness of Being*; but had he heard such a phrase, he could have woven a bitter sermon around it. For his congregation threw off more and more and more; the Temple's history was like a road taken by a fleeing populace, the shoulders of the road piled high with jewelry boxes, books, musical instruments, and other family heirlooms abandoned as people ran for their lives.

— ≡✦≡ —

He understood. It was not that he did not understand.

"We note the rise of anti-Semitism," he said one Saturday. "We see our people and their fate made into a world issue. We seek to escape the dangers of identification with the group whose fate is so precarious. We long to live the normal sort of life that being a Jew seemingly makes impossible. . . .

"For most of us being a Jew means merely a curtailment of happiness. I am a Jew. Therefore, I cannot belong to certain clubs. I cannot live on certain streets. I cannot rent a room in some hotels. I cannot send my children to many colleges. I am a Jew—therefore I cannot—my life is bound, my opportunity limited. . . .

"Why do we, when we hear 'Jew,' cringe with fear? Why does not the word summon to our minds a true connotation? Picture a Moses holding aloft the two tablets of stone. . . . Conjure up the image of Amos crying out to a hostile throng: Woe to you who grind the needy under your feet. . . . Why does not the word remind us that from the pen of divinely inspired Jews came the greatest lyric poetry the world has ever known? . . . That from the mind of Jews came the philosophy of a Spinoza, the statesmanship of a Disraeli? Why? Because we do not know. We are a generation ignorant of our own heritage."

Thus, he portrayed happiness: that they should sense to the core of their being the history, the shared destiny, the peoplehood (many got this far) and derive from it not shame and anguish but *pride*. He offered all this without God. He preached, in his early years, a Jewish version of the later black-is-beautiful movement. Not a holy people, but a respectable people. Jews Worth Knowing: Moses, Disraeli, Spinoza. Join Now and Find Yourself Related to Judah Benjamin and Jonas Salk.

"I have a conviction," he preached, "that our insecurity as Jews stems from *ignorance*." He then gave a sermon entitled, "How to Be Happy though Jewish."

⊶ ⊨♦⊟ ⊷

But they understood how things were. It was not that they did not understand. They were not sure the trade-off was worth it: to bring a more heavily Jewish definition to their lives in exchange for being related to Disraeli and Spinoza? It was not so easy being a Jew. Rothschild, in *his* circles, was not running into all the barriers they were: the graduate schools, law firms, neighborhoods, medical practices, banks, corporations, and country clubs automatically closed to them, no questions asked. Throw in Moses, Kirk Douglas, and Einstein, and it still was not an obvious swap. Besides, Spinoza was an excommunicated agnostic—and Disraeli? a convert.

In the first decade and a half after the end of World War II, people were not exactly falling over themselves to sign up as Jews, or as friends of the Jews. The Nazi persecutions and perversions were borne like shame by the survivors of the calamity not yet called the Holocaust, the Shoah. Jewish community centers did not honor the survivors in their midst in local memorial programs; there was no curriculum about it in the public schools. It was hushed, it was shushkied. Not till the 1967 war would the worldwide Jewish people begin to be able to look closely at what had happened. In the 1950s people still felt as if they were running for their lives.

And Rothschild did not give them enough credit, they felt, for being there for him to yell at in the first place. They were not abdicating, falsifying, converting. They were sticking by the Temple. They sent in their dues. They funded a dozen other Jewish communal and fraternal and charitable organizations, too. But they were Americans first, then southerners, then Atlantans, and, also, just happened to be, Jewish.

"There was anti-Semitism at all levels," said Charles Wittenstein, a Temple member, former area director for the American Jewish Committee, and former attorney for the Anti-Defamation League in Atlanta. "And it wasn't just the vulgar anti-Semitism of the J. B. Stoners, the George Lincoln Rockwells. There was also the genteel anti-Semitism of the prestigious law firms, the corporate employers. There was the social exclusion of the dining clubs, the golf clubs. There were neighborhoods off-limits to Jews—Lenox Park, Victoria Estates. There were hotels and resorts—like the Cloister Hotel on Sea Island—off-limits. It was genteel in that they didn't plant the bomb at your house. They showed you the door, without being rude about it."

"We were very aware of the Ku Klux Klan as kids," said Jane Axelrod. "We were never allowed to go near Stone Mountain—that was where they held their rallies and cross burnings. And we had a [KKK] grand dragon or whatever living in the Morningside area. You would cross the street rather than walk right by his house."

"I never knew what anti-Semitism was until I came to Atlanta," said Nancy Thal. "Back in the fifties, everyone was black or white and then there were the Jews. Down here, we knew there were boundaries and we knew that there was the Driving Club and there was the Capital City Club and it was, you know, a town where Coca-Cola was such a dominant thing. There was just an aura of WASPdom then."

"I owned a little cabin in Mountain Park, Georgia, in the fifties," said Sam Massell, a Jew, a native Atlantan, and the mayor of Atlanta from 1968 to 1972. A short, stocky, curly-headed, energetic bulldog of a man, he explained: "The City Executive Committee approached me about being on the executive committee: Mountain Park was the only place in Georgia you could hold office without being a year-round resident. I thought about it and said all right. They said, 'Come to the next meeting. We'll appoint you.'

"I went home to Atlanta. Came back up the next time, my neighbor came over, said, 'Sam, look here, you've got trouble.'

"I said, 'What's the problem?'

"He said, 'You're a Jew, right? Well, the executive committee has found out about it.'

"I went to my first meeting and they were all just as friendly, but they didn't get started, made no move to appoint me. I said, 'I understand you boys aren't for me now?'

"And they said—big smiles, just as pleased and friendly, 'That's *right!*' "

The stakes were high. In patriotism, in rationalism, in universalism, in democracy, they hoped to lose the cursed mark of the scapegoat. They embraced the ideal of the universal brotherhood of man, hoping to be thereby counted in. Letters, of course, chased behind Rothschild's "Let's be more Jewish" sermons. One urged him to read "some of the poems of Wee Robbie of Auld Scotia [Robert Burns]: The one which strikes a happy chord in the heart of any Jew is 'A MAN'S A MAN FOR A' THAT.' "

The Brotherhood of Man. Well, no rabbi could quibble with the Brotherhood of Man. But it was a longer and wider road than it may first have appeared to those who hoped to find, along its route, business opportunities, country clubs with nondiscriminatory clauses, neighborhoods without restrictive covenants.

The upwardly mobile Reform Jews were looking ahead, with hope, in the direction of the Capital City Club, the blue-chip law firms, the dental practices, the neighborhoods of stately hermitages, the debutante balls for teenage daughters. But behind them on the road, invisible for a moment as if around a bend, came a great mass of humanity. Black people also had their feet on the brotherhood highway, with their hearts fixed on larger, simpler realms: housing, education, jobs. While his congregants looked ahead, Rothschild, as if hearing somebody behind him, was starting to turn around.

2

Meanwhile, a delightful and fulfilling and busy life was lived on the narrow neck of land between Protestant exclusivity and Jewish orthodoxy. The Temple Jews lived almost like Gypsies on the fringe of society, within their own circle of wagons. But they lived handsomely, with rounds of fund-raisers, opera performances, bridge parties, golf games, tennis sets, and Christmas parties at the Standard Club.

William Schwartz said, "When we came back to Atlanta after I served in World War II, we'd end up at the Standard Club every Saturday night. . . . Even when we had dinner somewhere else, we'd end up at the club. In those days you couldn't buy a drink of whiskey in a restaurant in Atlanta, so if you wanted a cocktail, you'd go to someone's home or go to the club."

"The grounds were beautiful, the building was big, with wonderful rooms," Nancy Thal said of the Standard Club after its move to Brookhaven in 1949. "The golf course was wonderful—big Olympic-sized pool, nice locker rooms. It was just a plum spot. There was a big formal dining room, and there was a grill downstairs for the golfers, and the food was excellent—some of the best food in town. People had wedding receptions there, and sometimes they had the weddings there too. In other words, if there was, you know, a mixed marriage, they had the wedding there, if the rabbi would."

The Temple Jews owned their own companies and employed one another and their sons-in-law and their cousins (for success was not possible in gentile-owned firms). The Jewish-owned clothing and department stores, like Rich's, Leon Frohsin's, and Regensteins, were Atlanta's finest, so the people traveled to town and did their shopping (the store clerks greeted them by name) without leaving the magic circle.

The greatest German-Jewish success story in the city was the Rich family and Rich's Department Store, the largest such store in the Southeast. So great a success was Rich's that ultimately all Atlantans would know the store, but not its point of Jewish origin. The first (and for many, many years, the only) Jewish member of the Piedmont Driving Club was the Jewish wife (not a Rich) of the store's Christian chairman. "He converted to Judaism so Marx would marry them," said Janice, "then went back to Christianity to join the Driving Club. However, he chose a more upscale denomination than the one he'd left originally." So great a success was Rich's that descendants of the Jewish founder would mingle with the best Christians and die Episcopalian.

In 1867, Morris Rich opened a little dry-goods store in the ruins of Atlanta. A downpour came on the day he opened; the streets ran like muddy rivers; he laid down planks across the wet red clay to protect the footwear of customers he hoped would come. He offered fifty-cent corsets and twenty-five-cent stockings, and he accepted chickens, eggs, and turnip greens in lieu of money when necessary.

In 1882, M. Rich and Brothers opened up in new, larger quarters with great fanfare and publicity. The *Atlanta Constitution* hailed the new Rich's as "an emporium of fashion and design . . . acknowledged by all who have seen it to be the most complete establishment of its kind in the South, New Orleans, even, not to be excepted." In 1906 when the store enlarged again, the *Atlanta Journal* enthused: "Atlanta's womankind has received a most wonderful New Year's gift!" In 1895, Rich's helped to bail out the debt-ridden Cotton States and International Exposition; in 1917, it gave free merchandise to hundreds of families displaced by fire; in the 1920s, when the price of cotton fell ruinously, Rich's bought thousands of bales from

Georgia farmers well above market price. During the Great Depression, when the city of Atlanta ran out of money and could not pay its schoolteachers, Walter Rich—Morris's nephew, who succeeded his uncle in 1926—phoned the mayor and told him to pay the teachers in scrip; Rich's then cashed the scrip at full value, without requiring that any of it be spent in the store. In 1946, when 119 lives were lost in the Winecoff Hotel fire, America's worst hotel disaster, Rich's employees helped the out-of-town relatives find their dead and then brought to the bereaved, from the store to the hospital, new burial clothes.

With handsome gifts to the city—a radio station for the public school system, a clubroom for garden clubs, hospital wings and outpatient clinics, the Emory University School of Business Administration, the lab and computer center at Georgia Tech—Rich's was second in public esteem only to the Coca-Cola Company. "A derisive competitor on his way back to New York after an unsuccessful sortie into Atlanta . . . once charged that, to people in the South's Bible Belt, Rich's is 'the true church,'" wrote the *Constitution* columnist Celestine Sibley in *Dear Store*, her book about Rich's. While in genuine stature it was but a country cousin to the worldwide giant soft-drink distributor, to the German Jews of Atlanta, the Riches seemed to have attained the stratosphere: gentile acceptance and affection.

"Dick Rich was an attractive man," said Jackie Montag, the wife of the son of Rich's first cousin. "White hair, very neat, and he used to pride himself on the fact that he still wore the same size trousers that he wore when he went off to college. What he didn't know was that the people in the store altered them. It may have said size 14 or whatever, but it was not quite the same size he thought it was."

By the mid-twentieth century, Rich's had evolved into a sort of southern Disneyland. The only air-conditioned business in Georgia, it had wares more modern, alluring, and elegant than those offered almost anywhere else in the South. Ladies studied the New York fashions in magazines to know how to dress when traveling downtown. They rode down Peachtree Street by streetcar or automobile, met friends for lunch, then wandered through Rich's, browsing among a fabulous array of postwar luxuries: toasters, bedspreads, television sets, electric stoves, cocktail dresses. "I had a friend who headed the millinery department at Rich's," said Aline Uhry. "All the big socialites went there. And my friend said she hated it when two good friends came shopping together for hats, because the *minute* a hat was becoming to one person, her friend would comment that it didn't look right."

Uhry, a descendant of founders of Atlanta, lives in a modern, rectangular house filled with large glass windows and surrounded by old-growth trees. Carefully selected art is on display throughout the spacious, light rooms. But Uhry, an eighty-year-old sprite in stretch pants and a sweater, moves through it all with hospitable dismissiveness, as if she were saying about a dress, "*This* old thing."

"Rich's was like a family store. Some people in the Rich family wouldn't shop anywhere else. If they wanted something—this is true—from Davison's, they'd send a friend to pick it up for them. You knew all the salespeople by name and called them 'Miss Rose' and so on. My son went downtown with a friend of his, and it was before my mother's birthday, and my son went in the linen department (you could let children all around) and bought some guest towels and told the lady his name was Alfred Fox Uhry (which it is) and his grandmother was Mrs. Alfred Fox and she had an account there. And the lady gave him the towels and charged it to my mother.

"There were not many places to have lunch, but Rich's had the Magnolia Room, and there was the Frances Virginia Tea Room (my mother said they served yokel [countrified] food). At Frances Virginia, I remember one thing that was so special: it was green lime Jello with miniature marshmallows and crushed, canned pineapple, and a glob of mayonnaise on top with a cherry. That was *it*.

"And chicken à la king. Do you know chicken à la king? It's cut-up chicken, made nicely. They used not only milk but cream, thickened into a cream sauce. What I remember about the Magnolia was they cut up olives in it if it was fancy, and almonds, and served it on biscuits. People don't eat that way anymore. Some do.

"Rich's Magnolia Room tried to be uptown Junior League food. It wasn't black-eyed peas that now people love to go to eat.

It was chicken à la king. I mean fancy—all the molded things. Anything in a mold: Libby's fruit cocktail in a mold. Oh, a *big* thing was raspberry or strawberry Jello with bananas. See? That was big."

* ⊷ ▤ ⊶ *

"Our social life was Jewish," Uhry said, "a very tight little German-Jewish community revolving around the Temple and the Standard Club. It was an old colonial house ... and it had a ballroom and people ate there. It was the center of social life. The young people had dancing classes there, and do you know who taught the dancing class? Arthur Murray! My friend Joe Heyman said to me—we were at a party where people were dancing—he said, 'You know Arthur Murray sends me two hundred dollars a month?'

"I said, 'What's the joke?'

"He said, 'So I won't tell people he taught me to dance.'

"We had a Saturday night bridge-playing group for over forty-five years. At the height of it, we had twenty-three people. Five us went to Wellesley. We'd come to each other's houses for dinner. We'd get all dressed—cocktail dresses. You'd have drinks with hors d'oeuvres and candy and nuts in little silver dishes. The hostess would decide which bridge table you'd sit at. Usually two men and two women at a table (not married couples). Always get together on New Year's Eve.

"I think the Jewish lifestyle tried to copy the WASP style, in their own way. People say the Jewish clubs are exclusive, but they sprang up as a result of not being in the other. I had a lot of Christian friends at school; my school friends and my weekend friends were two different groups. I had one very close friend—Ruth. We walked to school together, studied together, ate lunch together, and she would come over to my house. One day her mother called on my mother. They sat down and had coffee and cake. And she said, 'Miss Fox, I just have to ask you a question. I know it's not true now, but I've been hearing from people in the neighborhood, I know it's not true, that you folks are Jewish.'

"Mama said, 'Of course we are.'

"Mrs. H. said, 'I just still don't believe it.'

"So then Ruth and I stayed friends at school, but we didn't visit each other's homes after that.'

"My husband and I lived on Woodhaven Road, and next door there was a family that used to borrow an egg or a Coca-Cola or something like that. The husband wanted to get in the Ansley Golf Club, which was not prestigious like the other ones, but it was Christian. It would have been his style of elite.

"And one day he came over to see my husband, and he said, 'Ralph, I wonder if you'd do me a favor. There's a man works for you who is president of the Ansley Golf Club, and I'd like my name to be put up for membership, but I've never been able to make headway. Would you say something to him about me?' Ralph said, 'Yeah, I'll do it.' So sure enough, Luther was taken into the Ansley Club. And he came over and thanked my husband so profusely. He said, 'Now, Ralph, if there's anything I can ever do for you, please call me.' 'Oh,' Ralph said, 'there's something you can do for me right now. I'd like you to get *me* in the Ansley Golf Club,' which of course was a joke, because he couldn't get in. He got that man in, but he couldn't get in."

"Dick Rich used to say he had a rule of thumb," said Jackie Montag. "He would invite non-Jews to his house *after* they had invited him, but he would never initiate it."

3

It was thus a cheerful, self-sufficient, old-time secret society that Jack Rothschild entered by taking the pulpit of the Temple in Atlanta. The Temple Jews were handsome, urbane, ambitious, and energetic. They founded and funded orphanages, hospitals, museums, schools, and university centers. "Reform Jews diversified," said Temple member Tony Montag. "The Reform Jews went out of the Jewish community into the Atlanta community as they became prosperous; they were involved with boards of banks and United Way, so they got the most print. Conservative Jews by and large stayed active within the Jewish Federation, B'nai B'rith, Jewish activities, so they had less visibility."

Pious Jews would, from time to time, revile their secularism, but the Temple members, bare-headed, in modern suits, unbound by ancient restrictions, felt themselves to be like young giants, with wealth and talent and new ideas at their disposal. They did good works, with good hearts, so they did not believe God would turn His face away simply because they were not huddled like their brethren over thin soup and yellowish candles. And even if the WASPs shuddered at their sudden ubiquity in civic life and retreated to their exclusive sanctums, these Jews still created skyscrapers, designed stadiums, and laid out a modern city. And after business hours they pulled back, returned to their circle of wagons on the fringe of accepted society, and enjoyed one another's lively company.

The members kept up the appearance of perfect contentment (and were, by and large, perfectly content) by insulating themselves against the petty insults, glass ceilings, and restrictive clauses of the outside world. Like ants in an underground kingdom whose scouts lug home a crumb of cupcake, leading to wild rejoicing up and down the tunnels, the Reform Jews of the South drew into their secret world bits of WASP culture— Christmas parties, golf courses, New Year's Eve balls—and covered them with their own interpretations and designs. "Even though my husband's father was president at the Temple and all this stuff, they had a Christmas tree," one woman recalled. "His mother told me that one time the rabbi came over, and she wouldn't let him in the front door. She yelled for her maid, and they pulled the tree back into another room before they'd let him in."

＊＊＊

Rothschild glided easily into the Temple social life, not because he was a rabbi (which would have won him respect, but not necessarily friendship) but because he could ride horseback, tell a good joke, and play bridge, tennis, and golf. "If people went to Temple, they went Friday nights," said Herb Axelrod. "Saturday morning services were at 10:30, but you had tee-off times at the Standard Club starting at 11:00. Rothschild teed off at the Standard Club at 1:30 on Saturdays."

Rothschild was gently chided about golf by his congregation—not for golfing on Saturday, but for having such a preposterous swing. "But I'm a Reform rabbi," he told them. "You wouldn't want me to have an orthodox swing."

"His best friends," said Janice, "the ones who took him up immediately, people his own age, were couples who were from important families where the men were on the board of the Temple. They rarely came to temple, though, and were not interested. But they were bridge players, as he was, and tennis players, as he was, and they found him a very personable addition to their social group."

The rabbi was single, folks noticed, *and* an intellectual, so a goodly number of the many dinner parties that included him featured the available young lady of the household: tan and robust from tennis, home on break from Wellesley; or fading and a little toothy, still unmarried at thirty, but well read. Janice Oettinger, age twenty-two, first noticed Rothschild as she sunbathed by the Standard Club pool and he was playing tennis. "Who is that?" she wondered aloud. When told it was the new rabbi, she replied: "That's ridiculous—Dr. Marx is never going to retire." "Besides," she said later, "all the rabbis I had ever known were way past their days on a tennis court, even for doubles."

Janice was the great-granddaughter of Edward Benjamin Morris Browne, the rabbi of the Temple from 1877 to 1881. She was related, by blood or marriage, to many of the best families, though her own family was not wealthy. Her father was a traveling salesman, and her mother was a free-spirit piano teacher, regarded by many as "the first hippie, before there were hippies."

They secretly began to date, the dates consisting chiefly of late-night telephone conversations (after Jack had returned to his room at the Biltmore Hotel from a dinner party), during which they worked the *New York Times* crossword puzzle. "We had a terrible time finding a time we could go out with each other," said Janice, "because he was booked up absolutely solid with people who had invited him to dinner, especially people who had young ladies to also invite for dinner."

In November 1946 he wrote to his friend and former professor, Dr. Jacob Marcus:

The other day I took a deep breath and asked someone to marry me. . . . I could go on to describe her in superlatives, but if I didn't feel that way I wouldn't want to marry her, so I presume you will take the missing superlatives for granted. In general, she is tall and dark and very young— 22, an Atlantan without a Southern accent. Without a place to live or furniture to put in it or money to buy it, we are planning to be married about the end of December.

"He exaggerated," said Janice. "He didn't actually ask me to marry him. Articulate as he normally was, in this instance he was silent and handed me a picture instead. It was a cartoon from the *Saturday Evening Post* depicting a young man on his knees looking up at a young woman primly seated on a sofa. The caption read, 'Go ahead, Harry. It's really very simple.' "

"We were married, with much misguided splendor, at The Temple on Sunday, 29 December," wrote Janice. "In the interim I managed to complicate Jack's life still further by drawing him into a series of social customs (parties, tidbits in the society pages . . .) that my mother and I had been led to believe were de rigueur for weddings in our circle. . . . He succeeded only in confirming Mother's opinion of him as an 'unpolished Northerner,' and confirming his own view of the South as a backwater of civilization still brackish with superficial courtliness and false values."

After a one-week honeymoon in New York, the newly-weds moved into Janice's parents' garage apartment. The post-war housing shortage made any move for the better seem unlikely, and when Rothschild received a letter from an out-of-towner asking about housing conditions in Atlanta, he wrote back: "I don't like to discourage you, but I've been here since July and have finally managed to secure the rear end of a garage—and I had to get married to be eligible for that." Back in his office, elbow-deep in letters again, he noticed that his rabbi-correspondents often signed off "Best regards from house to house." So Rothschild began signing his "Best regards from house to house which I wish I had one of."

To the organizers of an out-of-town conference, he wrote:

I received a mimeographed note that my application for reservations had been received and that I would probably have to share the room with some other rabbi. To this I don't object—but my wife, having met very few rabbis, is understandably skeptical. Anyway, she's coming along and if the house committee has no objections, I would prefer sharing a room with her.

And in October 1947, to Rabbi Ely E. Pilchik in Newark: "You will be interested to learn that my wife had a baby which we called Marcia, mostly because it is a girl." A son, Billy, followed thirteen months later. Now they needed a house more than ever.

They found one on a lovely, shady street and provoked an uproar in the neighborhood when word leaked out that Jews had looked at the house. A threat from the neighborhood was mailed to the Temple, though the Rothschilds had not even decided yet if they wanted the house. The seller wrote a letter of apology:

> I just want to tell you how very, very sorry I am about what happened in connection with your wanting to buy our house. It has shocked and upset me terribly and I know it must have hurt you deeply.
>
> I am a Christian—that is, I have accepted Jesus Christ as my savior and Lord. And I don't know how any true Christian can have any prejudice against the Jewish people. We owe so much to them. . . . I am a Canadian and do not feel very enthusiastic about becoming an American if this . . . is a sample of American democracy.
>
> I mentioned you to only one neighbor, but she certainly did a thorough job of arousing the neighborhood. We almost had a riot on our hands. Dozens of people called my husband at work and me at home. Then they started calling all the real estate agents. And later I learned . . . they actually stooped low enough to send you an anonymous letter. . . .
>
> I would still have sold you the house if you had wanted it, but I felt I must let you know the situation, for I couldn't bear the thought of your coming here and being persecuted by the neighbors. . . . I can truthfully say I would much prefer you as neighbors to many of the folks around here.

They had ventured outside the magic circle. Janice would reserve all her anger and criticism for the realtor who had led them to believe they were on safe, or prepared, ground. "While it came as no surprise that there were residential neighborhoods with de facto restrictions against Jews," she would later write, "we were astonished and amazed that a highly reputable realtor would be so careless (or callous) as to show us a house in one of them."

The Jewish people always knew, in a generally humbling sort of way, that there were people out there who did not like them. But they never knew precisely who—aside from the Ku Klux Klan—or why or where or when the antipathy might next reveal itself. Many Jewish southerners had what seemed the best of all possible worlds—a delightful life, a cultured life, a life of responsibility to the city and to the needy. But of all the unwritten by-laws of membership, the most important one was, When you step outside the known borders, watch yourself.

6

The Yiddish Capital of the South

1

"They were not *Jews* at that time—they were Germans," said a retiree, the son of a Polish butcher, speaking of the members of the Temple. "Today? With Israel? With all this patriotism and the homeland? Tut, tut, tut—today they're big supporters of Israel. They're Jews. But then? *Deitchen* (pronounced "Dye-tchen")—Germans."

"The Temple Jews weren't worth a goddam," said another retiree, the son of a Russian-born grocer. "We called them the *Deitch-yiden* (pronounced "Dye-tch-yee-din"). They wanted to be goyim. They worked and sent their children to school on the Jewish holidays. That was Marx. And there were a lot of good people among them."

"Let me tell you about the Temple Jews," said a retired grocer, the son of another Russian grocer. "They were German Jews, Austrian Jews. They didn't have nothing to do with the Russian Jews. The Temple was Jewish on the outside and whatever else you want to call it on the inside."

"The Jewish elite," said an elderly lawyer, "the *reich*—the rich, the Deutschjuden, believed they were Americans first and Jews somewhere down the line."

Not all the Jews in Atlanta had money and golf clubs (not even all the Temple Jews). Not all looked to the Episcopalians for role models. Not all the Jews in Atlanta denied any knowledge of revolution. And not all the Jews in Atlanta tried their hardest to avoid run-ins with bigots.

Across the city from the curving, tree-lined streets of Druid Hills and Ansley Park—where middle- and upper-class Temple families were vexed by the well-mannered exclusions of high-society anti-Semitism—lived the other Jews. Packed into boarding houses with three or four youngsters to a bed, these Jews, who lived hand-to-mouth, would have felt it rather a compliment to be snubbed by a gentile social club. They were, in fact, invisible to the Protestant glitterati, indistinguishable from the soot-faced masses of black, Italian, or Irish laborers. Had a Russian tenement Jew showed up on the velvet lawn of the Piedmont Driving Club, no elaborate explanations would have been offered at the door for why he could not come in: he would have been matter-of-factly directed to the side door for the hired help. In certain WASP circles, the Russians were known as the "black Jews."

Their fathers and grandfathers were not gentleman lawyers, retailers, and city founders, smelling of pipesmoke, like those of the German Jews. Their fathers were bearded immigrant poultry dealers, tailors, peddlers, tobacco dealers, liquor store owners, Hebrew teachers, and hatmakers, men who smelled of copper polish, of the slaughterhouse, of Shabbos wine. When the American-born sons went to war in the 1940s, they fought in the artillery, rode in tanks, flew in bombers. When, back in America, they encountered anti-Semites, their range of responses differed from those of the German Jews, who offered the ironic quip, the averted gaze, the editorial in a Jewish periodical, and the establishment of a separate country club.

The local anti-Semites were to find the Russian Jews a handful, for these Jews—especially the Socialists among them—were anything but genteel when it came to turf and race wars.

Behind the high wall of Yiddish (the first generation barely learned English), Atlanta's Russian Jews sold pots or shoes from pushcarts, and eggs and potatoes from hole-in-the-wall groceries. The Russian Jews were oblivious to the fact that there were *Jewish* country clubs that would not touch them. (Who ever heard of a Jewish country club, anyway? It sounded like a joke.) The eastern European immigrants who settled along Decatur Street in Atlanta among Greeks, Syrians, Chinese, Italians, Hungarians, and blacks would possess instead—like their New York City cousins—brass-knuckle, kike, pickle-barrel street stories. An Austrian-Jewish physician reported that the district was characterized by "dirt, filth, putrefaction, and noxious emanations."

Still, what the people had left behind in Russia and Poland had been worse: dirt, filth, putrefaction, noxious emanations, and *Cossacks*.

In the dark and crowded apartments, after hours, Old World Judaism grew and flourished like a weed, for life in Atlanta did not differ so much from shtetl life: birth, struggle, and death.

And Old World revolutionary idealism also grew and flourished. Two different organizations of Russian-Jewish Socialists thrived in Atlanta in the midst of the Orthodox Jewish world: one was the Farband, the National Workmen's Alliance, organized in Atlanta in 1913; the other was the Arbeiter Ring, the Workmen's Circle, organized in 1908, a fraternal order of freethinkers who had been associated with the Bund (the Jewish workers' movement) in Russia.

From such Jewish labor circles and revolutionary circles here and in Europe—of communal spirit, imbibing idealism with their daily bread, teaching their children Yiddish songs, bending the sacred humpbacked Hebrew letters to form Yiddish poetry, to make slogans, to talk of collectives and agriculture— came the early Zionists, the modern Jewish settlers of Palestine. Faced with the racial nationalism, the bloodline citizenship of politically awakening Russians, Germans, Poles, and Hungarians, they vaunted their own racial nationalism, their own birthrights, their own pure bloodlines, their own cocky heroes.

Judaism and revolutionary socialism—for lack of room or the means to segregate—lived side by side in the Russian-Jewish quarter of Atlanta, sometimes under one roof, sometimes at the same table.

"The Merlins were eight brothers and one sister," said Joe Jacobs, a labor lawyer and Arbeiter Ring member, pointing to a sepia photograph of eight black-eyed, fierce-looking men politely arranged by the photographer behind their seated mother and father. "This one was a Communist, that one was a Socialist, that one was an anarchist, some of them I don't know, and this one was so religious he ran the only kosher restaurant in town and sold religious artifacts."

"My uncles would come over to my father's delicatessen every morning," said jolly Sonny Epstein. She was the daughter of Lazar Aaron Merlin, the oldest and religious brother, and the niece of M. J. Merlin, one of the founders of the Arbeiter Ring. "They would come to papa's store and use the bathroom, and Papa subscribed to newspapers for each of them—the *Forward*, that's the socialist, and the *Freiheit*, that's the other side, the Communist. So one brother would come in and Papa would hand him the *Freiheit* on the way to the bathroom, then the other brother would come in and pick up the *Forward*."

The Arbeiter Ring and the Farband were two among dozens of fraternal orders, including the B'nai B'rith, in which the penniless immigrants enlisted. Most offered social functions, cultural events, and sickness-and-death benefits to Yiddish-speaking greenhorns without other affiliations. The fraternal orders, observed the historian Stephen Hertzberg, with quiet understatement, were "more hospitable than The Temple or the social clubs to Russian memberships."

The Farband and the Arbeiter Ring differed from the rest in strongly advocating Yiddish culture and socialism over traditional Judaism and Hebrew.

Jacobs reports in his old age to his downtown office, his arrival every morning a small miracle. In his slow-moving, gnarly fragility, he steers his old car down breakneck Peachtree Street, remembering depression-era factories, strikes, lockouts, and foodlines where today there are tiled fountains, people on Rollerblade skates, and ice cream boutiques. Yet he shows up every day (unless hospitalized or in Israel and on the days of the funerals of two of his sons) beautifully groomed and dressed. He soberly greets the secretaries and slowly moves down the hall.

He is erect and handsome, a Paul Newman in his late eighties possessed of a crinkle-eyed courtliness. Dressed in a starched pinstripe shirt, vivid tie, and dark suspenders, he has a long face, a straight profile, rose in his cheeks, and clean, straight silver hair boyishly parted and combed to each side. He once lit up the brown hallways of tenements he visited where ragged children peered down from the stairwells. He may have startled the cotton-mill strikers and the clothing workers who had been told a lawyer was on the way, who hoped for a smart one, prayed for an incorruptible one, and may even have anticipated a Jewish one, but could not have pictured this handsome, patrician-looking man. All this from the Alabama-born son of a Polish laborer and Socialist. Jacobs looked like nobility but was dead against it, and he spoke of justice for the masses in a soft voice that drew its accent from the lost Confederacy and from the lost Pale of Settlement. He had been in the forefront of the thankless century-long struggle to bring organized labor into the anti-union, low-wage, segregated-workforce, cotton-mill South.

Among *landsleit* (immigrants from the same Jewish regions and their children), Yiddish flowed from Jacobs like a lullaby: up and down, thickly up and down, making his hoarse voice raucously musical. Its gruff, wry, pained cadences were his own cadences: assuming the worst, commiserating, sarcastic, self-mocking, subversive, able to whirl within a sentence from suffering to a punchline. Within it there was sweetness, like a raisin inside a hard chunk of bread. In the lift of the tongue, the arch of the eyebrows, the sad sweetness of Yiddish curled around and under the inflexible codes and stern personages of Jewish tradition and softened them, as if gently chiding or teasing. In Hebrew, Moses is *Moshe* (pronounced "Mo-sheh"), the fiery, visionary patriarch hurling the stone tablets into the side of the mountain. But in Yiddish he became *Moishe* ("Moy-sheh"), after whom young boys were called Moishy, and you're having a glass of tea with the man already, you're passing him a plate of rugelach. In Hebrew, *Torah* ("Toe-rah"), the mighty mountaintop word of God, copied in ancient, perfect letters onto scrolled parchment, is the foundation of the faith, the fountain of truth for all eternity. But in Yiddish it became *Toyreh*, a *haimisher*, a homely thing; in that one curling syllable hid the love of ten million old and young men for the Law, men who prayed every day in rickety, wind-blown little synagogues across Europe, their toes and fingers freezing—in a moment they'll finish the prayers and bustle together around the wood stove—but first they must praise God for the gift of their own neighborhood Toyreh, tenderly wrapped in threadbare velvet and housed in a hammered-together ark.

Yiddish was the language created by poor people, Russia's untouchables, who lived for a thousand years in a realm of mud, persecution, and spiritual splendor. Because they had the splendor, they survived the poverty and the cruelty. In the religious imagination, even the least of them acted out their lives on a plane of sacred importance. It mattered to *God* whether they gossiped, whether they set aside a few kopeks for the poorest among them, whether they walked on Saturday rather than rode on their horse or cart, if they had one. A transcendent life of glorious expanse and exultation was thus constructed by poor people out of a few simple tools found around the house: a candle, a cup, a length of cotton, a satin cap, a loaf of bread, a book. Christianity, a thousand years younger, inspired the devotion of its people through art and architecture; magnificent cathedrals pierced the heavens and raised the hearts of Christian worshipers. But the Jews of eastern Europe—trudging home on mud roads between puddles, bargaining over potatoes, buttoning up against the cold even in their makeshift little synagogues—chatted with God.

If the southern factory workers, white and black, ever marveled at Jacobs's ability to understand and to express their misery, they would have grasped the source of his insight if they could have understood him when he spoke his mother tongue, for in Yiddish lay squirreled away centuries of poverty, exhaustion, and abuse, faith, rebellion, and wit.

"Where my people came from was the poor people," he said. "They were the ones who walked in *shmattes* [rags]. My folks lived in a freezing cellar over there. My father was a butcher from Lodz, Poland, a man that stood five feet two, very strong. He was a revolutionary. Poland was an anti-Semitic end of the world with pogroms and Cossacks. We occupied a status there: if a black man tells me, 'You can't understand how it feels to be a minority, . . . ' we had the same second-class, *tenth*-class status there. My parents were members of the Bund, the Jewish revolutionary party. My father was in the demonstration of 1903, went to jail for six months, came out, and got drafted. The young Jewish men had to serve in the czar's army. They were cruel to Jews. The religious ones couldn't keep kosher, and the radical ones didn't want to serve because they were revolutionaries. They wanted what we would call democracy, a government in which the people participated. Many of them, when it came time to serve, would inflict personal injuries, cut off a finger, cut off a toe, make themselves deaf. Sometimes it kept them out, sometimes it didn't.

"There were attempts to assassinate the czar. It was blamed on the Jews, and the czar sent the Cossacks out to annihilate the Jewish communities. Rasputin, the so-called mystic in the Russian Orthodox Church, stirred up anti-Semitism so deeply that many Polish people in the time of Hitler willingly turned the Jews in. My father took part in the demonstration of 1905; the police were looking for him again, so he and my mother left Poland. They moved to Alabama, where my mother's sister lived, and my father got a job making drainage pipes—tremendously heavy work—where they poured the concrete into the forms and came up with these great big pipes, rolled them, and loaded them on freight cars. He worked for five bucks a week, one of very few white men working alongside the black men doing this kind of work."

A lawyer with the southern drawl of the native-born, with a clear, serene face and high color, Jacobs certainly could have passed as a cultured, native-born white southerner. It was his integrity, his sense of self, rather than the cumbersome marks of the greenhorn, that kept him allied.

"On Sundays we used to go out to a lake with our families," he remembered. "There were city places you could go because that's open to everybody. We couldn't go some places in De Kalb County because Jews were not permitted there. We found Hard Rock—I think that's the name—where there were two lakes, private owned, a lawyer—Thomas somebody—owned them; one was for fishing with a boat and the other you could go swimming and lounge around, and they had sand and things.

"One bright day we're there and any number of us there, the Merlins, the Ruskins, the Russes, you name it. Now it's early in the afternoon, and Dave Merlin and his wife and kids are leaving. 'Steitch [his nickname], why are you leaving so early?'

" 'He doesn't want Jews here.'

" 'What?' I say. 'Wait! I know Thomas because he's a lawyer.' I go over there to him—he's sitting in the bar that he has there. He's already had enough beers or drinks so that he's like that. And I said, 'How come you're not letting Mr. Merlin's family stay?'

" 'Oh,' he says. 'We don't want them damned Jews here.'

"I said, 'What do you mean you don't want them damned Jews?'

" 'Oh, we don't want them Jews here. No, no.'

"I said, 'Well, you know, I'm a Jew too.'

" 'Oh, I'm not talking about you, Joe.'

"I said, 'Are you still telling me he's got to go?'

" 'Yes sir, we don't want 'em here. I told them get out of here.'

"I said, 'Well, we're all going.'

" 'Oh no, you don't have to all go.'

"I said, 'We're all Jews.'

"So we left. A few days later, I'm on the way to the courthouse, I run into him. 'Joe! Want to talk to you. I don't want my place to be the spot where all the Jews have to come to. Let them go someplace else. There are other places.'

"I said, 'Well, you know I came there. A lot of us came there, and we've been doing that for some time.'

" 'Oh,' he said, 'I don't mean you, you're a white Jew.'

"I said, 'There ain't no damned difference between me and them. They're my people.' "

Atlanta, in the first third of the century, was one of the Yiddish capitals of America, with two Yiddish schools (one Arbeiter Ring, one Farband), two Yiddish cemetery sections (one Arbeiter Ring, one Farband), Yiddish theaters, Yiddish lecture series, choruses, concerts, film series, libraries, and private loan associations. "When immigrants arrived," said Jacobs, "who didn't speak English, had no money, their relatives barely making a living for themselves—how can they go to work? So? The Arbeiter Ring did business with a little loan company: if three people signed, you could borrow five hundred dollars. We'd find a grocery store in a poor neighborhood, in a black area or near Fulton Bag and Cotton or the Piedmont Cotton Mill. We'd open up a little store and they were in business. Little by little they learned the language. For vegetables they had to pay cash, also for meat and canned goods. So we used to kite checks among ourselves. We met on Monday nights to determine which wholesalers had to be paid. If you kited the checks, it took two, three, four, five days for the check to get back to the bank. They didn't have the instant computers then. The Landau family who lived in Center Hill, we liked to kite checks with them. Why? Because they belonged to a bank at Bankhead and Marietta Streets, and it used to take a week for the check to go through there and come back over here to the Fulton Bank. That was the size of it."

Needless to say, from the point of view of the established German Jews of Atlanta, the black-clad, Yiddish-speaking, religiously Orthodox, pious Russian Jews were a headache enough: a challenge to any thinking American to get them into public baths, get them shaved, get them to an English class, and get them some new clothing (even if it was last season's donated clothing). Now here was a defiant core group, agitating within the ranks of the mild-mannered Orthodox: a careless bunch of left-wingers speaking Yiddish on the street and enrolling their children in Yiddish schools.

The well-intentioned Temple members were perplexed by people so much less eager to adapt to America than their own forebears had been. A handful of community leaders conferred among themselves and dispatched a delegation to the Arbeiter Ring. Given audience, they laid out a few civilized proposals and shared a few tactful suggestions. These were not warmly received.

"When we set up a school here to teach our kids Yiddish, we had a bus," said Jacobs. "On the side of the bus we painted Arbeiter Ring Yiddishe Shule (Workmen's Circle Yiddish School) in Yiddish, which is written with Hebrew letters. So the rabbis send a committee to us and ask us not to do this because it will create something. They said, 'Put down, "Workmen's Circle School" if you want to, but in English, not Yiddish.' "

The Arbeiter Ring members did not give it a moment's thought. As they faced the Temple group, each saw, in the other, good Jewish stock gone awry, decent people throwing the wealth of their full human potential on the ground.

"You got two types of Jews in the South," says Jacobs. "What *are* they? There's one type who is Jewish and they don't go around every time they say hello to you, 'I'm Jewish.' *But*, if the question comes up, they're Jewish and they let you know. On the other hand, there's the other one that says, 'I want to be like everybody else, so if we get into anything about Jews, I'm not going to mention it. We're not really different than anybody else. We get along.' "

Street Jews faced the uptown Jews. But the street Jews knew very well the origins of the uptown Jews. "They started out down here with the rest of the Jewish community," said Jacobs. "Washington Street, Capital Avenue, Atlanta Avenue: the Temple people started out in that end of the world, too. It's only later that they busted out and went north and got rich."

Exasperated and bewildered, the Reform leaders and the Russian rabbis departed. The Arbeiter Ring school bus with its brash Hebrew letters, its nose-thumbing, audacious don't-take-no-shit-off-nobody Hebrew letters kept banging through the streets of Atlanta.

⇥ ⇤⬦⇥ ⇤

Then Jacobs met the Ku Klux Klan.

Up his sleeve he had stories about them, stemming from his days organizing in rural areas.

"You know," he says, "the Klan in some places takes Jews in, and in some places doesn't take Jews but takes Catholics, but they don't take blacks in any. So the Klan in Mississippi rode into the little town of Stonewall—it's a little town with no paved road, but they have a damn textile mill. So the Klan begins to organize. They get everybody together. And Sam runs the only general store in town.

"And Sam has decided that he ain't going to go. His good

Baptist friend who runs the drugstore comes in and says, 'Sam, we didn't see you at the meeting.'

"He says, 'Well, I just didn't go.' You know, he's not going to make waves.

"So he says, 'We're getting organized. The filling station man is joining, insurance man is joining, all the business people are joining. You ought to join, too.'

" 'No,' says Sam, 'you go, you'll enjoy.'

" 'Sam, you ought to come.'

" 'Vell,' he says, 'I'll see.' Finally he goes. Everybody signs up and pays their ten-dollar membership and fifteen dollars for the sheets. Sam is still holding back. The pharmacist comes over: 'See, everybody's joining. How 'bout it? You ought to do it. For business you got to do it.'

" 'All right,' he finally says. So he goes over and signs up. The man who signs him up says, 'Sam, you see now, that ten dollars you just paid guarantees your daughter will never marry a black.'

" 'Really?' says Sam, cheering up. 'I'll tell you what: here's another ten dollars she shouldn't marry any of you goyim.' "

Jacobs was the lawyer for railroad brotherhoods, the International Ladies Garment Workers Union, and the Hatters Union. In the 1930s unions met in the Wigwam Building. "They had meeting halls down there, and when we had strikes, it was a very convenient place to meet," he said. "The hatters came along and had a strike, several of them, and we used to feed them lunch and hold their strikers' meetings there and review what had happened. We had Carmen Lucia down from Rochester, New York—the best Italian gal that I've ever met in terms of a firebrand and wonderful person. And when the strike came on, Max Zaritsky [the president of the Hatters Union] sent me down an Irish Catholic by the name of Huey Glover out of Jersey who came out of the men's hat division in order to take care of what we call the non-Catholics and the non-Jews and the non-Italians.

"Anyway, we're in there with our meeting one day. We look up, and here these characters come in Ku Klux Klan garb. They walk in the door, and we're all just sitting around the meeting hall. Carmen looks at me, and Huey Glover looks at me. We're looking at each other (and the Klan hates Catholics maybe more than they hate Jews), and these guys, they file in here through this door, . . . and then they head back out through this door. One, two, three, four, five: a dozen or more. In the sheets. And in the hats. And robes covered up and everything. So I don't quit; I figure we're there to carry on our business. We're carrying it on. Carmen's presiding. She even asks 'What? . . . ' and I say, 'Keep going, keep going, keep going, keep going.' So we keep going, and the next thing we know, here these men come marching back out. Don't say anything to us; we don't say anything to them.

"So then I find out that this is where their locker room is, and they're taking their costumes off. This is Ku Klux Klan [Lodge] General Forrest Number One. They robed up in the Wigwam Building.

"In the meantime, the Wigwam is in financial trouble—furnace needs fixing, roof needs fixing, nobody had taken care of it, let it get run down. Some of us bought stock in it through all the little organizations that met there. We have a meeting, I'm there representing the different brotherhoods, I talk too much, and they ask me to manage the building.

"I said, 'Yeah, providing you meet certain conditions.'

" 'What are they?'

" 'Number one: the Klan's gotta go.'

"They agreed to do it. I become manager. And then, of course, the first thing I did was notify the Klan to get the hell out. I sent it certified mail. I signed my name as secretary of the building organization.

"So they come to see me and protest because they had been meeting for years and years and years, and they didn't like it at all. And I told them, 'You guys and I stand for different things. You don't permit Jews to belong, you don't permit Catholics to belong, you don't permit blacks to belong. As a matter of fact, you're anti-us and you do anything you can to scare the hell out of us.' [There was a popular Jewish joke about the Ku Klux Klan: Why aren't Jews invited to join the Klan? Because they know better than to pay retail price for sheets with holes in them.]

"When I did that, they were not happy with it. They were not going to move. I had to put them out."

The Temple community now had another bone to pick with Jacobs. The Ku Klux Klan told the German Jews to call off Jacobs and cancel the eviction notice or there would be trouble. Rather than descend again into Little Russia, Reform leaders arranged to have Jacobs confronted on German-Jewish turf. To handle the meeting, they turned to their most successful coreligionist, the loftiest Jew in Atlanta, Harold Hirsch. A 1904 graduate of Columbia University School of Law, he was a senior partner in the firm of Candler & Thompson, the chief legal counsel for Coca-Cola, a member of the Coca-Cola board of directors, one of the designers of Coke's distinctive glass bottle, and one of the architects of modern American trademark law. He was a philanthropist, an endower of scholarships; Hirsch Hall at the University of Georgia was named after him, an almost unheard-of honor for a Jew in the 1930s. Hirsch dutifully summoned Jacobs to his office for a lordly browbeating.

"The next thing I know, I get a call from Harold Hirsch, the Coca-Cola lawyer. He's Deutschjuden too, at the big law firm. So when I got the call, that's just like the king saying, 'Come'— command performance, because he was the big man in the community. He was the top philanthropist and the big name who spoke for the Jewish community. Even the Seligs didn't speak for the Jewish community; even the Oberdorfers, because Hirsch was still bigger. You know, if there's a holiday, who do the newspapers interview? Do they interview a lay leader prominent in the Workmen's Circle? Of course not. They interview Rich because he's a zillionaire, or Hirsch, who was *the* man.

"His office was over in the Hurt Building, I think. When you walked in, they had this great big Coca-Cola bottle as tall as you are. And when you sat down, within a couple of minutes, a black man would come out dressed in a little vest and neatly dressed. 'Would you have a Coca-Cola?' and he'd open the thing there, and reach in and give you a Coca-Cola while you sat.

"Then Mr. Hirsch. 'So, how you doin'? How's your family? How you getting along?' We go through the pleasantries. Then he said, 'I had a visit from some men who represent the Klan, and they asked me to talk with you, to intercede with you about your action in ordering them out of the Wigwam Building, or they are planning to picket all the synagogues. I told them that I could not control you, but I would ask you. And they asked me what *was* my influence with you.' And then he says, 'I'm asking you to let them stay. They've been there all these years. We don't want picketing in front of the synagogues. We don't know whether they'll do it or not, but if they do, it will create problems.' Dit, dit, dit. So I listened.

"He was the *godol* [in Hebrew, *godol*, "big"; in Yiddish, *guddle*, "big wheel"] and I was a young whippersnapper.

"I explained how I had become an officer of the Wigwam Building on condition that the Klan goes, because I would not be an officer of an organization that permitted the Klan to carry on their kind of activities. And I said, 'With all due respect to you and I appreciate your talking with me, I'm not about to change my mind. And if they're going to picket, by God, let 'em picket. I'm not afraid of them.'

" 'Well,' says Hirsch, when we got through, 'I didn't think you would. But I've asked you.'

"He was pleasant about it. He really didn't want to ask me, but if I had said yes, I think he would have been much happier than if I said no. So I left. And the Klan never did a damn thing. Not one damn thing.

"They came and got their stuff. I checked behind them. But they were *mad*. Oi, were they mad. If they could have killed me, they would have done it. These are the same people who, when we tried to organize workers, beat up our organizers. But it taught me something: when you stand up, you stand up."

This quiet, handsome man with a noble bearing still subscribes to the view, now old-fashioned, that a person ought to stand for something. As Joe Jacobs became acquainted with Jacob Rothschild, he softened a bit in his universal condemnation of the Temple Jews. "Now Rothschild represented what I call the Jewish elite, the Deutschjuden, but, at the same time, he was one of the few voices that spoke up on the race question. It didn't make him particularly popular. I imagine some of the people would have characterized it by saying, 'We don't have enough problems among the Jews, he has to go take on the problems of the *shvartze*?' He had no real reason to reach into the black community, no real basis that I know of."

"One of the things I'm awfully discouraged about is that

we've let history pass us by. What has happened to the generation of immigrants who came to this country and what has
happened to their children? So many whom I'd hoped would be
good social thinkers and radicals and active in the political field
have been corrupted by our society, in which there's only one
objective: money. How rich can you get, and what do the Joneses
have? This is what has broken down our society." Jacobs's Yiddish penetrates even in the thick silences between his words and
causes more than the usual number of English words to tilt
questioningly up the musical scale: "Why?" "So?" And the ver-
satile, generic interrogatory "Nu?" There are many types of
human beings on earth, a divine variety, just as there are goats
and fish and chickens among the animals. And the type of
human being that he is, simply put, is a Jew.

Over this fact he never gnashed his teeth nor looked over
his shoulder nor tried to smooth out the wrinkles, no more than a
goat would try to resemble a fish. Whether Jews were a race unto
themselves he would leave, without curiosity, for the academics
and the anthropologists to puzzle. For him, they were a race—a
people. When he met another on the street or in the workplace—
a textile worker, a lawyer, a cotton-mill owner, or the man behind the counter at the delicatessen—racial knowledge passed
swiftly between them, a dark glance, wordless, unwilled, faster
by light years than a handshake and introduction. *Yid* (pronounced "Yeed" by Jews, "Yid" being derogatory). It did not
alter the course of business; the deli man had to be paid, the mill
owner had to improve conditions or face a strike, the stranger
on the street need not be chatted with. Still, regardless of their
status in life, Jews sensed a connection: I know what just happened to my people in Europe and I'm pretty sure I know what
happened to yours, and that goes for 1492, as well, and for
the twelfth century, and for 1000 B.C. Today we're in Atlanta,
Georgia, wearing hats, riding streetcars. Nu? What of it?
Our great-great-grandparents' ancestors had some work to
do involving pyramids. It was simple with Jacobs. He wasn't
superior or unique; there were many types of human beings
on earth; a Jew was a human being. He stood matter-of-
factly among the Scots-Irishmen, Italians, blacks, Anglo-
Saxons, and Chinese, without shame and without apology.

2

In time, many Russian Jews rose to local eminence: wealth, philanthropy, houses on deep lawns set back from quiet residential roads, their nearest neighbors wealthy gentiles, their children writing home from eastern colleges of specializations in drama, French, or anatomy. They built their wealth out of dry goods, groceries, liquor, scrap metal, and wallpaper. Max Kuniansky is a Russian-Jewish rags-to-riches story, a tough guy in a cashmere sweater, a fighter who learned early in life how to deal with hooligans—those on the street first, and later, those in the building trades. Born in Atlanta in 1917, the child of Polish and Russian immigrants, he grew up a burly little street kid, a Brooklyn type, who could organize the Jews, face down the ruffians from neighboring streets, and still manage to zip into his place at the dinner table just shy of curfew, thereby sparing his innocent mother the details.

"Yeah, I had a rep, a good reputation as a street fighter. I only got into fights when I was called a dirty Jew bastard or something like that. I had a few run-ins. When you play basketball on a Jewish team and you play against the cotton-mill teams, they call you dirty Jews and everything else. I wouldn't take it. I'd beat the hell out of them."

Retired, he lives in an elegant ranch-style house on a wooded lot in Atlanta's fashionable northeastern quadrant. "See? I made a little over the years," he says. "Didn't spend every penny I made. Nu? [So?] Now I live like a mensch." He is a balding, slit-eyed, hard-looking man, his round head like a brown nut, weathered, impervious. He sits quietly in a straight-back chair in his living room but keeps an eye on his wristwatch, giving the unmistakable impression that he still holds a few keys, that a short word from him into the receiver when the phone rings will speak volumes in various mercantile quarters. He still looks like the street fighter, the deal maker, despite having seen a good portion of his strength erode with age, less-than-robust health, and the bottomless grief of widowerhood. Underneath age and sorrow sits a Yiddish bulldog.

Because he made plenty of money as a builder of warehouses and a land developer and gave it away by the fistful, Kuniansky has a wall covered with plaques: he won the first

State of Israel Bond Award, the Abe Goldstein Humanitarian Award, and the Jewish Community Center's Lifetime Award; and he was the 1994 honoree at the Epstein School Founders' Dinner. Like other truly generous "big givers," he slights the honors with a wave of his hand and a dry spitting sound. He did not do anything with plaques in mind; *Helen*, his wife, enjoyed seeing him honored. He is unhappy these days when begged by his children to accept another proffered award. In deep loneliness, in the tomb of a half-empty, perfumeless walk-in closet, he dresses up, arranges a black silk bow tie, and listens for the honk of a car horn. He sits on a podium, picks at stuffed chicken breast and brussels sprouts, feels like a stuffed chicken breast himself, and looks furtively, through lidded eyes, around the ballroom, casing the joint, as they make speeches about him. This commemorative phase of life is not to his liking—he preferred the earlier, active phases, especially all the phases with Helen.

So it turned out he had had a head for business. He had kept what he needed to live well and raise his family, and the rest he had passed through to his fellow Jews. That's how he had been raised by his Warsaw-born mother and Russian-born father. Raising five sons and a daughter in Atlanta, they were labor Socialists, members of the Farband. Kuniansky attended the Farband school, was bar mitzvahed in Yiddish, went to work at fifteen in a produce house, then went to war as an aerial gunner. "I flew out of Italy in the Fifteenth Air Force," he said. "I had my gunner's wings. I flew in the nose turret of the plane." His four brothers fought in the war, too. Leon was a marine; Raymond was burned when a kamikaze hit his aircraft carrier. "I wore my mezuzah," Kuniansky said. "My oldest brother didn't want me to wear it. Said if I got shot down, it showed I was Jewish, see? I said to hell with it. They get me, I'm not going to deny being Jewish. Like they say, 'Shver tze-zan ah Yid' [Yiddish: 'It's hard to be a Jew']."

An elderly black housekeeper now sees to it that he takes nourishment and medicine; soup and hot tea sit on a TV table while he looks at his mail. The modern beige TV room is immaculate. Plate-glass windows open onto a small, sunny yard and woods. Tabletops teem with knickknacks: birthday presents, Father's Day gifts. Without Helen it all feels so damn retrospective.

He led his plane in and out of the flak, was shot up over Linz, Austria. "Nobody knew where we were when we got shot up but me. I knew where we were. We were disbursed and I led them all back to home base, safe. There were 148 holes in the plane." By war's end, Kuniansky was a captain wearing campaign ribbons from the European, the African, and the Middle Eastern theaters. He had earned bronze battle stars for the Rome–Arno campaign, for southern France, and for air combat in the Balkans campaign, and he had earned the Distinguished Flying Cross.

"Flying cross, yeah. That was quite an achievement."

On October 31, 1946, the Columbians—Homer Loomis and Emory Burke's Atlanta-based neo-Nazi outfit—rolled slowly through downtown Atlanta on the back of a sound truck, distributing anti-Semitic leaflets and advertising a meeting that night. "The JEWS are taking all the wealth and money in the nation!" said the leaflets. For whatever reason, a group of Jewish war veterans took this demonstration as the final straw.

"I went down and talked to Frank Garson and Abe Goldstein and got their permission to do what I wanted to do," said Kuniansky. "They were leaders of the Jewish community. I told them, 'I want to go down to the meeting and put a stop to it.' Kuniansky contacted Herbert Jenkins, then the commander of the uniform evening watch for the Atlanta police department. Jenkins said, 'That's just what we want. We wanted to run them out of town, and we needed an excuse.' I didn't go off helter-skelter.

"I picked up about twenty-five, thirty Jews that had been in the service, and we went down to their meeting. They were meeting at the corner of Pryor Street and Fair Street at a union hall. There was Loomis and there was Bright. Bright was one of the guys that was Columbian. They were doing just what Hitler was doing—they were speaking. One of them [J. B. Stoner] was a cripple just like that Nazi that was so crippled, one of Hitler's buddies.

"So what I did was—had a brother, Harry. He played football at the University of Georgia, Harry did. And he had a non-Jewish friend. And I took Harry and said, 'Don't let anybody out of here unless I tell you.' So we had them locked in.

"We went in and sat down at their meeting. We listened to them. They didn't know who we were.

" 'I hate the Jews because they have never become part of the American way of life,' " Loomis was saying, remembers Arthur Weiss, the commander of Jewish War Veterans Atlanta Post No. 112. " 'The Jew will die for what he believes in, but I've never seen one die for the American world. . . . Jews were the original Nazis.' "

"We didn't want any police there," said Kuniansky, the tough old man in the beige turtleneck. "Because if there was any trouble, we wanted to beat hell out of the Columbians. We were prepared to do that.

"They had about forty or fifty, and there were about thirty of us. So we sat for a while and listened to them talk about how the New York kikes came from New York and overcharged the poor white people for rent and they needed to get rid of them. So we listened to all that crap, and I got up and said, 'If you touch a hair on any Jew in the city of Atlanta, we're going to beat the hell out of you.'

"See, they didn't realize they had a crowd of Jews in the meeting hall. They found out, though. They didn't start fighting—we'd have killed them if they started fighting. We were strong enough to beat hell out of them. In those days you didn't have weapons. We didn't have anything. We didn't need anything. We were a tough bunch of Jew boys—you *had* to be in those days.

"So Loomis starts screaming: 'It's a lie! It's a lie!' I don't know the exact words to tell you. The meeting broke up when we told them they'd better not touch anybody.

"Now the Klan had a big following, but they were a bunch of idiots. They were trying to sell sheets and all. . . . We never took any stuff from the Klan. We would have cleaned them out in no time. But the Columbians made me angry listening to them. That was when I got a group of Jews together and we flushed them out."

3

The Columbians faltered and faded after that night. On November 2, two days after their disrupted meeting, Loomis and three other uniformed members were arrested for intimidating a black family that was attempting to move into a racially mixed neighborhood. Ultimately, three Columbians were indicted for unlawful possession of dynamite and were linked to a bomb plot targeting city hall, the municipal auditorium, police headquarters, and two newspaper offices. Others were linked to the patrolling of Atlanta streets and the intimidation of black citizens. Four were arrested for disorderly conduct and inciting a riot while picketing a black home in a white neighborhood. Loomis and Burke were charged with beating a black man into a state of hysteria.

"I happened to be at the station when they brought in five Columbians," recalled Captain Fred Beerman of the Atlanta police, the highest ranking of very few Jews on the force. "They had been on Crew Street rabble-rousing, I call it—on the porch of a house, rabble-rousing, trying to stir up the crowds, saying, 'We going to do this and we going to do that.' One of our officers arrested all of them. George Bright was there. He was arrested with them as I recall. He didn't know who I was, and I didn't open my mouth, but they were questioning him. George Bright was being questioned. Of course, he didn't know who I was, and I was just sitting.

"All mouth, I thought. Going to take over the government. 'We're going to take over the government.' They didn't. You know, when you're going to take over the government, you've got to have a plan, you've got to have something to offer. Not just that you're such a nice fellow that they'll jump out there and vote for you. But I'm going to say all mouth, no quality, no thickness, and no foundation."

In February 1947, Loomis was convicted of inciting a riot in the beating of a black citizen, and in March he was convicted of usurping police powers. Loomis's father, a New York admiralty lawyer, unsuccessfully defended his son in court with a two-hour speech to the jury—"my fair-skinned brothers"—during which he argued that his son was being "crucified like Christ by the Jews." Loomis received thirty months. Burke was sentenced to three years on three misdemeanor counts. The Columbians group was stripped of its Georgia charter in June 1947 and was added to the U.S. attorney general's list of subversive organizations in December 1947, but by then, with its leaders in jail, the Columbians as an organization ceased to exist.

Meanwhile, for future reference, the leaders had seen up close what Jewish Socialists looked like.

Like fetid smoke sitting in the air in the aftermath of a chemistry experiment gone awry, much that had been Columbian lingered in Atlanta. Bright avoided indictment and conviction. The Nazi-like uniforms, slogans, pamphlets, and books were available to copycat groups. And in the growing segregationist fervor of a city not yet nicknamed, by Mayor Hartsfield, "The City Too Busy to Hate," other lunatic-fringe types, other men daydreaming of fascism and race wars, roamed south into Atlanta.

7

Black Monday

1

The *Brown* decision in May 1954, which outlawed school segregation, fell upon the Old Confederacy with a heavy hand, like a reproof and punishment of biblical grandeur, like fiery hail or water turned to blood or death of the firstborn. All understood that the long-tacit agreement between the federal government and the South was over: Washington was no longer willing to stand by and let southern states govern their own Negroes.

A hush fell across the South in the immediate aftermath. Public spokesmen seemed at a loss for words. It was as if Newton's law had been declared invalid and apples ripening on trees henceforth should drop upward into the sky. The fundamental premise of southern life—the superiority of whites over blacks—was overturned.

A few public voices tentatively proposed acquiescence. "There is only one alternative," wrote Ralph McGill, "and that is secession by armed force." He then quickly reminded his readers that secession had been tried once before and had not worked out, so that his column should not be mistaken as a call to arms.

147

But McGill's moderate words and those of several other editors and a couple of border-state governors echoed eerily. No deep sound of assent was returned from the populace to the few leaders' calm remarks; no appreciative, approving murmur resonated in the chambers of federal power in Washington. Congress was silent and the White House was silent. "It makes no difference whether or not I endorse it," said President Dwight Eisenhower. Ultimately, he was heard to remark that his appointment of Chief Justice Earl Warren was "the biggest damnfool mistake I ever made."

Brown thus drifted over the South as words on paper, like an airdrop of propaganda leaflets over a besieged country, with no troops in evidence on the hilltops to back them up. Some citizens treated the words with deference, unhappily acknowledging the primacy of the rule of law in a democracy; but others ripped them to shreds.

During all this discomfiture of the moderates, the segregationists found themselves not at a loss for words. In the silence standing like darkness over Washington and the southern capitals, the bigots snarled their response, and their bitter retorts reverberated and multiplied.

"I've not yet met (and I've known tens of thousands of people) and I've not yet met one white person who wants to socialize or mingle with one of another race," said George Bright. "So it was really a matter of forcing a social condition on people who didn't want that social set-up. It has nothing to do with rights. Our neighbor down here can have all the rights he wants, but *I* should have the right not to associate with him. And I really should have the absolute right to segregate my children *from* anybody I wish and for any purpose whatsoever."

Representative John Bell Williams of Mississippi named the day of the decision "Black Monday," and the name caught on. " 'Black Monday' ranks in importance with July 4th, 1776," wrote Tom P. Brady of Mississippi, picking up the integration-is-Communist theme of the South in the cold war. "May 17, 1954, is the date upon which the declaration of socialistic doctrine was officially proclaimed throughout this nation."

"What is the real purpose of this?" asked Walter C. Givhan, an Alabama state senator. "To open the bedroom doors of our white women to Negro men."

Governor Herman Talmadge of Georgia promised to call out the state militia if necessary to safeguard the segregated schools. "So far as I am concerned," he said, "Georgia is going to resist mixing races in the school if it is the sole state in the nation to do so." The Georgia legislature passed a constitutional amendment to discontinue public education, awaiting only a public referendum. State Attorney General Eugene Cook issued his opinion that *Brown* did not apply to Georgia: "As I view it," he said, "the scope of this decision goes directly to our miscegenation laws. Carried to its ultimate effect it means these laws, too, could be struck down by proper legal attack. Once they are struck down, I foresee a [racial] amalgamation stampede."

Most white southerners regarded the *Brown* decision as arising from extreme malice toward the South and profound ignorance about blacks. At that time, schoolchildren were not seen, as they are now in popular culture, in movies, TV shows, and magazines, as bright, scrubbed, eager, happy, interchangeable little beings in a variety of colors, the skin tones and hair textures as harmoniously diverse as the colors of their shirts and caps. No such notion existed in the South in the 1940s and 1950s. Polls of the region in the fifties, conducted by northern universities and newspapers, confirmed that most whites saw blacks as inferior beings lacking in morality, responsibility, ambition, and intelligence. In 1956 the American Institute of Public Opinion surveyed the reaction to *Brown* and found 90 percent of white southerners disapproving. "Segregation is not a principle upheld only by louts and bullies," wrote the historian John B. Martin. "It is viewed as inherently right by virtually every white person."

In some respects, the *Brown* decision actually slowed the progress that was quietly being made. "Between the end of World War II and 1954, the reformers were making progress in the South," said Charles Wittenstein. "Certainly the reformers were making progress in Georgia, under Governor Ellis Arnall [1943–1947]. When the Supreme Court handed down *Brown*, it gave the segregationists a new lease on life. Then we had the Marvin Griffins, the Herman Talmadges, the Lester Maddoxes, the rise of all the people defending the ancien régime.

"Marvin Griffin [the governor of Georgia from 1955 to 1959] was campaigning for governor at the time," remembered Wittenstein, "and they had a celebration in his headquarters when the *Brown* decision came down. They knew that would enable them to holler 'nigger' for twenty more years."

Again, as just after World War II, a violent backlash ripped across the South: hundreds of whippings, burnings, and lynchings of black citizens. In Humphreys County, Mississippi, sixteen thousand black citizens had registered to vote. After *Brown*, under the pressure of economic reprisals and physical threats from the white community, the number of registered black voters declined to thirty-five. The Reverend George W. Lee, who had led the voter registration, was killed by shotgun blasts while driving his car. "The sheriff, at first inclined to believe that the lead pellets found in the minister's mouth and face were dental fillings, ultimately concluded that he had been murdered by another Negro in an argument over a woman. No arrest was ever made."

In August 1955, a fourteen-year-old boy named Emmett Till from Chicago, visiting relatives near Money, Mississippi, said, "Bye, baby!" to a white woman behind a store counter and ended up stripped, beaten, his eye gouged out, tied to a seventy-five-pound fan he had been forced to carry off a truck to a riverbank, murdered by a gunshot in the head, and thrown into the Tallahatchie River. As the killers drove away, they wondered whether anyone would notice the fan missing.

The defendants, brothers-in-law Roy Bryant, twenty-four, and J. W. Milam, thirty-six, later explained to the journalist William Bradford Huie in *Life* that they had not intended to kill Till when they dragged him from bed, but when he refused to repent or beg for mercy, they had *had* to kill him. "What else could we do?" said Milam, a burly, bald, cigar-smoking man. " . . . I'm no bully; I never hurt a nigger in my life. I like niggers in their place. I know how to work 'em. But I just decided it was time a few people got put on notice. As long as I live and can do anything about it, niggers are going to stay in their place. Niggers aint gonna vote where I live. If they did, they'd control the government. They aint gonna go to school with my kids. And when a nigger even gets close to mention sex with a white woman, he's tired of living. . . . 'Chicago boy,' I said, 'I'm tired of 'em sending your kind down here to stir up trouble. Goddamn you, I'm going to make an example of you—just so everybody can know how me and my folks stand.' "

Emmett's elderly relative, Mose Wright, testified at the murder trial and identified the defendants, and other blacks testified (prior to fleeing the state for their lives) that they'd seen the boy in the truck with the defendants, and heard him in the barn—"Who are they beating to death down at the barn?" one of them had asked at the time. Emmett's mother testified that the body returned to her in Chicago was her son's. The defendants did not take the stand.

It took the jury less than an hour to return the verdict of "not guilty." The jury foreman explained: "I feel the state failed to prove the identity of the body."

A few weeks after the *Brown* decision, Judge Tom P. Brady of Brookhaven, Mississippi, gave a speech entitled "Black Monday" to the Sons of the American Revolution in Greenwood, Mississippi. It was so well received that he was persuaded to make it into a little book, which he did: ninety-two pages long, it sold for one dollar and became the bible of the middle-class white resistance, the statement of opposition for those disinclined to join a lynch mob, but equally resolute to preserve white-only schools for their children. *Black Monday* sounded all the major notes: the inferiority of the Negro race, the sexual appetite of black males for white women, and the Communist plot behind the *Brown* decision. "It will take an army of one hundred million men to compel it," Brady wrote. "We have, through our forefathers, died before for our sacred principles. We can, if necessary, die again. You shall not mongrelize our children and grandchildren!" In speech and text he continued: "You can dress a chimpanzee, housebreak him, and teach him to use a knife and fork, but it will take countless generations of evolutionary development, if ever, before you can convince him that a caterpillar or a cockroach is not a delicacy. Likewise the social, political, economical, and religious preferences of the negro remain close to the caterpillar and the cockroach."

His portrait of "apelike niggers" wanting to go to school with "blue-eyed golden-haired little girls" expressed, albeit pornographically, the deepest fears of the majority of white southerners.

The White Citizens Council movement swept the South. Associations formed in every southern state, and local units sprang up in hundreds of towns and cities. The members were known as white-collar Klansmen or country-club Klansmen. "Their members are respectable citizens of the community, the quintessence of the civic luncheon club," wrote the historian David Halberstam in 1956. "At their meetings there is emphasis on speakers from the ministry and the universities." But the existence of the councils had the effect of suspending freedom of speech, he reported. "Before the advent of the Councils a man who spoke up against Jim Crow merely ran the risk of being known as a radical; today he faces an organized network of groups consciously working to remove dissenters—his job and his family's happiness may be at stake."

"The real conflict came after the 1954 decision," said Rothschild in a 1966 interview. "That is, the moderates abdicated. They didn't say anything and they turned over their power, which they really had, to the extremists."

"Integration represents darkness, regimentation, totalitarianism, communism, and destruction," said Robert Patterson, executive secretary of the Association of Citizens Councils of America. "There is no middle ground."

Forced to choose, with the ground opening up under their feet (there was no middle ground), hundreds of thousands of average white citizens—lawyers, accountants, homemakers, filling station owners, county commissioners—signed up with the White Citizens Councils. The ranks included those committed to preserving civilization and those compelled by family and friends to *act* as if they thought this would preserve civilization—those repelled by the sheets, hocus-pocus, fake regalia, and random violence of the KKK, but obliged to do *something*. Another hundred thousand, who liked the idea of torch-lit midnight gatherings, hoods, and bullwhips, joined the Klan. Although numbers are impossible to verify, perhaps altogether half a million white southerners enlisted in the Citizens Councils, the Klan, and other right-wing extremist groups in the wake of *Brown*, vowing to uphold segregation and protect the white race. They celebrated, with Confederate pride, their civil disobedience.

"I am not one of those who say, 'This thing will be solved, but not in my lifetime,' " said Brady. "I say this thing *will* be solved, and in *my* lifetime."

From 1946 to 1954, prior to *Brown*, suspicions of international Jewish interference in the racial politics of the region were discussed discreetly, by intellectual types like Bright. They imported literature from New York and applied it imaginatively to their local circumstances. It was a private perspective, a special insight belonging to a few associations of the extreme right. The Columbians was not the only Jew-hating organization in America: ninety-two anti-Semitic groups were operating at the end of the 1940s; at the start of the 1950s, fifty-seven were active. "Yet," writes Dinnerstein, "unlike prevous decades, the various accusations and charges against Jews attracted only a few malcontents and extremists and generated no significant anti-Semitic movement."

But on May 17, 1954, when the Supreme Court abandoned the separate-but-equal doctrine and outlawed the racial segregation of schoolchildren, segregationists and racists of every stripe leapt to the front lines of public discourse, including the extremists well versed in the literature of anti-Semitism. "The assault mounted by the white South to repel the forces of integration," wrote the journalist James Graham Cook in 1962, "has been accompanied by an outburst of anti-Jewish propaganda perhaps unmatched in the history of the region. . . . Only since the Supreme Court's school integration decision of 1954 have the masses of the white South been introduced in any really significant way to the rather more Northern notion that the source of America's troubles is 'the Jewish conspiracy.' "

"Anti-Semitic forces in the South, which have carried out bombings of synagogues, temples, and educational buildings, quickly tied themselves in with the organizations created to resist the Supreme Court school decision," wrote Ralph McGill. He continued:

Like the Communists, the anti-Semitics ride any vehicle which seems to be going in their general direction. . . .

Adlai Stevenson was attacked as a Jewish financed Red—a pal of Stalin's. The Rockefeller family was attacked as being in a conspiracy to rule the world in cooperation with Jewish financiers. Woodrow Wilson was found by these purveyors of lies to have been an international Jew in ancestry. Franklin Roosevelt, too, was so described. The Supreme Court, since the court decision, is a target by the anti-Semites who assert the court is controlled by Jews.

One may run at random through these hate pamphlets and extract phrases which reveal their technique of incitement: 'Plot, dirty, foul, debauched, vile, vicious, conspiracy, savage, Jew machine, counterfeit Americans, Jewish power, Jewish traitors, invisible government, sinister, subversive aggression'—these are the more familiar words. . . .

Uninformed, illiterate persons are deceived and satisfied with this sort of narcotic. They live on hate as a drug addict lives on his needle of heroin or morphine. Each pamphlet is a shot in the arm for the hate fringe. Some are so crazed thereby as to dynamite churches and schools.

A few wealthy men in the nation, always careful to keep their own names out of it, contribute to these various groups. But mostly, the income comes in a dollar or two at a time from those persuaded to "subscribe." . . .

The number of these anti-Semitic persons in the South has never been great. But by making their present pitch the charge that Jews favor desegregation, they have become an emotional menace.

"Most of my informants agreed," said a Jewish scholar about his interviews in a southern Jewish community, "that their picture of a quiet, mutually respectful existence began to fade with the Supreme Court's school desegregation decision. . . . Some Jewish leaders spoke to me of a 'paradise lost.' It used to be so quiet, the Jewish community used to be so respected, Jewish leaders used to be welcomed in the best society."

Brady, of the White Citizens Council movement, did not fail to dip his pen into the inkpot of Communist-Jewish conspiracy:

> Of all the nations which have ever been on this earth, the United States of America has been the kindest to the Jew. Here he has suffered but little ostracism—and he has brought most of this upon himself. . . .
>
> If [the Jew] is going to bow down and worship the Baal of Socialism and Communism the same fate of persecution and enslavement which has so often befallen him will again overtake him.

Brady claimed to have Jewish friends and to welcome Jewish members into the White Citizens Councils. He reiterated that it was only the Negro race for which mass deportation would be required. But the Jews, in the minds of perhaps tens of thousands of his followers, had become the evil twin of the black agitators.

"The NAACP is the worst organization to come along since the one that crucified Christ!" said a speaker at a Citizens Council rally in Memphis. "And I may as well say it: it's the same organization!"

2

Bright, like the Citizens Council members, eschewed the fake pageantry of the Klan, but he found that his political convictions lay to the right of the Citizens Councils' stands. He was keen to get to the heart of the matter, to the worm inside the rotten apple: the Jewish-Communists behind the smokescreen of school desegregation.

For several years after *Brown*, as the White Citizens Council movement grew in Atlanta and Georgia, Bright refrained from joining and contented himself with quietly receiving and disseminating literature and meeting informally with coworkers and fellow church members. "We were just common ordinary citizens who were becoming aware. We were in the churches, in the neighborhoods, in the workplace and restaurants and in the professional organizations—you just ran across someone every once in a while. There was no organization of opposition to the Communist party. No organization. There were just enough people who were educated and informed to tell other people and to get the word out with a printed book."

Then in May 1958, in Knoxville, Tennessee, two former Columbians, Edward R. Fields and Jesse Benjamin Stoner, created a new organization: the National States' Rights Party (NSRP). The group was described by the *New York Times* as "the ideal merger of Klan and Nazi philosophies" and by one observer as "the most active Southern-based organization with a Jew-baiting as well as Negro-baiting program." Bright was present at its inception.

"I went to find out what was happening," he said, "because here, finally, something is starting to gel so that there would be some kind of national concerted effort to support Joe McCarthy and Admiral [John C.] Crommelin and J. Edgar Hoover in their efforts. People came from all over the country."

Fields, born in 1932, had been introduced to Nazi philosophy at the age of fourteen. He was a middle-class white boy attending Marist, a Catholic prep school in Atlanta, when a friend offered to take him to a white supremacy group meeting. It was the Columbians. "We were enthused at what we saw," he later told an interviewer. "A huge Thunderbolt banner hung behind the speakers' rostrum. A record player blared out Nordic marching music. Then Emory Burke entered in uniform, followed by the other officers. He began by telling the audience of our racial heritage . . . and of the evil elements seeking to destroy white freedom and liberty.

"About that time a group of men wearing Jewish War Veterans' caps entered the hall. They began booing the speaker and tearing up Columbian literature. A scuffle broke out and the police entered. The meeting was ended by a police order that the hall be cleared. I walked up to a police captain and told him the meeting should not be stopped, that it was the Jewish War Veterans who should be arrested for inciting a riot. He replied, 'We have our orders.'

"I learned that persecution was expected and only through sacrifice would America be saved."

Fields worked on a "Free Emory Burke Committee" when the leader of the Columbians was jailed for usurping police authority and for beating a black man. He grew close to George Van Horn Moseley, an army general, a leader in anti-Jewish agitation since the 1930s, and an Atlanta resident, who wrote: "Although there are over thirteen million Jews of all classes in our Republic they have not, as yet, entered the life blood of our race so seriously that a purge is impossible." Through Mosely, Burke, and the Columbians, Fields was introduced into a national anti-Semitic network, which included John Kasper of Louisville; George Lincoln Rockwell of Arlington, Virginia; Bill Hendrix of Oldsmar, Florida; Maynard Nelson and Eustace Mullins of Chicago; and Peter Xavier of Dayton, Ohio.

When the first desegregation lawsuit was filed in Atlanta in 1950, Fields stood on the street handing out pamphlets headlined: "Jewish Communists Behind Atlanta's School Segregations Suit." That year he received a general discharge from the U.S. Naval Air Force for "unsuitability." Attempting to reenlist in 1951, he underwent a medical exam and filled out forms for the U.S. Naval Reserve, volunteering to serve, "but not in the U.N. police or any Jew-controlled international force." On his application he described himself as a self-employed "Anti-Jewish Crusader" and his job duties as "Distribution of anti-Jewish literature and organize youths for anti-Jewish action—Death to the Communist Traitors."

On December 15, 1952, a medical examiner filed a report of his examination of Fields, concluding: "Abnormal Psychiatric—Paranoid personality—is not qualified for induction: ... He states that Jews caused him to be expelled from both college and the Navy. He appears calm, unperturbed, and somewhat arrogant during the interview. ... He looks immature and he lacks the force of personality usually observed in paranoid individuals. ... He is seriously sick and his chances of eventually becoming frankly insane are excellent." The examining physician, disconcerted by his interview with Fields, contacted the FBI about him. An FBI report was filed, noting that the doctor was "quite anxious that someone with authority to commit this man to an institution be notified. We told him that we knew of no such person at the moment."

In Atlanta in 1952, Fields collaborated with Stoner to form the Christian Anti-Jewish Party; they picketed the White House with anti-Semitic placards. While studying chiropractic in Davenport, Iowa, Fields posted signs on local businesses: "This store is owned by Jews. Anti-Jewish Week, February 21–28." He later explained he intended this observance to correspond with National Brotherhood Week. By 1957 Fields was living in Louisville, Kentucky, an active member of the Citizens Council there and of the United White Party.

Born in 1924 and orphaned by age sixteen, Stoner was a survivor of polio who was exempted from wartime military service because of his limp. At age 18, he joined the Chattanooga Klan, discovered that Jews were the cause of his unhappy life, and was promoted to Kleagle. "Obsessive anti-Semitism," reported the *New York Times*, became "the center of his life." Wrote the author Elizabeth Cobbs of her first glimpse of Stoner in Birmingham in the 1950s: "I had expected an impressive and powerful person. But I found Stoner to be a creepy little wild-eyed man who appeared both nervous and leering." "A student of mine interviewed J. B. Stoner a couple of years ago," said Harvey Klehr at Emory. "Stoner was saying, 'No goddam Jew ever contributed a single thing to the good of mankind,' and the student, observing Stoner's disability, said, 'What about Jonas Salk?' He said Stoner got up and stormed out of the room."

In 1944, Stoner petitioned Congress to pass a resolution establishing that "Jews are the children of the Devil." In 1945 he organized the Stoner Anti-Jewish Party and worked toward legislation that would "make being a Jew a crime, punishable by death." In interviews with the press, he repeatedly described Adolf Hitler as "a moderate"—"I think Hitler was too moderate. He didn't have anywhere near the race problem we got." He declared that his own neo-Nazi party would eliminate Jews via gas chambers, electric chairs, firing squads, "or whatever seems most appropriate." He remained active in the Chattanooga Klan until 1950, when he was discharged for initiating a campaign to expel all Jews from Chattanooga. He moved to Atlanta, finished law school, and teamed up with Fields to create the Christian Anti-Jewish Party in 1952.

One of their leaflets read:

DEFEND THE WHITE RACE
The Great White Race Has a Right to Live

The Jews have destroyed Racial Segregation. . . . It has amazed some people to discover that the President of the NAACP is NOT a Negro BUT the JEW Arthur Spingarn. The NAACP was founded by his brother, the JEW Joel Spingarn. The national board of the NAACP has many Jew directors on it.

Jews Behind Race Mixing

All major Jew organizations are against Segregation. B'nai B'rith is the largest Jewish fraternal order in the world. The Jewish Anti-Defamation League of B'nai B'rith filed a brief with the Supreme Court in opposition to Segregation. It happily welcomed the decision against Segregation by saying, "the strongest victory yet" in the South in recent years. (P. 13, Chattanooga Times, May 18, 1954)

The Jew-owned Chattanooga Daily Times welcomed and praised the Court ban against Segregation in its own subtle way. Also it (P. 3, May 18, 1954) quoted a Jewish rabbi as saying, "When I heard this afternoon of the Supreme Court's decision I gave thanks to God."

The Jewish Rosenwald Fund spent $30 million financing organizations and writers that promote racial mongrelization. A race once mongrelized is lost forever. The Negroes are victims of the Jews—in politics and finance. The Jew plan of mongrelization (intermixing) would end the African race as well as the White. . . .

Don't Let the White Race Die

Do you want your children to go to school with Negroes? If so, they will eat together with them in the school cafeterias and use the same rest rooms. Do you want your children to dance with Negroes at school dances? Do you want your grandchildren to be part Negro? Do you want Negro schoolteachers to teach your children? Would you let your daughter date a Negro classmate? . . .

You can save Racial Segregation. You can Preserve the White Race. Join and elect the Christian Anti-Jewish Party to power and your children will NEVER have to go to school with Negroes. Our Party will solve America's racial problem in a strictly legal way—and in fairness to both races. Elect enough of our candidates to public office and we will enact a law or Constitutional Amendment that will give the Negroes a rich and prosperous country of their own in Africa. . . .

All White People—Protestant and Catholic, Native-born and Foreign-born, men and women, young and old: Do your duty for the White Race by joining and voting for our Party.

For an application blank send your name, address and phone number to:

CHRISTIAN ANTI-JEWISH PARTY

Edward R. Fields

Chief Secretary

P. O. Box 48   Atlanta, Ga.

Another leaflet read:

RALLY! December 4, 1954

SAVE WHITE SCHOOLS
Don't go to school with negroes.

MASS MEETING AT HAMILTON COUNTY
COURT HOUSE
in Chattanooga.

We White Christians refuse to sacrifice our precious White children upon the Jewish Altar of Race Mixing. . . .
Come to our Mass Meeting. Chattanooga will tell the world that our lovely, innocent, White Children will Never go to school with blacks.

CHRISTIAN ANTI-JEWISH PARTY

Only Whites Invited   Jews Stay Away

"SCIENTISTS SAY NEGRO STILL IN APE STAGE," stated another handbill illustrated with two simian creatures, "The Ape" and "The Negro." "Races Positively Not Equal."

— ▦ —

The National States' Rights Party was born out of the merger of the Christian Anti-Jewish Party, the United White Party, and other extremist organizations. It was significant on two fronts: first, it placed hatred of the Jews front and center in its anti-integration campaign; second, it represented a "super-organization" on the right, a confederacy of fringe groups previously unable to coordinate their efforts.

The thirty-six-point NSRP platform, hammered out in Knoxville, included the following principles:

We believe in the creation of a wholesome White Folk Community, with a deep spiritual consciousness of a common past and a determination to share a common future.

We favor complete separation of all non-whites and dissatisfied racial minorities from our White Folk Community.

We favor creation of a National Repatriation Commission, to encourage the voluntary resettlement of Negroes in their African homeland, with fullest financial and economic assistance toward that end.

We approve the removal of all alien minorities dissatisfied with our American way of life and the republic for which we stand.

We believe that immigration should be restricted to select white individuals.

We demand that all financial and moral support to the state of Isreal [*sic*] cease, as a basis for the rebuilding of Arab-American friendship.

The NSRP adopted the thunderbolt insignia of the defunct Columbians and published, under Fields's editorial direction, a monthly newspaper, the *Thunderbolt: The White Man's Viewpoint* (still in circulation thirty-five years later under a new name, *The Truth at Last.*) Headlines and stories reported Jewish control of the NAACP, the White House, the Supreme Court, and Hollywood; the Holocaust was denounced as a "GIANT PROPAGANDA HOAX," and Hitler was described as "a Whiteman [who] once meted out justice to the Jews." An anniversary issue celebrated the lynching of Leo Frank, the arch-segregationist Herman Talmadge was tarred as an "integrationist tool of the Jews," and the Anti-Defamation League was said to be holding political prisoners. The editorial stance on the *Brown* decision was that Chief Justice Warren and the eight associate justices ought to be put to death.

The NSRP would make headlines over several states and many years with its violent interference in the civil rights movement. There was the regionwide "Fire Your Nigger" campaign designed to drive blacks from the South; there was the 1960 presidential campaign slogan: "You can't have law and order and niggers, too."

In 1964, the NSRP nominated John Kasper of Tennessee for president, with J. B. Stoner as his running mate. They polled 6,957 votes nationally. "Brought before the House Un-American Activities Committee in February 1966, Stoner refused to answer any questions but infuriated congressmen with an editorial branding committee chairman Edwin Willis as 'part ape.' " In 1970, the NSRP nominated Stoner for governor of Georgia, but he won less than 3 percent of the vote. Two years later, he received 40,600 votes in a U.S. Senate race, and 71,000 supported him in his 1974 campaign to become lieutenant governor.

The NSRP credo was summarized in the campaign literature of John C. Crommelin, of Wetumpka, Alabama, a retired rear admiral who ran for vice-president in 1960 as the NSRP candidate. The Annapolis-trained aviator with the splendid World War II record was a hero of Bright's and the anti-Communist South's. The syndicated columnist Jim Bishop met the admiral once and described him as "a smiling, good-natured man who, in the Navy, served his country well. His current philosophy is summed up in a sentence: 'The Communist Jewish conspiracy is plotting the overthrow of white Christian mankind.' "

Crommelin distributed brochures that read:

> The ultimate objective of the Communist-Jewish conspirators is to use their world-wide control of money to destroy Christianity and set up a world government in the framework of the United Nations, and erase all national boundaries and eliminate all racial distinctions except the so-called Jewish race, which will then become the master race with headquarters in the state of Israel and in the United Nations in New York, and from these two communication centers rule a slave-like world population of copper-colored human mongrels.

In the postwar years in the South, this was not a widespread point of view. Few could have summarized it, touching upon all its aspects. With good cause, its aficionados met privately; in public they held their tongues. Southern Christians were overwhelmingly tolerant of the Jewish minority in their midst, and for several reasons. First, there simply were not all that many Jews living in the South. They were less than half of 1 percent of the population (representing 4 percent of the Jewish population of America). Second, Christian fundamentalism embraced the Old Testament. Although the overall impression of Jews was muddied by their portrayal as the killers of Christ, they also were called the Chosen People, and *Israel* was given a peculiarly southern and affectionate pronunciation—"Is-rah-aye-ell"—in Sunday morning sermons. Finally, the South already possessed in abundance a more obvious scapegoat: the more vulnerable, more easily recognizable, and more populous African Americans.

Besides, southern Jews had gone to great lengths to reform and smooth over disconcerting idiosyncrasies and to make themselves familiar and acceptable to the surrounding sea of gentiles. Most southern Jews in the 1950s were descended from Jewish southerners and considered themselves southerners *first*.

When the theory of Jewish-Communist subversion began to catch on in the white South in the wake of the *Brown* decision, it was adopted largely by people who either never had met a Jew or who had not really disliked the one or two they had met. The great majority of white southerners who, in the 1950s, would join an organization, subscribe to a newsletter, or attend a meeting in which the Jews were blamed for social unrest did not mean for their actions to be taken personally. "I have nothing against Jews as an individual," says Jason Compson in William Faulkner's *The Sound and the Fury*. "It's just the race. You'll admit that they produce nothing. They follow the pioneers into a new country and sell him clothes. . . . I've known some Jews that were fine citizens. You might be one yourself. . . . "

"No," says the man with whom Compson is drinking a Coca-Cola, "I'm an American."

"It was probably during their Egyptian sojourn that the Jews picked up their first traces of Negro blood," reported the booklet "Gallery of Jewish Types." In his research, Crommelin relied on this pamphlet, which was an attempt to synthesize the two arch-enemies. "A Negroid strain undoubtedly exists in Jewry; to it the frizzy or wooly hair, thick lips, and prognathous jaws appearing in many Jewish individuals are probably due." Crommelin thus referred to Jews as "jewlattos," as in, "Woodrow Wilson was a jewlatto." "The biggest lie of all," he said, "is the claim that the modern Jew is a white man."

These were crackpots; these were madmen. The extremity of their language was in inverse proportion to their numbers, in inverse proportion to the likelihood of their realizing their goal of purging America of all nonwhites and non-Christians. But in many locales, the crackpots did the dirty work of the power structure. And the crackpots had access to dynamite.

The majority of white southerners never advocated violence against Jews even after the *Brown* decision. In many southern towns, gentiles shopped contentedly in a Jewish market, wore suits and dresses offered by a Jewish ready-to-wear merchant, enjoyed bread from a Jewish bakery, or had their teeth polished by a Jewish dentist. Jewish mothers joined the PTA and helped stage the school Christmas plays; Jewish men became Rotarians, Lions, Masons, and Elks. Leaders of men in the South, editors, city councilmen, senators, governors, did not know or use words like *jewlatto*.

But they used words like *nigger* and opened the doors to the rest of it.

8

No Middle Ground

1

In his office, Jacob Rothschild (gaining pounds and losing hair with each passing year) was reading the Prophets. The Temple hummed like a Cadillac. In the outer office Eloise Shurgin answered the phone and typed letters. The postman came and went. Menorahs and kiddush cups gleamed on the shelves of the Temple gift shop. Best-selling Jewish books stood on a library cart in the hall: Henry Roth, Howard Fast, Leo Rosten, Harry Golden, Chaim Potok, Saul Bellow, Bernard Malamud, Leon Uris, and—who knows why?—Pearl Buck. A congregant and a florist visited the sanctuary to plan the color scheme for an upcoming wedding. "The years do fly," Rothschild wrote in a letter, "and each year carries me further from my vowed resolution that I will be gray before I'm bald."

Alone in his office with the door shut, he leaned back in his chair and read his English Bible.

Your new moons and fixed seasons
Fill me with loathing.
They are become a burden to me,
I cannot endure them,

166

said God to Israel, through Isaiah (Isaiah 1:14–17),

> And when you lift up your hands,
> I will turn My eyes away from you;
> Though you pray at length,
> I will not listen.
> Your hands are stained with crime—
> Wash yourselves clean.
> Put your evil doings
> Away from My sight.
> Cease to do evil.
> Learn to do good.
>
> Devote yourselves to justice;
> Aid the oppressed.

Rothschild did not, like the Orthodox, "lay Tefillin"—bind onto his forehead and forearm with leather straps the black boxes filled with prayers—he had never even seen this done. But he laid on his tongue every day slabs of the thick, bittersweet, ancient poetry; he rested his hand along the margin of the rough-hewn songs of righteous indignation. And with these he bound himself to God, to justice. Above the Temple dome the vast Georgia sky was a breathtaking blue, a Caribbean blue speckled with crows like the bright surface of a sea dotted with dolphins. In the sky out his window, in the free-flying clouds, Rothschild sensed God, the Jewish God, the God of history, over Georgia. He was finding his "personal God," the absence of whom had been evident to Rabbi Feldman a few years earlier. For Rothschild now, God was He who demanded justice.

Of course, a midcentury American Reform rabbi might well take to the Prophets. Unable, or disinclined, to perform, in the old way, traditional Hebrew benedictions, ablutions, supplications, and invocations; conducting Jewish worship in English, to the sound of the organ; aware, if he cared to think about it, of the skepticism in which his ecclesiastical title was held by the Orthodox rabbinate, such a Reform rabbi might well be cheered by

Isaiah's insistence (Isaiah 1:11–13) that God Himself was fed up with ritual and preferred justice to burnt offerings.

> "What need have I of all your sacrifices?"
> Says the LORD.
> "I am sated with burnt offerings of rams,
> And suet of fatlings,
> And blood of bulls;
> And I have no delight
> In lambs and he-goats . . .
>
> Trample my courts no more;
> Bringing oblations is futile,
> Incense is offensive to Me.
> New Moon and Sabbath,
> Proclaiming of Solemnities,
> Assemblies with iniquity,
> I cannot abide."

Yom Kippur, in Reform life, was but a half day or three quarters of a day. By late afternoon, congregants jovially broke the fast in one another's well-lit dining rooms around buffets of rolls, smoked fish, delicatessen meats, coffee, and soda, while uniformed black maids carried in trays of sugared pastries and cut-glass bowls of fruit salad. Some snuck out of the service midmorning to grab a bite at the lunch counter down the street.

But hear Isaiah's words (Isaiah 58:4–6) on fasting:

> Your fasting today is not such
> As to make your voice heard on high.
> Is such the fast I desire,
> A day for men to starve their bodies?
> Is it bowing the head like a bulrush
> And lying in sackcloth and ashes? . . .
>
> No, this is the fast I desire:
> To unlock fetters of wickedness,
> And untie the cords of the yoke,
> To let the oppressed go free.

Was there not, thought Rothschild, room here to bargain, to swap? Yes, he would tell them, you are welcome to your bagels, your lox, your sliced tomatoes, your Jello molds—the sun won't set for another five hours. But we'll call it a fast *if* you'll grant me instead the fast that God desires: "to untie the cords of the yoke." Let's ponder less our growling tummies and chasten ourselves with a hard look at the tin-roofed shacks and dirt streets of Atlanta.

Every Rosh Hashannah and Yom Kippur, he looked out over the wooden pews. His congregants looked like the sated, ornamented, perfumed haute bourgeoisie of any country, but their faces were hauntingly Jewish. When he wrote his sermons, he saw before him their Jewish faces, with their capacity for tragedy and, he believed, their inclination toward justice. He would not have swapped this colorful bunch for any other.

But he would not give them what they wanted on the High Holy Days in the few hours they were his prisoners—between the morning scramble to leave the house in time to find a good parking place and the afternoon stampede back outside to the parking lot. What he offered the congregants, captive in their pews, was his own anguished cry for justice, his own handmade verses.

For the hoarse, aggrieved words of Isaiah, Jeremiah, Ezekiel, and Amos had focused his mind. When he read the Prophets, it was as if the city were leveled by a wind blowing cold and straight across time from the Holy Land; all the confusion of neighborhoods, skyscrapers, and traffic blown away, so that he saw Atlanta like a dark stage emptied of scaffolding, backdrop, props, and costumes. What was left on the blank stage were ordinary men and women in street clothes, and those with black skin were brutally shunned, exploited, and abused. Shining the light of ancient words on the modern city, Rothschild understood the black citizens to be the wronged, the oppressed, the downtrodden spoken of by the Jewish prophets. And he heard the exhortations to help them.

But the terrible irony was that while Rothschild had found a path to righteousness open to the Reform Jews—allowing them to keep their Christmas parties, their Friday night symphony tickets, their platters of baked ham with pineapples, their shrimp creole—many still shrank from it. For the Temple Jews understood that their jumping onto Rothschild's racial justice bandwagon would render them—in the eyes of white Christian

Atlanta—more alien, more suspect, more *Jewish* than if the men were to grow beards and sidelocks and the women to don kerchiefs, all of them then trudging through downtown to sell pickles and used pots from pushcarts.

In January 1947, in his first public act, Rothschild agreed to cosponsor a protest rally at the state capitol. It was the moment of the famous, the absurd "Georgia Three Governors Controversy," an occasion for great hilarity in the northern press. In 1946, the infamous Governor Eugene Talmadge had won his reelection, then died. He had not been inaugurated yet. A free-for-all over succession ensued.

Three men claimed to be the rightful governor-elect: (1) M. E. Thompson, Talmadge's running mate, the lieutenant governor–elect; (2) Herman Talmadge [pronounced "Hummon"], the late governor's son; and (3) James Carmichael, who had run second to Eugene Talmadge in the general election.

Write-in votes further complicated the situation. Georgia was virtually a one-party state. Business was over by the end of the day of the white-only Democratic primary. Blacks could vote in the general election, but, by then, who cared? In 1946, however, kingmakers and insiders knew that Governor Eugene Talmadge was dying of cancer on the campaign trail. Several key groups urged their factions to return in November, *after* the primary, and cast write-in votes in the general election for someone other than Eugene. Political insiders believed that in the event of the governor's death, the winner would be whoever had run second to him in the general election.

The Talmadge faction, the innermost group, had hatched the plan and organized a write-in campaign for Herman: "You might call it an insurance policy," Herman Talmadge later explained. "If I couldn't keep Papa from dying, at least I could keep him from dying in vain."

"But the secret strategy didn't remain a secret," wrote the historian John Egerton; "others got into the act. All told, thirty-two people received write-in votes ... including one D. Talmadge Bowers, a north Georgia tombstone salesman."

When Eugene Talmadge died in December, the Georgia General Assembly agreed to declare the winner. They met to count the write-ins from the general election. "Milling about freely among the legislators and jamming the corridors and galleries were hundreds of lobbyists and state employees reinforced by a motley legion of clamorous partisans from around the state," wrote Egerton, "some of them armed, most of them drinking, all of them rowdily disruptive. 'Those were right squalid times,' Herman Talmadge later recalled." The count went on past midnight.

Because Georgians were unaccustomed to voting in general elections, the numbers were minuscule, but crucial: James Carmichael, the winner, had received 669 write-in votes; D. Talmadge Bowers, the Republican candidate, had 637; and Herman Talmadge had received only 619, throwing him out of contention.

At this point, one of those miracles of backwoods politics occurred. Just as the door was about to slam shut on Talmadge and his group, a heretofore uncounted pack of write-in votes turned up. In the Talmadges' home county of Telfair, 56 ballots, all for Herman, suddenly were discovered. They had been mislaid, it seemed, among the votes for lieutenant governor!

To this day, tales of the miracle are told under the Georgia dome: "They *rose* from the *dead* in Telfair County," it is told, in deep, reverberant tones, "*marched* to the polls, *cast* their votes for Herman Talmadge, and went back to their last repose, and they did it all *in alphabetical order.*"

"From a political science perspective," dryly comments the historian Numan Bartley, "the 56 voters who cast the newly discovered ballots were most interesting: the majority had precisely the same handwriting and some resided in graveyards."

Talmadge now claimed 675 write-in votes. The legislature, at 2:00 A.M. on January 15, 1947, declared him the new governor.

Governor Ellis Arnall flat-out refused to accept this ludicrous decision. He supported the liberal candidate, Thompson. He refused to yield his office to Talmadge. But the Talmadge forces, immediately after the legislative vote, exultantly marched downstairs to take possession of the governor's office, where Arnall unhappily awaited them. "Accounts differ," wrote Egerton, "on whether the aggressors banged the door in with a battering ram, took it down from the hinges, opened it with a key, or simply turned the knob and walked in. In any case, Herman made a dramatic entrance, flanked on one side by his mother . . . and on the other by Roy Harris. Standing before the embattled Arnall, Herman said, 'I presume you have been informed that I've been elected governor by the General Assembly.'

" 'Herman, you have no claim to the office of governor,' Arnall replied. 'I refuse to yield the office to you. I consider you a pretender.' A scuffle broke out between the teams of seconds; one of Arnall's men suffered a broken jaw. . . . Later, in the last hour before dawn, a Talmadge hit squad that included a locksmith and an escort of state troopers crept through the darkened halls, broke into the governor's office, and changed the lock on the door. Another team took over the empty governor's mansion."

Arnall tried to enter his office later that day and could not. He set up a desk for himself in the capitol rotunda. He yielded this desk to Thompson, "who set up a downtown office as governor in exile."

It was at this point that Rothschild was contacted by the Episcopal bishop of Atlanta and invited to participate in a rally at the capitol to protest the corrupt transfer of power.

Janice recalled: "Had it even occurred to him to question whether or not this action was 'good for the Jews' he would have concluded instantly that, whatever the risk, *not* to have been included on such a list would have been infinitely worse." The congregation's annual meeting fell on the night Rothschild's name first appeared in the newspaper as a planned speaker at the rally. The consensus at the meeting—not that Rothschild had asked anybody—was that religion should not be mixed with politics. "What's he trying to do, start Leo Frank all over again?" people asked. Officers of the Temple came up with a strategy for Rothschild: "Their advice was to say I'm sick, get called out of town, do anything at all so long as I don't show up at the rally tomorrow night," he told Janice. "I told them that if I should slip on a banana peel tonight and break my leg, and develop pneumonia in the morning, I'd have myself carried into the meeting on a stretcher, but I'd be there."

Governor Herman Talmadge served from January 14 until March 18, 1947. Ultimately, the state supreme court declared his election to be unconstitutional and made Thompson acting governor. Thompson served for two years and was succeeded by

Herman Talmadge, who won the governorship in 1948 and again in 1950. In 1956 he became a U.S. senator and served until 1980. "He . . . endlessly condemned the communists, the federal courts, the NAACP, and all the other outside meddlers and fellow travelers who were presumably seeking to disrupt Georgia's harmonious race relations," wrote Bartley, "and insisted that in Georgia 'the races will not be mixed come hell or high water.' "

Rothschild mentioned race relations in his first High Holy Day sermons in 1946 and 1947, and in 1948 he let them have it:

> How comforting this day might be! Here is the perfect opportunity to find ourselves forgiven. God's standard is too high for us. His law is too difficult. Our sins were just the expected failures of all mortals. All we need do, therefore, is come into His presence on each Yom Kippur, acknowledge our inevitable guilt, pray for forgiveness—and lo! We shall be forgiven. But . . . for Jews, life just isn't made that simple. We are held accountable for our conduct. We are responsible for our acts. . . .
>
> Don't rationalize your guilt by claiming that morality is too difficult for attainment by mere man. Don't pretend helplessness because the right way to live is placed out of your reach. Don't for a moment think that you can blame your sinfulness on the fact that goodness is beyond your grasp. Quite the opposite is true. . . . We must do more than "view with alarm" the growing race hatred that threatens the South. . . . The problem is ours to solve— and the time for solution is now. . . .
>
> We have committed no overt sin in our dealings with Negroes. I feel certain that we have treated them fairly; certainly we have not used force to frighten them. We have even felt a certain sympathy for their predicament. . . . No, our sin has been the deeper one, the evil of what we didn't do.

He reprimanded them as they sat (in dazed unhappiness, all dressed up and no place to go) about recent news items: a Kiwanis Club that refused to deliver the prize when the raffle winner turned out to be a black person; "the white man who went armed, to the home of a Negro who had dared to vote—

despite a warning—and was forced to kill the Negro 'in self defense' "; and the recent intimidation, by cross burning and violent threats, of three black college presidents who tried to attend a statewide meeting of the University System of Georgia. "Once again come the inevitable editorials," he said. "Writers 'viewed with alarm' . . . and enlisted the aid of all 'right-thinking citizens.' . . . Sometimes we wonder where these right-minded people are—and even if the writer of the editorials is one of them."

Deep-voiced, angry, looking back and forth from scripture to the black slums of his adopted city, Rothschild was in the grip of divine vision, of righteous anger. His loud voice was the frail instrument with which he tried to relay it.

"The law of righteousness is not up in heaven that we must wonder who will go there and bring it down for us and give it to us," he said. " . . . Millions of us must know the truth—but we keep silent, even though the word is in our own hearts. The problem is ours to solve, and the time for solution is now." And he said: "There is only one real issue: civil rights."

Asked more than once, in question-and-answer sessions and on call-in radio programs, to name his favorite Bible verse, he offered immediately Isaiah 6:8: "Then I heard the voice of my Lord saying, 'Whom shall I send? Who will go for us?' And I said: 'Here am I; send me.' "

For some members of the congregation, the fact that Rothschild felt God sending him was not good news.

First, there was the problem that the man had arrived fairly recently from Pennsylvania and did not really know what he was talking about. "Jack grew up in Pittsburgh," said the Atlanta police captain, Fred Beerman. "I don't guess he saw black till he might have been an adult. Well, hell, as a little old child I played with them, I fought with them, I was in their house. But a lot of people resented what Jack was saying."

Second, there was the problem that they didn't all agree with him. "Some of them thought it was all right, but I thought he was carrying it too far, too quick," said Beerman. "I could not conceive, nor could I accept, that a person was discriminated against for nothing he did but the way he was born. I guess that's my Jewish side. My personal view—as I say, I supported it—but I thought he was going too fast, too quick. If Jack had had his way, probably he'd integrated everything overnight. But you just can't do those things, you've got to move slowly. You integrate a neighborhood, then you integrate a school, then you put in some jobs. You do a step at a time, is my thought. You can't turn this world over overnight.

"I know I got tired of it, though. Every sermon was about integration. Every now and then—great. But not every dad-blamed one. And I got tired of it. What could I do about it? Didn't go as often."

"I think the majority of them for the most part didn't listen to him," said the attorney Herbert Elsas. "German Jews were not very observant—they weren't really there often enough for it to make an impression."

Third, there was the problem that those who did not agree with him—and some of those who did—thought Rothschild was moving way beyond his area of expertise. "I looked at Jack more as an ultraliberal social worker than as a real religious leader," said the businessman Richard Wasser. "Now, oddly enough, my son had a real strong sense of religion from Jack and admired him greatly. But my father-in-law and I used to become infuriated at some of the sermons where he went into social issues. I thought he needed to look after the religious views of the congregation and stay away from telling us which side of the garbage workers' strike to follow. Obviously, this is what made him famous.

Fourth, there was the famous problem that whether his congregants supported his integrationist views or not—and most of them did, to some extent, or came to—they had to wonder, "When a rabbi stands up in the Deep South and says, 'I'm for the Negro,' is it good for the Jews?"

━━◄◆►━━

A handful of Rothschild's congregants welcomed his words with an outpouring of joy and relief, for they had long found themselves drawn away from the mainstream by the terrible undertow of conscience. Three Temple members had been leaders of liberal thought on the race question in Georgia well before Rothschild's arrival: Josephine Heyman, Hannah Shulhafer, and Reb Gershon. All three were members of the Association of Southern

Women for the Prevention of Lynching (ASWPL), founded in Atlanta in 1930, and of the Georgia Commission on Inter-racial Cooperation. Gershon, born in 1899, was the childhood sweetheart and lifelong friend of Ralph McGill. In his memoirs, McGill paid tribute to Reb and her family:

> Through [Rebecca Mathis Gershon] a new sort of world opened up for one but lately come from an upriver farm. For all my enthusiasm, I was painfully shy. The Mathis family saw this, and when I came calling on their daughter, which was as often as I could, they took me in and made me welcome. Thereby was I introduced to music, paintings, books, and a culture older than mine. More, even than that, I was a part of conversations about issues, international and domestic. . . . The Mathis family gave me something I would not have found anywhere else in Chattanooga—an awareness of international events and of forces which were involved with them.

Their friendship lasted over half a century. "During the years of his loneliness after the death of his first wife," wrote his biographer, Harold Martin, "[McGill] would go to her house for dinner—and, going out to the kitchen, he would put on an apron and cook the meal himself. On the Saturday night before he died, he and his wife Mary Lynn dined at Reb's house. He arrived, Reb remembers, like Benjamin Franklin with his bread loaves, clasping a bottle of wine under each arm."

Meanwhile, Gershon became Rothschild's staunch ally and witty correspondent within the Temple community of Atlanta. She mailed him short, plain handwritten notes, cheering him on; the notes came with greater frequency as the going got rough for him.

"I was proud and pleased to see you quoted in this morning's *Constitution*," she wrote to Rothschild regarding comments he had made about school integration. "And as usual, you said it so well. For whatever it is worth, this is just by way of saying, 'I'm for you!' As if you didn't know. Reb."

"I appreciate your sentiment," the rabbi wrote back, "and can only say that 'I'm for you, too!' "

"Soon I will have used up all the phrases of congratulation and approval I know," wrote Gershon on another occasion, "and then I can only grab a banner and follow in your procession. . . . If any of your congregants take issue with your statement, count my approval as ten, I feel that strongly! Reb."

He wrote back, in a chastened mood: "It is particularly helpful to me to know that you agreed with what I said and that I have you in my corner."

"They were a little older than me and I was born in '09—I'm an old lady!" said lively, young-looking Miriam Freedman of Gershon, Heyman, and Shulhafer. "I was very fond of those folks. They were politically active and they made contact with the black community. As a matter of fact, the first time I went into a cultural program, I was with them and we did something that people didn't do in those days: we went down and had dinner in a black restaurant and then we went to a black concert. It was the early forties. We ate at a black restaurant near Atlanta University—we were the only white people there. We went to hear Marian Anderson, I think it was, with the beautiful contralto voice. We were the only whites at the concert. We were not uncomfortable. We were interested in the magnificent music. We did that to experience black culture in Atlanta. We were making a statement."

And there were people like Joe and Betty Haas, Leonard and Be Haas, Cecil and Hermione Alexander, Morris and Jane Abram, Brena Fry, and DeJongh and Phoebe Franklin eager for interracial contact and friendship. Leonard Haas—and, later, his cousin Joe Haas—served as general counsel for the Southern Regional Council, an umbrella organization for progressives across the South. "The Southern Regional Council . . . receives the lip-service of great numbers of our citizens," said Rothschild in a sermon, "but the actual labors of a pitiful few."

Morris Abram, a prominent attorney, worked for the release of Martin Luther King Jr. when the civil rights leader was jailed by a DeKalb County judge in 1960 for driving with an out-of-state license. When Mayor William Hartsfield set in motion a lawsuit challenging Georgia's county unit system and lost, Abram argued the case before the Supreme Court and won, ending the electoral stranglehold of rural counties on state government. King urged President Kennedy to appoint Abram solicitor general; though that position was not offered him, Abram did serve as the president of the American Jewish Committee, the president of Brandeis University, and a presidentially appointed member of the U.S. Civil Rights Commission.

Outside the Temple community, there were people like Abe Goldstein, the owner of Prior Tire, the first business in Atlanta that employed a black man as a salesman. The first hotel in Atlanta open to blacks while catering to a white clientele, the Peachtree Manor, was owned by Abe's cousins, two dentists, Irving and Marvin Goldstein. For these and others, Rothschild's words were a cause for celebration.

2

Rothschild was not the only southern rabbi in the 1950s to make a connection between the words of the Prophets and the blacks' movement for civil equality. A dozen or more southern rabbis stood for integration. They preached it to their congregations, cofounded interracial ministerial associations, worked to save public schools. Some presented their progressive ideas on the race question before Christian audiences, and one or two invited black ministers into their pulpits and black friends into their houses.

Because of these dozen, more or less, the phrase "prophetic Judaism" entered the modern lexicon of the Reform movement, referring not only to Amos and Ezekiel, but—across two decades—to the humanitarianism of a small group of rabbis manning frontier outposts in hostile territory. Foremost among them in the 1950s and 1960s were Julian Feibelman in New Orleans; Emmet Frank in Alexandria, Virginia; Alfred Goodman in Columbus, Georgia; Charles Mantinband in Hattiesburg, Mississippi; Perry Nussbaum in Jackson, Mississippi; Jacob Rothschild in Atlanta; William Silverman in Nashville, Tennessee; Malcolm Stern in Norfolk, Virginia; Allan Tarshish in Charleston, South Carolina; James Wax in Memphis; and Louis Youngerman in Savannah, Georgia.

Most southern Jews and southern rabbis, however, were paralyzed by anxiety about what the white Christian majority would think. "Isolated in their local communities and profoundly dependent upon local goodwill and friendly relations with local white Gentiles," wrote the sociologist Alfred O. Hero, "most of these Jews adapted themselves to prevailing values and habits. . . . As the generations succeeded one another, more and more Southerners of Jewish ancestry became virtually indistinguishable in ideology from the rest of the local power structure of planters and merchants." The majority of the rabbinate—like the majority of the rest of the Jewish population of the South—occasionally, and from a distance, lent moral support, but were little involved in the civil rights struggle. Their perception was that the white racists would just as willingly pursue the Jews. Why attract their attention? Why draw their fire?

"The Jew is quiet out of fear," stated Rabbi P. Allen Krause in his groundbreaking work, *The Southern Rabbi and Civil Rights,* submitted to Hebrew Union College in 1967, the result of his interviews and polls of southern rabbis, national Jewish leaders, and civil rights leaders. "Somewhat ambivalent about the whole issue, but tending toward *thoughts* sympathetic to the Negro," they sought safe, noncommittal ground. "Although many Southern Jews quietly supported the Black struggle for equal rights," wrote the folklorist Lipson-Walker, "this was primarily a theoretical stance."

"Let me say a word about the Southern Jewish party line," said Charles Wittenstein, of the ADL: "It was: 'Keep a low profile. If we espouse the cause of the blacks, the hostility will be turned toward us. The latent anti-Semitism that exists will explode. No matter what happens, it's going to be blamed on us.' And the Jews who were concerned that extremists would think that Jews were behind the desegregation movement were right: that *is* what the extremists thought. Their *mistake* was that in assuming that if Jews kept a low profile, the anti-Semitism *wouldn't* break out."

Whether or not the privately held attitudes of Jews were more "liberal" than those of their gentile neighbors is a subject of ongoing speculation. Southern Jews certainly perceived themselves as friendlier and more empathetic toward black people. "I think it is true and provable," said Rothschild in 1966, "that Jewish communities are more liberal on the subject of civil rights than comparable non-Jewish congregations." And the liberal-leaning silence of the majority of southern Jews ought not to be discounted entirely, for it represented an attempt to maintain civilized behavior in an anarchic world. Jews in small towns held, privately, moderate points of view and declined, with very few exceptions, to sign up with White Citizens Councils, despite the gales of racist backlash sweeping the South. Most were neither leaders nor followers of the segregation movement, but attempted to place themselves discreetly and politely on the sidelines, maintaining civil relations with both white and black.

Black leaders of the southern civil rights movement, trained by northern experience to look upon Jews as allies, were occasionally taken aback, and disappointed, by the steadfast forbearance, caution, and silence of most of the Jews of the South. "I think the majority of their congregations—I'm talking about the Deep South now—were real Southern," said the Reverend Fred Shuttlesworth of Birmingham, Alabama, a leader of the civil rights movement and the survivor of numerous attacks and bombings. "Not that the majority of their congregations would join a mob; but so far as being for the status quo, so far as voting against the interests of something that would move the Negro forward—the majority was negative." Still, the minister added, "the response of Southern Jews . . . certainly compares favorably with that of numerous other white groups."

Another black leader, Aaron Henry, said: "The image of the Jew in national civil rights activity has not rubbed off on the Jewish population of Mississippi. . . . This was the greatest surprise of my civil rights career to find that 'the Jews of Mississippi' were not with us, the Negro Community, in our quest for human rights."

"The national Jewish bodies have been most helpful, but the local Jewish leadership has been silent," Martin Luther King Jr. said in a 1958 interview. "Montgomery Jews want to bury their heads and repeat that it is not a Jewish problem. I want to go on record and agree that it is not a Jewish problem, but it is a fight between the forces of justice and injustice. I want them to join with us on the side of justice."

━━ ═◆═ ━━

The dozen pro-integration rabbis were more or less balanced by their opposite extreme: a dozen southern rabbis, representing perhaps 10 percent of the South's two hundred thousand Jews, dug in against the whole business. Some were out-and-out segregationists, comfortable with the "southern way of life." Others so greatly feared the backlash to their own communities if they were to side with the blacks' cause that they fell in step beside the segregationists. Of these it is impossible to know for how many the notion of racial inferiority was persuasive and for how many segregationism was one aspect of their protective coloration, their attempt to pass as ordinary white southerners.

The extreme right wing of the Jewish community and the great silent majority—dolefully searching for "middle ground"—agreed on one issue: the undesirability of northern Jewish interference in southern civil rights struggles. The southern Jews bitterly resented the meddling of the Union of American Hebrew Congregations, of the American Jewish Congress, and of the wild-eyed fanatics running B'nai B'rith's Anti-Defamation League (ADL), for these groups pretended to be speaking on *behalf* of southern Jews. Their statements and actions, like hosting Martin Luther King Jr. to be the keynote speaker at an annual rabbinic convention, turned up as news items in tiny newspapers in towns like Dothan and Florence, Alabama; Clarksdale and Natchez, Mississippi; Waycross and Augusta, Georgia—towns where Jews lived in total, vulnerable, and unarmed exposure. When a delegation of Reform rabbis flew into Birmingham to march with King, local Jewish leaders met them at the airport and begged them to turn back.

The southerners knew very well of whom they complained, for northern Jews threw themselves behind and into the civil rights movement to an extent probably unprecedented in American life. Jews were among the earliest supporters and board members of the NAACP; Jewish leaders helped support the Urban League; and the Jewish-dominated International Ladies Garment Workers Union and the Amalgamated Clothing Workers took the lead in organizing "our black brothers" for union membership.

In the *Brown* decision, the Supreme Court relied upon the findings of the black sociologist Kenneth Clark that segregation placed the stamp of inferiority on black children. His study had been commissioned by the American Jewish Committee; that organization, as well as the ADL and the American Jewish Congress, submitted amicus curiae briefs in support of desegregation. The Julius Rosenwald Fund, created by the president of

Sears, Roebuck, and Company, the son of German-Jewish immigrants, gave more than $20 million to programs for rural southern schools.

Young northern Jews enlisted in the civil rights struggle and migrated South; "as many as 90 percent of the civil rights lawyers in Mississippi were Jewish," estimated one black leader there. "Jews similarly were at least 30 percent of the white volunteers who rode freedom buses to the South, registered blacks, and picketed segregated establishments," wrote the historian Howard M. Sachar.

In 1964, when the bodies of three young voting-registration volunteers who had been murdered were discovered in Philadelphia, Mississippi, it was of little surprise to anyone that James Chaney, Michael Schwerner, and Andrew Goodman were one black man and two Jewish ones. "It made little difference, really," wrote Rabbi Allen Krause, "whether one-eighth or two-thirds were Jews. . . . 'Freedom Rider,' [the term for a protestor attempting to desegregate interstate buses and the terminals serving them] to many a Southerner, meant 'Jew' or one financed and stirred up by Jews."

From rabbis across the South, including Rothschild in Atlanta, came reports of the nearly totalitarian grip of segregationist thought in the 1950s; of the absence of neutral public space in which to exchange ideas; of the forced march everyone white had imposed upon them if they hoped to remain part of communal life. In short, the extremists were winning.

From Jackson, Mississippi, a rabbi reported that the White Citizens Council kept a card file "containing the racial views of nearly every white person in the city." In many communities, the local newspapers, reporting on a Human Relations Council meeting, concluded the article with the words: "The following people attended the meeting: . . ." "Dear White American," began a leaflet distributed in Hattiesburg, Mississippi: "Every dollar you spend at a Jewish business is helping toward the elimination of our White Anglo-Saxon race. . . . do you think the 'Freedom' workers who are invading our stores are here out of a heart of love? Make no mistake: There is only one thing that brought them here . . . the dollar. The JEWISH dollar."

In the 1950s, as the ADL began to issue public statements in support of civil rights, a few southern chapters of B'nai B'rith sent delegations to the north to ask the organization to soft-pedal its message. "When a rabbi from New Haven, Connecticut, takes part in such demonstrations," said a delegate from Macon, "you have no idea the position Jewry in our state is placed." The Waycross, Georgia, chapter of B'nai B'rith seceded from the national organization. "Every time one of you makes a speech," a southern woman told the ADL staff, "I'm afraid my husband's store will be burned up." At a meeting of the American Jewish committee, a lawyer from Memphis shouted: "If only you Yankee Jews would keep your long noses out of our business."

"The Jewish community was gripped by an overwhelming fear," recalls one Freedom Rider. "We met with the members of the Jewish Community Council who were most anxious to have us leave." And Rothschild, in a rabbinic journal article entitled "The Southern Rabbi Faces Desegregation," wrote: "If white Christians are fearful, the Jew is panic-stricken. He prefers to take on the protective coloration of his environment, to hide his head in the cotton patch in the dual hope that he won't be noticed and the problem will go away."

"I certainly agree that martyrdom is perhaps the noblest service which anyone can render to a great cause," wrote William S. Malev of Houston, the rabbi of one of the largest synagogues in the South, in 1958. "My only contention is that no one has the right to martyr somebody else for the cause he believes in. Certainly, the Jews of the South have the sovereign and unalienable right to become martyrs in the cause of desegregation if they so wish. I reject however any claim on the part of the national 'defense' organizations to impose martyrdom on the unwilling Jews of the South and to bask in their reflected glory of their self-sacrifice. It would seem to me that if they think so much of martyrdom, they ought to come down South and try it for themselves."

Or, as an Alabama rabbi told Rothschild: "I wouldn't risk the hair on the head of one of my members for the life of every *shvartzeh* [Yiddish for "black"] in the state."

━━◄═►━━

Contemporary surveys of southern Christian clergy found most of them hesitant, too. In October 1958, *Time* reported that nearly half the southern white clergy held segregationist views, while the other half generally remained silent "for various reasons—generally relating to the word 'fear.'" A survey of southern churches in 1964 revealed that only one Protestant denomination had desegregated—the Episcopalians—but the researcher was able to locate very few black Episcopalians. The Jewish columnist Harry Golden observed: "By and large, the Protestant clergy of the South abdicated its responsibility in this crisis. . . . Since May of 1954, the sermons in most Southern churches have been concerned with the virtues of happiness and the evils of juvenile delinquency." "They were confronted with opening the doors of their churches, their Sunday schools, their ladies' circles," said Rothschild, "while we don't have any Jewish Negroes in the South anyway, not many anyway."

"I knew clergymen who were committed to full equality, and wanted it, but didn't know how to pull it off," said the Reverend Dow Kirkpatrick, a United Methodist pastor, seminary professor, and lecturer, then at St. Mark's Methodist Church. "It can be a lonely feeling when you try to do it by yourself. Still, being in Atlanta, I felt I had ground to stand on, and it was safer for me than for the pastors all alone in towns in Alabama or Mississippi. We lost a few members—there were other Methodist churches that they could go to or they'd go across the street to the Baptist church. This issue was more important than theology. But I think most people want an opportunity to affirm that which is just and best. Silence is the only response many people are able to give until they discover they're not alone."

"In the fifties, people looked to the religious community to say something," said the Reverend Allison Williams of Trinity Presbyterian. "They don't do that anymore. Religion is sort of passé. There's very little of what I would call a willingness-to-be-crucified-for-a-cause type thing. Civil rights was perhaps the last clearcut kind of thing you could put your hand on and say, 'This is right and that's wrong.' There was a particular kind of courage that was called for, and a context which would receive that courage."

In the fall of 1957, white mobs rioted outside Central High School in Little Rock, Arkansas, as nine black students tried to enroll. Governor Orville Faubus warned that "blood [would] run in the streets" if the school was integrated, and he called out the National Guard to protect against the black students' entry. In reaction, eighty Atlanta Christian clergymen released a statement, the first of its kind in the South, which appeared in the *Atlanta Constitution* and came to be known as the Ministers' Manifesto. It read, in part: "Freedom of Speech must at all costs be preserved. . . . As Americans and as Christians we have an obligation to obey the Law. . . . The Public School System must not be destroyed . . . [and] hatred and scorn for those of another race . . . can never be justified."

Rothschild—who had been in on deliberations for planning the manifesto, but who refrained from signing it due to its explicit Christianity—honored the courage of the ministers in a sermon and in a newspaper article called "Eighty Who Dared: A Salute to My Christian Colleagues": "Inevitably ministers who confront the mores of their day with the timeless morality of their religious faith find themselves at best unpopular and frequently reviled and threatened. How could it be otherwise? If their people were in agreement with them, it would hardly be necessary for them to speak out at all."

3

In Atlanta the African American leaders also were pushing against the pillars of the southern way of life. The old guard of dignified Auburn Avenue leaders—NAACP officers, Republicans, circumlocuitous speakers and Sunday morning sermonizers—gathered at the Butler Street YMCA for their deliberations. Among them were the Reverend Martin Luther King Sr. of Ebenezer Baptist Church; the Reverend William Holmes Borders, the pastor of the Wheat Street Baptist Church; and Rufus Clement, the president of Atlanta University and the first black Atlanta school board member. Also participating were A. T. Walden, a lawyer and a patriarch of the black bar; C. A. Scott, the publisher of the *Atlanta Daily World*; and John Wesley Dobbs, a retired postal worker who organized a black Masonic Order and the Atlanta Civic and Political League and whose grandson, Maynard Jackson, would become the first black mayor of Atlanta. Warren Cochrane, the director of the Butler Street YMCA; Clarence A. Bacote, a historian at Atlanta University; Grace Hamilton, the executive director of the Atlanta Urban League and ultimately the first black woman elected to the state legislature; and Donald Hollowell, a lawyer, rounded out the group.

"Our experience here meeting with blacks was very different from that of whites elsewhere in the South," said Sam Massell, who would succeed Ivan Allen as mayor in 1968. "We had the black academic center of the country here. We had blacks who were well read and world traveled. You'd sit down to a conference table, for example, look up, and notice that all the blacks in the room were wearing Phi Beta Kappa keys."

Street action was not the style of the postwar black power structure. Nor was it the style of—nor comprehensible to—Mayor Hartsfield and his chief of police, Herbert Jenkins, nor of the key members of the business elite like Robert Woodruff, the chairman of the Coca-Cola Corporation; Ivan Allen Jr., the president of the Ivan Allen Company; Mills B. Lane Jr., the president of Citizens & Southern Bank; and Dick Rich and Frank Neely of Rich's. The black leaders cultivated, instead of a mass movement, a few key political liaisons; they made themselves known to Mayor Hartsfield and felt encouraged, by his civil reception when they called upon him, to continue to take their proposals and recommendations directly to the top. Thus, most of Atlanta's early civil rights accomplishments—the integration of the police force, the integration of the buses, the integration of the school board, the integration of the public golf courses, and eventually, in the most delicate and brilliant of the contrived scenes, the introduction of a handful of black students into a white high school—were handled sagely, with deft coordination, by men speaking in soft voices, wearing summer suits, and behaving with almost-exaggerated politeness. The necessary public actions—a touch of civil disobedience here, some arrests there—were secretly choreographed beforehand by the mayor, the black business leaders and ministers, the white business elite, and the white chief of police.

In 1955, for example, the city's golf courses were quietly and tactfully integrated. The desegregation of putting greens and sand traps may not have been a high priority in the rest of the country, but Atlanta was the birthplace and home of Bobby Jones (in 1930, the first man to win golf's grand slam in a single year). Also, Atlanta's mild climate made golf a year-round leisure activity, and there were middle-class black people eager to play. The black leaders interceding with city hall were nothing if not middle class.

"I would plow up all those golf courses and plant 'em in peas before I see them integrated," snarled Governor Marvin Griffin in response. "Emotionally the majority of the white community in the South, in Georgia, and even in Atlanta agreed with Governor Griffin's feeling," wrote Jenkins in his autobiography. "The Negroes must not be allowed one foot in the door and the iron curtain of segregation must not be breached." Having acknowledged the passionate views of the majority, the white elite and the black elite nevertheless met to plan a peaceable transition to black and white on green.

"Mayor Hartsfield hit on the idea of desegregating the courses on Christmas Eve of 1955. He felt that this was a good time for action on an issue that was not what could be called overwhelmingly popular." That day, Hartsfield and Jenkins drove around the target course: "It was a fine golfing day and, as prearranged, several Negro foursomes played on each course crowded with white golfers, without incident." There was unhappiness and dissent in white golfing quarters; to appease them, Hartsfield ordered the locker rooms removed to avoid integration in an intimate setting; on the other hand, there was the chastening image of mayhem in towns across the South. Golfing business leaders had to agree that none of them wanted to see a hysterical Atlanta featured in the national TV news. Thus, men in plaid slacks, white shoes, and pastel double-knit shirts were among the city's first reluctant integrationists.

("Come to Atlanta as your regional hub," whispered the city's promoters. "Come here rather than Little Rock.")

The Atlanta transit system also was desegregated without a ruckus. "On January 9, 1957," wrote Jenkins, "without warning (never before had the Negro leadership in Atlanta embarked upon a course of this nature without letting us in on it), a group of Negro ministers boarded a bus in downtown Atlanta and sat in the 'white only' section of the bus. The driver left his route immediately and drove the bus back to the garage, whereupon the Negroes got off and departed. . . . [Soon] Mayor Hartsfield was on the phone in one of his 'jumping up and down calls.' " The mayor was taken by surprise by the black ministers, who'd made their startling step in response to the pressure they'd felt emanating from King and Montgomery, and from hundreds of black students growing restive at the Atlanta University Center.

After calling a meeting of white business leaders, transit company officials, and the black power structure, Hartsfield proposed that a lawsuit be filed attacking Georgia's segregation law for municipal conveyances. To file a lawsuit, plaintiffs would be required. Jenkins was assigned the task of locating individuals willing to violate the law and make a test case. "I telephoned the Rev. William Holmes Borders, leader of the ministerial group, and asked him if he would mind being arrested," wrote Jenkins. "The Rev. Mr. Borders, a man of wide intelligence and vast understanding, replied that he was not happy at the prospect and would have some difficulty explaining it to his congregation. Then he asked me exactly what I had in mind."

Together they planned the time and place that black leaders would again board a bus, be led off by Atlanta police, and be driven away in the paddy wagon. "In due course," wrote Jenkins, "the federal court held the segregated seating law to be null and void and the city's transportation system was desegregated peaceably. . . . The whole community had won uninterrupted transportation service, for there took place no boycotts as in Montgomery."

("Come here, rather than Montgomery," whispered the ad men. "You'll prefer *us* to New Orleans.")

4

Rothschild was driving his young son, Bill, home from Sunday school one day and made a remark that pierced the child's memory. "We were listening to the radio," said Bill Rothschild, an attorney, rabbi, and teacher. "Some local civic leader was saying the public schools ought to remain open and we ought to obey the law because it would be good for business, and Dad kind of looked at me and sort of half looked out the front windshield and said, 'Why don't they do it because it's *right*?' "

"The Talmud asks the pertinent question," said Rothschild in a sermon in 1954: " 'Why did God create only one man—

Adam—when he made the world?' And answers its own question in these words: 'So that no man could one day claim, 'My father is better than yours, hence I am superior to you.' " When the legislature debated whether to shut down the public school system, he cried: "What man of intelligence burns down his house to rid himself of an unwanted guest?"

And as the mood of violent resistance darkened, and assaults on blacks and crimes against black homes and churches multiplied, he said: "It becomes increasingly obvious that unless decent people take up the burden, the South faces a return to the most primitive kind of bigotry and race hatred. . . . How can we condemn the millions who stood by under Hitler, or honor those few who chose to live by their ideals, when we refuse to make a similar choice now that the dilemma is our own?"

When he felt the congregation silently quailing at his words, wishing he would keep his voice down, fearing retribution, fearing an impairment of relations with white Christian Atlanta, Rothschild stormed at them: "One must understand that hysteria prevails, that there has been an abdication not alone of reasonableness, but of reason itself."

The congregants bowed their heads and endured the spray of his syllables and his tongue-lashings, and surreptitiously slid their sleeves up to check their watches. ("I don't mind them looking at their watches," a rabbi once said. "It's when they tap them, then hold them up to their ears that I get concerned.")

"[Rothschild] brought his congregation kicking and screaming into the twentieth century, both on Zionism and on civil rights," said Joe Haas. "He was a lonely man."

"I think it was difficult for him," said Aline Uhry. "They criticized him violently when on Friday nights or the holidays he talked about civil rights. They said they wanted him to talk about the *Bible.* Then they'd have fallen asleep."

In 1955, the Temple Sisterhood invited Rothschild's friend, Dr. Benjamin E. Mays, the president of Morehouse College, a nationally known black clergyman and educator, to speak at a Temple luncheon, and then, accompanied by Mrs. Mays, to sit down and *eat*. The Sisterhood was "bombarded with protests and dire predictions of what would happen should such a meeting be allowed to take place," said Janice Rothschild.

"Don't you know that mixed eating is against the law in this state?" said a furious congregant in an early-morning phone call to Rothschild's study.

"No, no, no, you've been misinformed, Sam," said the rabbi. "The Sisterhood luncheon isn't going to be integrated."

"Is Mays coming after lunch, to spare us the embarrassment?"

"Not at all. Both Dr. and Mrs. Mays will be with us for lunch, but they're going to be seated at the center of the head table and all us white folks will be segregated around them."

"What does Jack want to do to us," people said, "start the Frank case all over again?"

The Temple Sisterhood stood their ground: Dr. Mays came, he sat, he ate. "The program played to a packed house," said Janice, "and the Sisterhood received accolades from all segments of the Jewish community."

———

To give his congregants courage, Rothschild quoted the ancient rabbis in what was his favorite Talmudic passage: "It is not incumbent upon thee to finish the work, but neither are thou permitted to desist from it altogether."

In the warm vault of the Temple sanctuary, the scolded congregants listened. The rabbi described a world of human equality with such fervor that everyone could see *he* was convinced of it. With head raised, lips parted, and eyes slightly dilated, he described unseen landscapes as if he had just rocketed down from some glorious planet and would now give his report.

But, to his congregants, the rabbi seemed to be out of touch with their quiet daily struggles to keep at bay the pariah status surrounding Jewishness. They *might* have enjoyed hearing from Rothschild that he was working behind the scenes to end the religious barriers at the golf clubs, the law firms, or the dental school. But he mistook them if he thought that at this critical juncture they were concerned with the barriers to black progress.

Poised as they were between the ghettos of the past and the total equality of the American future, at this fragile point in their history, how could he imagine that they would want to turn back and link arms with the blacks? Come on, fellas! If they're letting us in, there's sure to be room for ten million colored people! You're not all literate yet? Don't have shoes? No problem, we'll wait.

Not likely.

In the dreaminess of a Friday evening at services, the congregants, seated under the creamy white dome as frilly as wedding cake frosting and listening to Rothschild's brave words clanging in the warm air above their heads, sometimes slipped into susceptibility for a moment and imagined that he might be right and that they could, through sheer moral force, overturn Jim Crow, seat Negroes at their lunch counters, and turn their black maids into salesclerks and their yardmen into bank tellers. But they were rudely awakened at the end of the hour when they pushed open the front doors of the Temple. Outside was a muggy night ringing with cicadas and crickets, heavy with the sweet musk of magnolias and azaleas; mosquitoes homed in on their bare arms and faces, and expensive cars, bulging with chrome, drove past along Peachtree Street. The night reminded them of where they were and who they were: descendants of European outcasts, scrambling to make a nice living on the red clay of the failed Confederacy. Stretching out on all sides were a million acres of cotton fields, tobacco fields, pecan groves, peach orchards, and cotton mills and carpet mills owned, by and large, by white Christians, and in which black Christians labored.

Their leather shoes and high heels made a muffled tap-tap on the blacktop of the parking lot. They found their cars in silence, started the ignitions, and pulled away. What Rothschild asked of them was not reasonable. It did not make good sense. Let the Presbyterian ministers ask it of the Presbyterians. Let the Episcopalian ministers require it of the Episcopalians. Ask the Baptists and Methodists to renounce the White Citizens Council members in their midst. But it was not fair or rational to ask what he asked of Atlanta's Jewish people. Didn't they have enough worries?

Rothschild also exited, stood on the hill beside the darkened Temple, headed for his car. He too felt the heat and weight of history—southern history. This was not history of his family's making, but he acknowledged it as the backdrop to the world in which he lived, in which he was raising a daughter and a son, and he accepted it as a legacy for which he was responsible. He had offered himself as an ally, and had been accepted as a friend, advisor, and intimate by Benjamin Mays, President of Morehouse, Rufus Clement, President of Atlanta University, and Reverend Sam Williams, President of the NAACP. He knew precisely where he stood: under the hot, close, dark sky in the center of the South in violent backlash.

He was, at this moment, not unlike George Bright, studying at his table five miles east of the Temple: Rothschild was at the left wing of the southern political spectrum; Bright, at the extreme, the fascist, right. Both were connected to the mass of white humanity by a slim thread.

The truth that was to Rothschild self-evident (the Negroes are our brothers) seemed to become garbled in his throat when he tried to transmit it. No matter how hard he worked on a sermon—scribbling out words with a pen, trying—like a biologist working with microscope and tweezers—to lift out vibrant words from Jeremiah and Isaiah and transplant them alive into his own prose—it was never enough. When he delivered the sermon—rising to his tiptoes in eloquence, pausing to wipe off his steamed-up glasses, his bald forehead shining under a mist of perspiration—he saw before him downcast faces that looked dull and unhappy. It was as if he were moving his lips soundlessly. It was as if he held aloft a spritzing, multicolored Fourth of July sparkler but the congregation saw only a burnt-out match. In the receiving line after the service, the men averted their eyes and offered limp handshakes; the women, with fake cheer, tactfully introduced an unrelated topic, such as a new book or a party to which they planned to invite him.

He shared with them the revelation that had altered—was altering—his life, and they sat browsing through the Temple bulletin, grabbing forty winks, startling awake, looking at their watches, and then tapping them.

9

Brotherhood Night

MAY 28, 1958

It was an Interfaith Night, a Wednesday night "Brotherhood" program of the sort that then took place in church basements under exposed pipes and foil-wrapped ductwork. A janitor clapped open a few dozen wooden folding chairs in the center of a vast, damp, subterranean room, and from around the city, church members arrived. Businessmen accustomed to private phone lines, roast beef, and late-model cars gave up their evenings at home watching television or playing cards. The wives mostly stayed behind, sponging off the counters after dinner as their husbands brushed off their shirt fronts, washed their hands, and went off to try to get a handle on modern times. On the small, creaky chairs they would fidget and take in what new information they could.

On this night, each from his separate corner of the city, Jacob Rothschild and George Bright headed for the large and prestigious First Baptist Church of Atlanta, where a proper social hall had been prepared for a meeting. A janitor dragged a table across the floor, flipped a white paper tablecloth across it, and

193

returned a few minutes later with a plug-in coffee pot and a package of cookies.

Rothschild, the guest speaker, had tucked into his breast pocket a soft set of typewritten three-by-five-inch cards for a talk about brotherhood entitled "Good Will Towards Whom?" Bright brought along a four-foot-by-six-foot sign reading "What Is the Christ-Killer Doing in Our Church?"

The church members made their way in from the parking lot. They stood near the coffee pot for the warmth of camaraderie, shaking hands and exchanging business cards. Well-fed, freshly tucked-in, good-natured men, most probably regretted that it was not Church Barbecue Night or Church Bowling Night instead. In a far corner, a mop stood dripping into a bucket with a sorrowful sound. Outside, Bright parked his car, got his billboard out of the trunk, and hammered it into the grass at the front of the church.

In the 1950s in the South, Brotherhood meetings—especially when they involved an interracial component—were, literally, underground events. They were staged in utilitarian chambers within churches or at the YMCA, in rooms overheated in winter and sweltering in summer. Visitors sensed they had crossed a frontier into a world of wild social experimentation and bohemianism. Men loosened their ties; women removed their white gloves.

"Brotherhood meetings" were excoriated in the right-wing media. A New York–based publication, the *American Mercury*, published a special issue in 1958 entitled "Poisoning These United States: You Are the Target!"

How the sinister Communist program of race mixing could advance so far without noticeably arousing the righteous wrath of American parents will probably forever remain a mystery. Doubtless much of the blame rests on the annual "brotherhood" farce. Initiated in 1934 as "Brotherhood Day" and becoming a full week's observance in 1940, "Brotherhood Week," under the nominal sponsorship of the self-styled National Conference of

Christians and Jews, has become a nationwide Hollywood-style theatrical stunt that plays up anything and everything but true brotherhood based on the fundamental doctrines of Christianity.

In the churches themselves, during Brotherhood events, all was seemly and gracious. In Sunday school classrooms glossy posters of the Holy Land fluttered, in which a robed, turbaned man might be seen leading a donkey along a pebbled road. There were libraries and studies equipped with handsome armchairs and ceiling-high windows, where board meetings and adult Bible classes were held; and there were airy sanctuaries where silver goblets and gold-tipped crucifixes and Tiffany stained-glass windows glittered in the silence. But these rooms were sealed and dark on Brotherhood Nights; the stairwells and firedoors leading to the meeting room were bolted. In this way, however inflammatory and unholy a tone might be generated, it would not penetrate the church proper. The anarchy and weirdness would be contained, the sanctuary would be uncontaminated, and the church would continue to gaze upon the street with its customary tall, paternal, and slightly benighted expression.

But on this night, in front of First Baptist, hiked a protester back and forth, complaining about the Jews. Before leaving home, Bright had visited his neighbor and shown him the notice for the meeting in the newspaper. "They're not only trying to put niggers in our schools, now they're trying to put Jews in our churches," he told Richard Carl Johnson. "A bunch of us are going down there to break up that meeting," he said and invited Johnson to join them. When Johnson declined, Bright responded, "We ought to go down and string one of them up."

Rabbi Rothschild emerged from the stairwell and began to work the room hand over hand, pausing only to shuck off his raincoat and drape it over the back of a chair. The church members, already comfortably seated, put their paper cups of coffee at their feet and stood, sighing, to go introduce themselves. Anyone could see he was an affable type, a regular guy; some might have said his "game" was to play the ordinary type. Their own assistant minister stood talking quietly with the fellow, telling some story while everyone else found seats again, and the minister's soft anecdote inspired a pleasantly drawn-out, deep-toned chuckle from the rabbi, who then stood smiling with suppressed laughter, wiping his eyes, while the minister approached the podium and offered the opening benediction.

Jewish people were so rare in the South that not all the church members had met one before. They had heard jokes and slang about Jews. The expression "jewed you down" was a standard business line meaning "to bargain" or "to cheat." (The definition of *to jew* and *to jew down* was offered in *Webster's Dictionary* that year.) "Jewish engineering" was the college slang for business administration courses; "Jewish cavalry" was army jargon for the quartermaster, or purchasing, corps. "There are good Jews and there are kikes" was one truism of the day; and there was a popular witticism, "A kike is the Jew who just left the room." In a column on anti-Semitism that would appear in the *Atlanta Journal* later that year, the columnist excluded from his list of anti-Semites "folks who have private convictions and indulge them in joke telling and private harangues."

The minister had offered his small joke to the rabbi in the first place to set Rothschild at ease, and to demonstrate to his congregants that two pastors of drastically different theologies could get along nicely. And the rabbi had chuckled responsively in order to give himself an occupation—subduing a bit of mirth—while he got his bearings and endured the words "In Jesus' name, we pray."

The jocular composure also gave him a moment to scan the audience and gauge the sincerity of the Baptist welcome. Rothschild had lived in Atlanta twelve years already and knew precisely the sort of commodity he was. He was in high demand for these ecumenical events, because Protestant clergymen—who had found themselves seated next to him at Rotary or Kiwanis meetings or at a meeting at the state capitol—had found him approachable, modern, well read, and witty, and thought to get some Brotherhood mileage out of the acquaintance.

"Dear Rabbi: This is to confirm and also to thank you for your coming to speak to us about your trip to the Holy Land," began a letter from "Men of Griffin, 'United for Service,' " in

Griffin, Georgia. "Last year for Brotherhood Month we had from the National Council of Christians and Jews, a Jewish and Catholic and Protestant layman all talking on the same program and we invited at that time . . . our Jewish friends and some Catholics as well and had a good time together. For this meeting we are having only one as the speaker and are inviting your people here to be with us and hear your talk."

Rothschild could answer thoughtfully, with no trace of fatigue or derision, and as if it were not the hundredth time, the question "Why don't the Jewish people accept Christ the Savior?" How to begin? Gently. But firmly. "The ancient hope for the world to be transformed at the coming of the Messiah was not realized at the time that Jesus claimed messiahship for himself. Even Christianity recognized that lack by envisioning a Second Coming to make up for it. . . ."

And the other inevitable question: "Why do you all call yourselves the Chosen People?" With humility: "We believe the Jewish people has been chosen not as a 'superior' people but as a people with special obligations, special challenges. . . ."

The rabbi was a superb placater of gentiles, in this respect a true successor to the distinguished old rabbi before him. He was thus a long-time veteran of interfaith meetings in drippy underground rooms, where he shouted from his note cards to be heard above the din of rumbling pipes and furnaces.

On the night of May 28, several of the church lay leaders, alerted by fellow members to the presence of the picketer and his sign, excused themselves from the meeting. They found George Bright on the lawn, not easily dissuaded from his mission. "We engaged in a small tug-of-war with him while trying to remove the anti-Jewish sign," said Hugh Edward Watts, a deacon of the church. Watts and another man pulled at the sign to uproot it, but Bright immediately began tugging at it from the opposite side as if to help them—"Let's get this thing off church property!" he said—while in fact his efforts obstructed all progress.

"Fellow, I don't believe we need your help," Watts finally told Bright.

"Rabbis and ministers have been preaching on brotherhood

since preaching began," Rothschild was saying inside, giving his talk on race relations. The men inside on the folding chairs, balancing cookies on paper napkins on their knees, missed entirely the spectacle out front. " 'Good will' would seem to be a term that can be used without fear of contradiction. As a matter of fact, it has become largely innocuous—until recently. Suddenly it has become a subversive doctrine."

The odd thing was that he most often was invited by ministers to speak to their congregations not on Judaism (which was what the audiences seemed most curious about) but on the race question, the Negro question.

"Dear Rabbi Rothschild: We would be very much pleased to have you talk to our Lions Club on Tuesday," began a letter from Cartersville, Georgia. You may use any subject you wish, but if you prefer to talk on racial discrimination or similar theme that will be agreeable." The ministers were nervous about broaching the subject with their own congregations, so they invited Rothschild to do it. So he spoke once again to white Baptists about racial coexistence. "Can good will be limited and remain good will? Have we now determined that brotherhood is no longer a desired goal of religious teaching? I would ask you—if you find it at all possible—to think with me without any reference to the 1954 and subsequent decisions of the Supreme Court." Then it was time for questions.

"Do Jewish people believe in heaven?"

And no matter how *passionately* he spoke about race relations, the questions always veered back to what clearly was felt to be the greater novelty.

"Does the Jewish church permit intermarriage?"

"Why don't Jewish people have Sabbath on Sunday?"

"Reverend Rothschild, is it true that your people don't accept Jesus as the Christ?"

"We dream of a messianic age, . . ." he began.

Then, harshly, from a thin, pained-looking man in the rear: " 'Rabbi,' would you tell these good people exactly what you mean by the 'Messianic Age'?"

"We believe that it will be a time of universal brotherhood and peace."

"Now 'Rabbi' Rothschild, aren't you leaving out a few details about how exactly this is to be accomplished?"

The young man, thin, pale, nervous, and intent, was Bright, who had abandoned his sign and come inside.

"It is traditional to see the prophet Elijah as the bringer of the news of the dawn of the messianic era," said Rothschild.

"Doesn't the Jewish Bible tell you to gather all the gold from all the Christians on earth before the Messiah can come?" asked Bright.

"No, no, we have no belief like that."

"Are you denying that you Jews are taught from earliest infancy to gather all the gold on earth?"

Alerted by the use of the word *Jews* (in an age in which *Jewish people* or *Hebrews* was the nonderogatory term), the assistant pastor, the Reverend William Arnold Smith, rose and said, "Thank you, sir. We need to open the floor now to other questions."

"Isn't it true, 'Rabbi'!" cried the young man. "Isn't it true! You need to own all the gold for the Messiah to come. It says so, in his own Bible!" he shouted to the audience who had turned in their seats to look.

"Rabbi, how many Jews are there on earth?" asked Bright, trying a new tack.

"Thirteen million," said Rothschild.

"I think you're leaving out a few million," Bright snidely replied. "There are sixteen million Jews on earth."

"Six million Jewish people were slaughtered by the Nazis."

"Yeah, well that's a bunch of baloney. Most of them were brought over here to the United States of America and they're living in New York right now."

It was the closest Rothschild had gotten to a white man in a paroxysm of race hate and superiority, like those on the television news and in the papers. Although Rothschild had launched his words like messages in sealed bottles upon the turbulent waters of Atlanta, he had not known if any had been intercepted by the opposing forces until tonight. The tone of Rothschild's voice changed not a bit, nor did his eyebrows lift in surprise. In truth, he had been braced for worse than this for a long time now, knew that black men, whom he admired from afar, endured a hundred times worse. As he stood holding the sides of the podium, and the heads of the seated church members swung to the front and to the back and to the front again, Rothschild was willing to continue the debate with the agitated man who stood in the rear. Like a submarine under bombardment, Rothschild pulled in vulnerable extremities, hooded the information-gathering apparatus, lowered his pressure, and concentrated his mental and physical force on comprehending, disarming, and returning the attack.

Rothschild could see that his very presence, his body, his face, his suit and eyeglasses, had a leeching effect on the rancorous man, drew poison from him. The man hated Jews. If he appeared to be sputtering, it was due to an excess of damning information, rather than to insufficient data. Rothschild, by his demeanor, tried to calm his distressed audience. This is an infinitesimally small fraction of the hate that is out there, he felt. So let's have it: see it, smell it, learn to recognize it. If it's present in yourselves, extinguish it. This small bit I, and you, can handle. We are more than equal to it.

But good manners prevailed. The folding chairs skidded and collided as men stood to stop the fight. They would not have their invited guest harangued and insulted. The heckler tarnished the church's good name.

Reverend Smith approached the overwrought man and asked him what the trouble was.

"I resent you having a Christ-killing Jew speaking in a Christian church, that's what the 'trouble' is," said Bright.

"If you'd like to come with me, we could discuss this privately in my office," said the minister.

It was not the first time Bright, then thirty-four years old, had felt himself shunted aside and shut down, and by his own kind. But the shabby treatment—bristly browed church officers now surrounded him, backing up their minister—troubled him less than the bald facts before him: that once again a double-speaking Jew was hoodwinking naive white Christians in furtherance of a vast and invisible plot. "Isn't it true, 'Rabbi'!" he called insolently over his shoulder from amidst the men who hurried him toward the stone stairwell. "It's in his own Bible! You can look it up! Someone ought to be hanged for having a rabbi in this church!" he cried as up the stairwell and out he went, ejected.

On the street he straightened his shirt, felt pleased enough with his overall effort, and drove back home in a satisfied frame of mind. It was all in a day's work.

"Rabbi Rothschild, do Jewish people celebrate Easter?" someone was starting up.

— ≡♦≡ —

"Yeah, Rothschild was the big chief," said Bright. "The most outspoken Jew in Atlanta. A Jew in favor of integration. He had a hold on the city. He had his organization. Their plan was to get the gold. That night he tried to dodge the subject. He would not admit that that was their own words, verbatim; in other words, that's what they are told from the time they are one year old: 'You will eventually have all the gold on earth. You will own everything.' He dodged the question and I didn't persist. But that made me mad to see him get up there in a Christian church and not tell the truth.

"Oh, he was attempting to espouse what the Jewish community was doing—doing all these good things for everybody and what the Jewish goal was. It was Rothschild's goal to tell how good the Jews were, because he needed to dispel or try to cover up all these facts that were going around the country. It was well known in Congress and in the armed forces. So he didn't mention any of that. He was just up there to tell what a wonderful organization the Jews had.

"But he made a couple of bad misstatements—*bad* misstatements—and I called him on it."

Bright later composed a typewritten, third-person account of some of his experiences, including the night at First Baptist.

The assistant pastor of the First Baptist Church in Atlanta, Georgia, invited a Jewish Rabbi by the name of Rothschild to come to the Baptist Church and explain Judaism to the Christian congregation. What sincere member of the Christian religion could even think of such a thing when all of her or his time should be spent explaining and learning her or his own chosen Christian religion. Anyway, George M. Bright, true to his chosen Christian religion decided to go into action for his Christian religion and carried a sign in front of the Baptist church in his disapproval of the Jewish Rabbi's appearance there. Members of the Baptist church, so-called Christians, took the sign away from George Bright and destroyed it. George Bright then entered the church and after the Jewish Rabbi's lecture on Judaism, during the open question and answer period, George Bright openly disagreed with some remarks and assertions of the Rabbi. Then the head man of the church at that time, assistant pastor Smith, ordered George Bright to leave the church. George Bright left the church.

Rothschild finished up the evening and headed out through a flurry of apologies and gruff pats on the shoulder. Outside, the city was quiet, bathed in starlight; crickets sang from the square front yards. Rothschild drove along peaceful streets, his tires droning on the cement, through working-class white neighborhoods. Who knew in which of the small wooden houses Jewhaters lived? These would not be eloquent or dangerous public anti-Semites like Bright, but everyday Americans, men who threw footballs to their sons on the grass and watched their daughters zigzagging down the sidewalk on roller skates, and casually, if it came up, told their children the primeval secret that Jews were Shylocks, nigger-lovers, God-killers. Jews were the only people on earth ever accused by others of murdering God, an accusation that attributed to them depthless evil and almost-infinite power. The ancient devilish indictment had chased the accused out of the fertile crescent and across Greece and Rome, hounded them out of Spain and England, sent them spinning back and forth across Europe, murdered them by the millions, and pursued them—him, Jack Rothschild, from Pittsburgh, Pennsylvania—into a church full of Baptists on Peachtree Street on a cool spring evening nearly two thousand years later. Behind the neatly drawn curtains of Bright's neighborhood, Rothschild imagined, were families whose feeling of being pinched by life caused them occasionally to turn resentful eyes on people named "Rich," "Goldstein," "Haas," or "Heyman."

At home he joked to Janice about the fact that someone had found him important enough to picket. But it was not just him. He was seen as a front.

Bright drove around Atlanta, too, that night, but he saw different scenery.

The streets of Rothschild's neighborhood—where houses were set back from the curb on manicured lawns, with two modern cars in the carport—were those seen as most dangerous by Bright. In Bright's Atlanta, the scary houses were expensive ones in which black-haired foreigners lived, lighting candles on weekdays, eating strange fishy foods. He imagined a city deviously controlled by millionaire Jews who had had unpronounceable names until they had changed them.

Bright saw through the Jews' facade, observed that they were passing most successfully as average white Americans while, in fact, serving a different master: mammon. He was sharp-eyed in their neighborhoods as he drove circling along quiet, hedge-lined roads; he saw easily past their friendly veneers when they greeted him in the downtown shops they owned, their thick eyebrows darting up in expectation when the small bells over their entrances jingled. Bright drove home keen in the conviction that the Jews were feeding and profiting on American commerce while secretly draining the lifeblood from it. They took cross-continental phone calls late at night, speaking in weird syllables, not English, and they riled up the blacks, filling their fuzzy heads with radical desires, and it all worked toward the Jews' own sly, international purposes.

And the Baptists? The Reverend Smith would continue on the path he had begun; he was one of the signers of the Ministers' Manifesto calling for a measured approach to school desegregation in Atlanta. Some of the others were of two minds: sorry for the congenial rabbi that the meeting had busted up, and faintly curious about the urgent young man's warnings about the Jewish Bible and Jewish gold. They were not curious enough to pursue the topic or to attend a local meeting on the subject, though they might leaf through an article about it, should one turn up in, say, *Reader's Digest* or *Life.*

Look had, in fact, recently run a long feature article on American Jews, with photographs of snappy-looking uniformed Jews who had fought for America and a "Who's Who" page of photographs including the actor Kirk Douglas, the cartoonist Al Capp, the Supreme Court justice Felix Frankfurter, the baseball star Hank Greenberg, the physician Jonas Salk, the musician Benny Goodman, and the writer Saul Bellow. The article profiled a Jewish family, the Hurands, living in Flint, Michigan: "Neighborhood kids, Hurand and sons practice football plays in the big back yard of Art's five-bedroom brick home," read one caption, the banality and normalcy somehow newsworthy. "Bess Hurand is a Cub Scout den mother, Art is in Civil Defense and the Chamber of Commerce," read another, "but, as in many American towns, the local country club does not accept Jews." One large photo showed the family and their friends laughing uproariously over a Jewish joke: "Art and Bess Hurand, Reva and Harry Ratner, and Marvin Levey enjoy an explosive laugh over a Jewish story." "In time," the writer concluded, "American Jews will no longer be regarded as 'different'—any more than Quakers are today."

It's unlike the Southern Baptists knew any Quakers either, or regarded them as anything other than extremely "different" if they did. Whether readers of the cheery article accepted Look's guarantee of the harmlessness, conventionality, and fun-lovingness of American Jews is impossible to know.

Truth was probably somewhere in between, most white southerners believed in those years. A cheery, middle-of-the-road, noncommittal approach was the safest route home from a Brotherhood meeting in the South in the 1950s.

10

Against the Chosen and Circumcised Elite

1

Discreetly, covertly they met, the spring and summer of 1958, the elite corps of the Atlanta branch of the National States' Rights Party (NSRP). First they converged on a two-room apartment in midtown Atlanta. Then, on an industrial road east of downtown that split soft, corrugated fields, they rented office space in a two-story building and drove out there on appointed nights. Hugging briefcases, they hurried across the gravel parking lot in their street shoes and took the lower stairs of the interior stairwell two at a time.

Most were men who held indoor jobs; their thin arms looked toothpicky and white, poking out of their short-sleeve business shirts. The clandestine fraternity realized that they might appear—to a truck-driving, shit-kicking type on a visit to Atlanta from Cordele or Jesup—to be a bunch of weaklings: George Bright, a cotton-mill engineer; Wallace Allen, a telephone salesman, handicapped from childhood polio; Chester Griffin, a perplexed-looking fellow who worked as an income-tax examiner for the state revenue office; L. E. Rogers, a slipshod janitorial

205

services man; Richard Bowling, a foul-talking, red-faced young drunkard known to rough up his mother for pocket change; and his brother, Robert Bowling, a sharp-dressing, Hollywood-handsome, dark-haired homosexual—the two of them, the Bowling brothers, known for having been fond of playing with dynamite as kids in Atlanta's public housing projects. They were hardened, their leaders felt, by their awareness of evil. Hitler they accepted, incorporated into their viewpoint; the Jewish people were evil.

In summer the earth tilted Georgia closer to the sun's broiler: African Americans in the cotton fields blackened, and white workers on the farms browned and burned like hard loaves of bread. On *behalf* of the sun-darkened white men in the rural counties—those who were shouldering hundred-pound sacks, steering tractors, slaughtering hogs, and shouting orders at niggers—on *their behalf*, the pale, time-clock-punching Atlanta men met after hours, shook hands, found chairs, and got down to business, distributing mimeographed sheets.

Around the collapsible table they met, drinking Coca-Colas from the soft-drink machine in the stairwell; some of them, bored, pressed the cold bottles against their hot foreheads, for despite the heat of the night, the leaders slammed the windows shut in case there were spies in the street. They spoke in clipped phrases and rugged voices—they were outlaws together, like the movie star James Dean. They chain-smoked and gave added emphasis to their snide remarks by jabbing cigarette butts into the new plastic ashtrays proudly fished out of a small grocery sack by one of the members. Their tough talk included: "Let's go kill a Jew" and "How many crosses could we burn in nigger town tonight without getting caught?" They cooked up far-fetched plans. They talked of going to the roof of the Fulton National Bank Building in downtown Atlanta with thousands of anti-Semitic leaflets and throwing them to the wind, to be carried to the far corners of the city. They planned to put leaflets inside newspapers and make them available in drugstores and at the public library. They discussed infiltrating the KKK in order "to put across the Anti-Jewish idea or to enlighten the white race concerning the Jewish conspiracy against the white people." One said he had traced the genealogy of Captain R. E. Little, the head of the bombing task force for the Atlanta police detectives, and had found him to be of Jewish origin: "He is a Jew and the FBI is completely affiliated with the ADL agents and is under control of the Jews." One told about Jews in a barbed-wire fence in Hungary who were sprayed with oil and burned alive; the men laughed and another of them said, "If local conditions ever develop between ourselves and the Jews we ought to just go to our homes and get our guns and go out and shoot them down on the streets, in the stores and shops, wherever we find them."

George Bright made himself available to escort John Kasper upon his release from federal incarceration. Kasper was a notorious segregationist and anti-Semite, a rabble-rousing speaker on the Klan circuit, the founder of the Seaboard White Citizens' Council, and the man largely responsible for the 1956 anti-school-integration violence in Clinton, Tennessee, which required the National Guard to quell it. Kasper served time in prison for anti-governmental violence and in 1964 would be the NSRP candidate for president. Bright drove with Rogers and a nineteen-year-old NSRP organizer named Billy Branham to the Atlanta penitentiary, picked up Kasper, and chauffeured him to the Biltmore Hotel.

One night a member reported that he had phoned Ralph McGill, debated him on the race question, called him a "dirty rat," and hung up. On another night the group's resident intellectual and inventor, George Bright, showed the men a state-of-the-art Japanese-made range finder, or telescope. He proposed that they aim it toward Jacobs Drugstore down the block from their office and observe the Jews.

Allen said he knew how to get a book by a Russian author: "It tells the intricate method for a small revolutionary group to effect a revolution," Rogers recalled him saying. "Lenin started his movement with a small group of people and he was able to take over Russia because of the printing press; he was able to unite small parties and therefore effect a complete overthrow of the existing regime and take over the country."

"The government of the United States is outmoded and archaic and fit for horse-and-buggy days," said Allen on another occasion. "It lacks the means to maintain a white society due to the Jewish conspiracy against the white race and the Jewish control of the press."

"We met," George Bright said simply, "to discuss what the

local Communist Party was doing and how to combat it." (In fact, there was no local Communist Party.)

"The primary objective of this group," said Rogers, "concerned not integration or segregation but the Jewish question."

Where had these men come from? How had they found one another? For those hoping to get involved, those Americans infuriated by what they read in their newspapers or saw on TV, a national network of secret resistance societies was taking shape in the 1950s; names and addresses were shared among regional headquarters of like-minded organizations. One phone call or letter was sufficient to establish contact. Griffin later explained how he had been included in the loop: "I first became interested in these organizations around the time that the Supreme Court handed down its decision in 1954 on segregation," he said. "I had prior to that time supported Strom Thurmond for president and been a strong believer in states rights and segregation." Griffin, thirty-two, who worked for the Georgia State Revenue Office, had a bland, open-mouthed face and an unfocused look in his eyes, and he favored checkered short-sleeved shirts and greasy, back-combed hair; most of the other men thought him dopey. "Chester Griffin was just a loner," said an old acquaintance, "and was just looking for a place to know somebody. He was a typical Southern boy, old maiden aunts put him through school, too lazy to do anything but eat, never did anything but run his mouth."

Griffin liked the sound of John Kasper. "During the Clinton controversy in 1956," said Griffin, "I contacted John Kasper and other people up there—I got their names out of the *Knoxville Journal*—and they wrote back. I heard from the Seaboard White Citizens Council in Washington, D.C., Kasper's organization and from the Iowa Constitution Party and it had Ed Fields' name on there. I wrote Ed Fields. And then, November of '57, I got a letter from a Kentucky White Citizens Council telling me about a big meeting they were going to have in Louisville, and asking me to attend. I was unable to do so, and shortly after that, I received a letter telling me about a meeting to be held at Knoxville, Tennessee, by the United White Party. . . . Then, one night in March of '58, I got a knock at the door, I went there, it was Billy Branham. He introduced himself and said he had been sent down by Ed Fields from Louisville."

Matt Koehl, the national NSRP organizer, had targeted Atlanta. He assigned a staff member, nineteen-year-old Billy Branham, to do initial footwork, including contacting the man, Chester Griffin, who had written to Fields. Then Koehl drove down himself in May 1958 to speak to a small cadre of men at a series of night meetings.

At the founding meeting of the Atlanta unit, Koehl addressed a small band of men—George Bright and his brother, Albert Bright; Wallace Allen, Chester Griffin; and L. E. Rogers— who gathered in Branham's apartment to listen. A few sat on kitchen chairs; someone sat on the bed. "Matt Koehl was engaged in political activity in behalf of Admiral Crommelin, who was running for Governor of the State of Alabama, and he was discussing with the group his method," said Rogers. "Matt was telling us about how they had been successful in getting some TV time, and without any hopes of really gaining any votes, but it was to expound and explain the Jewish question and to acquaint the people of Alabama with the Jewish conspiracy against the white race." Suddenly, interrupting discussion, George Bright jumped up, grabbed his flashlight, and dashed outside. "I went with him," said Rogers, "and he went out shining it up in the trees around the house. I asked him what he was doing and he said he was looking up in the trees for FBI men. He thought maybe FBI men were listening to the meeting."

Once the excitement died down, Koehl returned to the prepared agenda. "Matt Koehl had a sheet from the local newspaper, *Atlanta Journal* or *Constitution*, I don't recall which," said Rogers, "and it had a picture of the synagogue where they were tearing it down to make way for the expressway, and there was a large headline that said: 'Shed no tears. It is progress.' When he showed me and the group [we had] kind of a round-robin discussion that the group had a sympathizer in the composing room of the *Atlanta Constitution*."

Rogers was a chunky man with dark hair that stood up in short spindles all over his head, like that of a freshly cropped young boy. Forty-one years old, a ninth-grade dropout, divorced and remarried, he had a chronic weight problem and a chronic cash-flow problem. His wardrobe was apparently in decline—socks mismatched, business shirts wrinkled and stained—and he could be counted on to bum other men's cigarettes. He was a small-time janitorial services contractor who employed a few black men and cleaned offices after hours, but he had also recently driven a laundry truck, worked at the Mohawk Rubber Company, done maintenance work at Children's Hospital, worked at Lockheed Aircraft, and cleaned the Hurt Building. Everywhere he went, he found himself met by the same mild aversion: men who looked up when he opened the door quickly looked down. Even in these closeted circles of the extreme right-wing, Rogers managed to seem overeager and without finesse. He was the sort of man who fabricates a social life not from "By Invitation Only" events, but by turning up at meetings of organizations so desperate for members that they will take anybody.

The group elected officers at their first meeting. Nearly everyone present won a post. Branham, the local organizer, was elected temporary chairman at their first meeting; Griffin, vice-chairman; Rogers, secretary-treasurer and security officer; Allen, local organizer; and George Bright, security officer.

The Atlanta bunch promptly argued for local autonomy. They objected to the Thunderbolt symbol, wanting to invent their own. "We informed Koehl that we wanted to maintain control over it," said Griffin, "over the strictly local actions here. A week later a meeting was held at the same place—Matt Koehl again spoke to us. We decided that until we became stronger it was best to be secret about our existence, knowing that we would be smeared and knocked down before we ever had time to gain any strength, before people would understand our objectives were legal and above-board. At this meeting we decided to rent us an office. L. E. Rogers volunteered that he would help to rent that office."

--- ═◆═ ---

The first two meetings at the fledgling group's new headquarters, on Flat Shoals Road east of Atlanta, were devoted to cleaning up the place.

"We cleaned the office and swept the floors and wiped down the blinds and what not," said Rogers. "And when we finished cleaning the office George Bright and Chester Griffin checked the building over, they felt the brick in the fireplace and tapped the tile in the floor and the baseboard and checked the hinges on the doors on the inside for secret mikes that the FBI might have hidden in the office to overhear conversations that might take place." The group authorized George Bright to purchase seven chairs.

The history of the founding of the Atlanta unit of the NSRP goes on and on in this vein, absurdly disingenuous, a true founder's tale, consisting not of thrilling speeches, stirring public appearances, and swelling ranks of men, but of the frequent annoyance of having to cough up five dollars of nonresidential rent money and of the strain of heaving a secondhand desk up the stairs to the office with too few men on hand (and those few not athletic types) to get it hoisted without placing the members in brief physical jeopardy in the stairwell.

Griffin recalled:

> The next meeting we held was back over at Billy's, and at this time we talked about getting equipment for the office and getting it in shape so we could use it and there wasn't anything said much about any political activities, it was chiefly devoted to getting the office in shape. Then, the next meeting towards the last of May '58 . . . we discussed a press release, whether or not we should release a statement to the press about our existence and our activities and our aims, and that was the chief topic of discussion and, other than that, the only thing we discussed was taking up money to pay the rent because it was due again, and we broke up fairly early.

Most great endeavors—social movements, the founding of nations—are generated from just this blend of fantastic ambition, on the one hand, and rented halls lined with empty folding chairs, on the other, where only six people have shown up out of the metropolis to hear the much-heralded speaker, and one of those has mistaken it for a gathering of ornithologists and another has to leave early to get to his bowling league. The NSRP mistook its own vast and dark designs for political power; the members wavered confusedly over whether they should maintain secrecy while growing in strength, or call a press conference and announce their presence so that the populace could be prepared for the takeover.

Griffin said:

> We carried the desk up which L. E. Rogers had given to us, and had waited for Billy Branham and George Bright to fix us a sign. We had a short meeting this time because our light fixture, our light, wasn't fixed yet so we broke up early and went on home, and last meeting was Wednesday night at Billy Branham's house and L. E. Rogers agreed to get the management to get our light fixture fixed and George Bright was to get us some chairs and I was to get some ash trays before the next meeting.

Could not Tom Paine, Vladimir Lenin, Theodore Herzl, and Mao Zedong share similar memories?

> Then our next meeting . . . we again met over there at the office and this time we had chairs and a light fixture—our lights had been fixed and plaster had been fixed, and we all worked on a decal on the door. . . . We had two new men there, and I don't know what their names was, they stayed only a short while. We explained our platform and we discussed the book, 'Know Your Enemy' and outside of that there wasn't much of any other subject taken up. . . .
>
> On June 17 we again had a meeting at the office and [talked about] whether or not we should obtain an American flag since Alaska had recently been admitted to the Union and [the flag] might be shortly changed and we agreed to take that up at the next meeting.

At a meeting at the end of May, George Bright said he was in the process of inventing a portable folding cross that could be easily transported by car, quickly erected at a target site, and set afire. He was designing it for a movie theater on Ponce de Leon Avenue that was about to be leased—or so rumor had it—by a black man. At the July 2 meeting, the men discussed spraying a grass-killing chemical on the lawn of the Jewish Temple on Peachtree Street in the shape of a swastika.

Two of the men drove to the Atlanta airport occasionally: a real undercover job! They wore sports shirts and strolled amiably through the terminal, hands in pockets, jingling their change and looking cheerily about, then laid their hands on a wrapped box waiting for them in the package department and beat it back to their car. The package was their lifeline, the literature for study and distribution mailed to them by the national leadership. The materials they received bore the imprint of "The National Committee to Free America from Jewish Domination" and included brochures entitled "The Jewishness of World Communism" and "Are Jews Communists?"

Some were like children playing at war with peeled greenbean cans for walkie-talkies and stockpiled pecans for an arsenal, who bark out movie phrases like "Cover me, Joe!" and draw maps in the dirt with sticks. They felt ready to go to war: here were the headquarters and the mean, warlike talk to prove it.

But they were not all bumblers, weekend warriors, foulmouthed slanderers who would not hurt a fly. They did not all devote months of meetings to getting the lights turned on, to assigning this sublieutenant to bring some ice to the next meeting and that one, some pretzels. There were those who did not mistake the NSRP for a sort of gun-toting Kiwanis Club, or Cub Scouts for adults. The national leaders of American grassroots fascism, including several men in the Atlanta area, were not playing. Their veiled letters and ambiguous statements concealed cross-country transfers of hate literature and money and the technology of bombs. They saw themselves as an intellectual elite fully capable of governing America. With their bombs, they thought to strike at the vipers' nests, at the headquarters of those who were ruining the country.

2

Long after business hours, the NSRP crowd, like-minded, disenchanted, disconnected men drifted around Atlanta, running into each other on street corners and at all-night diners where they took time to repeat and reaffirm their maddened ideology, handing around from the trunks of their cars the latest literature, the newest scientific findings. Absent serious purpose, they had to create the illusion of serious purpose; thus, in the middle of the most banal, time-wasting, mind-numbing hours of the hot and pointlessly wakeful night, George Bright and his regulars—who, by the summer of 1958, included Allen, the Bowlings and J.B. Stoner—spontaneously set up shop and argued race and Jews and Communism while waiting for the waitress to bring their eggs, steaks, and Coca-Colas. In the larger society they were known, generically, as "race agitators," but no one seemed as agitated as they themselves: jittery, chain-smoking, loud and interrupting, peripatetic, insomniac.

Richard Bowling was tall, with wavy blonde hair, and smoked a pipe. He was a former member of the Christian Anti-Jewish Party and had picketed the White House in 1954. Robert, more reserved, dark-haired, was the frequent sidekick of Stoner. "When Richard was sober, he had lovely manners," said an old acquaintance. "Their grandmother's money sent him and Robert to Catholic school till they set the mattresses on fire. Richard was a wolf in sheep's clothing. Robert was never involved in any criminal way with that whole crowd. A top musician at the Atlanta symphony kept him, a very talented man. Robert had tickets to the symphony."

Allen lived in a ranch house north of the city and did advertising work for the Atlanta United Automobile Workers under the name Allen Advertising Agency. He, like Stoner, walked with difficulty as a result of childhood polio. The bitter-looking thirty-two-year-old could have been handsome. His smooth skin was pulled tight over high cheekbones and jutting forehead and bald skull, and his deep-set eyes looked out from within this clean, rocklike promontory of a head. But he kept his jaw tight, eyes slit, thin lips compressed, an expression on his face as if he were swinging a heavy club against an approaching enemy while feeling himself backed up by idiots. And, with one leg shorter than the other, he was forced to wear a leg brace, a sore point all his life. He was married to a delicate woman. Sammie Margaret Summers Allen, then thirty-one, was "small as a porcelain doll, [with] a whispery voice, reddish hair and glasses." They had two small children at home and a third on the way.

As a young man, Allen had won a scholarship to the Pratt Institute in New York. He had hated the city. On Christmas Eve one year he had leaned his crutches against the wall in a bar, and the crutches had been stolen. Without cab fare, he had had to drag his bad right foot through the city back to his rented room.

He held passionate, explosively expressed beliefs about society—his angry talk was littered with the epithets "Jews" and "niggers." "His politics," a reporter once observed, "in my opinion are slightly to the right of slavery." He was by nature a loner; he loved his wife and children fiercely, but he lacked the capacity to be either a leader or a follower of men. Mistrust was primary with him, so that he found conspiracy theories to be as plain and obvious as principles of natural science; his personal disasters and the decline of civilization seemed entwined. He would see plenty of both, for he was in for a difficult life: infant polio and lifelong physical handicap; parents divorcing; his first son, Matthew, born in 1956 with ruined kidneys, promised only a short life, then hit by a car while bike riding and killed at the age of nine.

Allen respected some fine pristine notion of "America," recognizing it chiefly in the breach. His elemental cynicism kept him aloof. He had sought out the NSRP in Tennessee, Texas, Kansas, and now Atlanta, in the faint hope of channeling his bitter furies into some central purpose; he showed up and listened in case a miracle should occur and someone should utter an intelligent thought. In IQ he was the peer of Bright, Fields, and Stoner, while the majority of the right-wing extremists seemed to him to be fools, blowhards, chatterboxes, double agents, or lonely guys hungry for a welcome. He limped away from these meetings as disgusted as ever. "My husband felt that when he made contact with Chester Griffin and the Bowling boys at the NSRP meetings," said Mrs. Allen, "that it was like the tar baby, hard to get loose of them." In September 1958, however, Richard Bowling began working for Allen as a telephone salesman, earning commission. He visited the Allens often in the evenings "just for conversational reasons."

As he sold ads for union newspapers, Allen worked with

Jews, but he despised them as a group. Since 1954 he had believed that they were behind desegregation. He believed civil rights to be destructive of America and a plot of Jewish Communists. "Very intelligent, loquacious and highly nervous," was the impression of an Atlanta police detective. "Thinks the Jews are responsible for present integration program; that the Jews are Communistic at heart; hates the political activities of the Jews; does not hate the Jews as such; his concern is to preserve America for Americans and to maintain segregation."

"He had strong ideas, but he was real gentle in his way," said Mrs. Allen. "He had plenty of faults, but he didn't do anything violent. He had decided opinions about what was going on in our country. He just didn't believe that we were all alike. I really think he was a misunderstood person. I didn't agree with a lot of the things he said but I think a person ought to be able to associate with any kind of person. I feel like Jesus was accepting of everyone."

Trapped in a state of furious paralysis—wanting chiefly to strike out at everyone and everything, but to do so in intelligent company—Allen found it necessary to kill time. He later gave an account of a typical evening with the NSRP crowd:

> I went to the Plaza Drug Store at the corner of Highland and Ponce de Leon. I called George Bright just to talk to him and he said he would be right over. We talked on the street corner for awhile, then went in the drug store about 10 or 12 o'clock. We had not been there long when a woman came up and said she saw me everywhere she went, or something to that effect. One of us, I think George, asked her to be seated. She was there about ten minutes when I noticed she was becoming hostile for no reason. I asked her to leave and she refused so I asked the policeman on the beat who came in to ask her to leave. He did and she left, George got up and followed her out. I drove down Ponce de Leon. A car was stalled in front of me so I had to wait through a green light. As I waited, J. B. Stoner and the Bowling boys drove up beside me. We both pulled our cars over to the Gulf station. J. B. had a book called "Our Nordic Race" and we discussed its contents for awhile. We then got into my car and we

drove to the Magic Grill to eat. I had soup and the others had steak or something. We then drove back to the Gulf station. J. B. & Robert said they were sleepy and I remember someone commenting on the lateness of the hour which was three o'clock.

The woman who irritated Allen—whose decibel level fell somewhere between "spunky" and vulgar—briefly interested George Bright. Marilyn Craig was in the process of a messy separation from her husband, Pete Craig. Their two sons, ages sixteen and ten, lived with their father. Within the month, Pete Craig would commit his wife to a mental institution on a sanity warrant and she would be declared incompetent; she would later proclaim the whole mess to be the result of the animosity generated by their pending divorce. Forty years old, she was a night owl like Bright and his confederates, and often felt the need for a newspaper or a pharmaceutical supply at midnight or 1:00 A.M. She would drive from her house north of the city into town to visit the all-night drugstore on Ponce de Leon, Plaza Drugs. "They *happen* to be open all night long. It's the only one in the city of Atlanta that is," she said defensively, feistily, in the gritty voice of a hard-luck, chain-smoking woman who finds herself to be full of pluck, though others may find her to be simply ill bred. "I had gone there at late hours of the night on many occasions. At that particular time, I went to obtain a newspaper after having tried several different spots out on my own side of town. . . . At eleven o'clock at night what did you ever find open? Quite frankly, I would get also a cup of coffee. Sometimes I would order a sandwich. I frequently chatted with the cashier. Many people do that."

She recalled the origins of her brief nonaffair with Bright: "On this particular night, when I was leaving the pharmacy, someone whom I knew slightly . . . someone I do know by sight slightly . . . Wallace Allen stopped me and asked me sort of a general question and said, 'I would like to have you meet a friend of mine.' He and George Bright were seated at a table. Mr. Allen and I had a slight little disagreement. It didn't amount to too much. He asked me to sit down and I sat down on the outside, and he said something to me. Anyway, I gave him the answer and he said, 'Leave, if you don't like it.' He said, 'Just *get* up,' and *I* said, 'Listen, my friend, you invited me to sit down, and I'll be damned if you are going to make me get up.' I was a little provoked at the manner that he used." Allen called over a police officer to throw her out, but Craig then stood and said: "Well, he certainly don't have to. I was leaving anyway. I *just* had a little discussion with him."

Bright courteously pursued her to make amends. "George followed me out and apologized to me, and we sat and talked for quite a little while. Might even stretch it and call that a pick-up. It *could* be called a pick-up, or we might even call it the other way around, because we left in my automobile. You could say I picked him up if you want to. If you want to, it wouldn't bother me in the least."

They spent the first of several mornings before dawn organizing themselves to observe an extraterrestrial event. "We found we had a mutual interest which happened to be in . . . satellites. We observed the stars [for] quite a little while. The rest of the evening . . . we were together. Part of the time we were riding. We were parked for a very short while, roughly about thirty or forty minutes. Holding hands? Yes, we did hold hands. It was a cold night . . . By that time it was Sunday morning. We went to Bradshaw's and had breakfast. We then spent most of the day at my house; and that night I do not exactly recall except that we were together. . . . I did see a good bit of him over a period of two weeks."

◄ ═◆═ ►

Bright went home one night and, feeling spiritually inclined, wrote an invocation, with which he opened the next NSRP meeting: "Our Heavenly Father, we beseech Thee to know that we will fight this battle to our last ounce of energy and the enemy's last drop of blood."

In May, Bright picketed and heckled Rothschild at the brotherhood meeting at First Baptist Church.

In July, the NSRP prepared for its first "action," the picketing of the offices of the *Atlanta Constitution and Journal*.

3

The Atlanta group had been personally encouraged to picket by George Lincoln Rockwell, probably the best-known anti-Semite in the country, described by the newspaper columnist Drew Pearson as "the young führer who lives in Arlington and displays a Nazi swastika inside his home with the door open every evening." A forty-year-old World War II navy pilot, a husky, dark-haired man with a buzz haircut, the son of a famous prewar radio comedian, "Old Doc" Rockwell, George Lincoln Rockwell had reentered the navy during the Korean War and had been sent to Iceland. It was there that he had become obsessed with the world Jewish conspiracy and read *Mein Kampf* for the first time. He married the niece of the Icelandic ambassador to the United States and honeymooned with her at Berchtesgaden, the Bavarian town in which Hitler, Göring, and Bormann had maintained fortified mountain retreats.

Rockwell was a printer and national distributor of anti-Semitic materials. On his basement printing press he turned out the pieces marked "National Committee to Free America from Jewish Domination." In a newspaper interview in 1958, he explained that he was not *anti-Semitic*, because that term would also include Arabs. "I am anti-Zionist and anti-Communist Jews and any other form of treason. I'm pro-American Republic. We derive our idea from Adolf Hitler. We admire him for his genius, his ideas. We are not German Nazis and we do not believe we should exterminate Jews." He emphasized that he did not condone violence, but agreed that he was opposed to "Jews as a group." He called the Holocaust "a monstrous and profitable fraud" and circulated the disinformation that the six million "later died happily and richly in the Bronx, New York." In correspondence, Rockwell used code words to elude detection: *Eskimo* meant "Jew"; *Eskimo land* was "Israel"; and *Eskimo conquest of Russia* was "the Red Revolution." In 1959 he founded the American Nazi Party. He remained a leader of American anti-Semitic activities until 1964 when he was shot to death by one of his own troops.

In July 1958, Rockwell phoned Wallace Allen to let him in on plans for nationwide picketing against America's Jew-slanted approach to the Middle East. Rockwell had worked for Allen a few months the previous year, moving his family to a trailer park in Atlanta to do so, but Allen had considered Rockwell a tremendous financial drain and had severed ties with him. The phone call therefore startled him. "Rockwell was heavily in debt and needed more money than he could make with [my] husband," said Allen's wife. "[My] husband remarked that he was surprised that Rockwell would consult him considering the differences they had had," she said, "but since they held basically the same political beliefs about the Middle Eastern situation (the time that Ike sent the troops into Lebanon), [he said] that he would see what he could do."

Rockwell had located a wealthier benefactor than Allen had proved to be, and he was eager to boast to Allen about his new friend. Harold Noel Arrowsmith Jr., the rich son of the late canon of Baltimore's Episcopal cathedral, was a self-described anthropologist who had a spare twenty thousand dollars to spend on anti-Communist and anti-Jewish activities. At the University of Mainz in Germany, he had studied the origin of the races, attempting to demonstrate that the Nordics and the Mediterranean people were not the same race; in the Library of Congress he pored over microfilm searching for proof of the Jewish-Communist conspiracy.

Enthused by Allen's civil response on the phone, feeling flush, Rockwell followed up the phone conversation with a letter:

It was wonderful to talk to you on the phone! Made me realize how feeble and uninformed most of the so-called "hardcore" is, just by contrast.

So please forgive the lack of amenities and proper narratives of how all this happened. Suffice to say that we are finally beginning to DO what we have all so long talked about, mostly thanks to ONE "Fat Cat" as X used to call them, who is putting his $$$ where his mouth is, God bless him.

The Enclosed "hate-mongering" [leaflets and posters] will give you an idea of the caliber of material we are preparing to roast the Jews alive in the fire of truth as it were.

[We will go] all out on the stickers, which are the ultimate weapon against the Jew, because he can't see where he's getting hit from—the technique he himself has been using to knock us all off.

People who won't even publicly admit that there are such things as Jews have been sneaking up to get a supply of these "Communism is Jewish" stickers to put up privately in the right place.

The big blast is all set for either next Sunday or Saturday, if there is local ordinance forbidding picketings, etc. on Sunday

There are three items for handbills:

1. An inflammatory explanation of WHY we seem to be having trouble in the Middle East, coupled with an announcement of the picketing and an invitation to come and hoot at the Jews with us.

2. A documented, damning INFORMATION sheet to hand out at the "ceremonies" to establish exactly what Israel has done and is doing and generally to anger the citizenry at the traducers of our country and traditions, etc.

3. Membership applications for The American National Committee to Free America from Jewish Domination—local chapter—(the results of this will be all yours in your area—if you want to and can handle it).

There will also be a sort of information sheet to be sure that all the demonstrations are well COORDINATED and OBVIOUSLY NATIONAL in scope. We think the Jews are just a little off balance for once right now—and a NATIONAL and EFFECTIVE blast at them right now will, we hope, tip them just enough so that they will come out from behind some of the brotherhood a bit and let Americans see their dirty soul.

All the rest will be coming along following this— and, I hope will bring a glow of warmth to your cheeks as you realize we are about to kick hell out of these who have been driving us into the ground for so long. The worm has turned, and is armed with CASH!—a very powerful weapon in our present society.

... It will be wonderful to be working with you again. ... We both want you to know we have nothing in our hearts for you and ———— but the warmest feelings of gratitude and respect and friendship. Our "differences"— as you called them—were the result of the same old relentless pressure of imminent starvation (etc.)—which in turn are the results of the operations of the Chosen and circumcised elite whom we are about to start on their way to their reward.

The "big blast," Rockwell later explained, under dour questioning by the Atlanta police after the Temple bombing, referred to the planned picketing.

Allen affably wrote back:

Dear Linc,

Congratulations on having obtained arms to fight the enemy. I hope the "Fat Cat" realized the necessity for a continuing and relentless assault as, for instance, a weekly attack by TRUTH against the DAILY LIARS.

The exact method we will use here is still undecided and is entirely dependent on existing conditions which will be examined thoroughly. You will just have to trust we will do the best job possible with the means at hand. The Israeli consulate is next door to the F.B.I. if there is any significance to that. The Temple would be wrong since it relates to the religious rather than the political. Next is choosing picketers who are the most immune from Jewish economic retaliation, Etc. But I'll figure out something.

The Stickers are great but I'll have to criticize some of the other. The piece from the American Hebrew is too subtle for the ordinary Goyim mind.

Allen called a meeting with Bright, Griffin, Branham, and Rogers to propose the picketing to them.

The men drove to the airport on Sunday, July 27, 1958, to pick up picket signs shipped by Rockwell. Identical signs had been used by Rockwell to picket the White House. The signs were part of his campaign to enlist Arab allies in their fight against international Jewry. Rockwell reportedly sent letters and photographs of his propagandistic activities to President Gamal Abdel Nasser of Egypt, though no evidence exists that Nasser repaid the attention. When Allen saw Rockwell's signs, he was revolted. One said "Save Ike from the Kikes" and pictured a cringing Eisenhower at the feet of a gun-wielding Jew. "[My] husband disapproved of the signs—he considered them entirely too radical," said Allen's wife, meaning, most likely, that he found them obvious and stupid. "[He stated] that he would have nothing to do with any picket demonstration in which those signs were used. . . . When [my] husband refused to have anything to do with these signs, they printed signs of their own to use. They were mainly concerned with suppression of the news by the *Atlanta Journal & Constitution* concerning the Middle [East] crises."

On July 27, 1958, the *Journal and Constitution* building became the first local target of the NSRP. Five pickets—including Bright and Griffin—protested, bearing signs that said: "Nasser outlawed the Communists and jailed his Reds, but your Jewish press lies that the Arabs are Reds" and "Jews Control Press, Suppress News" and "The Jewish-Controlled Press Lies about the Middle East."

Allen had stayed home. Bright, Griffin, and Luther King Corley were arrested. "We picketed only a short while," said Griffin, "before the police swooped down in typical Gestapo fashion. [This was an odd complaint, coming from a neo-Nazi.] They wanted to know if we were armed and what we were trying to do—start a riot? and a lot of ridiculous assertions and absurd questions, and instead of following the example of Washington, D.C., where the police furnished protection to the picketers, these police were bent on making us victims of persecution and so they loaded us all into a police car and carried us down to the police station where we were interrogated and insulted and called Communists and all manner of abuse was heaped on our heads."

Allen hired the attorney James Venable to represent the picketers. Arrowsmith sent two hundred fifty dollars to Allen to help defray the attorney's fees, as did Russell McGuire, an editor of *American Mercury*. The men were sentenced in municipal court to thirty days on a prison farm. The sentences were appealed, and the men were released.

Griffin very nearly lost his job at the state revenue office as the result of his arrest and conviction, though he was unaware of this. Revenue Commissioner T. V. Williams later said that he had considered removing Griffin from the payroll at that time and had not done so at the request of some Jewish leaders who did not want to stir up unnecessary trouble.

The *Journal* printed an editorial to remind readers: "Atlanta's Jews are among the best and finest citizens in the city and Atlanta would not be what it is without them." And Rothschild's sermons were being reprinted by the Atlanta newspapers. "If it is religion's province to speak out on social issues, then what does it have to say on the subject of racial equality?" he asked in a sermon carried in the Sunday paper. "The spirit of the Bible—both Old Testament and New—is clear and unequivocal: All men are created equal." He, too, wrote an invocation that he offered to the readers of the *Journal and Constitution*: "O Lord, quicken us to work with the righteous of all nations and creeds, to bring about Thy kingdom upon earth, so that hatred among men shall cease, the walls of prejudice and pride separating people shall crumble and fall, and war be destroyed forever."

No wonder Bright felt he ought to go home and write his own damn prayer.

4

To resist and expose the Jews' vast and sticky web, the men of the NSRP had only themselves and their thin network of like-minded souls and benefactors. They had less than only themselves, really, for this was no brave, tight band of loyal knights: a few of them were surveying the others around the table with disappointment and contempt. Although Rockwell had stated, "There is just one problem with our movement: 90 percent of the members are lunatics," Bright or Allen might have said it differently: "The main problem with our movement," either might have said, "is that 90 percent of our members are morons."

"My husband thought Chester Griffin was not mentally

competent," recalls Allen's widow. "He did not think highly of Bobby Bowling. His brother, Richard Bowling, had the intelligence but he was mixed-up. My husband would go to attend the NSRP meetings, but he didn't join anything. He wasn't a joiner. . . . My husband felt the group had been infiltrated and these others just weren't aware, and he didn't want to get tangled up in things with them."

Allen was especially suspicious of the motives and behavior of L. E. Rogers, the owner of the janitorial services company. Allen wrote down his recollections of an NSRP gathering on the weekend of August 30, 1958. In red ink on mint-green stenographic pages, it reads:

> A social gathering, at a home on Dixie Highway in Louisville. We were all in the backyard (which was also a parking lot)—people were talking and taking pictures of one another—Rogers called me aside—over to his car and complimented me on the fine "hardcore" we had here, he said he had a "hardcore" of his own. I said that's fine—I thought he was referring to Segregationists—he then said, "Don't spread it around that I'm the Commander of the Confederate Underground" [a collective name for members of any of numerous right-wing extremist organizations, but not a single established group]. I thought he was either kidding or crazy. He then said he would like to get recruits from the N.S.R.P. I told him that this was a political group. He said he had an out-of-state nigger who could be depended on to do any dirty work and who knew how to handle explosives. He then got in his car—jumped up and down in the car seat and blew the horn five to six times. I considered him to be a harmless nut at that time and thought nothing further about the incident.

Allen was not the only one perturbed by the behavior of Rogers over that August weekend. The young NSRP organizer, Branham, recalled: "Mr. Rogers asked me, if I had the opportunity, would I kill a group of Jew babies? I answered no. He then said, 'Well, that's what it's going to take because little rats grow to be big rats.' "

J. D. Chapman, a Klansman of the J. E. Johnson #61 Marietta Klan, whose unit Rogers also joined, wrote:

> In the summer of 1958, he made the statement occasionally at several different meetings that Hitler had done a good [job] exterminating Jews. Because he did it in masses as we in America would have to do it singally [sic] until we could get a force big enough to take the masses. That you couldn't look to the Federal Government any more for the enforcement of constitutional government. He made the statement after meeting that we ought to go out and kill a Jew or blow up a nigger house. He said, "I wonder how many crosses we could set on fire in the nigger quarter and get away without the law catching us?" I reminded him of his oath as a Klansman never to violate the law and never to do anything to intimidate any one and never to advocate violence. In July or August of 1958, he made the statement that Hitler did a good job of "exterminating" a million or so Jews and what we needed was a Hitler in this country. . . . He also made the statement that the head of the NAACP is a Jew. . . . He many times advocated violence and hatred toward the Negro and Jewish races which is against the principals of the US Klans, Knights of the Ku Klux Klan.

"He said it was too late for prayer—what we needed was action," recalled another Klansman. "He spoke of how Hitler killed Jews in Germany, that he wished he had gotten over here for a while and we wouldn't be having the trouble we are having now with the Christ-killers."

Rogers's extremism and careless speech led more than one of his comrades to suspect that he was working for the other side. Such misgivings about Rogers expressed by NSRP members and Klansmen were endemic to resistance movements. In fact, so common was the thought that there were those in one's midst working for the enemy that one sentence crossed over into common humorous parlance: "The only ones paying dues here are the FBI spies."

5

On November 11, 1957, during services, eleven sticks of dynamite were found at Temple Beth-El in Charlotte, North Carolina.

On February 9, 1958, an overnight bag containing thirty sticks of 60 percent Giant Gelatin Powder, Atlas Explosive, was found at a synagogue in Gastonia, North Carolina. The fuse stuck out of a hole drilled into the top of the case; the rest of it lay coiled inside on top of the dynamite. The fuse had burned to within two inches of the cap.

A bomb severely damaged an Orthodox Miami synagogue on March 16, 1958, despite the fact that the rabbi carefully had refrained from public comment on the Negro question; a second rabbi in town, Abraham Levitan, received a threatening phone call on that day warning that his synagogue would be next if he did not stop preaching integration; and a third Miami rabbi, Tibor Stern, was told to remove a menorah from the front of his temple or his would be next.

Also on March 16, a bomb exploded at the Nashville Jewish Community Center, and Rabbi William Silverman of the Temple in Nashville received a phone call from "the Confederate Underground" warning him that his temple also would be bombed, that "nigger-loving people" would be shot, and that Federal Judge William Miller would be murdered for enforcing integration decisions.

On April 28, the Jacksonville Jewish Community Center was bombed, and Rabbi Sanders Tofield received a call from "the Confederate Union" warning that Jews must be "driven out of Florida except Miami Beach" or they would die.

Also on April 28, 1958, undetonated dynamite with burnt-out fuses was found at Temple Beth-El in Birmingham, Alabama. A black janitor found a blue canvas zippered bag containing fifty-four sticks of Giant Gelatin 60 percent dynamite. A fuse had burned down to five and and a half inches from the bag, and the second had burned down a bit closer. The caps were determined by detectives to be live caps.

Birmingham's commissioner of public safety, Eugene "Bull" Connor, who apparently possessed a softer spot for the Jews than for the blacks in his jurisdiction, took immediate investigative action following the discovery of the unexploded dynamite at the Birmingham temple. The investigation quickly centered on Stoner and his circle. On May 8, 1958, a former Klan leader from Montgomery visited Connor and said: "Mr. Connor, I believe I can tell you who put that dynamite at the Temple Beth-El and at the Jewish synagogue in Jacksonville. If he didn't do it, he is the kingpin who had it done. . . . I want to get a promise out of you on the square that you will never mention my name to anyone because this is the most dangerous man that I have ever known. . . . This man will do anything against the Jews and the Negroes, and especially against the Jews. He hates the Jews."

"He went along in his conversation," said Bull Connor in a statement dated July 16, 1958, "explaining to me on the numerous occasions that he had met him and how wild he was. Sometimes he would get so excited talking to him about the Jews that he would have to quiet him down so that the people across the street from his house could not hear him. He also told me the name of an organization that he thought he headed up, of which there were not over six or eight members. . . . He said that this man has an alibi for every bombing that he has ever had anything to do with. . . . He told me this fellow's name was J. B. Stoner."

Connor and his detectives, using this man as a go-between, worked out a sting operation for Stoner. Knowing that Stoner was "desperate for money," they let it be known that a Birmingham group had a bomb site in mind and would pay good money for the job. "On June 16, 1958, we asked him could he get Stoner to come to Birmingham and talk to our detectives, whom we were going to claim were interested in having some place in Birmingham bombed." The place they wanted bombed, they would say, as a lure, was the church of the civil rights activist the Reverend Fred Shuttlesworth.

On June 21, 1958, Stoner pulled into Birmingham in a 1956 Studebaker to meet with Connor's undercover men.

One of the detectives wrote:

> I opened the conversation with the remark that I had lately come into this local activity, that I had been opposed for many years to any violence, but for the past three years local conditions continued to be so bad among the negroes; that Rev. Shuttlesworth and Lamar Weaver

had gone to the Terminal Station and sat in the White Waiting Room and were protected by the police. . . . I stated that we had elected Commissioner Connor hoping that he would do something about the negro situation and that we were a little disappointed in him. . . . Mr. "S" commented that all the politicians were influenced by the growing negro vote. Sergeant Cook and I told Mr. "S" that all the people here had left it up to us to decide in selecting a responsible person who would arrange for Rev. Shuttlesworth's church to be blown completely off the map and not leave a brick standing. We also told Mr. "S" that we didn't have quite enough money at this time, but that there were some big business people that had promised to come through with some substantial donations to the cause, but that they must be satisfied that it would be a thorough and complete job and not a dud, such as was set off at the Bethel Jewish Church. . . . Mr. "S" 's reply was that 54 sticks of dynamite would certainly have destroyed the building, but that perhaps (and he smiled when he said this) "the Jews were attempting to raise money" [meaning the Jews had bombed their own temple as a fund-raising and sympathy-generating ploy].

. . . I stated to him that I did not want to know who would set the bomb, but I had been told by the informer that he, Mr. "S" could have it arranged for $2,000.00. Mr. "S" agreed that he could have the church completely destroyed for $2,000. . . . I told Mr. "S" that we hoped the total destruction of that church would persuade Shuttlesworth to leave Birmingham and go up North where he belonged, but if that did not work our group would be willing to go further with another job that would eliminate Rev. Shuttlesworth completely. Mr. "S" 's reply was that some people would set out bombs and some would do other type of work, but he could arrange either or both type of jobs. Sergeant Cook explained again that we did not have the $2,000 but we had a few hundred. . . . We promised to let Mr. "S" know, by contacting the informer, when we would have the $2,000 needed and told him we were sure we would have the money within the next ten days or two weeks. . . .

Through the whole interview with Mr. "S" he was careful to avoid any incriminating admission about any past acts. We mentioned that the damage to the Jewish church in Jacksonville was very slight and we wanted a complete job. He only smiled as he did in discussing the failure of the bomb to go off at Bethel in Birmingham.

When discussing the possibility of Shuttlesworth not leaving Birmingham after his church was destroyed and that it might require eliminating Rev. Shuttlesworth, Mr. "S" reminded [us] that several years ago two negro NAACP leaders in Florida were blown up and eliminated, and he smiled when he mentioned this. . . .

Mr. "S" stated that he had seen the bomb and it was made up and could be brought to Birmingham on short notice. . . . He also said that any bomb that was put down and did not explode that we would not be charged for it, but another would be set off.

The ethics of using Shuttlesworth and his church as a baited trap in this sting operation were highly questionable, needless to say. His parsonage had been bombed once already, on Christmas night 1956, as he lay in bed. For that bombing no one was ever arrested or prosecuted. "As pastor of Bethel Baptist Church in North Birmingham and leader of the Alabama Christian Movement for Human Rights," the minister later wrote, "I can say that very few people have suffered more physical Klan brutality than I have. . . . The list goes on, with mobs and beatings, bombings, jailings, and water hosings. . . . At one point, I honestly felt as if I would not live to reach age 40."

On June 29, 1958, a detective stationed at the Greyhound Bus Station in Birmingham observed the arrival of Stoner and Robert Bowling. That night Shuttlesworth's church, the Bethel Baptist Church, exploded. Windows were shattered, but no one was injured.

Realizing there had been a major foul-up here, Bull Connor went to Washington to ask for help and, perhaps, exoneration. He told the FBI: "[We] called our informer long distance . . . and told him of the bombing and asked him if he thought Stoner had had anything to do with it and he said no he didn't believe so. About twenty minutes later, our informer called back and said

Stoner had just called him long distance and told him that they had bombed this church and he wanted him to get some money out of us for the job. Our man told our informer that we had never told him that we *would* give him any money to bomb any place or church. We said we *might* could get some people to give us some money. He said he told Stoner that those people had not told him that we would give him any money to bomb this church."

Warily, sensing that his own police department had just seemed to have arranged for the bombing of a black church, Connor—no friend to the blacks, but fond of his own job— pleaded: "There is no question in my mind after reading their statements and talking with my informer for eight hours Sunday that we have just about come to the end and we have got to have help from the FBI to catch [Stoner] because he or his crowd do not live in the state of Alabama and we do not have men that we can put on to tail him 24 hours a day.

"I think this is one man who must be tailed every hour until he is caught or he and his crowd are going to do a lot of damage in the Southeast."

6

The evil nexus described by the NSRP members by the late 1950s involved more than Communist Jews riling up southern niggers, as the conspiracy was perceived in the 1940s. In weird antithesis to the power actually possessed by a decimated world Jewry, the influence and might attributed to them by intrigue-minded right-wingers grew and grew. Not just blacks, but the newspapers; not just Mayor Hartsfield and Police Chief Jenkins, but J. Edgar Hoover and the Justice Department; not just Hollywood and the Supreme Court, but the White House; not just America, but the Soviet Union and the Middle East, all had fallen or were falling, all becoming tools of the nefarious Jews. The fact that the NSRP members were arrested for picketing the Atlanta newspapers and were described as un-American in those same papers, while Jewish citizens were praised and Jewish sermons and prayers were reprinted was simply too much to bear: conspiracy was the simplest explanation.

Jews were less than human and, at the same time, more

than human. In imagination the Jew, swearing his loyalty oaths only to his own kind, was swelled with power and greed, prepared to feed—figuratively and literally—on American Christians. Like the behemoth helium balloons in Macy's Thanksgiving Day parade, Jews grew—in the underground literature—frighteningly large, heedlessly knocking against the bulwarks of Christian civilization, manipulated with ropes held by men unseen by the masses.

⁕

Janice Rothschild began to fear for her husband's safety, as he persisted in accepting speaking engagements to gentile groups and black groups around Atlanta and across the South. Trying to persuade him not to speak to a B'nai B'rith lodge in Jackson, Mississippi, about civil rights, she showed him a newspaper article reporting that Mrs. Nat King Cole had convinced *her* husband to cancel a concert in Mississippi out of fear for his safety. Rothschild replied: "I'm neither famous nor black so forget it."

"Bombings have shocked and bewildered us," Rothschild said in a Friday night sermon in May 1958, entitled "Can This Be America?" "Synagogues and centers have been bombed in such widely scattered southern cities as Miami, Charlotte, Gastonia, Nashville, Jacksonville. An attempt was made on a conservative synagogue in Birmingham. It doesn't seem possible. We'd like to ignore the whole thing. We think, 'Maybe if we talk about it, we'll be bombed, too.' But we must face the facts:

"It's a pattern without rhyme or reason. Bombs were placed indiscriminately whether they represented a point of view on the desegregation issue or not. Thus—Nashville—where some leaders are urging that the law should be obeyed, was bombed. But in Jacksonville there had been no mention at all. Even in Nashville, it was the rabbi of the *Reform* congregation who was the most outspoken, but his Temple was *not* bombed. It would indicate that hate is hate, and violence is directed against all minorities when it becomes possible and fashionable to use it. . . .

"Why the bombings? To create an atmosphere of intimidation. Bombs are used to frighten people and thus deprive them of their rights as citizens of a free land.... This is the way of anarchy....

"What shall be our course of action?" he asked them, knowing they silently prayed for his answer to be that perhaps he ought to refrain from making integration speeches all over the place from now on. Of course, this was *not* his answer. "Our first duty is not to allow ourselves to be intimidated." The congregation sighed. "We are a vulnerable minority. What we do makes no difference in how we are treated. Whether we speak our conscience, or hide and remain silent—we will be attacked.

"It's hard to believe that it could happen here. Nashville, Miami, Jacksonville all believed it inconceivable that such a thing could take place in their cities.... Above all, we must resolve not to surrender to violence. Or submit to intimidation."

So Rothschild—increasingly the recipient of warnings from fellow southern rabbis that he should be careful—failed to hold his tongue. One southern rabbi pleaded with him not only to temper his own comments, but "as a bright and intelligent young leader of the colleagues . . . to lead the red-hot boys to be a little more prudent and cautious," meaning: make the northern Jews pipe down.

Rothschild wrote back, in May 1958, that in his opinion the concerted silence of every Jew, North and South, would have not the slightest effect on the security of Jews in the South because "the lunatic fringe doesn't really care who it bombs."

"If this is dangerous," he added, "then I shall have to live dangerously. Because, I firmly believe, that this is my responsibility as a rabbi. And even if I weren't a rabbi, it would be my responsibility as a human being.... Don't think that I like endangering the security of our institutions—and even my family—God forbid. But I'm here, and life requires it—and so be it."

PART II

11

When the Wolves of Hate Are Loosed

1

OCTOBER 12, 1958

"There was a huge shockwave," recalled Richard Wasser, "a loud noise that I could hear. I felt the windows rattle; I heard them rattle. And that was the night the Temple was bombed. The next morning I read in the paper about the explosion and said, 'That's what I felt last night.' "

The Temple gaped open. The hole was like a toothless mouth—the brick rubble like fallen teeth—in the face of a stunned giant socked in the jaw. Cords and pipes dangled into the black cavity, like tendons and ganglia exposed. Detectives stood deep in water and mud; rubber-neckers stopped traffic on Peachtree.

The bomb that blew a hole in the Temple's outer wall broke into the psyche and dream life of the congregation for years to come. This most private place, this place where they gathered in order to be among Jews and to behave as Jews, had been stalked.

At 8:30 that morning, children dressed up for Sunday school appeared in their kitchens, but phone calls canceled their

237

car pools. They lingered dreamily over the funny papers, then were ordered by parents with drawn faces to go back upstairs, change into play clothes, and stop asking questions. The bombing was, like the lynching of Leo Frank, a subject ripe for "shushkying" by parents and grandparents who had known shushkying in its heyday; but the bombing proved impossibly large and immediate. At any rate, the half-undressed children hung from banisters, crept down hallways, small natural investigators, little pitchers with big ears.

"I was sheltered from the bombing," said Marcia Rothschild, Jack and Janice's daughter, now a specialist in educational computer software. "I had to get up and ask what was going on. It was the day before my eleventh birthday. I remember waking up to a lot of commotion. I didn't hear the phone, but I could hear arguing and whatnot going on. Dad was in the bathroom and Mother was in the bedroom, and they were hollering back and forth and I was on the other side of the door. And he left. And I remember going in and asking my mother what was going on, and she said the Temple had been bombed. The only thing I knew about bombs was what I had seen in movies: bombs come out of the sky and destroy everything. I had no concept. In the next few days we saw pictures in the papers and on the news, and then I understood that a hole was in the side of the building and not in the roof.

"Their effort was to keep everything as normal as possible for us. I had classes that I took at the community center on Sunday afternoons, and I went. My brother had plans to spend the day with a friend from another synagogue, and he went. Now I kind of wish they hadn't done it. I wish we had been included. Children did not belong in these situations. Well, what happens is, your children don't learn what living is all about. I really think it was a mistake on their part, but that's what people believed about childrearing."

Rothschild stood stolidly in the rubble, knelt when asked by detectives to kneel and comment on some item in the detritus, then he stood again, with crossed arms. His demeanor was quiet. He was allowing himself to be instructed by the message delivered to him in the night. So wary was he of exploiting the moment, of capitalizing improperly on this graphic act of cruelty, that he would refrain from public comment for many months, other than the sermon he would give his own congregation the coming Friday night. He declined hundreds of invitations to speak about the bombing. "National television wanted me on," said Rothschild, "and I refused. I wouldn't go out of the city for six months after it happened because I didn't want to capitalize on it. I was interested in making something valuable come out of this experience. And I felt very strongly that public exposure for personal reasons was not the way to do it."

The beautiful Temple, which he first had seen on a summer day while bounding up the driveway on his way to introduce himself to Marx, now listed left, a hole in its side, its innards blown 150 feet across the next-door parking lot of an insurance firm. (Would Marx comment, as he had when the Eternal Light went out: "I don't know what to tell you. The Temple never blew up while *I* was rabbi"?)

The words Rothschild had pronounced from inside the sanctuary had been taken by certain groups as the opening volley in a war, and this was their return shot. But he had not aspired to heroism. He had aspired only to be civilized, to compose and recite the words that a civilized man ought to say in evil times. For this Rothschild had found no better blueprint than the Prophets. Isaiah was his morning newspaper, Amos his north star.

＊＊＊

And what were his private thoughts? Of course he hated the cruelty and the destruction, but, at the same time, with a small portion of his soul, he found he had to tip his hat to it: it had got his attention. It registered the wrath of untold hundreds, maybe thousands. His temple had become a seismograph: "This morning in Atlanta the white racist backlash hit 9.4 on the Richter scale. . . . "

Rothschild could not but detect within himself, along with the anger and fear, a strand of vindication. Atlanta had felt itself above the violence and mayhem exploding in other southern cities; the attitude here had been, "What we don't see doesn't exist." Atlantans, it had seemed, did not have to change their ways, for their city was an oasis. But they were wrong. The hatred Rothschild had said existed *did* exist.

He was a bit like a young day-camper run by his counselors through a bogus "snipe hunt," who has set out a bait of sugar cubes in his cap, who hides and waits behind a bush while the other boys, learning the search was a hoax, return to camp; and lo and behold, the snipe comes!

Rothschild had lured the snipe out of Tennessee or Alabama. It had taken a chunk out of his building and had melted back into the night, but it had left its marks, as easy to read as the abominable snowman's footprints. From now on, no one could say that it did not exist, or that it did exist, but not in Atlanta.

There was an element, too, of having survived a hazing, of having weathered an initiation. There is not much point in being fearless if you are invulnerable. To share the blacks' burden, truly, it was necessary to be vulnerable. In his heart he offered his bombed Temple first to God—a bonafide burnt offering—and second to all of the civil rights leaders and all the taunted black schoolchildren: "I . . . we . . . stand with you."

"Here am I. Send me."

Perhaps it was an initiation for the bombers, too—who knew? Young men possibly, acting on orders, running with explosives through darkness on a dangerous mission based on misguided loyalty, proving their mettle as white men, as brave soldiers in the race war. Or were these senior officers, veterans of other bombings? At any rate, the intent was clear: Up the ante in Atlanta, abandon talk. We'd as soon kill you as have to listen to you anymore, said the bomb, so *shut up*.

Now it was Rothschild's move again. In reply it was necessary, he felt—given that he was not likely to heave dynamite back at them (though Jewish fighters had been doing just that since 1948 in Israel, and had done so in 1943 in the Warsaw Ghetto)—to talk and talk and talk, ever louder and clearer and more specifically.

＊＊＊

Mayor Hartsfield—a decent, cheery, older man in fedora and glasses—showed up at the bomb site. He had the tour, then gestured to the newspaper, radio, and television reporters to come closer as he made his statement: "Atlanta has prided itself in being a beacon of tolerance and racial and religious decency in the South. This shocks and amazes us. We cannot help but feel this is the work of an out-of-town gang operating southwide. . . .

"Looking at this terrible demolition I cannot help but realize it is the end result and payoff of a lot of rabble-rousing in the South. Whether they like it or not, every political rabble-rouser is the godfather of these cross-burners and dynamiters who sneak about in the dark and give a bad name to the South. It is high time that decent people of the South rise up and take charge."

Although Hartsfield offered a one-thousand-dollar reward from the city of Atlanta for information leading to the arrest and conviction of the bombers, his statement did not lead to anyone's arrest and conviction. But the mayor's statement was a rallying cry, an attempt to reach the vast proportion of the citizenry who wrongly believed that their silence on the race question was an adequate, even a moral response.

The only two positions on race easily identifiable to moderate Atlantans in 1958 were held by extremists. To hazard a bit of support for one perspective or the other appeared to lead one promptly to the slippery slope at the foot of which one found oneself arm-in-arm with Klansmen or with those called "nigger-lovers." As long as the exploding black churches and Jewish synagogues were blowing up in other cities, it was comfortable to assume that Atlanta was the capital of moderation.

Sunday newspapers all over the city still lay on front walks and yards, but with peculiar irrelevance—the men hurrying to the scene of the crime, knotting their ties as they ran, galloped across them without pause. In an instant the still-folded newspapers had become relics of an older, peaceful Atlanta. The new Atlanta—torn by violence like Birmingham or Selma or Little Rock, *those* poor relations—would roar onto the front pages on Monday, October 13: "JEWISH TEMPLE ON PEACHTREE WRECKED BY DYNAMITE BLAST; ARMY OF POLICEMEN HUNTING BLASTERS; GODLESS BOMBING AIMED AT ALL ATLANTANS, 'SICK AT HEART'. RABBI ROTHSCHILD ASSERTS." But in the Sunday papers, the violence in the news was still far away, in Clinton, Tennessee, for example, where an integrated high school had been destroyed that week by dynamite. "We have a choice of education by democracy or education by dynamite," Tennessee's governor, Frank Clement, had said. "We *will* have law and order in Tennessee. So help me

God!" And Atlantans would have read those words over coffee and toast and wonder at the decade's insanity, yet complete their breakfasts feeling themselves, and their city, personally untarnished.

Until October 12, 1958, the resistance to integration in Atlanta appeared to many as peripheral to their lives, a subject for discussion in the legislature and on the editorial page, but not the day-to-day concern of refined people. Nearly everyone, by the late 1950s, had acquaintances who professed to feel passionately one way or the other. Fighting words could be read in the newspapers; campaign slogans often included the word *nigger*; liberal ministers preached on "Brotherhood Sunday" and scowled and made eye contact when they came to the word *brotherhood*, as if they were trying to relay something deeper. But moderate people, people of quiet goodwill, civilized people could sidestep it all, as if the race question itself were not quite worth their notice, as if the subject of Negro rights was somehow slightly obscene.

But silence was, in fact, a *retreat* from decency, Mayor Hartsfield said in effect; there was no middle ground. As the majority waffled between the two extremes of compliance with *Brown* and violent defiance of *Brown*, the power of the latter—who did not indulge in silence—was in ascendance. The white Christian mayor stood in the ruins of his city's Jewish temple, called it unacceptable, and invited fellow white Christians to join him in condemning the act.

When the Temple on Peachtree Street exploded, the first reaction among middle-of-the-road white people was that it was the work of outsiders. Some even said foreigners. "Communists" was hinted. The paper called them "the haters." The mayor had called them "an out-of-town gang operating southwide." An editorial described them as "some slinky cowards posing as members of the human race." But regardless of who the perpetrators were, one was forced somehow, suddenly, to form an opinion. Either the bombing was a step in the right direction or it was not. For the vast majority of Atlantans, it turned out, it was *not*.

"Most of Atlanta's best people had been moral zeroes," wrote Lillian Smith, a Georgia novelist, essayist, and white champion of black rights. "The bombing of the Jewish Temple

. . . was a small price to pay for bringing about the sharp change in the moral climate that occurred, afterward. People who had been morally paralyzed stirred, spoke out, protested. The cagey ones stopped being quite so cagey. . . . They began, at least, to say they were 'against bombings, violence, and for obedience to law.' They felt terribly brave to do so.' "

The bombed Temple gave most people their first close-up view of the world that would result if defiance of the law became commonplace. If the *law* were to be abridged, the landscape that ensued would be one of anarchy and violence. The segregationists—from lowly street-corner vendors hawking racist newsletters, all the way up to the governors, congressmen, and senators pontificating on state's rights—seemed to promise that a return to a simpler way of life was possible, a simpler time when white meant white and black meant nigger. How far back might the southern time machine journey, if law were overthrown? Back to 1896, *Plessy v. Ferguson* (the decision affirming separate-but-equal policies) certainly, but why not further back, why not back to the centuries before the Fourteenth Amendment, when trade in human chattel made the world turn?

The bombed Temple announced to the middle-of-the-roaders in Atlanta: *This* is what it will look like—shreds of blue robes from a children's choir in the flood of blasted pipes—this, and *not* Scarlett O'Hara's Tara. For many, many decent white Atlantans, the bombing of Rothschild's temple was an awakening. And it offered them their initial opportunity to condemn an act of hate-filled violence. "Well *now* there," they might say, "this thing has gone too far."

Rothschild installed the title for his upcoming Friday night sermon on the bulletin board at the foot of the Temple hill, in time for Monday morning commuters and curiosity-seekers to see it. The sign read: "And None Shall Make Them Afraid."

━━◆══ ━━

As the day wore on, Rothschild began responding with his trademark wisecracks. As ever, they bought him time, or privacy. When people asked, "Is Janice upset?" he said, "She sure is. She's upset with me because she's been telling me all summer that the downspouts on the front of our house needed painting and I neglected to have it done. Now [thanks to the TV news] she says the whole world can see how bad they look."

And when, on Monday, a synagogue in Peoria, Illinois, was bombed and reporters asked Rothschild if he had a message for that rabbi, Rothschild boomed: "Welcome to the club!"

＊ ＝✦＝ ＊

Hartsfield's statement also accomplished the work of soothing and comforting the Jewish people of Atlanta, especially the Temple congregants, who felt—some of them for the first time, that day—an old fear. Into their hearts pricked the cold memory of isolation. Although they assumed that the bomb did not speak for the vast majority of southern white Christians, who had lived for generations amicably side by side with them as neighbors, business associates, partners, and friends, they understood that an extremist fringe sought to separate the Jewish people, with this bombing, from the wider community; to blow a chasm between them and the moderate white majority.

In Alfred Uhry's play *Driving Miss Daisy*, the Atlanta Jews particularly loved—and howled with self-recognition at—one line (a line deleted by Hollywood for the movie). Told that the Temple has been bombed, Miss Daisy, annoyed and bewildered, snaps: "Don't they know we're *Reform?*" by which she means: "Don't they know that we're really quite similar, in our lives and religious practices, to *them*, unlike our Orthodox brethren, who really are, it must be admitted, a little extreme?"

Well, they didn't know. Plus they didn't give a shit.

The Jews of the other Atlanta congregations and of the Arbeiter Ring and the Farband had more experience than did the Temple Jews with what it meant to be cut off, to be called alien. Leo Frank's lynching had taught an older generation, and the destruction of European Jewry had shown everyone it touched, that Jewish cries for help usually were not answered. Edward Krick, president of Atlanta's Congregation Shearith Israel, wrote to Rothschild, "We feel very keenly the implications involved and feel that it is a blow directed at us all." But the rising civic stars of the Temple had flourished in this modern city. Some were on a first-name basis with bank presidents and with the senior partners of major law firms; their rabbis played golf with ministers. Marx for sixty years had cast his congregants as virtually the same as Christians; Rothschild for twelve years had believed his congregants to be so much the same that he felt entitled to speak publicly on gentile affairs. Now, with a bomb and a phone call, the self-styled Confederate Underground had said—and the newspapers printed it—"Jews are hereby declared aliens."

So the gut reaction of the Temple congregants was "*US?!*"

And the gut reaction of the eastern European Jews was "*THEM?*"

When Frank had been arrested in 1913, given his kangaroo trial, convicted, sentenced to die, seen the death sentence commuted, and then lynched, Atlanta's Jews had absorbed the events with grief and horror; Frank's treatment had left behind a profound taste of powerlessness and of detachment from the white community. The eastern European Jews then in Atlanta had watched in amazement: that this could befall a Deitchyid was not good news for anyone.

Now something had happened to the Deitchyiden again. Again the eastern European Jews watched with anxious concern. Now that the Temple Jews had been publicly singled out as Jews—out of all the Jews in Atlanta, *them*—where was their success? Where was their power? Where, in a word, were their gentiles, now?

And the Temple Jews wondered most of all. When old-timers occasionally lamented, "It's Leo Frank all over again," what they meant was "We're alone in this. Something horrible is happening, and no one in the wider society is even interested. We're cut off from decent folk."

As the first waves of news of the bombing expanded from the crime site that Sunday morning, ringing the Jewish houses, the thought within each was Does anybody care? Is this a crime against Atlanta, or only against the Jews?

So when Hartsfield turned up immediately and stood beside Rothschild for newspaper photos and made his television statement, it was felt to be a great, great moment in Atlanta's Jewish history. It meant that the years of vaunted solidarity with the whites, with the gentiles, with civilized Atlanta, had not come to naught, were not all illusion, that the Temple was an important Atlanta institution. And it was only the beginning, for an avalanche of condolences, public statements, sermons, letters, and contributions followed. "That morning," said Janice, "in churches throughout the city, preachers angrily denounced the crime. Politicians hastened to be seen and heard making similar pronouncements. Reporters and editors ran to their typewriters to do likewise. . . . Offers of help came from all sides. Contributions began to pour in, despite repeated announcements that the damage was fully covered by insurance. . . .

"To Bible Belt southerners . . . the desecration of a house of worship was an abomination. That its members were Jewish made no difference. That they were well known and white probably did."

Even President Eisenhower, approached by reporters for his opinion of the bombing, rather safely offered: "I think we would all share in the feeling of horror that any person would want to desecrate the holy place of any religion, be it a chapel, a cathedral, a mosque, a church, or a synagogue." A few days later he went further out on a limb and described the "Confederate Underground" as "a bunch of Al Capone gangsters who soil the good name of the Confederacy." "For hoodlums such as these to describe themselves as any part or relation to the Confederacy of the mid-19th century is, to my mind, a complete insult to the word," said the president. (The question of whether the esteemed Confederacy might not be due for a second look was left for a later era.) But he did send in the FBI, the first time that agency officially was dispatched to investigate a bombing.

The mayor's $1,000 reward offer grew, by the end of the week, to more than $20,000. The *Atlanta Journal and Constitution* pledged $5,000 to the reward fund; the First National Bank of Atlanta pledged $2,000; Southern Bakeries Company, $1,000; Governor Marvin Griffin, $250; the Atlanta Biltmore Hotel, $1,000. The Atlanta Board of Education unanimously offered nearby school facilities for use by the Temple.

Pat Watters of the *Journal* wrote: "Even as the thundering echo of the explosion of 50 sticks of dynamite at Atlanta's Jewish Temple still rumbled, there came yet another noise, one not heard much of late, one often drowned out. It was the still quiet voice of the moderate heard once again in the Southland."

The African American community of Atlanta—the opinions, statements, and contributions of which were not solicited by the media—was riveted by the bombing. Their initial reaction was not unlike the initial reaction of the eastern European Jews, as both groups contemplated the damaged Temple: *Them?*

The black leadership knew and had worked with Rothschild. Ministers sermonized against the vandalism, and the *Atlanta Daily World*, the famous black daily published on Auburn Avenue, covered the bombing, investigation, and trial with front-page headlines and with editorials. "These assuredly are times," said a *World* editorial, "in which the wild oats of a certain brand of politician are coming to harvest." On guard against the possible announcement by police of a black perpetrator, the paper warned: "It would be quite un-Godly for those who would follow the pattern of 'covering' up their tracks to attempt the old pattern of involving a Negro 'suspect.' "

Many African Americans, including those who had not heard of Rothschild before, assumed that the bombing was about race, and even that bombing the Jews was another way of attacking the blacks. "We hope you will accept our small gift," came from the maintenance department of Temple Rodef Shalom in Pittsburgh, "although it is not much but every cent is from our hearts. We feel this is one way we can answer the race-haters. . . . As Negroes we understand the agony of life in the South." Said Julian Bond: "I thought immediately the bombing of the Temple was about civil rights, that whoever did this is striking at these people because these people are close to my people. Or these people are sympathetic to my people. That was my thought immediately. I'd never thought about sympathy from them before. It just came to me when the Temple was bombed. It felt like a proxy attack on my interests."

The Herndon Foundation sent a check for five hundred dollars to Rothschild, with a note from the chairman, N. B. Herndon: "Men free in mind and soul must rid our nation of those forces who would destroy us from within."

→ ⋈ →

The morning of the bombing, Nancy Thal—then Nancy Braunfield Mantler—a thin, dark Jewish beauty, a husky-voiced divorcée with two children, was scheduled to be married. The night before, Nancy's family and the groom's—the Thals of Dayton, Ohio—had stayed out late at their rehearsal dinner at the Standard Club: "I was now thirty and getting married for the second time," she said, still a long-faced beauty, long accustomed to life in affluent settings, her voice full of surprises. "And you know, all my family was in town: Mother and Daddy, my brother and his wife, and all Aaron's family in from Dayton, and various cousins and uncles, everybody down at the Biltmore Hotel. It was the only really nice hotel in town. And Aaron's folks had given us a beautiful party at the Standard Club, so everybody was out late.

"I had a housekeeper named Rose Perry—eight feet tall, you know, and wonderful!—helping me and the children. I had all their things laid out for the next day—Mother and Dad had gotten marvelous dresses for them in New York. Everything was laid out for them. My luggage was all ready to go on a honeymoon trip to Mexico. And we had had this party and, as I say, I got in real late, so I told Rose Perry, 'Now, Rose, please, don't wake me up until the last minute. You know, we were out so late tonight, I really want to get a good night's sleep for my big day.' Little did I know how big.

"So anyway, at 7:00 the phone starts jingling, and I think, 'Who in God's name could this be?' The wedding was to be at noon in Jack's study, with a big luncheon and reception later at the Standard Club.

"And it's Janice. And Janice starts rattling on about, 'Nancy, I've got to talk to you, it's very important.' I said, 'Geez, do you know what time it is? What is the matter with you?' And I started really laying into Janice, and she's getting very uppity with me. She said, 'I'm *trying* to tell you that the Temple has been bombed!' And I said, 'Oh my God.'

"A little while later, Mother called and said, 'Now, Dear, I don't want you to read anything into this.' In other words, she was afraid I would call off the wedding because I might have thought it was a little signal from God that maybe I'd better not get married.

"Then the old Jewish humor started in: that Bud Mantler (my first husband) did it; or that Aaron did it because Aaron had never married before and he was a carefree bachelor taking a

At the Temple, the South's flagship Reform congregation, bar mitzvahs, Hebrew, and yarmulkes had been rejected in favor of confirmations, organ music, and Sunday morning worship. COURTESY OF THE TEMPLE, ATLANTA

"So far my war career has disillusioned me on two fronts," wrote Chaplain Jacob Rothschild from under bombardment on Guadalcanal. "To wit: Spam, and South Sea Island Paradises." COURTESY OF WOODRUFF LIBRARY, EMORY UNIVERSITY

"You will be interested to learn that my wife had a baby which we called Marcia, mostly because it is a girl," wrote Rothschild to a friend. A son, Billy, followed 13 months later. COURTESY OF WOODRUFF LIBRARY, EMORY UNIVERSITY

"Devote yourselves to justice/Aid the oppressed," said the prophet Isaiah, stirring Rothschild to action. He saw the African Americans as the poor and oppressed who are spoken of in Jewish tradition. His congregation was less clear on this point. COURTESY OF WOODRUFF LIBRARY, EMORY UNIVERSITY

George Lincoln Rockwell, "the young führer" of Arlington, hoped to free America from "Jewish domination." COURTESY OF AP/WIDE WORLD PHOTOS

Members of the National States' Rights Party drifted in and out of all-night establishments like Plaza Drugs, discussing the Nordic race, the Jews, and the "Negro problem" over steak and eggs. COURTESY OF EDWARD T. M. GARLAND

A nitroglycerine bomb equal to 50 sticks of dynamite hit the Temple in the middle of the night. The "Confederate Underground" phoned the press: "We are going to blow up all Communist organizations. Negroes and Jews are hereby declared aliens." COURTESY OF AP/WIDE WORLD PHOTOS

Mayor William Hartsfield stood in the wreckage and called for the South's "decent people. . .[to] rise up and take charge." COURTESY OF THE ATLANTA JOURNAL CONSTITUTION

Rothschild, home asleep when the bomb hit, later said: "What message was the explosion meant to deliver? 'You [Jews] are not wanted here. . . . Law is dead. We are the law.' " COURTESY OF THE ATLANTA JOURNAL CONSTITUTION

From left: George Bright, Wallace Allen, Luther Corley, Chester Griffin, and Robert Bowling were indicted. Defense counsel Jimmy Venable (far right), Imperial Wizard of the National Knights of the Klan, tried to block Jews from testifying. COURTESY OF AP/WIDE WORLD PHOTOS

Corley, front left, was freed by the Grand Jury. Bowling (in dark suit), Bright (smoking cigarette), Griffin (checked shirt), and Allen (white tie) were escorted by detectives through the city jail. COURTESY OF AP/WIDE WORLD PHOTOS

Richard Bowling, also indicted, and his brother Robert were known in adolescence as "the bomber brothers." COURTESY OF AP/WIDE WORLD PHOTOS

The flamboyantly attired Reuben A. Garland Sr., flanked by his younger son, Edward, was one of the best-known, most successful, and most expensive criminal defense lawyers of his era. COURTESY OF EDWARD T. M. GARLAND

During the bombing trial, Garland practiced a few of his famous shenanigans, including a feigned heart attack. Here George Bright confers with Garland outside the courtroom. COURTESY OF EDWARD T. M. GARLAND

The city's response to Martin Luther King Jr.'s 1964 Nobel Prize for Peace: "There's good news and there's bad news. The good news: an Atlantan won a Nobel prize! The bad news: it's *King.*" From left: Ralph McGill, publisher of the *Atlanta Constitution;* Dr. Benjamin E. Mays, president of Morehouse College; Paul J. Hallinan, Roman Catholic archbishop of Atlanta; and Rabbi Jacob Rothschild cochaired the dinner to honor him. COURTESY OF WOODRUFF LIBRARY, EMORY UNIVERSITY

"You are Atlanta," said Rothschild to the packed audience at the Dinkler Hotel. "You—and not the noisy rabble with their sheets and signs now slogging sullenly the sidewalks beyond these doors." Here he presents the city's gift to King. COURTESY OF WOODRUFF LIBRARY, EMORY UNIVERSITY

woman and two children—you know: 'Who needs this? I'm going to bomb the Temple.' And then my group came in and said, 'No, Nancy did it—she got cold feet about Aaron.' So everybody had their ideas about who did it.

"However, the phone was just ringing off the hook that morning with what we were going to do. Janice said we had to change the plans as far as the ceremony was concerned because there was just no way. The police had the Temple surrounded. So we decided to get married in the Ellman Chapel at Ahavath Achim. We were the first couple to be married there. Rabbi Epstein was there; he was lovely. Still, everybody was very nervous. You know, it's amazing what the human spirit absorbs; even when events are terrible, you just go ahead and do what you have to do, whether it's getting married or whatever. I think everybody was very edgy, though, because it was just such a dastardly sort of deed to absorb. The kids, of course, added a nice levity to a serious situation."

Rothschild came running in straight from the bomb site to perform the ceremony. As he jogged in looking disheveled, he took one look at the bride and groom and their dressed-up relations and children, and the comic angle on his morning suddenly revealed itself. He drew close to the bride and snarled: "You and your weddings!"

"Jack was always so funny," Thal said. "He had a great sense of humor. When he said, 'You and your weddings!' I just said, 'Jack, please.' (He hadn't even officiated at my first wedding.) So we got through that hurdle and got on with it and it was a lovely ceremony. My mother and daddy stayed on in Atlanta with the children, and Aaron and I went to Acapulco."

2

Janice Rothschild stayed home Sunday morning, when the rabbi drove to the Temple, to begin the telephone calls canceling Sunday school. She spent the morning on her telephone, calling and calling and calling, and when morning lengthened into afternoon, she stayed at the telephone, answering and answering and answering calls from well-wishers as the news spread across the country. It did not occur to Janice that she herself might be in danger—that rabbis' houses also were seen as fair game—until a call she answered in the late afternoon.

"By that time I was tired and numb, hardly aware of what I was saying to the friends and strangers who kept calling from all parts of the country to offer sympathy." Her friend Julie Weiss had joined her to help with meals and children and phone calls—Bud Weiss was the president of the Atlanta Jewish Community Council and a Temple vice-president. "With me still on the telephone, [Julie] found some leftover spaghetti in the refrigerator and heated it up. . . . When a call came in that was different from the rest, I heard myself say, 'Thank you very much,' the same as I had been saying to others. I must have looked stunned, though, for Julie asked me what the caller had said and I, still in a trance, told her word for word, in front of the children, 'He said he was one of "them" that bombed our church, and he was calling to tell me there's a bomb under our house now and it's lit. He said we have five minutes to get out and save our lives.'

"When I came to my senses, I was standing in the doorway, purse and car keys in hand, irrationally wondering whether or not to go back inside to save some priceless heirloom, and, if so, which one. Julie, five months pregnant, had scaled the retaining wall behind our garden and was standing in the woods beyond, holding onto Marcia and her own child [Billy was at a friend's] and yelling at me to get out of the house. . . .

"I joined them and went with them to our next-door neighbor's house. . . . We notified Jack and Bud and the police, and then tried to settle down and regain our equanimity. It wasn't easy. Our neighbor, who had been drinking heavily, yelled that he wasn't going 'to let those sons-of-bitches run you out of your house' and strode toward our house, permitting his own young son to accompany him. . . .

"Jack, Bud, the police, and FBI agents arrived shortly. Bill Schwartz [the Temple president] came, too, but stayed only a moment because his own home had just received the same type of call." The newspaper offices also received a call: "This is the Confederate Underground. You nigger-loving *Atlanta Journal*—the Negro churches, the Jewish churches—we're going to blow all of you up."

"All of us realized," said Janice, "that the calls were probably hoaxes, but we were shaken nonetheless. And tired. Very, very tired.

"While one team of agents checked the premises for a bomb, another questioned me about the call. I repeated what I had heard, describing the caller's voice as male, not very well educated, probably from middle Georgia. When my questioner seemed puzzled at my ability to give such detail, Jack explained that I was a theater buff, having studied drama in college, and that I enjoyed trying to identify regional accents. The officer seemed even more startled at this explanation but continued with his investigation. When it was finally determined that we were safe, the crew departed, leaving two officers in a patrol car in our driveway to guard us through the night."

At ten o'clock Sunday night, Rothschild realized he had not eaten all day and was hungry. He and Janice, and Bud and Julie Weiss, went out to get dinner—while police guarded the house, and the children, Marcia and Billy, were sent home with friends to secure their safety.

The Rothschilds and Bud and Julie Weiss drove to Seven Steers, a hamburger place in Buckhead. "They had wonderful, wonderful hamburgers," recalls Janice. "This was before McDonald's. They had a sign out front with a cowboy lying flat on the ground with his legs crossed and a sign over his head saying, 'Hep stamp out home cookin'!' " But there, Rothschild found himself suddenly reminded (in a way he had somehow *not* been reminded by the bomb, which had showed him that he was effectively passing for black) that he was a *Jew* first, and peculiar to most southerners. He suddenly realized that the liberal ministers—his local allies in the day's disaster—must have given sermons that morning along the lines of "The Jews are our brothers," as he sermonized about blacks; and that when they (or he) said it, it was a theological statement first, a statement of belief in the unity of creation. With time, the imagination leapt to keep up with the credo and pictured the oppressed other as the same as oneself. Long after that, if you were lucky (as Rothschild had been with a few African Americans) you made friends with real people and no longer felt compelled to harp on common humanity and sameness, but began to notice and relish the differences.

That night in the booth, momentarily bereft of chitchat, their faces sagging with fatigue, their clothes rumpled, waiting quietly for their meals to be brought, the Rothschilds and the Weisses sat in a sort of warm mutual gloom amidst the rowdy soda-pop western-kitsch decor of the place. They felt themselves highly conspicuous, recognizable as Jews to the strangers packed into booths and tables all around them. It was a new, and not pleasant, feeling. They sat, feeling themselves watched and—what was almost worse—feeling suspicious of their jolly fellow diners. "I remember looking around at the people sitting at the other tables as we waited for our food, wondering if any one of them had been the person who had called, or who had bombed the Temple, or if any of them hated us enough to contemplate such actions," said Janice. "It was just a strong feeling, wondering about all these people I'd lived among all my life— 'Does this one hate me? Does that one hate me?'—because I had never thought like that before.

"I mean if people didn't like me, I always assumed there was something wrong with *me*. I mean I *knew* there were people who didn't like me, and who didn't like Jack, but I always attributed it to something we had *done* or *said* rather than the fact that we were Jewish. I knew that anti-Semitism existed, but I never really felt it in these terms. And certainly never imagined that anyone would hate us enough to do something like that.

"I realized I was being melodramatic in even entertaining such thoughts, but they persisted. Jack and the Weisses were being so quiet that I suspected that they were having similar thoughts."

The discrepancy was too great: the Rothschilds in a state of shock and mourning, and all around them people digging into their meals with hearty appetites, talking with their mouths full, snorting with laughter. Finding no correspondence to their experience in the restaurant—for though they had imagined that they needed "escape" and "distraction," what they really hungered for was explanation and meaning—they finished eating, paid, and went home.

The night was not over. The phone was still ringing. Police checked the house. After midnight, wound up, Rothschild poured two drinks. Janice said: "That was the only time I ever remember Jack taking a drink for other than a purely social purpose. He poured a Scotch for himself, a bourbon for me, and we sipped them quietly as we tried to put our minds in order.

"The whiskey had helped, but we were still left with a long, unwelcome stretch of time in which to think before we slept. I lay there wondering if we would ever wake again, if someone would bomb us while we slept, if soldiers in a battle zone had similar thoughts each night as they tried to sleep, if Jack had had such thoughts when he served on Guadalcanal. . . . I didn't ask him, of course. I hoped he was comfortably asleep.

"The telephone jarred us awake an hour later. I grabbed it, hoping to keep it from disturbing him. The call was from New York. It was a reporter asking to speak to the rabbi. I whispered that the rabbi had just fallen asleep and I preferred not to wake him. That was too polite. The caller insisted.

"I held my ground, still whispering. I explained that the rabbi had had a very trying day and needed his sleep. It did no good. My adversary claimed that his paper was holding its presses for him. He had to get a story for the early edition.

"By that time Jack realized he would do well to get it over with as soon as possible. Reaching across me for the receiver, he said, 'This is Rabbi Rothschild. What can I do for you?'

"From the other end of the line came the question, 'Was that Mrs. Rothschild I was talking to?' "

Awake, and already guarding—as was his instinct—his true thought, Rothschild responded with a wisecrack: "And if that *wasn't* Mrs. Rothschild, do you really think I'd tell *you?*"

3

In the days following the Temple bombing, there was a scramble among politicians and phrase makers for the moral high ground. The South politically was split in half: you were for segregation or you were against it; so the wily leapt up from each side to define the meaning of the bombing. For the segregationists, the bombing represented just one more attempt—as Eisenhower, in his caution, had expressed it—to soil the good name of the Confederacy. Segregationist leaders imagined a "conspiracy to bring national discredit upon the South at a time when it is fighting against integration of its public schools." They took this opportunity to state for the record that Jews, categorically, *were* white and that their status as first-class citizens was disputed only by a very small minority even further to the right. The segregationists carefully distinguished between the bombing of Jewish centers and harassment of Jewish citizens and the bombing of black churches and harassment of black citizens. The latter strategies were referred to only in euphemism. Macon attorney Charles J. Bloch, the vice-president of the States' Rights Council of Georgia and the state's most prominent Jewish segregationist, gave such a euphemistic public statement: "I do not believe there is the slightest connection with the bombing and those of us who have been fighting for constitutional government." Bloch later termed "perfectly preposterous" the idea that violence may result from disagreement with the Supreme Court. "Those of us who believe in constitutional government and those of us who think that the decision of the Supreme Court . . . was wrong have just as much right to test that decision as the NAACP and its allies had to test *Plessey vs. Ferguson.*"

In several bursts of imagination, segregationists pictured the Jewish people as their close friends and allies. The White Citizens Council of Dallas County, Alabama, sent a donation for repair of the "Jewish church"; unwilling to accept it, Rothschild forwarded it to the mayor for reward money. Roy Harris of Augusta, Georgia, the president of the Citizens Councils of America, deplored the bombing and added, "We've got a hell of a lot of Jew members." A *Constitution* article recalled the Jews' fondness for the Confederacy: "The Atlanta Hebrew Benevolent Congregation, whose temple was bombed Sunday morning, was organized from a group which cared for itinerant Confederate Soldiers after the War Between the States. . . . " Governor-to-be S. Ernest Vandiver (a protégé of the Talmadge faction in state politics who ran for governor on the pledge that "neither my child nor yours will ever attend an integrated school during my administration—no, not one," and thereby gained the nickname, among blacks, of "No Not One" Vandiver) expressed shock and sympathy: "I regret that we have had this happen within our state." And he added—apparently without sarcasm—"It is a tragedy that would seem to be an attempt to violate the Constitution."

But even the most heartfelt condolences from the segregationist leaders seemed to require a bit of agility, for men who had sanctioned violence and defiance of law out one side of their mouths looked a bit shame-faced and awkward when hastily trying to condemn such acts out the other side of their mouths. The moral high ground triumphantly and eloquently was seized this time by the liberals, and the Temple bombing, to this day, is understood as *they* described it, as a defining moment, an act that enabled even the timid and the political newcomer to take a stand.

"A Desecrated Temple Cries Out to Heaven" was the title of a *Journal* editorial on October 13. "The Sunday bombing of The Temple defiled Atlanta and Georgia as well as that holy edifice. . . ."

But the column that nailed the segregationist leaders—that "ripped" them, to use the phrase of the day—came from the pen of Ralph McGill. Returning to his house that Sunday afternoon from a speaking tour in the north Georgia mountains, he had been met at the door by his wife, who said his office had been trying all day to reach him. She told him the Temple had been bombed. "Soon after, in his office, in twenty minutes of furious, uninterrupted writing, he produced three typewritten pages that smoked with anger and with shame."

A Church, a School

Dynamite in great quantity ripped a beautiful temple of worship in Atlanta. It followed hard on the heels of a like destruction of a handsome high school at Clinton, Tennessee.

The same rabid, mad-dog minds were, without question, behind both. They are also the source of previous bombings in Florida, Alabama, and South Carolina. The schoolhouse and the church were the targets of diseased, hate-filled minds.

Let us face the facts. This is a harvest. It is the crop of things sown.

It is the harvest of defiance of courts and the encouragement of citizens to defy law on the part of many southern politicians. It will be the acme of irony, for example, if any one of four or five southern governors deplore this bombing. It will be grimly humorous if certain state attorneys general issue statements of regret. And it will be quite a job for some editors, columnists, and commentators, who have been saying that our courts have no jurisdiction and that the people should refuse to accept their authority, now to deplore.

It is not possible to preach lawlessness and restrict it.

To be sure, none said go bomb a Jewish temple or a school.

But let it be understood that when leadership in high places in any degree fails to support constituted authority, it opens the gates to all those who wish to take law into their own hands.

There will be, to be sure, the customary act of the careful drawing aside of skirts on the part of those in high places.

"How awful," they will exclaim. "How terrible. Something must be done."

But the record stands. The extremists of the citizens' councils, the political leaders who in terms violent and inflammatory have repudiated their oaths and stood against due process of law have helped unloose this flood of hate and bombing.

This, too, is a harvest of those so-called Christian ministers who have chosen to preach hate instead of compassion. Let them now find pious words and raise their hands in deploring the bombing of a synagogue.

You do not preach and encourage hatred for the Negro and hope to restrict it to that field. It is an old, old story. It is one repeated over and over again in history. When the wolves of hate are loosed on one people, then no one is safe.

Hate and lawlessness by those who lead release the yellow rats and encourage the crazed and neurotic who print and distribute the hate pamphlets, who shrieked that Franklin Roosevelt was a Jew; who denounce the Supreme Court as being Communist and controlled by Jewish influence.

This series of bombings is the harvest, too, of something else.

One of those connected with the bombing telephoned a news service early Sunday morning to say the job would be done. It was to be committed, he said, by the Confederate Underground.

The Confederacy and the men who led it are revered by millions. Its leaders returned to the Union and urged that the future be committed to building a stronger America. This was particularly true of General Robert E. Lee. Time after time he urged his students at Washington University to forget the War Between the States and to help build a greater and stronger union.

For too many years now we have seen the Confederate flag and the emotions of that great war become the property of men not fit to tie the shoes of those who fought for it. Some of these have been merely childish and immature. Others have perverted and commercialized the flag by making the Stars and Bars, and the Confederacy itself, a symbol of hate and bombings.

For a long time now it has been needful for all Americans to stand up and be counted on the side of law and the due process of law—even when to do so goes against personal beliefs and emotions. It is late. But there is yet time.

Ten months later McGill received a telegram from Grayson Kirk, the president of Columbia University: "I HAVE THE HONOR TO ADVISE YOU THAT COLUMBIA UNIVERSITY TRUSTEES HAVE AWARDED YOU PULITZER PRIZE FOR EDITORIAL WRITING." He had won for his columns on the Temple bombing and other hate bombings.

"Naturally he won the Pulitzer Prize," said George Bright. "If you call that a prize. I don't. Pulitzer was just a Jew. It's a Jewish prize to all of the people who do good for the Jews." He laughed. "The Jew will give a prize to anybody who helps the Jewish community. The more you help them, the bigger Pulitzer Prize you get. They were glad to have Ralph McGill on their side. 'Here's a reward, Ralph.' "

4

On Monday morning, October 13, letters and telegrams began arriving at the Temple by the sackful, as if Rothschild were Santa Claus and this were Christmastime. From the most remote and handsomest churches in Atlanta, whose thresholds, one suspected, never had been crossed by a Jewish or black person, came statements, board resolutions, contributions, and offers of assistance so heartfelt that one suddenly wondered whether one had misjudged the people. A cry of anguish and sympathy rose from Atlanta's stone churches on their green lawns studded with magnolias. "This is not who we are! We are not in support of your being bombed out! We have many fine Jewish neighbors and friends!" A shout of sympathy went up from Atlanta's brick or wooden black churches, fronting sidewalks; in these, too, boards voted, resolutions were issued, and contributions for the Temple were collected. Much of the Christian South spoke, deploring the violence. Some of the ministers who wrote were among the eighty who had signed the Ministers' Manifesto, and some were not. Businessmen and shop owners wrote on their letterhead stationery, enclosing money; some of these were Jewish, and many were not. Schoolchildren wrote, as did veterans, widows, rabbis, Quakers, physics professors: a collage by Norman Rockwell might have captured such a thing in oil for the cover of the *Saturday Evening Post* as a true American moment. Rothschild had hit the postal jackpot. He was like a child who dutifully answers every chain letter, stamps and mails his five postcards, and puts his name on the bottom of the list with the promise that someday five thousand postcards will arrive (they never do arrive). For Rothschild, they arrived.

━ ⊯◆⊯ ━

The Reverend Harry Fifield wrote immediately to offer the facilities of First Presbyterian. And Custer Avenue Baptist Church wrote: "Fret not thyself about the wicked—God will repay." "YOUR FRIENDS AT TRINITY PRESBYTERIAN CHURCH . . . THIS MORNING ASKED GOD'S BLESSINGS ON YOUR CONGREGATION," came by wire. Telegrams also came from Brookhaven Methodist,

St. James Methodist, Druid Hills Baptist, Morningside Baptist, Covenant Presbyterian, and the Discussion Class of Northside Methodist Church. "WE ARE GRIEVED FOR YOU AND DISTRESSED BY THE FORCES THAT THREATEN THE RELIGIOUS FREEDOM OF ALL IN CHRISTIAN FELLOWSHIP," wired Grazener Trinity Baptist. "WE LAMENT THE TRAGIC DYNAMITING OF THE JEWISH TEMPLE," came from Audubon Forest Methodist Church.

The Congregation of the United Liberal Church sent regrets, as did "the entire membership of St. Mark's Methodist Church." "OUR HEARTS BLEED OVER THIS VILE AND CONTEMPTIBLE TRAGEDY," wired the Reverend Candler Budd of Glenn Memorial Methodist Church. "MAY THE GOD OF ISRAEL SUSTAIN AND GUIDE US ALL." "THE BRUTAL DYNAMITING OF THE TEMPLE IS CAUSE FOR THE MOST PROFOUND REVULSION TO ALL GOD-FEARING AND DECENT CITIZENS," wired the board of the Atlanta YWCA. "Those of us who have come to know you in Atlanta know so well that, of all people, you and yours do not deserve to be so badly hurt," wrote the Reverend Robert E. Lee, of the Lutheran Church of the Redeemer.

"Dear Sir:" came on a small folded piece of notepaper. "I do hope this may help somewhat to rebuild. I am filled with shame for the people who did this to your Temple." Signed: "An Episcopalian." Inside were three dollars.

Five dollars came from the Columbia Theological Seminary; $5, from "a Central Presbyterian family"; and $100, from the South Pine Nightwear Company in York, Pennsylvania, the owner of which wrote: "I do not think that words have yet been coined to express my true feelings."

Five hundred Methodist ministers and laymen adopted a resolution expressing "deep concern as well as great alarm at the tragedy at The Temple." Contributions arrived from Gate City Table Company, the Pershing Hotel, Josiah Sibley Real Estate, DG Machinery and Gage Company, Alan L. Ferry Designers, RabTree Transfer and Storage Company, and Henry Robinson, a professor of mathematics at Agnes Scott College in Decatur, Georgia. "As a gentile, Protestant, white Southerner, I deeply regret the unfortunate occurrence of the past weekend at your Temple," wrote a Ralph D. McWilliams. "Christian friends whom you do not know" sent a note of condolence. The Fulton

National Bank added thousands to the reward money and offered: "Should you have need of temporary financing in handling repairs, we shall feel honored to have you call upon us."

The outpouring of sympathy and fellowship from Christian Atlanta inspired Janice Rothschild to name the crime "The Bomb that Healed." Healed, forgiven, forgotten was the abandonment in 1915. The earth had orbited the sun forty-three times since Leo Frank, and, in that time, Jewish-Americans in Atlanta once again had endeared themselves to the Christians, as their forebears had when Atlanta was a raw settlement.

For the moment, few—besides McGill, Rothschild, a small handful of Temple congregants, and observers from the black community—pondered the meaning of this crime in relation to the civil rights movement. It was felt by nearly everyone in the city to be an act of pure anti-Semitism. "It was just hate," said a Temple member. "It was just a message of pure hate."

The blessed shower of telegrams and letters said, in effect: "You are like us. We feel as if one of our own churches had been bombed."

At the time, it was what the Temple Jews most wanted to hear. At least in this city, they were not being held responsible for the civil rights movement. Calling it an act of pure anti-Semitism meant "They hate you just because you are Jews, not because of anything you have or have not done."

"Please accept my small gift to help in the rebuilding of your Temple that was destroyed by some narrow-minded bigots," wrote Arthur H. Tuber of Levittown, Pennsylvania, enclosing ten dollars. "Long proud of my lineage and traditions, both of which are deeply bedded in the South, I hang my head in deep shame at the hideous act of desecration of The Temple," came from M. C. Langhorne.

Congregation Or Ve Shalom in Atlanta wired "HEARTFELT SYMPATHY." Telegrams and letters arrived from Rodeph Shalom in Rome, Georgia; Temple Oheb Shalom in Baltimore; Congregation B'nai Jeshurun in Newark; Temple Israel in Boston; Temple B'nai Israel in Oklahoma City; Congregation Shaarai Zedek in Tampa; B'nai El Temple in St. Louis; Temple Emanuel in New

York City; Temple Bethel in San Antonio; and Kahal Kodosh Beth Elohim in Charleston, South Carolina. And "HEARTFELT FRATERNAL SYMPATHIES" arrived from Rodeph Shalom in Philadelphia.

The mayor of Baltimore wrote, as did the Society of Friends from Westport, Connecticut, the Firestone-Goodwin Advertising Agency of Minneapolis, and "the Negro prisoners of the Atlanta city jail."

"Your handling of yourself and your congregation in this critical hour reflect credit not alone on you and your people, but all of us who bear the name Jew," came from Philip M. Klutznick, the president of B'nai B'rith.

"Many of my very dear friends of many years are of your faith," came from El Dorado, Arkansas. "I am sure you must know Dave Grundfest in Little Rock?"

"PS—You look good on TV!" came from a Chicago friend. Rothschild wrote back: "I must tell you that I don't look any better on TV than anywhere else—I'm just further away."

—— ⊪✦⊫ ——

Jewish citizens across the city experienced an outpouring of sympathy and support from Christian neighbors and business acquaintances, people with whom the topic of Jewishness never had arisen before. A German-Jewish refugee couple who ran a deli in stylish northeast Atlanta reported unprecedented business the day after the bombing: the store filled with customers coming in to express their regrets. A former employee of Rich's took a call from her former boss, with whom she had been out of touch, inviting her and her husband to dinner: "He was just trying in his bumptious way to show friendship." "After the bombing, the principal at E. Rivers Elementary School gave all the kids a letter to take home to their parents," said one-time Temple member Babette Ferst Herzfeld. "In a beautifully written letter, in a tone of friendship, he reminded parents how the Temple had let them use its Sunday school classrooms after a fire at the school. He wrote that it was time to return the hospitality and contribute to the rebuilding fund. It was a small elementary school, maybe two hundred kids, but the kids went home and raised five thousand dollars."

Jewish shop owners and newspaper columnists around the country found themselves the recipients of unsolicited contributions. The owner of Saul's in Griffin, Georgia, was handed twenty-five dollars by a customer, as was Hy Esserman, of Essermans and Company, in Rome. Alfred Segal of the *Cincinnati Post and Times Star* was mailed twenty-seven dollars, and a stockboy at Jacob's Drugstore in Atlanta handed five dollars to his boss.

From the daughter of the slain NAACP director in Florida, came a letter of sympathy to Rothschild, in which she mentioned that she and her sister had been in the house when their parents were killed by a bomb thrown from a passing car. "This one reminded us bitterly," said Janice, "that no such attention had been accorded black victims of such acts—and there had been hundreds throughout the South within the past few years."

"This is the segregationist answer to the prophetic pronouncements," wrote Rabbi Newton J. Friedman from Beaumont, Texas. "It would not be amiss to have the activities of your fellow Atlantan Grand Wizard of the KKK checked. His speech in Macon in April 56 was more anti-Semitic than anti-Negro."

"MAY THIS ACT OF VIOLENCE ALERT AMERICANS TO THE FACT THAT BIGOTRY UNLEASHED THREATENS ALL WE HOLD SACRED," wired Rabbi Arthur J. Lelyveld of Fairmount Temple in Cleveland. (A few years later this rabbi would be assaulted and beaten while demonstrating for civil rights in Hattiesburg, Mississippi, and seriously injured.)

"What can one write to you from Jackson, Mississippi?" wrote Rabbi Perry E. Nussbaum of Beth Israel Congregation. "The pattern is fixed. . . . I doubt if my own Congregation will escape." (In 1967 both Nussbaum's temple and his house would be wrecked by bombs.)

"This outrageous deed certainly makes us feel sick," came from the JCC in Nashville. "It is difficult to express ourselves even though we have had the same identical experience."

And from Rabbi Victor E. Reichert in Cincinnati, came the telegram: "ISAIAH 43 SUSTAIN YOU." The passage: "Fear not, for I will redeem you; / I have singled you out by name. . . . "

5

On Friday night, Rothschild spoke. A huge crowd filled the damaged, cordoned-off temple, despite thoughts that there might be some danger. "They came out stronger than ever," said the police captain, Fred Beerman. "The first Friday night service that Rabbi Rothschild had after the bombing, it filled that place up like it was High Holidays. I mean full. Usually on Friday nights you got 50 or 65 people there, 100 on a good night maybe. But I think it holds 747 people, and it was packed. I mean *I* went, and I *rarely* went. I think it made him stronger. If he got a boost, that was it."

"The next Friday night after that Sunday, the Temple was overflowing," said Schwartz, the Temple president. "The point is that it woke up those people who were on the fence. People were angry. Many of them who had been opposed to what Jack Rothschild had said from the pulpit were very supportive now. In other words, it really rallied everybody together."

"Even though all of us realized there would be extra protection for us at the Temple that Friday night, we could not stamp out a tiny ember of fear that some further act of terror would take place," recalls Janice. "In spite of that fear, a huge crowd filled the sanctuary, gathering as a family might in time of trouble. . . . Jack and I were amazed and thrilled to see so many people sitting in that damaged hall, with panes still missing from its windows and doors still askew on broken hinges.

"I never heard anybody say, 'That's what we get from Jack's sermons' or anything like it," said Joe Haas, the attorney and Southern Regional Council board member who had encouraged Rothschild from the start in his venture into civil rights. "I think they felt that Jack was a leader and that he probably stimulated something in some crazy group, but I don't think there was ever any feeling of blame by any means. If anything, it really cemented Jack's relationship with his congregation. The outpouring of the community had a lot to do with that too. It showed that the community had the greatest respect for him and for his words."

As the congregants absorbed the fact that the Temple had been attacked, they responded ardently as Americans. Not *shver tze-zan ah Yid*—"it's tough to be Jewish"—but outrage at the challenge to Rothschild's freedom of speech. Yes, he was a pill;

yes, he went on about the blacks too much; yes he had been almost totally distracted, since day one, from the purpose for which he had been hired, whatever that was, and had spent a lot of time running around the city like a second Jeremiah. But he was the rabbi, and if he believed that the race question was what a rabbi ought to talk about, then by God, they were paying his salary and they expected him to talk about it. He said they might be bombed and they *were* bombed, which meant, obviously, that the argument over the equality of blacks was a deeper one than they had paid heed to.

Of course he had told them, but his warnings had been *sermons*, after all; and if they knew anything at all about religion, it was that the words pronounced inside a house of worship had no relation to the world outside. For ultramodern *hommes d'affaires* southern Reform Jewish people like themselves, to enter the Temple sanctuary with its gold griffins and ornate ark and high dome was to enter an almost-imaginary world, a through-the-looking-glass fairy-tale world where reason was suspended, where boys with dark curls felled giants, where powerful kings demanded lullabies, where men cried to God from out of fish bellies. In *that* world, far removed from the streets, Rothschild had told them about justice and what was required of them to live justly. And it was very nice and poetical, and he gripped the podium and deepened his voice, and then it was over and time for pink punch and vanilla cookies with candy sprinkles in the social hall.

But now they had been assaulted for these words, for Rothschild quoting Isaiah at them, for their listening to Isaiah for half an hour before having their refreshments. The world of illusion dropped away. The bomb blew a hole in a real wall, not a biblical, nor metaphorical, one. So they responded first as Americans, and turned out by the hundreds to listen to Rothschild again, to say, above all, to the city: he has a *right* to say it; we have a right to hear it.

⇥ ⩔ ⇤

They packed into the Temple on Friday night, their cars double- and triple-parked in the parking lot. They overflowed the pews and leaned against the walls. They were nicely dressed, but it did not feel like Rosh Hashannah. Eight hundred Jews in fancy clothes were locked into a sanctuary with planks of wood nailed over broken windows, and uniformed police were standing guard outside. It was impossible not to recall, fleetingly, Germany. Had not people who looked like this been locked into similar rooms a dozen years before, then set afire? "This is the last empty building we will bomb in Atlanta," was the message the bombers had phoned into the papers. The congregants had to think it, so they thought it: Are we likely to get hurt here? Still, the resolve to be there was profound, deeper than common sense. As Joe Jacobs would say, "We're all Jews." They had been attacked; it was no time to scatter. So they smiled absurdly at one another, straightened their ties, adjusted their pearls, and faced forward. Americans and Jews.

And, feeling indulgent toward Rothschild for once, protective of him, fond of him, proud of him, they let down their guards a little and allowed themselves to be nudged along a tiny bit as moral people and as Jews: not only that he should say it and they should hear it, but that they should *act* on it.

If *Negro equality* were fighting words, and since they had willy-nilly entered the fray already, they might as well say the words themselves and put up their dukes. Not to stand by the rabbi now would be cowardly, and they were not cowards. They'd stand by him. Him and his Negroes.

So thought a great many.

Rothschild approached the lectern, placed his hands on either side, looked out over the crowd, and emitted a wisecrack: "So, *this* is what it takes to get you to Temple!"

Oh, *Jack*, mouthed the women knowingly, and settled back. The world had not changed completely.

Rothschild opened with the Sh'hechiyonu, a prayer of thanksgiving that God has allowed us to reach this day. Like all his words, it was double-edged: thanks for everyone's having survived the attack (to which the congregation could say "Amen!") and thanks for being given this event upon which to build better lives (to which the congregation could think, "Fasten your seat belts, we are going for a ride.")

Rothschild spoke:

What message was the explosion meant to deliver? What effect was it supposed to have? Its intent was clear enough. This was an act designed to strike terror into the hearts of men. It was intended to cause panic and confusion. It was to say to an already fearful minority: "You are not wanted here. Don't speak; don't preach the ideals of your religious faith. You are second class citizens marked for a life of fear." And more than this. It was to say to all the bewildered and confused people of America: "Terror is at hand. We have the means to spread terror and rule by force. Law is dead. We are the law."

Never was a message so garbled in its transmission. Never did a band of violent men so misjudge the temper of the objects of their act of intimidation. For this is what really happened: Out of the gaping hole that laid bare the havoc wrought within, out of the majestic columns that now lay crumbled and broken, out of the tiny bits of brilliantly colored glass that had once graced with beauty the sanctuary itself—indeed, out of the twisted and evil hearts of bestial men has come a new courage and a new hope. This single act of devastation has taught lessons which all words, all prayers, all pleas had been unable to teach. . . .

The first of them is that this must be a land ruled by law and not by men. . . . Once man decides that it is within his personal province to decide which laws he will obey and which he will ignore—then there is no law at all. . . .

And that law must be the moral law. . . . It is not easy to live by the rigorous demands of our spiritual forebears. Yet, it is more dangerous not to. For every time we stray from the paths they have set for us, we bring ourselves near to danger and destruction. The difficult way is still the safest way, after all. . . .

Who is to blame for the wave of violence that has swept across our land? The guilty ones are not alone the political leaders whose words fan the flames of hatred and incite to violence. Not even those who perpetrated the very acts themselves bear all the blame. Responsibility rests equally with those good and decent people who choose to remain silent in such a time.

And his congregation heard him and his congregation agreed. A symphony of accord was concluded, in which Rothschild had played his one deep melody, and sounded it again, and sounded it again, and now finally the orchestra picked it up, each instrument trying the melody in its own way, in its own clef: the melody was taken up and played en ensemble. They silenced the dissent among themselves and thenceforth stood publicly as Rothschild's allies.

"As I look back upon that hectic time, most of it runs together now in an indistinguishable pattern of chaos and excitement," Rothschild said many months later to his congregation. "Only one event stands out in bold relief. It was the sight of the sanctuary filled to overflowing. . . . Your coming was spontaneous and unplanned. No special notices were sent, no campaign for attendance was conducted. Nor could the sermon have drawn you—there was precious little time for the preparation of a sermon at all. Why, then, did you come?

"Essentially, I think, to reaffirm your allegiance to Judaism. . . . It was no longer enough to be just a dues paying member of the Temple. You had to be—for that one night—a participating member. You wanted to pray—to join with other Jews in heartfelt prayer. For years you had been secure in the comforting belief that your only obligation to Judaism was to contribute to the physical maintenance of its religious embodiment. Now, someone had threatened the existence of that symbol of your religion. And you needed to demonstrate to yourselves and to the world that the symbol was important—not in itself but as the tangible evidence of your own living faith. So, suddenly, attending a religious service became the most important event on your calendar—more important than a football game, more important than some social engagement. All the customary excuses somehow didn't sound so convincing: you were tired after a hard day's work—but not too tired; the movie was a good one—but you could see it another night. You came to Temple because you needed an hour of spiritual renewal—needed it more than anything else in the world."

"Alas," he continued on that Friday night many months later, as he looked out over a sanctuary of mostly empty pews, "the need disappeared. . . ."

The leaders of the white resistance had moved to step two of what was proving to be a four-tier strategy for eliminating opposition: step 1—verbal warnings, threats, speeches, leaflets, and other written propaganda; step 2—more garish threats, like victimless bombs and cross burnings; step 3—physical assault of individuals, with beatings, floggings, and so on; step 4—murder. Within five years the church and temple bombers were generating victims: four young teenage girls crushed as they sat in their Sunday school lounge in Birmingham in September 1963 (so that the choir robes of the Temple children in Atlanta would seem to have been an ominous portent); untold dozens of bodies of murdered black men dumped into lakes. A violent underground cruised the South; demolition pros made themselves available to local groups; the same names turned up in separate investigations in different bombed cities. Chattanooga, Birmingham, and New Orleans were headquarters for violent men who had long since thrown off the constraints of law and order. The explosion of the Temple was part of a pattern. Hate bombs had not yet spilled blood, but they were capable of it. "Looky what *we* can do," said the Confederate Underground. "Might is right."

12

"If It's the Bombing You're Interested In, I Don't Know Anything about It"

1

As in the wake of any startling crime, what was most vivid in the minds of the local citizens crept over them at nightfall: that felons were loose. It ruined the illusion that men and women all over the city were preparing for a peaceful night's sleep. For on the previous night, a sleepless band, dressed as if for work at three in the morning, had driven through oblivious neighborhoods and wreaked havoc on a dignified and silent building.

In reports from small towns across America where a horrific crime has occurred for the first time, a bystander is certain to offer the observation: "We never even locked our doors before this." And what she means is that in the thousand thoughtless daily housekeeping motions—whistling the dog in for the last time that day, unstringing the laundry from under darkening trees, yanking down the garage door, turning off the downstairs lights—there is an unhappy, new self-consciousness. The first nausea of fear and an awareness of cruelty have intruded.

Discomfited, Atlantans closed and locked their doors on Sunday against the bronze-leafed autumn night, where in a darkly turquoise sky a million stars came peering.

For the well-being of the citizenry, it was necessary to make arrests promptly, to fix the leak in the roof of the collective sense of security.

One hundred officers were assigned to the case, given highest priority by Chief Herbert Jenkins. FBI laboratory technicians were flown in from Washington. Police departments in Alabama, Florida, and Tennessee opened their bombing files to the Atlanta police. Atlanta detectives were paired with FBI agents to visit hotels and railway, bus, and air terminals; they set up roadblocks on Peachtree and questioned drivers; and knocked on doors in a block-by-block search of the area around the Temple.

On Monday, detectives announced the recovery from the rubble of a piece of brown wrapping paper, which they turned over to the FBI. In an announcement to the press, FBI laboratory experts confirmed that this paper was "similar to that used in wrapping dynamite."

This was the extent of the information collected at the crime scene.

If modern FBI and Alcohol, Tobacco and Firearms (ATF) experts could have visited the Temple on October 12, 1958, they might have recovered chemicals, gunpowder, fuse fragments, footprints, and tire markings; within a few weeks they could have known precisely the kind of nitroglycerine used in the bomb, how much of the substance was at large in America, the names of people with access to it, how it came into Georgia, and whether it had been in any of the houses or vehicles of the suspected men. They would have known what type of timing device was used and in what other locales such a device had been employed.

While the 1958 experts announced the recovery of a piece of brown wrapping paper that they felt resembled paper often used to wrap dynamite, 1990s experts would have known pre-cisely. Not all brown wrapping paper is identical. The bit of brown paper retrieved from the crater might have opened out encyclopedically to modern experts, might have been imprinted with a grain of gunpowder, a fleck of skin, a hair follicle, or a fingerprint that might have caused computers to whir and lights to flash back at headquarters. If modern detectives could have been airlifted in, via time machine, the dark history of the South could have been altered. Where there were no arrests, there might have been arrests; where there were arrests but no convictions, there would have been convictions—if and where the power structure permitted them. The children killed in Birmingham by crashing wallboards and plaster now might be women in the prime of life, raising children in a more integrated world, for the criminals who bombed them might have been identified already, might have been serving time for their earlier crimes. Vague, shifting alibis sound even more feeble beside the poster-sized blow-up of the defendant's fingerprint on a timing device.

It was not to be.

Thirty-five years ago, the chief thing the police detectives could say was that they felt someone knowledgeable in explo-sives had planted the bomb, because all the sticks of dynamite detonated; that they believed funding for the bombing came from sources outside the South; that they believed the bombing was linked to other bombings around the South; and that the dyna-mite had been wrapped in the sort of brown wrapping paper in which dynamite often was wrapped. "The bombing was defi-nitely done by somebody who knew his explosives," said one detective, I. G. Cowan, in a press conference. "An amateur tends to set the fuse so that only one or two sticks explode and the rest just scatter." That definitely narrowed the field of suspects to several thousand army veterans and munitions experts.

Still, it was a widely respected police force, an award-winning police force. Murders were solved, speeding autos were waylaid, drunks and transients were sent on their way. Under the dogwood trees, order was maintained. In the 1950s, the secret of exposing wrongdoers lay not primarily in the sterile retrieval of microscopic detritus from a crime scene (though the FBI was making great strides in matching bullets to gun types, and Detective W. K. Perry solved a rape case in 1957 by matching pubic hairs and underwear fibers). The emphasis was on the character arts: being able to spot a bad apple, to recognize a suspicious demeanor, to make out an alibi as cheesy, to break a suspect.

Good, upstanding, moral character radiated from the top: from Hartsfield (whose late-in-life divorce from his wife of forty-five years and May-December remarriage were widely forgiven), and from Jenkins, and from all the clean-cut, straight-arrow, square-shouldered police officers, white and black, on street patrol (for the force had been integrated under Mayor Hartsfield and Chief Jenkins, since 1948). Social deviants in the community stuck out like sore thumbs—perhaps especially in Atlanta, where a civilized accommodation to the Supreme Court's ruling on integration was being ventured in the highest quarters—while, elsewhere in the South, mayors, police chiefs, and city councilmen were cutting themselves loose from law, with long lines of social misfits enthusiastically following their example. Where community leaders publicly thumbed their noses at Washington and the federal courts, it was like opening the doors of the insane asylums: Klan-robed riffraff paraded through the streets, bribed and accepted bribes from public officials, and knew themselves to be untouchable. But in Atlanta, the names of known rabble-rousers appeared on lists on the police chief's desk, where Jenkins scanned them from time to time, knowledgeably frowning, and police cruisers were instructed to drive slowly in certain areas, on the lookout for trouble.

At the top of Jenkins's list of suspects in the Temple bombing were the men arrested that summer for the anti-Semitic picketing of the *Constitution*: George Bright, Chester Griffin, and Luther King Corley, all members of the extremist organization founded by Ed Fields and J. B. Stoner, the National States' Rights Party.

As the Atlanta Police Department moved toward locating, detaining, and questioning these men, the local FBI agents were reviewing their own files. They, like Jenkins, had kept tabs on the known asocial characters in Atlanta, but they had gone a step beyond the police chief's methods: the FBI had placed an informant within the NSRP, almost from the beginning.

Wallace Allen was right: the group's security had been compromised. While George Bright shined his flashlight up into trees and tapped on walls and placed his ear against the chimney, one man in their midst had been drinking in all their talk and committing it to memory as fast as he could. Allen was right about him, too: L. E. Rogers, the overweight, out-of-pocket, compulsive, and vulgar janitorial services man, was an FBI spy—or, in the language of the day, a sneak. He had joined both the NSRP and the KKK for the purpose of relaying inside information to the FBI—he had done it for the highest motives of citizenship, he later would aver. Meanwhile, he earned $50 to $75 for each report, had grossed $1,150 by October 1958, and had filled the local FBI files with reports of discussions such as the one in May in which NSRP members had fantasized shooting down Jews in the streets.

The FBI therefore concurred with the Atlanta Police Department's list of suspects and contributed three more names: there was a pair of brothers—Richard and Robert Bowling—known since boyhood for troublemaking and experimenting with explosives, who lately had been spotted in the company of some of the South's most dangerous extremists; and there was a telephone salesman—Wallace Allen.

Thus, by Sunday night of the Temple bombing, though on-the-scene detectives held in their hands paper particles and fuse device fragments they would not properly be able to decipher for another twenty-five years—like hieroglyphics before the discovery of the Rosetta Stone—the "character arts" and good old-fashioned undercover work produced the names of six likely suspects.

2

On Monday, October 13, the day after the bombing, police detectives were dispatched by Jenkins to arrest them.

In some cases this was more easily ordered than performed.

Robert Bowling was apprehended without incident. From his house police recovered a transcript of the municipal court trial of the NSRP picketing of the *Constitution* and *Journal* offices, and newspaper clippings of recent bombings. But Chester Griffin and Richard Bowling had disappeared.

The moment Griffin, the slightly dim-witted state revenue examiner, learned of the bombing, he surmised that he himself was the target of a massive manhunt and that his name was being broadcast over radio and television, and he took off.

He had gone to bed around ten o'clock on Saturday night, he remembered, having gone to a movie at the Fox. At 9:40 A.M. on Sunday, he was awakened by a telephone call from Rogers, who asked, "Did you just hear the news?"

"No. What happened?"

"The Jewish Temple just got it."

"I can't help it," said Griffin, and hung up. He looked both ways before leaving his house, yelled for his brother, ran to the car, and zoomed out to Stone Mountain in search of James Venable, the Imperial Wizard of the National Knights of the Klan, the lawyer who had represented Griffin and the others when they were arrested for picketing the newspapers.

"Knowing the warped minds of the F.B.I., the Atlanta Police, and the Anti-Defamation League, and the Atlanta newspapers," said Griffin, explaining why he had fled, "I well anticipated what lay in store for me, and they had already broadcast the fact that regardless of whether I was guilty or innocent, they were going to come over and try to pin anything that happened on me. So naturally this made me a bit uneasy, and after I ate, why I had my brother drive me out toward Stone Mountain and I tried to get in touch with Mr. Venable so that I'd know what to do in case I were to be picked up."

But Venable was out. Griffin delayed returning home. "I decided the best thing I could do was to lay low and try to get in touch with my attorney first thing bright and early Monday morning," he said. "So I went out to East Point and saw a show, and then I come back to Atlanta and caught a cab and went over to Highland Theater and I saw it was the same one I had already seen, so I just stayed around that drug store at the corner of Highland and Greenland until the show over at the Plaza was due to come on, and finally around eight o'clock, I went on to that show and it was a long one and it was about 11:30 before I got out, and I walked across the street, caught a taxi at the

Briarcliff Hotel, went home. When I got home, there was two FBI men and a City Policeman surrounded me and they didn't—they tried to prevent me paying the taxi operator and it was necessary for me to shove them out of the way before I could do so, and I hollered for my brother to where he would know what was happening and be able to do something about it, and I demanded they show me a warrant for my arrest, which they did not have, and they commenced questioning me about where I had been."

Detective W. K. "Jack" Perry drove forty minutes north of town to arrest Wallace Allen. Allen was home when the detectives appeared. He let his dog loose on them.

"Well, we had a warrant to go up there and arrest him," said Perry, later the chief of homicide. A loose-limbed, white-skinned, soft-drawling man, Perry lived in a modest farmhouse at the crest of a scrappy-looking hill in Conyers, Georgia, filled with elegant sideboards and glass-topped tables made by Perry for his wife in his spare time. "We got up there and he had a chain link fence right up against the sidewalk, and the gate was closed. He had a pretty deep front yard to his house and he was on the porch. I told him I had two uniform men with me and then my partner was with me. I started to open the gate, and he told me not to come in the yard. He was real arrogant. And I told him who I was, and I said, 'I got a warrant for your arrest.' About that time he turned a German shepherd loose on us. He called him Adolf—that was the dog's name—and the dog started running toward the gate. Well, I knew I was going in that gate, so I off and told him, I said, 'When that dog *gets* to the gate, I'm going to kill it.' So I pulled my gun, and the dog stopped just before it got to the gate. He hollered at him, and he stopped, because I would have shot him.

"But anyway, we went on in, and he had a picture of Hitler over his mantle with electric little candles burning underneath it. I remember leather, or something about leather, like riding crops, some kind of leather laced together. There was a good bit of leather there. And he was in the printing business. He had all kind of pamphlets that he would print. And one of the others told me that he was in the printing business. We were looking for explosives, or anything pertaining to it, but we didn't find it.

"He was very arrogant and belligerent, and he wouldn't tell you nothing. He wouldn't tell you the time of day. And he had that picture of Hitler and that dog named Adolf—he worshiped Hitler. But he took that ride anyway. He come on down."

Allen protested to the police: "If it's the bombing you're interested in, I don't know anything about it. I've never even seen a stick of dynamite."

From Allen's house the detectives removed anti-Semitic literature and drawing paper. "We interviewed people at a restaurant in Roswell," said Perry's partner, the Atlanta police detective C. J. Strickland, "who said that Allen would come in and use up the napkin dispenser doodling swastikas." In the drawings taken from his house by police, pages were covered with swastikas, Nazi flags, and a variety of hooked noses, in profile.

Luther Corley was released for lack of evidence. Richard Bowling still was being sought by police. He was not located until Saturday, October 18, at which time he was arrested and his car was impounded. No one found out where he had been hiding—police merely reported that he had been "on the dodge" since the bombing. In the car, police found a mimeographed sheet signed by the national commander of the Knights of the White Camellia, which read, in part: "The Jew is the sworn enemy of white Christian America. . . . This is a life and death struggle which we must win legally if possible, but violently if necessary."

Meanwhile, the mother of the Bowling boys, Katherine S. Bowling, protested their innocence to the press. Forty-two years of age, divorced from their father since Richard was one and she was pregnant with Robert, she had raised them alone by working as a clerk in a luggage store and as a secretary. "She says that she doesn't like Jews," reported the syndicated columnist Jim Bishop. "She does like Negroes 'if they are kept in their place.'

"She admires her sons enormously. When she reads about Bobbie being arrested for bombing a Jewish house of worship, she automatically thinks of the time he found a butterfly in the house. He refused to kill it. 'He just got a piece of paper and he scooped up that butterfly, and set it free outdoors.' "

3

Practically the only person in the city of Atlanta who claimed to have missed hearing about the bombing of the Temple for a full day and a half after it happened—though it ate up radio and television programming all day Sunday and was plastered across Monday's *Constitution and Journal*—was Bright. "I didn't have a paper at that time," he recalled many years later, seated in the front room of his small stone house. "No, unfortunately I did not hear about it or read about it or wasn't aware of it until I was told that I was under arrest for it."

The first he knew, he says, was when he opened his door to a policeman on Monday afternoon and was arrested.

"I was dumbfounded," said Bright, laughing. "I had no idea why they arrested me. I was amazed that somebody would accuse me of it. I was surprised. I thought it was awfully stupid of somebody to accuse me of something I had absolutely nothing to do with.

"The police questioned me for a long time," he said, still finding it funny. "It didn't frighten me. I thought the whole thing was a stupid undertaking on their part. Mainly they wanted to know my connection with other people. When I had no connection with other people, they couldn't do anything.

"Well, I knew L. E. Rogers," he said with a disparaging snort made dragonlike by the effusions of cigarette smoke that flowed from his mouth and nose. "L. E. Rogers, Leslie E. Rogers, turned our names into the FBI. He merely picked out some names from the anti-Communist movement, especially out of the National States' Rights Party, picked those five names out and turned those five names in. And those were the five that were indicted. When the indictment was publicized naming these five who had been arrested, then we knew Rogers had turned these five names in. We knew that.

"Rogers was an infiltrator into the anti-Communist activities either as a paid informer or as an opportunist. He may have been a Communist himself. Who knows? Who cares? I don't know who he was working for. L. E. Rogers was apparently an orphan, because he left no record. He was self-employed. He traveled around the country quite a bit. His background was not known. There were no legal records. You know, we tried desperately to find out where he was born. We don't know if that was his real name. He would go around and attend all the anti-Communist meetings, and then report to the police department or the FBI or the ADL or whoever it was. Who and what. But he was too nosy, and he would disappear during the meeting and come back later and say that he had been someplace different. We checked him out—he wasn't there. So undoubtedly he was up at the police department reporting.

"It wasn't a shock to me because what Rogers did was pick five out of the most effective anti-Communist organization—we had doctors, lawyers, generals, businessmen. In other words, he wanted to kill it.

"Ah, you know, come to think of it, that wasn't the reason at all. The damage to the building was superficial," Bright continued, chuckling. "It wasn't intended to kill anybody nor to destroy the building. It was superficial damage—just to an entranceway, I believe. In other parts of the country people were being killed by bombs. Churches were *destroyed*—burned, and so forth; totally destroyed. So I think it was sabotage: either by the Temple in order to blame it on the anti-Communists or by L. E. Rogers to get these people *now*. 'Get these people in jail now before they become even more active because they're doing too much harm to our movement, the Communist movement.'

"The police listened to Rogers because he was a smooth talker. Chief Jenkins was just so stupid. There wasn't any evidence to be presented to the grand jury to indict. Absolutely none. It was just hysteria over the Jewish Temple. My golly, Rothschild had control over Jenkins and over the city. Golly, it was well known that when Rothschild said, 'Jump,' they jumped. The newspapers jumped when he said, 'Jump,' because he could have all the advertising withdrawn from the newspaper. That's the power of the advertising. Rich's was the main source of income. Rothschild was worried about our party; he wanted our party singled out. He knew who I was. I debated him in church one time.

"Look, if someone had wanted to do real damage, they could have. We weren't worried about the Temple. I have no doubt the National States' Rights Party was *not* behind this bombing. It hurt our organization. I have no evidence that any group was behind it. It wasn't their kind of tactic. It accomplished nothing. It would be negative to do such a thing."

Bright puffed at his cigarette and chuckled, and puffed and chuckled, as he spoke. One can only hazard wild guesses as to where the humor lay for him. Was it amazement, even after all these years, that the police could have been so ill informed as to accuse him of an act of violence? Was it the insult that he could be accused of so ineffective a bombing? Was it satisfaction that, after all these years and all he was put through, whatever he truly knew about the bombing and the bombers was not drawn out of him in interrogation, so that the police, in his memory, could not help but appear a bit Keystone Cop–like, while he, the race warrior, kept his cards close to his chest?

"I really think J. B. Stoner could have done it—and Bowling was a hothead—no, L. E. Rogers could have done it. Yeah. Because I'll tell you what—it made sense to us after, we discussed this afterwards. It made sense to us that since there were some bombings prior to that, that if we could be undermined by a gratuitous bombing and be blamed for it, then that would be a way to destroy us. So L. E. Rogers very well could have done it. Or the Communists themselves. Or the Jews themselves. They could have bombed their own temple. They didn't want us around.

"Oh yes, and there was Rothschild. He was supporting civil rights in order to feather his own nest. There's no reason to be involved in the rights of others unless it's going to net me some gain eventually. He knew the blueprint on how everybody else was going to be mongrelized interracially so that everybody else would be the same color (a gray color) and his race would remain pure. His race—the Jews—would be the only pure race left. Of course that would have motivated Rothschild—that his own race would stay pure. Rothschild was the most influential. He told Ralph McGill what to print."

In a warranted search of Bright's house, police retrieved a draft of a letter from May 1958 addressed to Rabbi Jacob Rothschild, which read, in part: "You are going to witness one of the most terrifying experiences in your life."

4

On Monday afternoon, October 13, 1958, the day after the Temple bombing, Atlanta police detectives Strickland and Perry broke the case.

They took a confession from Griffin, whom they had picked up the night before. They listened to his story first outside the jail, because he was afraid to talk inside it; and they listened to his story again when he told it to Sergeant Marion Blackwell and to the police stenographer who recorded it.

"Wallace Allen and George Bright were both of them hardened fanatics, like J. B. Stoner—no way you were going to penetrate," said Strickland from his home in Fort Pierce, Florida. "Allen and Bright were entirely different from the Bowlings, from Chester Griffin. Griffin was the weakest link. You could look at him and tell it."

Strickland is an Atlanta native and a World War II army veteran from the Forty-first Infantry Division; he was with the first troops to enter Hiroshima after the atomic bomb was dropped. He graduated from the Atlanta police academy in 1948, and then served as a vice-squad detective and a homicide detective before his promotion to sergeant. Promoted again, he served as a lieutenant of homicide and lieutenant of the vice squad; promoted again, he served as a captain of homicide and robbery, and for a year as a major of criminal investigation. In 1973 he was appointed by Commissioner of Public Safety Reginald Eaves as his administrative assistant, and in 1976 he assisted in the investigations by the U.S. House of Representatives Select Committee on Assassinations.

"Only thing Griffin had was a broke arm when we arrested him," said Perry in Conyers, Georgia. "He had his arm in a cast. It was already broke. But you know you can look at people when you start to interview them, and you can always tell the weakest link. And that's who I go for. And it paid off. Eventually, he told us all about it. This was a man where the elevator wasn't stopping at the top floor."

Perry, also an Atlanta native, joined the police department in 1952. Having worked in vice and in traffic, he was, by 1958, a homicide investigator. Like Strickland, he moved up the ranks from detective to sergeant to lieutenant to zone commander in the field and then to chief of homicide, a rank he held for ten years until his retirement in 1979.

Perry was a man of deep intelligence and intuition. Slow-moving and affable, he naturally hid the quick workings of his mind. Unlike northern geniuses who sometimes seem to be banging around in haste, firing rapid torrents of words, leaving offices full of papers rustling in their wake as they tear through, Perry was a discreet man who buttoned his shirt slowly, took his time backing carefully down the long gravel driveway from his modest wood-frame house out in the country, and had the patience to garden and to make furniture. He thought things through. He made the time to call repeatedly on a suspect and seemingly indulge in long, sociable chats. Accepting a glass of iced tea, he made himself comfortable in a kitchen chair and sympathetically listened to impulsive confidences that occasionally lurched willy-nilly and exposed, to the detective's gentle brown eyes, true guilt or innocence. His hobby was cabinet making—not so far, really, from his profession—for here, too, impossible planks needed to be fit together to make a proper whole. From bits and pieces of lumber and hardware he built smooth, subtle, glass-paned sideboards; and in the crimes to which he was assigned, he built—from bits and pieces at the crime scene, and from talks with the suspects—the true history, no matter how improbable.

"I was working with Strickland when we got the call on this case," he said, in poor health the spring of 1995. "Homicide worked anything of violence like that. I was working day watch on Sunday morning when this thing came in, and we was on West Peachtree Street, me and my partner, eating breakfast at that Magic Grill. They had looked for that bombing all through the night. Somebody called in—a lot of people called in—said they heard a loud explosion. But they couldn't find it until someone came to the church that morning. And we got there, and of course we was assigned to the case then. And then, of course, they called in everybody. And the FBI was there. I was assigned to the FBI; well, me and my partner both. Once this thing happened, for about three and a half months I didn't go to the Atlanta police department—I went to the FBI.

"We started, you know, interviewing," said Perry. "You got to interview, interview, interview everybody around the place. And the States' Rights Party, they was automatically suspect, which George Bright was a member of and the rest of them. But a lot of it was more or less harassment: we harassed. You know, that's the way you do. Now, for example, Robert Bowling lived with a fellow. I don't remember his name. He was a suit salesman for Muse's, and he was a homo. And we were trying to get information through him, and of course he wouldn't tell us nothing. So I got him fired at Muse's, and he'd go somewhere else, and I'd follow him wherever he'd go and I'd go get him fired. I'd tell them, 'He's connected with this group here,' and they'd fire him. There was three places I know he went to, and every time he'd get a job, I'd get him fired. Used it for harassment. You know, you harass somebody sometimes so long, and they'll tell what you want. I don't think he was involved. He was just living with Robert, and Robert was living with him. He was on up in age way back then. He was much older than Robert.

"George Bright was already in jail when Griffin made his confession. But George Bright wouldn't tell you what time it was. We knew that we weren't going to break him. We interviewed him, but he wouldn't tell you nothing. You know, you were just spinning your wheels. He just wouldn't talk to you at all.

"But looking at Griffin, he didn't look like he was working with a full deck. And, you know, you got to study people. We knew the rest of them wasn't going to say nothing. The others were tougher. He was the weakest, Griffin was."

Griffin told the detectives he would talk to them, but not inside the jail, which was sure to be bugged, where the other men would find out he had talked, and kill him. Perry and Strickland drove him to a restaurant and invited him to confess there, but Griffin was still frightened. "He told us that if he were to talk, they would kill him," said Perry. "So we took him out, got him out of the jail, thinking he would talk. Took him to a restaurant on Ponce de Leon, and he thought maybe the booth was bugged. So we'd go somewhere else, and he'd say 'Man, ya'll got this bugged, too.' So I said, 'We'll go to Grant Park.' Now Grant Park is where the Cyclorama [a three-dimensional exhibit about the Battle of Atlanta] is at, out there in the east part of town. It's a huge place. There's parks and benches. And I said,"—the patient, drawling, almost fatherly voice, the kind eyes, and the first hint that you may be getting toward the bottom of the man's tolerance— " 'Now *you* pick the bench or the swing. We don't have them *all* bugged.' And he, you know, searched us to make sure we didn't have a bug. And he finally determined that there was a swing that wasn't bugged. He didn't want nothing bugged, you know. So that's where we broke him, was at Grant Park."

On the tall metal swingset in the chilly shade of Grant Park, Griffin talked. "I'm sure he had in mind that he was in deep trouble," said Strickland, "and that if he unloaded and told the whole story, it would be in his favor. We had to go to the swings and sit down where he could see all around him.

"He told us George Bright was the one set it up. George Bright was the one that built the bomb. He described everything that each one did, and he went into detail with George Bright. I think George was more or less the leader of that thing. And they was getting a lot of coaching from J. B. Stoner. J. B. was more or less an advisor to them. Of course, he belonged to that outfit too."

"We came back to the station," said Perry, "and took him to the fifth floor, and we had a steno come up there in a part of the jail we didn't use. And he dictated and signed a lengthy statement as to what took place."

⊷ ▰◆▰ ⊶

"I was present at a meeting of the National States' Rights Party, at 524 Flat Shoals Ave., S.E. in the second week of May, 1958," Griffin's confession begins. "Also present were Billy Branham [the nineteen-year-old Atlanta NSRP organizer, in whose apartment the men first met], George Bright, L. E. Rogers, and Wallace Allen."

During the course of this meeting, Wallace Allen brought up the subject of dynamiting the Jewish Synagogue on Peachtree St. He stated that J. B. Stoner could be counted on to go to Anniston, Ala. to pick up the dynamite from KKK there. And that Billy could be a watcher while Wallace was in the get away car and the two Bowling boys would plant the dynamite and one of Ace Carter's men from Birmingham, Ala. would set the fuse to it. I opposed such a move.

One sees here why Griffin displayed simultaneously a craving to talk and a fear of talking: he was fairly bubbling with concurrent knowledge of guilt and innocence—his own innocence, of course, and the others' guilt. He offered to police a type of confession considered, in legal circles, to be generally reliable, in that it brimmed with names, places, dates, and incidents, a dense content unlikely to have been invented out of thin air one day after the bombing and on the day of the man's arrest. He simply had not had the time to fabricate such a lengthy story.

George Bright was to draw the diagram to place the dynamite and Wallace would case the building for the job. Wallace stated that he would be able to obtain the dynamite. And that 20 sticks should do the job. Wallace Allen stated that J. B. Stoner could be counted on to bring the dynamite in a suitcase at night. The suitcase would be a cardboard type. He was to bring the dynamite to Wallace Allen who would then go with the other members of the party to plant and set off the dynamite.

Such details as the cardboard suitcase are of special interest to legal experts. Is it conceivable that such minutia was discussed five months before the bombing? In the horrific cases of murderous car bombs destroying buildings, have the conspirators debated what *color* rental car or truck should be detonated?

J. B. Stoner was to leave town and go to Chattanooga while this was going on. No definite date was set for the bombing. No more was said in regards to this bombing there at subsequent meetings. We had approximately 8 meetings after this one and this bombing was not discussed with me. I believe that after I objected to the bombing that I was left out of the plans.

Typical of confessions of this sort, Griffin was careful to exonerate himself. But the fact that Griffin absolved himself left the case ajar, muddied the prosecution, and made the statement less a confession than an unsworn accusation.

> After we were arrested for picketing in front of the *Journal* Bldg. [in July], we had an open air meeting at Piedmont Park. We discussed means of increasing membership and of the legal aspects of the picketing. It was decided to suspend future meetings for 4 or 5 weeks. Richard Bowling contacted me one time to state that L. E. Rogers was a spy and not to trust him. That is the only time that I contacted the Bowlings after the Piedmont Park meeting. He stated that Rogers was an ADL spy, "Anti Defamation League." I have not contacted Wallace Allen for at least 4 weeks, I have seen George Bright and L. E. Rogers about once every ten days. I went up to Louisville with L. E. Rogers on Labor Day weekend to attend the National States' Rights Party Convention. While up there I fell over a concrete divider strip in a parking lot and broke my arm. I have not seen or contacted Billy Branham since his departure from Atlanta one week after the picketing. He went to Detroit to stay with his parents and attend school up there. Around the first of May I had a conversation with Billy Branham at the Rebel Drive In at which time he stated that extreme measures would be necessary in order to fight the enemy. He stated that he had an uncle in eastern Kentucky, at Harlan, who owned a mine and had access to dynamite. I, at that time, stated my objections to such an idea.

Griffin was a saint, it appeared, a man who would not abide hate talk in his presence.

> Billy Branham stated around the first of June that it might be necessary to take drastic action in case the Henry Grady High School became integrated. During the discussion of the dynamiting of the Jewish Synagogue on

Peachtree St., it was suggested that one of the charges should be put behind a column. . . .

At a meeting it was suggested that it was best to bring outside men to do the jobs instead of the local members and to use black unknown cars as get away cars. The Nights of the White Camellia of Tallahassee, Fla., of which Bill Hendricks [*sic*] is affiliated, believes in using drastic means to achieve their aims. . . .

Rogers' phone call [Sunday morning] was the first inkling I had had that such a bombing was to occur or did occur. I had not been in contact with any of the members of the organization except Rogers and Bright. I had not phoned nor seen Wallace Allen, J. B. Stoner or the Boling [*sic*] boys during this period of time and did not know of their plans or preparations. Billy Branham had stated on more than one occasion the Bowlings were too hot to handle at regular meetings but could be counted on to do the necessary work. The implication being dynamiting.

Signed: Kenneth Chester Griffin

"The bomb was a very shrewd thing," said Perry. "The way it was described to me by the one that told us all about it, George Bright took a piece of wood like so. All right, he has an open book of matches stuck in the end of the wood with a thumbtack. There's a wad of cotton saturated with lighter fluid also tacked into the wood. From that the fuse comes across, goes to the bomb, the dynamite. All right, they light a cigarette and open up that matchbook, and they light the cigarette and lay it in there and it takes about five minutes for that cigarette to burn back to where it hits the matchbook. Then it makes a flash. The flare ignites the cotton, which is impregnated with lighter fluid, and that starts the fuse. That gives them time to go. They can be, in five minutes . . . they can be anywhere, away from the area. And he said that was the type device that they used. We turned the statement over to the solicitor general."

On Friday, October 17, five men were indicted by the Fulton County grand jury under an 1897 code reading: "The willful and malicious destroying or injuring of any dwelling house, storehouse, barn, depot, or other house or place of business or lodging . . . with or by the use of dynamite, powder, nitroglycerin, or other explosive substance or compound shall be punished with death." The indictment charged that the five—George Bright, 35; Wallace Allen, 32; Chester Griffin, 32; Robert Bowling, 24; and Richard Bowling, 25—"did willfully and maliciously destroy and injure a house of worship known as The Temple . . . by using some explosive substance and compound which is to the grand jurors unknown."

By Saturday, October 18, all five were in jail. One already had confessed. The detectives rightfully felt proud of their first week's work on the case.

"At that time we were trying to act like professional investigators and police officers," said Strickland. "We satisfied to our own minds that we did the best we could: we broke the case, now it's in their hands—the FBI and the prosecution—let them do the best they can."

13

"The Jewish Race Is Not on Trial in This Case"

1

The elite corps of the Atlanta branch of the National States' Rights Party was lodged in the Fulton County jail.

"They wouldn't set a bond," said Bright. "I was in jail 101 days. It was rough. The worst part was malnutrition. Terrible food. I wouldn't feed it to my dog."

James R. Venable, who had represented the NSRP members arrested for picketing the *Journal and Constitution* in July, was hired by Chester Griffin to defend all five arrested men.

Defense attorney Venable—"Jimmy"—was the imperial wizard of the National Knights of the Klan, a member of Georgia's most prominent Ku Klux Klan family, and the mayor of Stone Mountain, Georgia, (east of Atlanta) from 1946 to 1949. The Venables once owned Stone Mountain itself, the largest granite outcropping in North America, on which likenesses of the heroes of the Confederacy—Robert E. Lee, Stonewall Jackson, and Jefferson Davis—were carved: a southern Mount Rush-

288

more. The Venable granite business paved Atlanta's streets and made the family wealthy. At the summit of the mountain, rallies and cross burnings were held in 1915 to signal the revival of the Klan—reactivated by the Leo Frank case. Members called themselves the Knights of Mary Phagan. A Klan rally and cross burning were held on or near the mountain on every Labor Day weekend for half a century, from 1931 until 1981. In 1936, Venable cofounded the National Knights of the Ku Klux Klan and named himself imperial wizard; he led the Knights until 1987, when he was eighty-four. He claimed to have known every imperial wizard except General Nathan Bedford Forrest and often said that he "longed for the good old days when the Klan was a real power." He recalled when his rallies brought to the mountain town "a line of Greyhound buses five miles long and full of Klan."

In 1966, Venable was subpoenaed before the House Un-American Activities Committee. He testified that he kept no membership records. "Let me get this straight," said the acting chairman, Joe R. Pool, of Texas. "You are the Imperial Wizard and you don't know where your Imperial Kingdom is?"

"That's right," Venable replied in as thick a drawl as the committee could want. "Klan members are like filling stations; they pop up, and then they disappear."

Jimmy Venable was a peaceable fellow, according to family friends, with no particular bones to pick with Jews or blacks; he just happened to have been born into the world of the Klan in 1903. "Half of America was under a sheet then," said a close friend of the Venable family. "The Klan was booming: just a lot of people didn't want to be told by the government who they had to mix with. Mr. Venable had the best sense of humor; he saw nothing wrong with anybody really; he'd be kind to the worst person in the world."

As the mayor of Stone Mountain, Venable donated land for the city's first black cemetery; as a defense attorney, he represented many black clients and spoke at black colleges. He won an appeal for two black Muslims in Louisiana convicted on charges stemming from a police raid on their mosque. "He always said, 'The Negroes don't have any trouble with me,' " reported the family friend. " 'I keep the courts from running all over them.' " To his white critics he replied: "I'd represent

Martin Luther King if he paid me enough. I'd represent Nikita Khrushchev."

A benevolent fellow or not, Venable in 1971 wrote and had published a book entitled *Choose Your Side, or The Thinking of the Ku Klux Klan*. The book is a history of America, from a unique angle, opening with a long list of Christian saints like "Saint Pope Gregory IX, who in 1233 issued an Edict concerning Jews," and "Saint King Edward I, of England, who in 1290 Expelled the Jews from England," and which concludes with "Saint Adolf, of Bavaria, the greatest anti-Jew since Jesus Christ and the Greatest White Champion"; and "Saint George of Virginia, who died for the White Race, a Military Veteran of the United States who could not be buried in a National Cemetery because of Jew objections." Venable discussed at great length "The Jews' Disease":

> Jews "resolved" themselves much as is the case in a Breed Of Cattle, except the Jews did it in an Enclosure of their own making . . .—and they think it has all been "GREAT,"—but they have in fact, long ago, created and Established themselves (bred to a Conformation of certain Inner Human Traits)—as truly A KIND OF CATTLE, sincerely posing as "SUPERIOR" HUMAN CREATURES,— but being really A CATTLE with a certain kind of MENTAL DISEASE or PSYCHOSIS that is found, in some measure, in probably 99% of all Jews. This disease is Paranoia . . . and its unmistakable symptoms are **Delusions of Greatness**, or **Grandness**, or **Genius . . . Coupled** with **Delusions of Persecution. . . .** This **special Jew Disease** has for countless generations **presented a World Health Problem.** It is **quite clear** to all Non-Jew students of World History, Past and Present, **that the Jews are the Mental-Health Problem of the Whole World!**

And so forth. For six hundred pages.

Venable practiced law out of a disheveled office across from the DeKalb County Courthouse in Decatur, Georgia, and carried abbreviated forms of his client files on three-by-five-inch cards in his pocket, alphabetized for ready reference. Toward the end of his life, suffering from Alzheimer's disease, he resigned the practice of law as the result of a state bar petition to have him disbarred for incompetence.

2

One of Jimmy Venable's first acts as defense attorney was to assist Chester Griffin in the retraction of the statement he'd given police the day after the bombing. In that statement, extracted on the chilly swingset at the foot of a grassy slope in Grant Park, Griffin remembered that he'd overheard talk of bombing the Temple, but had himself declined to participate.

In his *new* statement to police, under Venable's direction, he'd heard nothing, remembered nothing, knew nothing. He denied that any conversation about bombing the Jewish Temple had ever taken place at any meeting or anywhere else.

In the new statement, Griffin's eagerness to talk to police and his fear that everything was bugged were transformed. Now it appeared that Detectives Strickland, Perry, and Blackwell had harassed him for days.

When we got to the Station, they tried to be nice and said, "Now, we just want to merely ask you a few questions and then we will turn you loose." So they proceeded to ask about the Bowling boys to which questions I said I hardly know those boys. . . . I don't believe, however, they were mixed up in any kind of bombing, I am quite sure they aren't.

And they wanted to know about Billy Branham, and I said I had not seen Billy Branham since he left [town] shortly after the picketing. . . . Then they wanted to know about Wallace Allen, and I told them I had not seen Wallace Allen in at least eight weeks and I didn't know what he was doing, but I was sure he didn't have anything to do with any bombing.

Then they wanted to know about George Bright, and I said, "George I know is not connected with anything like that." . . . The only thing we had talked about was mailing out some literature, we never mentioned any bombing [or] dynamite in any shape, form or fashion. . . .

Finally they appeared to be mad and they said, well, send him on back, and they sent me on back to the finger-printing room . . . and this fingerprint man was kind of a bit of smart alec and he grabbed my sore thumb and twisted it—twisted my thumb belonging to my broken arm, it ached all night long, and I was unable to get any sleep the rest of that night. . . .

The next morning I was woke up around five o'clock and they came around, old salty piece of bread and old salty piece of meat, and two pieces of bread and one toasted and one wasn't, and wasn't fit for a dog to eat.

The police refused to let Griffin see his lawyer, he said, and they threatened that he would lose his job if he did not talk. The detectives assented to the truth of the latter half of this statement: threatening job loss was their typical strategy.

I kept repeating I wanted to see my lawyer, and all they would do would be to make a sneering remark about he is on the run, he can't help you, what you want to see him for, and not any other lawyer will take this case, and your only hope is just to tell us all you know. They started smearing Wallace Allen, they said that Wallace Allen was getting rich off this, I was just a sucker, and that George Bright was getting the money off of this, also. . . .

Finally about two o'clock they said, "You haven't had anything to eat, have you?" I said no and so they said, "Why come on with us, we will get you something to eat," and so they carried me out, without having any Court Order to do so, and carried me over to Evans Restaurant on Ponce de Leon, and bought me a dinner, and they were fairly licking their chops in anticipation of the juicy information I was going to give them, and I told them that I was not, and so I clammed up on them, I didn't know anything, and this made them mad and they finally took me back, got back about 2:30 to the cell. It wasn't but a little over an hour until they came again with the same old business and they—by this time—they had me practically out of my mind, constant questions to try to scare me, worrying the life out of me, and so, they set in on me again, and after about an hour or two, I decided the only thing to do was to give them a false story so that I could get out and they shut their mouths up and I might get hold of a lawyer.

The source for all the detailed facts, dates, and places in the first statement, Griffin then revealed, had been a dream:

> I had had this wild dream one time about a bombing, and [it] is substantially the same story I told them, and Blackwell added a few little twists of his own on to it. . . . They carried me off again without having any Court Order to do so, and we went over to Grant Park.
> They came back and they lit on me again about two or three hours trying to get me to make a statement, and finally, after being worn out, I consented to sign it.

The detectives urged Griffin to testify before the grand jury, but he refused: "They started in on me trying to get me to say I'd testify before the Grand Jury and they'd let me off and I said I am not going to testify against these boys because they are innocent, they are innocent, you just tricked me into signing that statement there, and it is not true and I am not having any part in any Grand Jury testimony."

The police then administered a lie detector test, but it was inconclusive. Griffin said: "They made it too tight around my chest purposely to where it would show up bad and then kindly emphasized certain questions and kept repeating the question over and over—four times and more times instead of four, and they took it, they came back in with it with the tale that I was lying to them and would I take the test over. I told them no, I wouldn't take the test over." Suspecting that Griffin may have been the one to phone the Rothschild's home, the police made a recording of Griffin's voice.

As to the presence in Griffin's first statement of Asa Carter and J. B. Stoner and Bill Hendrix—all likely masterminds of the southwide terrorism—"I just created that," Griffin said now, "in trying to send them off on a wild goose chase."

Detectives Perry and Strickland believe, to this day, in the veracity of Griffin's first statement. Granted, Griffin might have crammed into his first statement every name and place he thought the detectives *wanted* to hear. He implicated a number of major players in the segregationist backlash.

On the other hand, there is Griffin's mad dash to hire a lawyer as soon as he learned of the bombing, an action powerfully suggestive that there was at least some truth in the first statement: Griffin probably had heard or knew *something*, else why the panic?

And Venable researched, on Griffin's behalf, the question of conspiracy: "The crime is completed," according to the law, "when an overt act to effect the object of the conspiracy is done by at least one of the conspirators." The legal research proceeded, in other words, as if Griffin's first statement had been true: that at an NSRP meeting in May, the Temple bombing had been discussed in Griffin's presence, and that the subsequent bombing of the Temple had made Griffin a conspirator.

3

Venable confidently felt that the Temple bombing case was one he knew how to handle. It presented itself to him in an outline as familiar and homely as an old wood-handled plow. Without investigation he could see what the machinery of the case hinged on: the perfidy of the Jews. It was an old, old story; he knew it well; he took it by both handles.

In jail he backslapped, chuckled with, and winked at the indicted men, as if to let them know a fix was in, a cosmic fix: that he, the imperial wizard, well acquainted with midnight, born to the knowledge of a mystical mumbo-jumbo spellbinding to the masses, his gleaming robe decorated with the ribbons and badges of increasingly secret orders (the innermost secret circle, truth to tell, consisting of himself and his wife, children, and TV set in a modest den most evenings), required only half a fistful of old tricks to win this case. For this one, a minor bit of wizardry, the least of his magic, thrown like fairy dust or sand into the jurors' faces, should do.

The theory of the defense was that the Jews themselves were behind the bombing: that they gained far-reaching sympathy and considerable financial gain from the victimless crime; that the true victims were the unjustly accused patriots of the NSRP. Venable's case strategy was to demonstrate that five innocents had been ensnared in the Jews' sticky nets, one of which nets was the Jew-controlled Atlanta newspapers.

Venable's law partner, Essley Burdine, gave a statement to the press: "The five men have been tried, convicted and hung by the Atlanta newspapers through information furnished them by a group of publicity-happy officials of the Atlanta police department."

A bail petition prepared by Venable charged that the men were held on "pretended charges of vagrancy with the aid of Solicitor General Paul Webb and the Anti-Defamation League known as the Jewish gestapo."

The five men were brought from their jail cells in the Fulton County Jail and permitted to make public statements while the court considered whether to set bail.

Allen, high-cheekboned, gaunt, said: "Well I just want to tell you that I'm not guilty of being connected with that bombing or any other bombing of any kind. I don't know anything about bombings. I just feel like that the *Atlanta Journal* because of all this pressure being put on them to find somebody that they are trying to convict anybody and that they have left themselves more or less on the spot by bragging that they had captured the people but I'm not guilty of it. I've never participated in any meetings where bombings were discussed. I've never advocated it or condoned it and I don't believe in it and I'm just innocent, 100 percent—1,000 percent innocent, so help me God."

Griffin, in a checkered shirt, his thick, straight, dark hair standing up around its cowlick, desperately anxious that his codefendants might learn about his first statement, said: "I have never taken part in any dynamiting of the Jewish Temple. I have never taken part in a discussion of a dynamiting. I do not know who had a part to play in this. I have not got any idea, unless it would be some Communist. . . . I am loosely associated with these other boys and we do not act as a group. I am sure, however, that none of these boys would do such a thing and I am quite positive that they are innocent. . . . I have been subjected to great pressure and intimidation in an effort to frame me for this dynamiting, of which I had no part."

Robert Bowling, handsome in a fine suit, said: "I am not guilty of the charge against me. The indictment was pressured by the Atlanta newspapers and by the Jewish Anti-Defamation League of B'nai B'rith. . . . I was at home in bed at the time it happened. I am not connected with any anti-Semitic organizations and hardly know the other defendants in the case."

Richard Bowling, his red-faced brother, said, in part: "They have to have a scapegoat and they are going to try to get anyone they can. The evidence against me does not warrant an indictment. My name has not been mentioned by anyone in connection with any violent acts. My political beliefs have been the whole cause of the action taken against me."

Bright, calm and condescending (unlike his nervous, swearing, fingernail-picking associates, he had spent his time in jail reading) said:

Gentlemen, I deeply appreciate the opportunity that you have afforded me. This is the first act of kindness that I have seen since I was picked up Monday afternoon. I've been under very heavy interrogation and I still, and always have, protested my innocence. I say repeatedly, and I stand on this with no qualifications whatsoever, that I am entirely innocent of the bombing that took place over last weekend or any other violent acts or any violence whatsoever in my whole life. I have always and do now stand 100 percent for the Constitution of the republic of the United States of America. I have never, in all my life, ever condoned, discussed, planned, or participated in any deeds, acts, or thoughts of any violence whatsoever.

That is my stand for my whole life as a Christian and I say this as a Christian with Christian principles. I'm a baptized Baptist and I have stood on the principles of the Ten Commandments all my life. . . .

Now I do know this, and this is public knowledge. It should be by now, in case the people of the country do not know this. For some time there has been brewing a threat of the integrationists to break the barrier of segregation in this city.

I've known this for about a year, I think. And I have been active in voicing my opinion for the continuance of segregation. I have been active in voicing my opinion for the continuance of any truthful knowledge and facts that come to the newspapers and other press and the radio.

I have said, even with public display, that I do not believe that newspapers in general give a fair picture of not only politics, local, international, and national, but of this present situation. . . . I say without reservation, to my full knowledge, that any accusations and all accusations that have been put to me as accusations by the gestapo, that is to say the local authorities and the FBI, trying to accuse me of these bombings have been barefaced lies.

I think they realize that I am 100 percent innocent of this incident—the bombing—and all others that might have taken place regardless of when or where. . . .

Where are my civil rights today? Where is the Justice Department and Mr. Eisenhower, who have such beautiful statements concerning civil rights? Where are my civil rights today? I don't believe it's possible under this government of the republic of the United States for my civil rights to be so denied me.

But they have been time and again. All my rights have been taken away. I did not even get a right to defend myself, to see my accusers at the indictments. The whole thing was rushed through and I'll say this: That I believe with all my heart and truthfully that the local authorities are trying their best, for other reasons, to deny me any civil rights that I might have had or might have in the future.

Bail was denied.

On Saturday, October 18, the Confederate Underground threatened the foreman and the assistant foreman of the grand jury that had indicted the men. The foreman was warned: "You're going to pay for it." The assistant foreman, Robert C. Van Camp, was told: "We're going to kill all of you who indicted those innocent men. This is the Confederate Underground." Van Camp was warned that his house would be blown up in seven minutes.

A caller from the "Confederate army" gave the newspaper offices fifteen minutes to evacuate before being blown up. The Associated Press was warned that Jewish homes and "Jew-loving" newspapers would be bombed at future dates. A wave of phony bomb threats disrupted classes at five schools in Atlanta, including Emory University and Georgia State University, caused evacuation of a theater, and created airline delays. "What recourse do we have but to shut down classes?" asked an angry official at Georgia State after an anonymous caller told him: " 'Buddy, your building is going to be blown up in half an hour.' A prank or a crackpot, maybe, but we can't risk the lives of 2,000 persons."

In New York City, the Stephen Wise Free Synagogue in Manhattan, Streit's matzo factory on the Lower East Side, and the New York Guild for the Jewish Blind all received telephone threats from the Confederate Underground. A headless effigy of a male figure was hung in front of the Emanuel Synagogue Youth Center in the Bronx. Windows were shattered at the Mapleton Park Hebrew Institute in Brooklyn while people were in the building, and windows also were smashed at the Ahavis Achim Synagogue in Brooklyn. St. Patrick's Roman Catholic Cathedral received two bomb threats.

⊷ ⊨⊫ ⊶

Meanwhile, the right-wing extremist press was not accepting at face value everything reported in the *Journal and Constitution* and the *New York Times*. The voices of the newly emerging moderates in Atlanta were not the only voices, nor Rabbi Rothschild the only hero. An editorial in a neighborhood paper in Atlanta, the *North Side News*, called the emergence of the moderates "an affront to public intelligence," while other papers made a hero of Chester Griffin.

This is an effort to give the nation the impression that Atlantans have no desire to stand solidly with their fellow Georgians on many state's rights issues. . . . Those who have incited this hullabaloo would have the nation believe that Atlanta is a captive city within a stubborn Georgia, and that all Atlantans are ready and willing right now to bend the knee to those who would have us integrated.

This . . . blast from the integrators was far more evil than the bombing of The Temple, in its misrepresentation of the true character of Atlanta and Georgia citizens.

The defense theory that Jews and integrators stood as the most likely beneficiaries of the bombing caught on across the country.

"SYNAGOGUE BOMBING A FRAUD" was the headline of the California-based news monthly, the *American Nationalist*, with the subheading, "Jewish Groups Use Bomb Incident to Confuse Gentiles."

Atlanta—While the *American Nationalist* has never condoned the use of violence in any form against Jews, and has in fact been emphatic in its condemnation of the Atlanta synagogue bombing, we are equally opposed to the frame-up of patriots on false charges simply because it is alleged that they are "anti-Semitic." Such a situation exists in Atlanta, Georgia, today where five patriots have been arrested at the instigation of the sinister gum-shoe organization known as the Anti-Defamation League of B'nai B'rith. . . .

One of the five did, it is true, sign a pre-fabricated "confession" (since repudiated), but he did so only after third degree torture methods were applied continuously for more than two days and two nights by Atlanta police, who reportedly twisted the victim's broken arm as an inducement to sign. . . .

So long as the Atlanta five remain on the hook, the identity of the real bombers, who in all probability were Jewish fanatics, will be conveniently forgotten. This is an important consideration, propaganda wise. As indicated elsewhere in this issue, there has been a magical transformation in Southern public opinion since the bombing. Before that, Southern whites were displaying increasing bitterness toward the Jews as it became known that most of the impetus behind the integration drive was supplied by Jews and Jewish organizations—including the ADL. So bitter was this hostility becoming that even Southern Jews were shaken by it, and many openly questioned the wisdom of their national organizations. . . .

The bombing of the Atlanta synagogue saved the day. Instantly Southern Jewry rallied behind the ADL with renewed fervor. . . . But not only was the rank and file of Southern Jewry brought back into line by the temple bombing; the gentile public was also profoundly affected. Throughout the South, indignation against the Jews and their pro-Negro agitation was instantly replaced by compassion and sympathy . . . gentile public opinion toward the Jews underwent a wholesale transformation. And last but certainly not least, the bombing served to discredit those critics of Jewry (the so-called "hate groups") who had been exposing their pro-integration activities. . . .

The practical result is that in many areas of the South today you cannot criticize Jewry for any reason without giving rise to the suspicion that you are a potential synagogue bomber.

The *American Nationalist* offered its own reward—"Reward Offered for Real Synagogue Bombers"—of $250 for information leading to the arrest and conviction of the individuals responsible for bombing the Temple in Atlanta. This reward carried an interesting codicil: "An additional reward of $250.00 (making for a total of $500.00) will be posted if the individuals guilty of the bombing are revealed to be Jews, or in the pay of Jews."

4

On December 1, 1958, the state named the defendant who would be tried first. On that Monday morning in the Fulton County courtroom of Judge Pye, Assistant Solicitor Tom Luck announced that he would open with the case of the *State v. George Bright.*

At the courthouse, Venable now pushed into motion the

cranky old machinery of the anti-Semite's defense. He filed a plague of subpoenas with the hope of uncovering Jewish domination of the media and Jewish control of elected officials, Jewish profit resulting from the bombing, Jewish involvement with the bombing itself, and Jewish cover-up of the Communist-Jewish nature of the crime by the Jewish "defense organizations."

From the Anti-Defamation League office in Atlanta, he subpoenaed the names, addresses, and occupations of every member living in Atlanta, and any "investigators offering evidence or information concerning or pertaining to the alleged bombing of the Jewish Temple." ("Alleged bombing" was itself a strange usage: usually it is the perpetrator, not the perpetration, receiving the qualifier "alleged.") From the American Jewish Committee he required the names and addresses of all contributors to the investigation and the building fund. From Rothschild he demanded the names and addresses of all Temple members (this, coming from the imperial wizard of the Ku Klux Klan, was received particularly unenthusiastically). He required also the names and addresses of all persons, firms, and businesses making donations, gifts, or contributions for repairs. From WAGA-TV, Venable subpoenaed "the names of firms, corporations, business houses, retail outlets owned, operated and controlled by persons of Jewish faith or birth who buy time segments, shows or spot announcements . . . [and] the amount of each contract purchased by persons of Jewish birth or faith." From the *Atlanta Journal and Constitution*, specifically from McGill, he demanded the names of all advertisers of Jewish birth or faith, and records of all financial dealings with individuals of Jewish birth or faith.

Judge Durwood T. Pye was a crusty little old segregationist, but one who took the Southern high road, so to speak: he took pleasure in books on Confederate history, collected watercolors of the boys in gray, and worked to close the public schools rather than integrate them, but he preferred Southern Negroes to home-grown Nazis any day of the week.

As scrawny, scrappy, drawling, and political as Venable himself, Judge Pye began quashing Venable's subpoenas. He allowed to be subpoenaed into evidence only the membership lists of the Temple, the insurance records of the Temple, the name and address of the architectural firm (Finch, Alexander, Rothschild, Barnes and Paschal), of the contractor called in for the rebuilding, and the estimate for repairs: $96,908.07. Ralph McGill also was ordered to furnish records.

The tall old courtroom windows filled with winter sun like the cloth sails of wooden ships whitening in the wind. By daylight, under electric ceiling lamps and wearing a wool business suit, Venable displayed the craft he most often practiced by torchlight, on top of the granite mountain, under the stars. There, he kicked about inside his satin robe and hood, his moist breath returning foully back upon his face; hundreds of other men inside their humid face masks stormed about, shouting words out through their mouth openings. Until they removed their hoods, they were like a regiment of men with buckets over their heads. But Venable—with a crotchety voice, like an old grandpop on a TV western—could catch their attention, silence and instruct them. Before judge, jury, and courtroom he could do the same: for the audience's edification, and for the good of his innocent clients, he cast suspicion on the government's motives in this case and outlined the far-reaching influence of the Jews.

With a flourish of invisible robes, Venable began the voir dire, the process of questioning prospective jurors. Many a case is won or lost in voir dire, both because of the final choice of jurors, and because of the notions subconsciously planted by innocent-seeming questions. Prospective jurors who might have surmised, like the rest of the population, that the bombing of the Temple was a random act of pure anti-Semitism, heard here for the first time, in the sneer and odium in Venable's words, that the old, large, simple categories no longer applied. If they had thought, humanistically, in 1950s-era enlightenment, of their Jewish neighbors as average white Americans just like themselves who attended a different church, they heard here that there was more to it: the truth was darker, and hidden; the roots of the Jews were all knotted up with Communism and black liberation; the ways and needs of the Jews were so devious and labyrinthine that they may well have vandalized their own building for a quick fix of Christian sympathy and charity.

"Are you or have you ever been a member of, or donated to, or knowingly given aid to or sympathized with the National Conference for Christians and Jews?" Venable asked the naive white citizens summoned for jury duty.

"Are you or have you ever been a member of, or donated to,

or knowingly given aid to or sympathized with the NAACP? . . . the Urban League? . . . the Southern Regional Council? . . . any organization having to do with Jews or Judaism? . . . any interfaith organization? . . . any interracial organization? . . . any organization cited as Communist and subversive?

"Have you ever purchased or urged others to purchase bonds for Israel? . . .

"Have you any relatives or close friends employed by the Atlanta Newspapers, Inc., Davison's, Rich's, J. P. Allen or any of their subsidiaries? . . .

"What church do you attend?

"Have you any relatives employed by a Jew or Jews?

"Have you any close relatives who could be, and could you be intimidated in any way by Jews or Jewish organizations, or the Atlanta newspapers, or Rich's, or Davison's? . . . "

"Mr. Venable," commented Pye in the midst of this, "the Jewish race is not on trial in this case."

The spat-out, slanderous questions of Venable's voir dire, stained with unspoken accusation ("the mongrelizing Communist Jews are behind this whole damn thing," is what the lawyer wanted to say—*would* have said, given rocky terrain, firelight, chewing tobacco, whiskey) culled from the herd those citizens admitting to normal interactions with Jewish people. These were thanked and dismissed. "During selection of the jurors," reported the *Constitution*, "the defense Monday struck all prospective jurors who said they had dealt with Jewish merchants . . . or who said they had feelings against bombing of churches." The twelve winners of the jury selection took their seats, and it was then evident that the defense had had to dip toward the bottom of the well of humanity to find white men in Atlanta beyond the range of the *Constitution*, WAGA-TV, and Rich's Department Store. After the jury was empaneled, one of them admitted to being a former Klansman. Another later remarked, "You know, it wasn't but two hundred years ago that the blacks were eating each other in the jungles of Africa." And a third, an elderly fellow who entertained the jury panel during deliberations by telling filthy jokes, many of which seemed to include the word *snot* in the punchline.

The hatreds and conspiracy theories behind the Temple bombing ascended to the courtroom like smoke from an outdoor pyre blown into the windows. A rogues' gallery of characters took the stand. A judge presided, but the defendants' lawyer was little better than the defendants, and the defendants' pals and neighbors packed the spectators' seats.

Jewish people stayed away; Rothschild had asked them to. He feared the impact on the jury of a courtroom full of aggrieved-looking Jews. He did not want the jury to mistake *State v. George Bright* for a case that might be considered *The Temple Jews v. George Bright*. But this was an error, he learned later, for the atmosphere in the courtroom soured, and the jurors felt the eyes of Klansmen and NSRP members upon them, and felt the crowd's swift empathy with the defendants' testimony. "Jack and I couldn't help being revolted by the faces of the friends of the accused," said Janice Rothschild. "They were faces the likes of which I had seen only in movies and newsreels." Leading figures in the KKK and the NSRP arrived from around the country to observe and to give character testimony on behalf of Bright. Eldon L. Edwards, the imperial wizard of the U.S. Klan, Knights of the Ku Klux Klan, Inc., was spotted by reporters in the courtroom:

> Snappily dressed in a dark blue suit and wide-brimmed hat, and wearing a reddish mustache and smoking a big cigar, Edwards said he was there simply to observe.
>
> Asked his opinion of the blasting of the Jewish temple, the Klan leader said:
>
> "I'm just as much interested in things of this nature as the law enforcement officers themselves. Nothing can be accomplished by such an outrage as this. It is foolish to pull stunts of this nature."
>
> Asked his personal attitude toward Jews, he answered:
>
> "Personally? You might say neutral."
>
> He said the men who are suspects in the bombing are not Klan members "and never will be."
>
> He said he thought everybody—whites, Negroes, Jews—were deserving of the protection of the law. "We

all live under the same constitution and we should observe it," he said.

As interpreted by the Supreme Court? he was asked.

"No," he answered crisply.

Suddenly, to Venable's everlasting regret and aggravation, looking as colorful and rotund and plumed and pleased with himself as a puffin on a rock island, Reuben A. Garland Sr., age fifty-six, the state's preeminent defense attorney, popped up. And from the first day of the Temple bombing trial there was no shaking him.

Reuben A. Garland Sr. was a red-faced, short-legged, short-fused, vociferous little man, vain about his wavy silver hair, which he smoothed back lovingly with both hands. He could have handled another half-foot of height, for he possessed style, swagger, and volume enough to equip the largest man. His grand style thus overflowed his inadequate proportions and adorned his wife, house, car, two sons, and office with ostentation and splendor.

He was all ebullience and flowery language and exaggerated courtroom etiquette; his big, square, rosy face with its twinkly blue eyes and silver tresses ballooned onto the sketch pads of the courtroom artists, eclipsing Venable's short-cropped, hanging, craggy one; and his thundering basso profunda resounded for all to hear, leaving Venable's scratchy old-man's voice sounding like second fiddle. His sumptuous Cadillac was parked out front; his vassals, in the row behind him, stared straight ahead like secret service agents awaiting invisible commands, responding to no voice but that of their potentate.

What, one might well ask, and Venable certainly did, was Garland *doing* here in the opening ceremonies of Venable's greatest case?

He had launched a rival colonizing mission. He was making the case his own.

For a defense attorney, especially one as flamboyant and successful as Reuben A. Garland Sr., there was no place on earth he preferred to be that week than in the courtroom at the trial of the accused Temple bomber. For though everyday citizens would balk at linking themselves to such a man, or to a man accused of such a crime, for a defense attorney it was the optimum encounter, the only connection worth having: if his name had not been first on the lips of the accused, there'd been a misstep.

"For a criminal defense attorney, especially in the days when bar associations outlawed any type of advertising, the only way he could market himself was in the courtroom," said Donald F. Samuel, an Atlanta-based lawyer, president of the Georgia Association of Criminal Defense Attorneys. "It's still true today: the only way you get publicity for the next big case is to try this big case." The public's gut reaction—to stay far away from an individual accused of a terrible crime—is counter-intuitive for a defense attorney, who hopes to become the accused's best friend. "We're not playing to the public, trying to pander to the public," said Samuel; "only people accused of a crime are going to hire us. We're trying to look good to the next person accused of a crime.

"To be perceived as fighting hard, to appear every day on the front page of the *Constitution* or the *New York Times* waging your client's battles, is like gold. And if you win? it's platinum."

Reuben Garland wanted in on the Temple bombing case.

James Venable did not want the more well known and popular Reuben Garland anywhere near him *or* his five clients.

"I will tell you, dear, that Mr. Venable did not at any time want Reuben Garland in that case," said a former assistant of Venable's. "He and his partner, Mr. Burdine, had all the law. I adored Reuben—he entertained the hell out of you. I saw him one day walking around in a red hunting jacket and black patent leather boots up above his knees; now anyone who's that kind of entertainer is interesting to people. But Mr. Garland would go down to the jail to drum up business—it's a matter of record. He just violated the gentleman's code of conduct of the bar association, and he would just walk in on anything he wanted."

By the opening day of Bright's trial, Reuben Garland had gotten himself hired first by one, then by another of Venable's five bombing clients, and he was working on a third, and a fourth was in the wings, and he sincerely had his heart set on the fifth: Bright himself. While Venable read his law and handwrote his subpoenas and appeared in the courtroom on *State v. Bright*, Garland, brimming with sympathy, Latin, and fine manners, worked the halls and waiting rooms of the courthouse and the jail where the families of the other defendants anxiously were marking time.

Allen was the first to hire him.

"My husband knew of him and admired him and had a lot of respect for him," said Sammie Allen. "He told me to see him. We were both unhappy with Venable and Burdine. Venable was very childlike, a very innocent type of person. Neither one of us thought he could handle something like that. We were both unhappy with him from the very beginning. Most of his cases were little petty crimes, not the kind that made headlines, talking about execution. We didn't think he was the type to handle this big a case.

"I liked Mr. Garland and Mrs. Garland very much. I usually went to their house to talk about the case. I think he was delighted to have the case.

"Mr. Garland was very kind to me and very supportive. It was a pretty high fee for us—he didn't want to do it for nothing, by any means. My father paid the downpayment. I think Mr. Garland knew that my husband was innocent because my husband was not begging him to take the case, was not coming to him with a hat-in-hand attitude."

Garland invited Sammie Allen to sign a statement attesting to the fact that he was now Wallace Allen's lawyer. "I have this day employed REUBEN A. GARLAND . . . for the defense only of WALLACE H. ALLEN. . . . " A copy of this he furnished to Venable.

Then he set his cap for Robert Bowling. "My husband knew Richard and Bobby Bowling, and they knew Venable," said Sammie Allen. "Richard and Bobby didn't want to change attorneys; it was only through my husband's insistence that they changed attorneys."

Venable had reached the mountaintop, only to find that Garland was hollowing it out from the inside.

In court, from day one, they tangled. Beaming, a fresh flower in his lapel, redolent with expensive French aftershave, Garland engaged in a public tug-of-war over Venable's clients. The *Constitution* reported:

> The opening minutes included a debate between defense attorney Venable and Reuben Garland over who

would be in charge of the defense of defendant Robert Bolling [sic]. . . . Mr. Venable had announced that Mr. Garland would be "associated" in representing Robert Bolling. . . .

There was a young lady of Niger / Who smiled as she rode on a tiger . . .

Mr. Garland called the mother of the two Bolling defendants up before the judge's bench. She went outside a few minutes later after the judge ordered the two attorneys to settle the thing among the three of them.

When they came back from outside, Mr. Garland announced that he would be in charge of the defense with Mr. Venable and Mr. Burdine "associated."

They came back from the ride / With the lady inside / And the smile on the face of the tiger.

Shortly thereafter, Garland acquired Richard, as well, and "the mother of two of the defendants, dressed in a black velvet coat and white gloves, then sat back down in the spectators' section of the court."

Throughout the trial of Bright, Garland was there, harrumphing, gesticulating, lighting his cigar, offering points of law, popping up and down, pretending to confer with Burdine and Venable, who shooed at him as if at a mosquito. Making and Venable, who shooed at him as if at a mosquito. Making strident objections, acting in every way like an annoyingly prodigious, brownnosing student who waves his arm frantically with the right answers while his classmates sit sullenly, Garland horned in.

W. Whittier Wright, an engineer on the faculty of Georgia Tech who specialized in classified work on electronics, was chosen for the jury. The most educated and cultured juror, he slipped in possibly because of his fondness for the views of the 1920s-era Fugitive Agrarians, an intellectual movement based at Vanderbilt University that celebrated the preindustrialized South. An elegant, tall man with white hair parted down the middle and bushy salt-and-pepper eyebrows, he remembers Venable as "a high-class redneck," but what he chiefly recalls from the trial was watching Garland "pulling out this handkerchief he kept in his breast pocket and flailing it around."

Meanwhile, the papers reported:

While the [examination] was going on, Attorney Reuben Garland, representing two others in the bombing case, was at the defense table talking to Attorney Burdine.

Prosecutor Luck objected to his presence, pointing out that he was not associated in the Bright case.

"Have seat, Mr. Garland," Judge Pye said. The lawyer sat down.

The prosecution opened its case. Solicitor Luck, a rangy, good-natured man, greeted the jury and promised them: "We will show that George Bright had violent anti-Semitic feelings, that he participated in a conspiracy that planned many violent acts, and that the conspiracy culminated in the Temple bombing. The state will prove that George Bright not only planned the bombing but assisted at its execution."

Testimony began for the prosecution. The court heard from the Temple janitor who had discovered the damage, and from witnesses to Bright's heckling of Rothschild at the First Baptist Church in May. George Lincoln Rockwell's letter to Allen was introduced into evidence, prompting newspaper articles and much public speculation about the "fat cat," the "mysterious money man," the "bombing financier," and the "big donor from Baltimore, MD," ultimately identified as Harold Noel Arrowsmith Jr. And individuals testified who had heard the bombing: "I had gotten out of bed and gone to the bathroom," reported a Mrs. Paul Hamilton Asher, "and had returned to the bedroom and was raising the window when the explosion went off. It nearly scared me to *death.*"

As the prosecution prepared to introduce Jacob Rothschild, Venable leapt to his feet to block his testimony. He protested that Jews could not reliably be sworn in. He conjured up medieval folklore surrounding the Kol Nidre prayer of the Jews. Kol Nidre, chanted on the eve of the fast of Yom Kippur, originated in the Middle Ages to invalidate oaths sworn by Jews while under the threat of torture. It is a prayer for forgiveness for oaths made to God, and has no bearing on oaths sworn between human beings.

"It invalidates any other oath the Jews have taken during the year!" cried Venable in his objection, for the misuse of the Kol Nidre, like the *Protocols of the Learned Elders of Zion*, had circulated widely in the right-wing press. "It says all other oaths will be made of no effect."

Again, Pye cautioned Venable: "We're not trying any religion in this case and counsel recognizes that." In fact, the tactic of disallowing a Jew's testimony had been outlawed by the Supreme Court of Georgia in 1873. The court asked, in *Donkle v. Kohn*, "Has it ever, at least in modern times, been contended that a Jew was incompetent? That a want of belief in Jesus, as the Saviour, was a ground for the exclusion of a witness?" It was held: "We think not . . . [A] Jew is competent at common law."

Rothschild testified about having been heckled by Bright during a talk at the Baptist church on May 28. "Bright asked a question about the number of Jews in the world and when I answered 13 million, he took exception and insisted there were three million more. It soon became apparent that he was not really interested in the number of Jews, but he became belligerent and antagonistic." When Rothschild reminded Bright that Hitler had exterminated six million, he said, "Bright challenged me on that."

During cross-examination by Venable about the same matter, the defense attorney asked Rothschild: "I guess you don't think very much of Adolf Hitler and his methods for exterminating Jews, do you?"

"I didn't think any civilized person did," said Rothschild.

The rabbi also testified about the damage to the synagogue before being dismissed.

Excused from the courtroom, he returned to his duties at the Temple, willing to allot to the trial of George Bright no greater portion of his attention than he had allowed Bright and his group before the bombing. The public conversation in which Rothschild was engaged—in which he had placed himself, and his Temple, on the side of the Negroes, on the side of law, on the side of *right*—ought not to be sidetracked for too long a time over one bombing of a temple, he thought, even though the temple was his own. Rothschild had read Jewish history; he had absorbed his peck of Jewish suffering, and he was reluctant now to let the Jew-as-victim again steal to center stage in the hearts of

Jews, eclipsing all other stories. For he was fighting for their attention, for their hearts: that they should live as Jews by directing their attention outward, to the oppression of others. Almost perversely, he thought: The fact that this congregation had been bombed did not necessarily mean they had *deserved* to be bombed. Let them come forth from this tragedy and *earn it*.

He left the courthouse in fast strides, shuddering from the obscene contact with Venable, which he put out of his mind. Profoundly uninterested in playing the role of victim, he returned to work and to the struggle at hand.

Janice Rothschild testified about the threatening phone call she had received on the day of the bombing and the fact that she had heard this voice again on a tape played for her at police headquarters. The voice she selected as familiar belonged to Chester Griffin.

"It was exciting being called by FBI agents and taken to their office to help in an investigation," she said later. "Aware of my tendency to romanticize, however, I could not trust my opinion when one of the voices did sound like the one I remembered from the night of the bombing. To further my suspicion—of both the voice and my romanticism—that particular man had been the only one to stumble in his reading of the transcript. After identifying himself and stating that he was reading a prepared script at the request of the FBI, as each of the others had done, Chester Griffin paused and said something like, 'Gee, somebody might really think I did this.' Then he continued reading, but not without some hesitation during the part relating to his alleged conversation with me.

"I told myself to stop playing amateur psychiatrist, but still felt obligated to tell the agents that I did think Chester Griffin's voice sounded familiar. They thanked me, assured me that I would not be called upon to testify to it in court, and escorted me home.

"Two weeks later I received a subpoena to testify. . . . When I mentioned my apprehension to a friend, one of the leading attorneys in town, he told me to relax, that even if I was asked about the tape, it was highly unlikely that the defense would make it difficult for me. He explained that it was considered counterproductive 'to badger a lady—especially if she's a preacher's wife.' "

She testified simply, was thanked, and dismissed. "My first experience in the witness box ended with no ill effects."

Captain R. E. Little Jr., the head of the bombing task force for the Atlanta police, testified that Bright had admitted writing a note found in his house telling Rothschild, "You are going to witness one of the most terrifying experiences ever in your life." He said that Bright could not explain the meaning of the note. Little testified that Atlanta detectives had investigated Bright's alibi for the night of October 12—that he was in the company of a Mrs. Marilyn Craig—that police had confirmed that Bright and Craig had spent time at an all-night drugstore, but that the corroborating witnesses could account for only a portion of the night.

Washington-based national correspondent Jim Bishop wondered, about this time, whether or not the state had up its sleeve a "big witness who points the finger at the five and says, 'I was at the Temple the night of the bombing and these men were with me.'

"If the state doesn't have that kind of testimony," he wrote, "it doesn't have much of a case."

＊＊＊

On days four and five, the state presented their two "star witnesses."

The first was none other than the FBI-paid informant, Leslie E. Rogers, the annoyingly chummy loner, the man singled out—even by outcasts—as a loser. He had approached the FBI in Atlanta in November 1957, volunteering his services, because, he said, "I was disturbed about the publicity in the paper concerning the general unrest throughout the South." He detailed the NSRP meetings he had attended with Bright and the other defendants. "The purpose of this organization was expulsion of the Jews from the government and extermination and persecution of the Jews," he said.

"Is it true you're a police pimp?" asked Venable.

"No, I wouldn't call it that," said the witness.

"Mr. Venable, see if you can find another word," sighed Pye.

"Isn't it true you're testifying now in hope of getting part of the reward offered for the conviction of the bombers?"

"I don't know anything about rewards, other than what you read in the newspaper, I couldn't tell you the amount because reward doesn't enter my mind, it is rewarding enough to me if we can just have peace and people go out and have freedom of worship and our schools and our democracy can just get back to normal, that is certainly rewarding enough for me."

By the time Rogers was excused, the state had established that Bright was an active member of the virulently anti-Semitic NSRP and that typical conversations at meetings included imagining some violence the group could do to Jews. On the other hand, Venable had effectively portrayed Rogers as a "sneak," suggested that he had a financial motive in testifying, and established that he had no direct knowledge of the event.

Rothschild then received word from the prosecuting attorney's office asking him to reverse his advice to the congregation to stay away from the trial. "They called and said, 'Rabbi, please get some of your people to come down," said Janice Rothschild. " 'The atmosphere in this courtroom is so permeated with hate and rednecks, that we really need to balance it.' " Accordingly, Jewish women in flowered dresses, pearls, and white gloves appeared shyly at the tall wood doors of Pye's courtroom and bravely squeezed into seats along the benches among rough-talking men who had sworn blood oaths to expel their ilk from America.

On Friday, December 5, the state introduced their chief witness, the man whose testimony would place Bright at the scene of the crime, the man whose story was the backbone of the prosecution's case.

"He told me he planned and led the Temple bombing," the witness said. "He told me he didn't do the actual bombing, but that he rode as a lookout."

It was not Griffin, who had so thoroughly debunked his first statement that he had made himself useless to prosecutors. No, the big witness was Jimmy Dave DeVore, thirty-three, an assembly-line worker at a Chevrolet plant and a former filling station mechanic who had been jailed for violation of state sales tax laws and forgery and was housed in Block Three–East, Fulton County Jail. His cellmate was Bright. The star witness, in other words, was a "jailhouse snitch"—of all types of witnesses, probably the least reliable.

Nervous, intimidated by the crowds, DeVore testified that Bright had spoken to him at great length in jail, sometimes in two- or three-hour stretches.

> Well, sir, I met him when he came in the door; I was standing in the door and he and Mr. Moss, one of the turn-keys at the County Jail, were having a few words about some fingerprinting or something, and he told him to come on in and he wouldn't come in and he stumbled in and fell in my arms, I was standing in his way, a little piece in front of the cell door, and that is the first time that I saw him. . . . We sit in the cell and talked at different times. . . . I didn't threaten him and when he came in the cell, I just started talking to him, and we asked him what he was in there for. . . . There were between 27 and 30 men in the cell, I guess. . . . He had a newspaper in his hand and I asked him what he was doing with it. . . . He had a pencil and he was marking out some kind of a name, had his name in it wrong; I believe they had it George Allen Bright in the newspaper and he said his name was George Michael Bright and he was marking out the Allen, I think, and putting Michael above it.
>
> I mentioned to him, I said, they got you on a pretty bad thing, bombing that Church out there. And I asked him what they was holding him for, what evidence they had against him, and he said he thought maybe they might have found some nitroglycerine or dynamite dust in the back of his car . . . and he thought they had a letter that he had wrote to Rothschild, Rabbi Rothschild, threatening him, and they also thought they might have found a set of plans . . . plans for the Temple . . . he said he was an architect or something, draw mechanical drawings, I don't remember exactly what he said about it, and that he had drew it and marked it in red, drew the plans to the

Temple in blue and the place to put the bomb for it in red, and X-ed it.

In the course of "numerous, or several" conversations of "four to six hours a day" over a three-week period, the events of the early morning hours of October 12 were revealed to DeVore: Bright had been picked up from Doby's Grill, an all-night diner on Ponce de Leon, by Allen and others in the middle of the night and "carried out on Spring Street." Three cars parked along- side the Standard station at the Spring Street intersection of Peachtree; Bright rode with Allen. A fourth car, a Pontiac, was left by Richard Bowling at the side of the ramp going up to the expressway a short distance from the Temple, with a jack under a rear wheel to simulate a flat tire, for use as a getaway car. Bowling ran across the rear parking lots of the neighboring buildings to the Temple, laid the dynamite, then ran back to the car on the ramp. The car was driven off the jack, without getting the jack. After the bomb was deposited, Bright went to Doby's on Ponce de Leon Avenue, had a steak, and picked up a girl.

The crowded courtroom grew quiet as he talked.

"And he told me all five of them had ironclad alibis," added DeVore.

"And Bright said he had made a trip to Decatur with Ven- able and paid off a check to get Bowling out of jail one time. And that was supposed to be a partial payment for Bowling's partici- pation in the bombing, and the balance of it would come later.

"I'm not the only one who heard all this."

"Mr. DeVore," said Venable sweetly when he stood for cross-examination. "Wouldn't you like the court to believe this story so that you could get your hands on some of that reward money? Aren't you turning George Bright in for the money?"

"No, I don't want any of the reward money and I wouldn't have any if they offered it to me," said DeVore. "I was the one trying to protect him. I told LeRoy Mays not to hurt him. They cut up his t-shirt with a razor blade. They were all mad at him. They called him 'The Bomber.' "

"Isn't it true that if you cooperate with the police, you'll get some help with your own forgery case, which hasn't gone to court yet?"

"No, sir."

But that is precisely the problem with the jailhouse snitch as witness: an accused criminal has nothing to lose. He is in jail already and is bored out of his skull, with no end in sight, nothing to offer, nothing to make a deal with. Then a celebrity suspect is tossed into his cell and looks and smells like manna from heaven. The key questions to ask when considering the testimony of the jailhouse witness are these: First, what does he know, when claiming that his bunkmate has "confessed," that every subscriber to a newspaper or owner of a TV does not already know about the facts of the case? In other words, has the suspect "confessed" to new material, or only to the facts as already printed in the papers read by the jailhouse witness? Second, if there is new material here (as there surely was in DeVore's story), can it be verified?

Bowling's car jack, abandoned on the expressway ramp in this account, was never found. That does not mean events did not happen the way DeVore said—or that they did.

On Friday afternoon, the state rested, and Venable put up the case for the defense.

Mrs. Albert Bright, George's sister-in-law, said, "George was at home all evening, but he left home sometime after midnight."

The Atlanta police officer Paul Green said: "I saw George Bright at Plaza Drugs at two o'clock in the morning the night of the bombing. I went off duty and didn't see him after that."

Ann Blackwell, a cashier at Plaza Drugs, said, "George Bright left the store in company with a woman about 2:30 A.M."

It was curious that the defense attorney, to a far greater extent than the prosecution, established that Bright was roaming around the city unaccounted for after 2:30 A.M. the morning of the bombing.

The defense case continued into Friday night and resumed on Saturday morning, December 6. Men then took the stand to praise Bright and to impeach the testimony of Rogers.

KKK Imperial Wizard Eldon L. Edwards, from College Park, Georgia, said: "L. E. Rogers has a bad reputation. I would not believe the man under oath."

John Felmet, the Klan treasurer, echoed his words: "I would not believe L. E. Rogers under oath."

Wesley Morgan, the exalted cyclops of N. B. Forrest No. 1, U.S. Klans, Knights of the Ku Klux Klan, agreed.

Arthur Cole of Lafayette, Tennessee, the sixty-seven-year-old chairman of the NSRP, said, "I met Leslie Rogers at a NSRP convention in Kentucky on August 30th and 31st, 1958. Rogers asked me where he could buy dynamite." He explained that the purpose of the NSRP was to resist integration.

"What about anti-Semitism?" asked Luck on cross-examination.

"No, no," said Cole. "I've got some awful good Jewish friends."

The next few impeached DeVore's testimony. Fellow cellmate Leroy Mays, whom Devore had named as having also heard Bright's tale, said he had heard no such thing. D. M. Harris, another prisoner, also refuted DeVore's account. So did Arnold O. Brannan, another cellmate. Homer M. Collins, the owner of a service station where DeVore had once worked, said he would not believe a word the man said. DeVore's brother, Elrod DeVore, testified, "I wouldn't believe Jimmy under oath."

Bright sat in court with his shoes removed, his stockinged feet resting on a sheet of newspaper and no emotion showing in his face. Finally he was called to testify in his own defense. "Bright, wearing glasses and dressed in a dark blue suit and light tie, took his seat in the witness chair and waited while Judge Durwood Pye instructed him as to his rights," reported the papers. Then Bright began: 'If it please the court, gentlemen of the jury, I am George Bright.'

"Then, in a scholarly, controlled voice, the 33-year-old bachelor launched into what he said would be an account of his innocence and a complete refutal of the state's case."

He went back into time, into his family history, and detailed his own life through the years. This took more than six and a half hours. He attacked Mayor Hartsfield and Police Chief Jenkins as being pro-integration. He characterized Rogers and DeVore as liars. Told by Pye to use a different word, he switched to "prevaricators." Jack and Janice Rothschild stayed for a few hours of it, to comply with the prosecutor's request, grew restless, and went home. Bright's central argument was "I have a spotless character and the state's case against me is completely false."

Then he gave his own account of the events of that night: On Saturday night, October 11, he was at his brother Albert's house until around midnight. Then he went to Plaza Drugs on Ponce de Leon, where he met Marilyn Craig, a woman he knew. They left the drugstore a little after 2:00 A.M., rode around, bought some food for breakfast, and spent the rest of the night at Craig's house, in separate rooms.

"The first I knew of the bombing was a report on the radio at Mrs. Craig's house." (Years later he would remember that the first he knew of the bombing was when police came to arrest him for it on Monday afternoon.)

"L. E. Rogers planned the whole Temple bombing scheme and framed me and the four other men indicted. . . .

"The red and blue pencil drawing referred to by DeVore as a diagram of the Temple was in reality a drawing of a new-type riveting machine invented by me. . . .

"The solicitor doesn't know the first thing about Communism," he said at one point. "I challenge him to explain the first thing about Communism. He doesn't even pronounce anti-Semitic correctly. He pronounces it anti-Semeetic; that shows how much he knows about it. . . .

"I have no hatred for the Jewish people. I served in the Army in World War II with Jews, worked for Jews, worked with them, and always got along harmoniously with them."

Near the end of the day, however, he added: "Virtually every great man in Western civilization has made statements unfavorable to the Jews," he said, then read quotations from seventeen writers, philosophers, and historians, all derogatory to the Jews, including Cicero, Thomas Carlyle, Voltaire, Saint Thomas Aquinas, Goethe, and Nicholas of Russia.

"Truth has been on my side," he said in conclusion, "and God above won't let anything but a just verdict be rendered in this case."

As the trial drew to a close, Venable successfully blocked the admission into evidence of the results of a polygraph test given Bright by FBI experts. With the jury in recess, Leo Gormley, an FBI agent, told the judge that he had asked Bright several critical questions twice. "Each such question brought an immediate response on the polygraph," he said.

"What determination did you make?" asked Luck.

"That the reaction observed on the polygraph indicated that Mr. Bright was lying," the agent said.

The defense argued that there was no legal authority for the admission of such evidence, and Pye had to concur that the evidence was inadmissable. Results from lie detector tests did not become admissible in Georgia until 1977, and only then if both the state and the defense agreed in advance to the admissibility of the results.

* * *

"George Bright is a dangerous man smart enough to kill," said Luck in his closing argument, urging the jury to return a guilty verdict.

"This man is on trial because he advocated segregation," argued Venable.

In his charges to the jury, Pye explained that the jury should find one of three verdicts:

1. Guilty, requiring a sentence of death in the electric chair
2. Guilty, with a recommendation of mercy, requiring a sentence of life imprisonment
3. Not guilty

At 11:00 P.M. on Saturday night, the jury began deliberations. At midnight they were driven to the old Briarcliff Hotel on Ponce de Leon, across from Plaza Drugs, where they spent Sunday in seclusion. They resumed deliberations in a locked jury room at the courthouse 9:30 Monday morning, December 8, and sat together all that day and into the night.

On Monday night, after seven hours of deliberation, the foreman of the jury advised the judge that they were "hopelessly deadlocked." At 10:00 P.M., when they retired for the night, the deadlock held at nine to three, though no one revealed whether the majority stood for conviction or for acquittal.

In the outside world, death threats were phoned in to

DeVore and to his children, to Rogers, and to the Fulton solicitor general, Paul Webb, who was told, "We'll get you if Bright is convicted."

On Tuesday the jury deliberated all day, completing twenty-two hours of sessions without reaching a verdict. In the outside world, the other four defendants began to be released on bond. Bowling was released on $1,000 bond and Allen on $5,000 bond. In a subsequent indictment, Robert Bowling's name was dropped altogether.

On Wednesday morning the jury resumed deliberations.

"Yeah, well, there weren't any deliberations," said Wright, the bushy-browed Georgia Tech engineer and jury member. "Of course, the judge would say: 'Gentlemen, you may resume the deliberations.' And neither phrase was appropriate: we weren't gentlemen; we weren't deliberating. Judge Pye was a sort of formal, scholarly type person and treated us with a dignity which we didn't deserve. I did; I don't know about the rest of them. We had, for example, the elderly fellow, a dry sort of old man. He was the one who told the filthy jokes. I can't remember them specifically, but they were unbelievably vile. One juror laid down and went to sleep on the jury table. Literally. It was incredibly boring. I remember looking out the window and counting the bricks in the wall of the building across the street.

"Back at the hotel, we had the deputy sheriffs who were sequestered with us, who ate with us and lived in the hotel with us to keep us separated from the outside world. We couldn't make any phone calls to our wives. When we were first sequestered, the sheriff had to call our wives and ask them to carry a suitcase of clothes over. They had televisions in their rooms, but we weren't allowed to watch television, so the sheriffs tried to entertain us with stories about their escapades, which were really nuts. For example, they told us that for fun sometimes they would go out and find some park in a black neighborhood, creep up on a car and find two blacks making out, and they'd shine the flashlight in and say, 'We'll let you go if you continue.' Of course, they were calling the blacks 'niggers.' I mean that was one story I heard them tell. Meanwhile, Judge Pye sent us some nice old *National Geographics* to entertain us.

"So among the jurors it was mainly a discussion of, 'How quick can we get out of here?' And there were no deliberations after the first day or so. Now, you're not supposed to discuss the case until you adjourn the case. But, of course, jurors do that anyway. You're sitting there, you're divided up in a room with somebody, and you're going to discuss it to some extent. You have nothing else in common. So I don't know when we reached a deadlock. We were probably deadlocked before the case was even given to us.

"Nobody liked George Bright. And there was a lot of pressure at the time to come up with a scapegoat—to find somebody and have a conviction. Although we didn't see the papers or television, I think probably the jury knew there was a lot of attention focused on the bombing and that somebody had to pay for it. But I don't think they were really interested in justice. They just wanted to get somebody and get out of there. No, nobody liked him. Frankly, going back over the trial, I think the thing in my mind that hurt the prosecution was the witness they brought in, somebody who had been in jail with Bright. It was a setup, you know. He was a slimeball. His performance on the stand was really unacceptable. I mean, compared to Bright—Bright was really sane.

"But to me they had not proved their case, certainly not without a reasonable doubt.

"I may have been the only one to begin with, but when we ended up there were three of us against conviction. The rest, their logic was unbelievable: 'You know the FBI. They're not going to say he's guilty if he's not.' But you don't send a person up for life, I said, just because you don't like him or because this guy is a despicable character and nobody likes him or even because the FBI says he's guilty. They haven't *proved* him guilty, was my argument.

"Of course, all that did was polarize the jury, and I've learned since that the better way to do is to keep quiet. Don't say a thing. It may be obvious to you what the situation is. Say, 'What do you think?' and 'What do you think?' and let everybody say what they think. And then at the very end say, 'I think you're exactly right and I think you're right. But here's so and so and so,' and then you can resolve it.

"Instead, I had everybody saying, 'If it weren't for you, we could go home.' "

At 11:15 Wednesday morning, after twenty-six hours of

deliberations, court was convened, Bright was brought in, and the jury returned to the jury box.

"Mr. Foreman, does the jury wish to communicate with the court?" asked Pye.

"Yes, sir. We are still deadlocked. We seem to be hopelessly deadlocked," said Ralph C. Castleberry, the foreman.

"How do you stand numerically?"

"The count is nine to three."

"How long has the count been nine to three?"

"Since 11:00 A.M. Monday."

"Do you think there is a chance of ever reaching a verdict?"

"No, sir. I don't think this jury will ever reach a verdict."

"Which of you believe a verdict can be reached by this jury?" the judge asked the jurors. No one moved. "Which of you believe a verdict cannot be reached?" In their only show of unanimity in eighty-four hours, all twelve raised their hands.

"What I thought?" croaked Pye three and a half decades later, slumped way down in an old dusty couch in his filthy front room with newspapers and books so banked in around him it appeared that he himself had been there, forgotten in the trash, for several months already, except that the newspapers were current, and the books were brand-new hardbacks freshly un-boxed from the History Book Club. "Now I did not reach any conclusion about their guilt or innocence because I had no re-sponsibility at that time on that subject. I would be responsible for passing on the guilt or innocence only if they were convicted and a motion for a new trial was filed. So as the case progressed, I did not undertake to reach a conclusion."

"The court," said Pye, "declares a mistrial in this case." The jurors were paid six dollars per day for their efforts and released.

14

"I Am One of Them That Bombed Your Temple"

1

Reuben A. Garland Sr., born in 1902 in Fort Gaines, Georgia, was the state's preeminent defense lawyer. Carrying a gold-headed walking stick and giving it a twirl, he was no stranger to the fresh flower in the lapel, the gold pocket watch, the black cloak for the opera. He was outfitted in breathtakingly expensive suits by London clothiers. Proletarians on the street could spot his latest Cadillac. "He was a very jocular guy," said the attorney Joe Haas. "When you met him on the street, he was very expansive. His personality was all over the place."

"I rode in the car with him—*once*. Now *that* was an intimidating experience," said the attorney Gene Reeves of Lawrenceville. "He had a big black Cadillac, and he would ride down the street looking everywhere and talking and talking and not seeing anything that was going on. Miraculously, he never had a wreck, but I was staring at him in sheer horror."

Garland was, in short, a great presence in Atlanta; anyone

in trouble thought of him first. And when he was loose in the courtroom, it was like the day the circus came to town. "Whenever Reuben was on trial in the courthouse, everybody knew it," said Earl Hickman, a former superior court clerk. "The young clerks would all try to get out of what they were doing to go listen to Reuben Garland. It didn't make any difference whether it was a big case or little case—he was flamboyant and spectacular; he was colorful and had a reputation of usually getting his man off. I guess he was the premier criminal lawyer in this part of the country."

His cases and exploits were written up in newspapers and true-crime magazines. His voice was pebbly and rough and deceptively contrite at the low end of a couple of octaves, and like the outraged scream of a mountain lion at the high end. With it he could call the hunting dogs home from the woods, rally election-year crowds (he often ran for office, but never won), and cause grown men to weep on the witness stand.

"It was something always going to happen when Reuben was there," said the Atlanta attorney John Nuckolls, a former district attorney. "If you had a file and somebody at the preliminary hearing noted that Reuben was representing the defendant, that was enough to make that case a lifetime experience. And they would always lay on extra deputy sheriffs, because you could expect there'd be a huge crowd if they heard that Reuben was going to be in the court."

"He had this entourage that followed him," said Nuckolls, a handsome man with salt-and-pepper hair, fond of Izod shirts. "He had Harris Bostick, his black investigator who later became a lawyer and a city court judge. And Bostick might have had him an assistant. And there was a white investigator. And there was Charlie, who was indentured to him forever, I guess. Charlie stabbed his wife something like twenty times, and Reuben got him acquitted for justification and Charlie worked for him for years. So Reuben would come into court with his entourage— those three and another twenty people that he just rounded up somewhere to come into court. Whether they were actually witnesses or not you never knew; he might have brought them into court to intimidate the D.A. And of course it was effective on me as a young prosecutor. I was scared to death because you just didn't know.

"Even if it was for an arraignment where there was no need to do anything at all but walk in and plead 'not guilty,' he would always come in with this entourage of assistants and witnesses and make this dramatic appearance. He always demanded 'formal arraignment,' which at that time was an archaic litany that would go on, 'How shall ye be tried?' It was in Old English that had been done away with probably hundreds of years ago, but in Georgia it was referred to as 'formal arraignment.' The defendant's response was supposed to be: 'By God and a jury of my peers.' It's a fairly long process. And Reuben would *insist* on it."

Garland saw to it that the cut of his broad-bellied figure and the ornate trappings of his person made the point that here was a man of wealth, worldliness, and distinction. "He was a bigger-than-life kind of guy," said Nuckolls, speaking in an old-time country Georgia accent. "I remember one of his suits, a light blue silk suit; it was just an electric blue. And he wore white shoes with it, a white silk shirt, and a blue tie. He had this white silk handkerchief hanging out and this white mane of hair."

A letter survives from Garland to his haberdasher, dated September 23, 1959:

> I have just purchased from you a black gabardine material at the price of $175 to be made up in a suit. I told you that I wanted the finest gabardine in existence on the face of this earth and you assured me that none was finer than the material I purchased.
>
> After I had purchased it, you stated to me that you probably had it in stock. If there is any material, out of stock or in stock, of gabardine texture that is finer than this suit, I do not want the suit.
>
> Doc, I am not interested in saving $5.00, nor $105.00, nor $5,000, nor $5,000,000. . . . I am only interested in getting the best gabardine there is, and I believe it should be tailor-made. . . . It is not often that I buy a suit, and when I buy a suit, I want the best.
>
> Relying upon your representation that the cloth ordered is the finest, I have agreed to pay the price.
>
> Yours truly,
> Reuben A. Garland

Nuckolls said: "I have seen him in court in a cut-away: long tails and spats and a cane and a top hat. I mean, that was the way he treated a case. I don't think he could take *a* case. It was always *the* case. It was going to be *the* event."

Garland lived, rather stuffily, under twenty-foot ornamented ceilings in an Italianate mansion built in 1912, which he acquired in 1956, with oil paintings of gentleman forebears and fox-hunting scenes on the cracked walls. The house was filled with antebellum armoires, canopied beds, a silver tea service, a butler's pantry, a suit of medieval armor mounted on the second-floor landing, and the family crest hanging above a stone fireplace. He had married the daughter of Judge E. T. Moon of La Grange, Georgia. Named Fauntleroy Winston Moon, she had matured into an ample woman with a warbling voice and powder-white skin of a quality that once upon a time in the South was sheltered on bright days by a parasol. When Fauntleroy gave parties, pianists bent to the grand piano in the far corner of the living room; a gowned soprano placed a plump white hand on it and launched into song; and black waiters in white jackets offered drinks from silver trays. The waiters included gold-toothed Charlie, the acquitted wife-killer.

Fauntleroy Winston Moon Garland, in her mid-eighties, had had her memory slip, like eyeglasses sitting askew, on a great many subjects, but on the subject of her own lineage, and that of her late husband, she was crystal clear and emphatic: "Of course, some of the family came in the 1600s—that shows up in the DAR records," she said, thick-voiced and drawling, "—but my branch of the family, the Winstons, immigrated in 1730. They came to Virginia. Winston was from the House of Marlborough, a younger son; one of the Winstons, Sarah Winston, married a Henry and became the mother of Patrick Henry." She knew by heart the intricate bloodlines, family trees, and marital alliances of the high South, out of which grew invitations to tea, to dinner, to engagement parties, to debutante and charity balls.

"Now Dolley Madison's mother was a widow; she went to Philadelphia and ran a boarding house. . . . Now Alexander Stephens [the vice-president of the Confederacy] and my grandfather thought they saw a way to get the plantations free and clear, and they were opposed to the war. After the firing on Fort Sumter, a message was sent to Woodlawn—my grandfather's country place—where he was closeted with Stephens trying to stop the war. . . . "

＊＊ ⊷◆⊷ ＊＊

Reuben Garland began the practice of law in Atlanta in 1922 at the age of eighteen. In 1977, he could brag about a career that included the highest personal injury jury verdict for a white man in Georgia ($169,627.81, for an automobile accident case); the highest personal injury jury verdict for a black man in Georgia ($28,000); and the highest "pain and suffering" jury verdict in the *world* at that time ($50,000, in *Thomas Newton Cook v. Singer Sewing Machine Company*).

He claimed the second fastest "not guilty" verdict from a jury in a murder case in the state of Georgia: six minutes. He also claimed the *fastest* "not guilty" verdict in a murder case: two minutes.

These days, buffoonery is the province of late-night TV comedians, in broadcasts from small smoky stages, who make weird sounds into microphones held right against their mouths and build successful careers on their ability to do unexpected things, sudden bodily contortions or something peculiar with their faces or clothing. It is in their interest to be thought slightly mad. Garland was a performance artist of the first rank, and he did his act in the course of representing murder defendants in courtrooms across the Deep South. And no one, not even his closest associates, could swear absolutely that he was not slightly unhinged.

On occasion he feigned a heart attack when cross-examination of his client by the prosecutor was going poorly. On occasion he employed the famous "cigar trick." "Reuben would run a wire through a cigar so the ash wouldn't drop off," said Nuckolls. "And during the prosecutor's argument, Reuben would sit there and light this cigar and smoke. No ash would drop. By the time he was fifteen minutes into the cigar the ash was half a foot long. Eventually one of the jurors would see it; ash would be out to there and it still hadn't dropped; and the jurors quit paying attention to the final argument. They'd all be sitting there looking at that ash on that cigar. I know that for a fact. He did it just to distract the jury."

"Reub was defending a man for murder," recalls the Atlanta attorney Elliott Goldstein. "A group of black men were shooting dice and they got in an argument, and this fellow pulled out a pistol and shot one of the men. So they tried him for murder, and a witness was on the stand testifying what had happened. The gun had been put into evidence. So Reub was cross-examining the witness, and he said, 'Do you recognize this gun?' He picked it up by the barrel and handed it to him, so the fellow involuntarily grabbed the gun by the stock like anybody would. Reub *jumped* back and started screaming: 'There he sits! There's the guilty man! He's got the gun in his hand! Look at that guilty look on his face!' This poor guy was standing there trying to throw the gun away. The judge held Reub in contempt."

"I'll give you an idea of some of the little nuances he was good at," said Gene Reeves, a former client and a former colleague of Garland's. "Reuben once represented me in a case, and the man who was the chief witness against me was named Dorfman. Reub called him Dinglehoffer, Dorfhead. Finally—at that time, Eichmann was being tried—he got all mixed up and called him Eichmann. But he knew what he was doing. There is a lawyer named Paul Cadenhead, and we tried a case against him one time and Reub called him Mr. Keghead."

"There was a lawyer from Decatur named Schley Howard, the grandfather of Lieutenant Governor Pierre Howard, who had a trick that he would pull on the judge," said the retired superior court judge Durwood T. Pye. Bony, uncombed, unkempt, and hard of hearing, he pronounced his own name in a shout: "PAH!" "He was a good lawyer, excellent lawyer, but when the judge would rule against him, he would cry. CRAH!" exclaimed the old judge, nearly weeping himself at the hilarious memory, buckling over on his decrepit sofa to laugh and laugh. "Just let the tears *roll* down his cheeks. He tried that on me. I just sat there and looked at him, and then *smiled*, you see." And the old judge nearly popped his galluses, so hard did he laugh to recall it.

"Now Reuben Garland's technique was to try to make the judge *angry*," said Pye, "and to try to create a situation where it looked like the judge was picking on him. One of his tricks was this: the jury would go out during a recess and when the court ordered the jury to come back, during the time it would take for the jury to come from the jury room into the courtroom, Reub would start addressing the court with some inconsequential, absurd proposition—the idea being that the judge would order him to stop, refuse to hear from him. So the jury would come in while the judge was admonishing Reub, you see. Reub was being bawled out by the judge, you see. By the time that happened three or four times during the trial, the jury would get the impression that the judge was picking on Reub—taking advantage of him. That was just one of his tricks. But I knew that trick. He tried it on me. I just looked at him and didn't say a word, and finally he shut up." In a dim and filthy living room, banked with papers and teetering towers of books, with untouched and tepid dishes delivered by Meals-on-Wheels on a plastic tray before him, the old judge joyously laughed.

"I once saw him cross-examine a witness for half the morning about a color," said Nuckolls. "In the police report, a witness had described the perpetrator's car as gold. On the witness stand, she called it yellow. And Reuben cross-examined this poor woman on the difference between gold and yellow and why she *had* said it was gold and why she was lying now. And when it started out, it was such an innocuous point that I'm sure the jury could have cared less. But it became more and more of an issue. He *made* an issue out of it. He had the poor woman so confused and mad and finally he said, 'Well! *tell* me! Was it *go-o-o-ld*? or was it *y-e-e-llow*?'

"She looked at him and said, 'I . . . don't . . . know.'

"He turned to the jury and said, 'I thought not. Thank you.' And sat down. And we didn't get the murder conviction."

———— ✄ ————

"I tried a case," said Nuckolls, "involving a defendant who was charged with murder. He was a little pimp and a street hustler and gambler who had killed a security guard at a country club. Luther Alverson was the judge. I was the prosecutor. And there was a period from maybe 9:30 till 12:00 where Reuben controlled the courtroom like I've never seen in my life.

"As prosecutor, my desk was the closest to the jury box. The witness was straight in front of me, so that by standing at my desk, I was looking head-on. The defense table was at my left. Now Reuben was scooting in his chair toward my table so he could see the witness a little better. Then he started glancing through the things on my table as I was examining the witness. And being a young lawyer and not realizing there wasn't a thing in those files that was important, I immediately moved them further away where he couldn't see them, thinking that the district attorney's file was sacrosanct and should not be compromised by defense counsel.

"I think he realized then that he had something going there. So as I was examining the witness, he moved over a little further and a little further and eventually was seated right behind me; and then he switched to *my* chair where I'd just been sitting, and began thumbing through the files on my desk. So I said, 'May we approach the bench? . . . 'Your Honor, Mr. Garland is at *my* desk, reading *my* file.'

"Judge Alverson instructed Reuben not to do so. And Reuben had this very effective voice in the courtroom. He couldn't speak quietly. It was just an absolute bellowing voice: just *loud*. And he adapted sort of an English accent. He loved the English jurisprudence. So, although we were supposed to be at a sidebar conference, Reuben's voice could still be heard anywhere in the courtroom: '*Well, may it please the court*, the prosecutor is communicating with the witness by hand signals, and Ah demand the right to be able to see the witness's hands.'

"There wasn't much the judge could say. 'Well, get where you can see the witness full face on.' So Reuben took the seat behind my desk. Oh, within thirty seconds after I started back, he started going through my file again. I protested to the judge again. This went on for an hour: I asked a question; the moment my back was turned, Reuben flipped through my papers; the judge ordered him to stop. I'd start again; Reuben would turn back to my files; the judge would stop him. Finally Judge Alverson interrupted us, sent the jury out, called Deputy Thomas, and ordered him to take a piece of chalk and draw a line from the base of the bench out the rail, down the center of the aisle, and out the back door. And he said, 'Mr. Garland, you stay on *that* side of the line. If you cross the line, you're in contempt of court.'

"The jury came back in, and immediately they could see this line, and they had a pretty good idea of what had gone on.

So I get up and I'm examining the key witness. Reuben's sitting in his chair on his side of the line, looking like a choirboy. He could have this absolute cherubic expression at times. And then he moved over a little. And Alverson, who was sitting there, could not wait to hold him in contempt of court. You could see him tensing. Then Reuben scooted in his chair a little nearer to the line, and a little nearer again.

"By now, there isn't a juror in the courtroom paying any attention to what I'm getting out of this witness. And *I'm* looking at Reuben, totally frustrated. Then he brings his chair right up *to* the line. And so the next move (clearly he was going to cross the line), he stands up halfway, holding the chair close to his bottom, getting ready to spring—Alverson is already starting out of his seat. Reuben leaps into the air, throws his chair across the line, then squats down on his side of the line and doesn't move.

"But by then, it was too late. Alverson had already screamed, 'Mr. Thomas, arrest Mr. Garland! He's in contempt of court!' And the jury is sitting there looking, and Reuben very calmly, very stately, says, with that British sort of accent: 'May it please the court, let the record show that Mr. Garland's *chair* may have crossed that line, but his *ass* did not.'

"We had a hearing for an hour as to whether or not Reuben's ass crossed the line, the judge insisting that it did, and Garland calling *me* as a witness and asking, 'Did my ass cross the line?' The whole concept of the trial had been lost by this time in this little subscenario. In a very cold, calculating murder case, a man got off for manslaughter."

⊷ ≖⊹≖ ⊷

"When he first started practicing law," said Nuckolls, "I'm not sure that a black man was entitled to an attorney at that time. I do know that Reuben was the first significant or known attorney to represent blacks other than in an appointed case. He had the ability to get the black community involved, and the church, of course, was the center of the black community. He would go in and get the church to raise his fee. And he would get *enormous* fees in cases that you couldn't believe would come up with the money. Some poor, downtrodden mill worker or pulpwood worker in south Georgia would be charged with rape-murder of a white woman, and Reuben would get the black community together and they would hire Reuben Garland. And they wouldn't have anybody else in the world but Reuben Garland. To be able to retain Reuben Garland was a part of your stature. If you were able to retain Reuben Garland, you had done the right thing for your community. They all wanted Reuben.

"He has told me of going into towns and having deputy sheriffs pull up alongside of him and shoot out the tires in his car, and of having to sleep at night on a pew in a black church with armed guards. I think that's when he developed this tactic of it was him against the world defending this poor black man, and everybody including the judge was against him. And he would bait the judge and create an atmosphere of sympathy for the defendant. He won verdicts that he never should have won probably. And maybe rightly he won them, I don't know.

"Back before there was NAACP Legal Defense, Reuben was the NAACP Legal Defense, in effect. But it was done for an outrageous fee, I'm sure, because he was terribly expensive."

In fact, recollections of Garland's costliness and ferocious bill collecting color some accounts of him. A story is told of his wrestling a set of car keys out of the grip of his client as the two of them sat at the defense table. Reuben refused to make his opening statement until he possessed the man's car, parked outside the courthouse, as his fee.

"Reuben," said a long-time acquaintance, "would have mailed Jesus a bill."

"You couldn't put him in today's setting," said Reeves. "He wouldn't fit. He lived in the time he lived; he was the last, I would say, of the great orator-type lawyers. He didn't profess to know the law. He had no idea. That's what he hired us for—look up the laws, see. He didn't practice law in the sense that he had a great legal mind. All he professed to know was human nature and attitudes and ways. And the law supported it, fine, that was even better. If it didn't, well, he'd find a way around that."

"Dad told a story of being in class one day at law school," said Edward T. M. Garland in Atlanta, "with the professor calling on everyone about, 'What is *stare decisis*?' And he asked different people, and he finally asked Dad what stare decisis was. Dad gave some answer, and the professor said: 'Mr. Gar-

and, if you were standing in the middle of the road and the law came down the road and the law ran completely over you, you would have never known that it had come nor that it had gone.' That was a story he told."

2

George Bright's new trial was set for January 12, 1959. The state believed their case against Bright was the strongest—and a conviction in his case might lead to his cooperation in prosecuting the others or might induce the others to plead guilty in exchange for lesser sentences—so they went with their case against Bright, again.

Reuben Garland was hell-bent on being the counselor at the defense table beside him.

James Venable clung in wretched futility to his star client.

Bright had consented, when asked during his first trial, to having Garland "associated" with the case. He left the decision of who would be lead attorney up to the two lawyers.

Venable wrote to Garland:

Dear Mr. Garland:

Mr. Burdine and myself do not need any help in the preparation and trial of the case of The State v. George Bright. We have obtained the law necessary for this case and our pleadings are in shape and we have the case already prepared for trial as to the law, the evidence and the witnesses.

During the last trial of the Bright case, I was greatly embarrassed and humiliated by your interference therein, as well as in the Bowling case when the calendar was called. You made open remarks that you were leading counsel, which no doubt led the public as well as members of the bar to consider that I was incapable and not competent to be the leading counsel. I resent this very deeply.

Failing to get a satisfactory response, Venable was blunter in a second letter:

The defendant in the case approaching trial of State against George Bright employed us and Bright himself has not fired us as his counsel, and therefore we are still Bright's counsel of record in this case, and he yet owes us a balance on his fee.

Very truly,

James R. Venable

Garland was not unduly flustered by this correspondence, for he had in his possession a more precious letter: in shaky green handwriting on a small sheet of onionskin, mailed from Rochester, New York, on January 5, 1959, more valuable than a mountain of letters from Venable, it read:

To Mr. Ruby Garland

Dear Sir:

As per our phone conversation I am sending to you my certified check for $3500.00, $2000.00 of which is your fee for defending my son George in his forthcoming trial, and $1500 is to provide bail for him if it will be allowed.

If the bail is not allowed the $1500 will be returned to me.

Mrs. Bright and I plan to be in Atlanta as you suggested.

Sincerely yours,

A. G. Bright

"At the prisoner's side when he again faces the bar of justice Monday will be Reuben Garland," reported the papers. " 'Attorneys James Venable and Essley Burdine, who defended Bright in his first stand against the bombing charge, withdrew from the case Saturday,' Burdine said.

" 'Mr. Venable and I have just withdrawn from the defense of George Bright. We could not agree on the type of defense to be used with the family of the defendant. There is no question of the innocence of Mr. Bright and we are sure that whoever represents Mr. Bright will establish this fact.' "

In preparation for jury selection, Garland did not rely on

crafting insinuating and anti-Semitic questions for prospective jurors, as Venable had. Rather than using that slapdash technique, he approached the problem as he would a scientific inquiry. He assigned investigators to research the background of each potential juror. They prepared for him a document of several typewritten pages, which read, in part:

Suggestions to STRIKE FROM JURY PANEL

No. 1   David H. Goodwin, clerk, 1st Nat'l Bank
Possibly Jewish, says he is "for segregation" but would he say he is for integration?

No. 5   Marvin M. Allen, carrier for post office
Has written pro-integration letters to the editor of Atlanta Journal

No. 8   Grady J. Conn, Calvert Iron Works
This name is suspiciously jewish but that's all to go on

No. 14   Clarence J. Hood, Jr.
Lives in a neighborhood where there are several Jews

No. 16   Joe L. Hopper, VP—Hopper & Neely Pharmacy
Jewish Firm. Neely is probably Jewish.

No. 20   Hessel H. Holland, Manufacturer's Agent
Most customers of Mfg. Agent are usually Jewish

No. 24   Ivy W. Duggan, VP Trust Co. of Ga.
Bankers naturally under Jewish Compulsion

No. 96   John W. Stanton, Secretary, Atlanta Baseball Club
Employed by half jewish firm. Hal Aaranson, jew owns ½ Atlanta Crackers

No. 107   Arnold J. Rich, Barney's Liquor Store
JEWISH. JEWISH FIRM. JEWISH NEIGHBORHOOD.

No. 137   Fred Scheer
          JEWISH

No. 141   Herbert D. Roth
          JEWISH

No. 170   Rufus L. Lolley, Jr., salesman, Atlanta Beverage
          DEFINITELY NOT. HE IS EMPLOYED BY JEW-
          ISH FIRM.

Once Garland got involved in the Temple bombing case, his reputation, from the perspective of the Jewish population of Georgia, forever took on the stain of an anti-Semite. His younger son, Ed, recalls competing during the trial in a high school wrestling match at the Hebrew Academy. When the Jewish students in the stands learned whose son was on the mat, they began chanting, "Kill him! kill him!" Certainly Reuben knew how to tap into southern distrust or dislike of Jews. "Anytime he had a Jew on the other side of a case," said the Atlanta attorney Miles Alexander, "it became Shylock on trial." Garland represented the wife of the pest-control millionaire Otto Orkin in a divorce action (while Morris Abram represented Orkin, a Latvian-Jewish immigrant). "I predict that my defense of the lovely, sweet, Christian character that I represent," said Garland, "will be the longest and hardest fought case of my forty-year career." But Garland was a showman, an actor, a defense attorney. "I suspect he was just being a criminal defense lawyer, if I have to guess," said Alexander.

Unlike George Bright, who assumed a dry just-the-facts attitude when assailing Jewry, but whose entire field of vision was clouded by race prejudice, Garland's just-the-facts approach to trial preparation and jury selection served one simple goal: the acquittal of his client. In this case, Jews were the number one undesirables for the jury, and—he had been told—perhaps the number one suspects in the crime. If the accused had bombed an Irish-Catholic cathedral, Garland would have applied himself, with the same bulldog straightforwardness, to unseating Irish people from the jury box. It was the most elemental step in jury selection, and Garland's own feelings were not bitterly mixed in, as Venable's had been.

If Bright had been a Jew in a similar three-ring circus of a trial, Garland *still* would have been first in line, when jail opened in the morning, to get hired by the man.

With a Jewish client, Garland could be just as abrasive from the opposite point of view and manipulate local prejudices to his own advantage. In the 1930s he defended the New York mobster Jimmy Rosenfeld, alias "Jimmy Rose," in the murder of an Atlanta man, and played very different strings: "Rosenfeld is a Jew!" he cried, insinuating bigotry on the part of the jury. "This man can't *get* a fair trial in the Deep South."

Robert Lipshutz, the White House counsel for President Jimmy Carter, recalls that as a young man fresh out of law school, he could not find a firm that would hire him or even rent him office space. "There were barriers," he said. "The big firms simply wouldn't hire you; religion was a barrier—there was no secret about it. Reuben Garland—who was at that time already a very flamboyant criminal lawyer—offered my partner and me office space. We didn't accept the offer, not wanting to be identified with him so closely, but it was a very nice offer."

For a public unaccustomed to the notion that an attorney could devote his highest and best energy to a cause in which he did not personally believe, Garland was forever tarred by the linkage with Bright.

⊷ ⋇⟐⟐ ⟐⊷

Meanwhile, he assigned to his staff research questions into Jewish arcana. Perhaps hidden within ancient Jewish law and mysticism lay secrets to the bombing on Peachtree Street; perhaps there *was* a world Jewish plot to acquire all the gold and enslave the gentiles. He wanted to know the meaning of *Talmud,* of *Gemara,* of *Mishna.* His assistant reported back that the Talmud was written in "Aromatic," instead of "Aramaic"—an odd slip, given the penchant of right-wing columnists to allude to the odor of Jews.

One of Garland's associates, perhaps thinking that more mileage could be gotten out of the Kol Nidre angle than Venable had managed to get, submitted a note to the boss:

Mr. Hambrick was with the police force for 25 years and knows you very well. He has a copy of the Kolnidre, that is the one where they take the vows and the oaths at the beginning of the year and any vow or oath they take they can throw out in their minds. It is authentic and is exact word for word. It is not a copy that he made up but the real thing and you may have it if you want it by calling him and telling him so and he will mail it to you. He said he wished you all the luck in the world on your clients and if he can be of any help let him know.

Similar offers of help poured in from around the country. Whether he welcomed this class of allies or not, Garland found himself the new golden boy of the leaders of American hate groups and the editors of hate sheets, many of whom wrote to bring him up to snuff on the Jewish question. With Garland on their side, they hoped this clash might end in victory for their side for once, that at last the Jews would be publicly exposed and censured. They wrote to Garland with urgency, feeling he could not possibly fathom the evil powers he was up against. "THIS PICTURE DEFINITELY IDENTIFIES RABBI ROTHSCHILD AS ASSOCIATED WITH ARCH ENEMIES OF THE SOUTH," said an anonymous note; enclosed was a newspaper photo of Rothschild standing with Senator Jacob Javits and Senator-elect Kenneth B. Keating of New York on their campaign-promise tour of southern temple bombing sites.

William Stephenson, the editor of the *Virginian*, wrote helpfully to Garland: "It is indeed reassuring to have a man of your caliber interested in the case. . . . If I may just make a suggestion, it has occurred to me that a useful purpose might be served if the self-styled 'Anti-Defamation League of B'nai B'rith' could be scared at least a little prior to the trial. . . . There is strong evidence that the ADL is one of the prime movers in this whole affair and I assure you that they can't stand up to close investigation. . . . Years of experience have taught me that they are almost everything except what they pretend to be."

The editor enclosed, for Garland's perusal, a photocopy of a stolen document: the American Jewish Committee's 1953 budget. ("If it is absolutely necessary I will endeavor to secure the original.") He enclosed, also, back issues of the *Virginian*, a sort of quickie correspondence course on American Jewry. "If you have not previously read material of the kind which you will want to read to prepare your case, you may be disagreeably surprised by the harsh language we sometimes use. If so, I will say only that we are writing primarily for people who know our subjects almost as thoroughly as we do—and *they* know that our language really is mild, in view of the facts. . . .

"Being innocent, the defendants have nothing to hide and can only profit by a trial. But quite the opposite could be said of the other side. They have much to hide, and the further you go into their history and activities the worse you will discover it to smell."

Garland wrote to thank him for the offer to help. He expressed interest specifically in any documentation Stephenson might gather to establish Rogers's affiliation with the ADL: "[Wallace] Allen thinks he is Jewish," Garland wrote, "and is working with members of the ADL and other radicals to falsely accuse and frame those indicted for something that Rogers and his confederates did themselves in order to discredit the States' Rights movement in the nation."

The NSRP organizer Matt Koehl wrote to Garland, and the NSRP chairman, Arthur B. Cole, wrote to Garland. Edward R. Fields, the information director of the NSRP, wrote to say, "The Jews have a deep-seated hatred for you." Russell Maguire, the editor of the *American Mercury*, sent him reprints of articles outlining the Jewish origin of Communism and the Jewish corruption of the American justice system. These articles apparently were read closely and appreciatively by Garland, for he immediately began a correspondence with Maguire about "the Jews and their allies."

3

On the first day of court, resplendent in a silk suit of robin's egg blue, bursting with satisfaction to be in the eye of the camera outside the courthouse and on center stage in the crowded courtroom, he demanded, as was his wont, the straitlaced proceedings of "formal arraignment." "The defense waives nothing," trilled Garland, with the slightest affectation of a British accent.

"Let the issue be joined," intoned Judge Jeptha C. Tanksley. A 1943 graduate of the U.S. Military Academy at West Point, he had served during World War II in Italy as a first lieutenant in the infantry and had been injured by a German mortar shell falling close to him. He had lost both legs and an eye. He had retired from the service as a captain, returned to Atlanta, graduated from Emory Law School in 1949, and served as a trial attorney in the solicitor's office for four years before his election as a superior court judge. "There was standing room only for the whole two weeks of the bombing trial," he said. "The courtroom was packed. I just don't think people generally like to see someone mistreated, certainly just on the basis of their religion."

Garland might well have felt invigorated. He was in a position of singular advantage vis-à-vis the prosecution, for he knew what was in the state's case. There was no criminal discovery in the 1950s—a defense attorney did not learn the content of the prosecution witnesses' testimony until they were on the stand—so Venable had gone into court blind at Bright's first trial, without a clue of what lay ahead. Garland, on the other hand, had sat through Bright's first trial. He knew the whole script. The state, coming into the trial with Garland, was now the blind partner, for Garland had an entirely different game plan.

Days before he would give his closing argument, Garland offered a preview of his defense of Bright in the questions he asked prospective jurors. He had a list of names in his briefcase of which jurors lived within the dark realm of Jewish influence and ought to be struck; thus, he was not obliged, like Venable, to ask questions the gist of which was "Who hates Jews? Raise your hand." At any rate, Garland's taste ran counter to packing the jury with rednecks. He preferred blue bloods; the scaled-down anti-Semitism and racial bigotry of thinking men, of middle-class and professional men, was more to his purpose. The intent of Garland's voir dire was to sell the jurors subliminally on the existence of a secret Jewish-Communist conspiracy to undermine America; to impeach the witnesses who were going to testify against Bright, including FBI agents; to portray Bright as a patriot; and to offer up a more likely perpetrator.

"Do you believe that the Communist movement is an international conspiracy?" he asked them, strolling back and forth before the box, his hands clasped behind his back. Who could possibly answer anything but yes? Immediately the prospective jurors found themselves in some agreement with him. The correct answer to all of Venable's questions was no, but more than half the time Garland looked for nods, assents, yeses, solidarity, trust.

"Do you believe," he trolled musically, "that this conspiracy affects the relations between races and groups in the state of Georgia?"

"Do you believe," he cried, whirling upon them and allowing his voice to cascade down a roller coaster of notes, ending in a whisper, "it is possible that Communists or criminals have provided the FBI with information and while doing so or afterward committed illegal acts or subversive activities?"

"Do you believe that if a citizen provides information to the FBI that this places his personal life and activities *above suspicion*?"

"Do you believe that it is possible for $85,000 in reward money to affect a person's testimony on the witness stand in a court of law?"

"Do you believe that convicts in jail who provide information for the FBI are actually innocent of the crimes for which they have been convicted?"

"Do you believe the FBI is infallible?"

"Do you believe," asked Garland, posing a question that brimmed with tantalizing drama, "that the Communists will commit acts of violence to further their objective of world domination in such a way as to avoid detection and to throw the blame on innocent persons?"

"Do you believe that the Communists are *masters of deceit*?" (Picture Garland leaning conspiratorially close to the jury box; see him end with a roar, making the men jump back.)

And, the patriot defense: "Do you believe that any American has the right to carry a sign on the public streets displaying to others his belief and opinions?"

"Well, I'll tell you why I got caught on the thing," said the World War II veteran and retired Ford worker Manley R. Morrison of Lithonia, Georgia, who served as an alternate juror. He is gruff voiced and beer bellied, with a deeply creased but somehow impish face; he looks fifty and claims to be seventy-seven. "I know the Lord's blessed me. I like people, and I try to do right in life, and I feel like that's the reason I'm seventy-seven and still kicking and going." He lives in a brand-new neighborhood of winding short streets and cul-de-sacs. In the war he had spent sixteen months "assigned to Old Blood and Guts"—Patton. In his den are brass eagle lamps, a Laz-E-Boy recliner, and a big TV topped with photos.

"I know exactly why Reuben caught me and put me on that jury. I didn't want to get on that. You could tell it's going to be a long, drawn-out thing. Of course, they didn't put any ladies on it, you know. But anyhow, they put us in there, and they were going to pick out two more jurors. So he's interviewing and asking several questions, and he asks me and probably the rest of them too, 'Do you know that all magazines have carried articles about this case?' Of course, I couldn't let that go. I says, 'I do not know that *all* magazines carried an article about the case. Nobody knows that.' You know what I'm saying? It's a trick question, and he's trying to find out who's listening and who isn't. Well, that's lawyer business.

"So he's finding out who's going to listen and who isn't and who can understand the difference, because words intimate a whole lot of things. And that was the reason I assume he picked me, because I said I did *not* know that all magazines carried this article."

Morrison was chosen as an alternate, but he was in one respect a ringer: what slipped by Garland's investigators was that in 1945 Morrison was store manager for one of the Paradies dime stores and he had gotten along fine with Paradies, a Jew. He had even been invited to the boss's daughter's wedding and had enjoyed himself at a reception at the Standard Club.

"We will show that the defendant has strong anti-Semitic tendencies," said Luck, much as he had the first time around, "that he participated in a plot to exterminate the Jews, and that he is linked to the actual bombing of the Temple as a planner and lookout man."

"This is an innocent man!" cried Garland to the newly seated jury. "He was arrested because he participated in a picketing of the *Atlanta Journal* building last summer. Mayor Hartsfield and the *Atlanta Journal* conspired to lay this charge against this man because of that picketing. And all the time, Mr. Bright was an innocent bachelor-man who felt compelled to work for what he considered a good cause: separation of the races. . . .

"We're going to show you who *really* bombed the Temple!" he boomed. "It was actually the state's star witness, L. E. Rogers! *He* bombed the Temple as part of a plot to collect the reward money."

Where previously there had been only the dry proceedings entitled *State v. George Bright*, it was "The Reuben Garland Show!" opening live onstage.

Bombastic, swollen with pride, expensively groomed down to his pink fingertips, his silver hair flowing backward as if windswept, he took control of the courtroom. "During the Temple bombing trial, Charlie was there," remembers Ed Garland. "He chauffeured Dad back and forth to court and ran around to open the car door for him. He parked the black Cadillac right in front of the courthouse and got out and ushered Dad in and carried his bags up to the courtroom and was there to pick him up at the end of the day."

Garland was a one-man band for whom all traffic had to stop. He was a fabulous obstructionist, who brought Luck's case nearly to a standstill and infuriated Tanksley, who saw in Garland's shenanigans not brilliant defense work but blatant nose-thumbing, disrespect for the court, and defiance of the authority of the bench. Even city hall suffered a work slowdown, under the avalanche of subpoenas launched by Garland, who demanded the appearance in court of half the police force, including the entire vice squad, all FBI agents in Atlanta, Police Chief Jenkins, and Mayor Hartsfield. Once he opened his briefcase on day one of the second trial, it was as if a huge, aggressive, multicolored rooster had been uncaged in the courtroom and began flying from pillar to post, roosting on ladies' hats, on the judge's gavel, on the inside ledge of a tall window, cocka-doodle-dooing every time the prosecutor and the witnesses opened their mouths to try to speak.

"COCKA-DOODLE-DOO!"

THE COURT: I overrule that objection and permit the testimony that the witness gave to remain in the record. Now go ahead, Mr. Solicitor.

THE COURT: Mr. Garland, the Court instructs you, sir, to yield to the Court when I attempt to make a ruling.

THE COURT: Gentlemen of the jury, Mr. Garland's description of the Court's conduct is highly improper. You gentlemen can form your own opinion about the Court's conduct.

THE COURT: Mr. Garland, the Court has made several requests of you. You did not follow instructions. I want to inform you again, I expect all attorneys to follow instructions.

"Cocka . . . doodle . . . doo."

THE COURT: It is not necessary at any time that you apologize to the Court, Mr. Garland. The Court is not interested in apologies.

Tanksley, weary of reprimanding Garland every time the effusive defense attorney opened his mouth, began privately to keep track of Garland's offenses. As the record built toward a finding of Bright's guilt or innocence, a parallel record was made regarding Garland's contempt of court. It included the following exchange:

"May I ask that the witness not be exposed to the face of Mr. Garland at such close contact?" said the prosecutor during an examination.

"What is the matter with my face?" cried Garland. "My face is not contagious."

"Go ahead with your testimony," said the judge.

"I am, Your Honor," said Garland, "just as rapidly as my feeble brain will permit."

"We didn't laugh," said Morrison. "No, we had to be dignified. Really we didn't try to show any emotion at all. If there was something funny, we didn't laugh because we were trying to do the right thing."

⸻

Like Venable before him, Garland would impeach the testimony of state witnesses Rogers and DeVore by portraying them as socially unstable and financially unproductive men motivated by yearning for what he described as a "quarter million dollar reward." (He added a zero whenever possible; the reward was twenty-five thousand dollars.)

The threatening letter seized by detectives from Bright's house, in which Bright warned Rothschild that he would soon witness "a terrifying experience," was introduced by Garland in its entirety. It thereby lost a good deal of its oomph. Garland required Police Captain R. E. Little to read Bright's letter aloud:

> Mr. Rothschild: You have brought to us a glowing account of Judaism, glowing because you planned it that way. You are right now telling yourself that these people here tonight have just witnessed a most gratifying experience. In just a few seconds, you are going to witness one of the most terrifying experiences ever in your life. In fact you have been chosen to be the star performer. We are going to have a question and answer period and you are going to star with your answers.

Bright's ominous warning, it now became clear, referred to the public grilling he was planning for Rothschild at Brotherhood Night at First Baptist. Like Rockwell's letter to Allen—which briefly had created a flurry among detectives and reporters because of its reference to a "big blast" and which truly only referred to the picketing of the newspaper office—the letter was set in the war-zone language and siege mentality of a pacific, white-skinned man.

The first important witness in the state's case took the stand Wednesday morning, January 14, 1959. It was Janice Rothschild, age thirty-four, whose Mediterranean beauty and ladylike hauteur made a pleasant impact on the jury and on court watchers. "Mrs. Rothschild was impressive," said one juror. "She was obviously a first-rate, high-class person; long, smooth black hair. Swanky." Janice planned to testify simply and briefly, as she had in the first trial, that she had received a threatening phone call at her home on the day of the bombing and that she had later recognized the voice as Chester Griffin's in a "voice line-up" at the police station.

If the state's case against Bright can be seen as a length of knitting, then placing Griffin at the other end of the phone line from Janice Rothschild was the first stitch looping the needle. The prosecution needed Griffin's phone call to begin to knit the story; Griffin tied the NSRP into the bombing.

But Griffin's phone call could not stand alone, one little wooly stitch. Griffin's phone call was a crucial piece of probative evidence, evidence that gives rise to an *inference* of the defendant's guilt. But Griffin's phone call was not *sufficient* evidence on which to convict Bright, for such a man as Griffin could have made the phone call anyway, on a lark, for a thrill, for a laugh, regardless of prior knowledge of a plot or acquaintance with Bright or membership in the NSRP. Proving that Griffin made the confessional phone call was not the same thing as proving the *truth* of what he had said over the phone.

Once the fact that Griffin made the phone call was secured on the needle, the state would have to knot into place four more stitches: First, that what Griffin said—"I'm one of them . . . " was true—that there was a "them," a conspiracy; second, that the "them" was the NSRP, which his phone call did not reveal ("them" could have been him and his wife, him and a Klan unit, him and his bowling league); third, that Bright was a member of the "them," of the NSRP; and fourth, that Bright had carried out the object of the conspiracy by bombing the Temple.

Griffin—about whom other men said, "The boy hasn't got both chopsticks in the chow mein"—had become a central protagonist in the trial of Bright. For Griffin had prematurely and carelessly tipped his hand twice: on Sunday when he had called the Rothschild house (if he had called), and on Monday, when he had jabbered to the detectives Perry and Strickland.

Garland weighed his options. Perhaps he should allow the state to prove Griffin to be the phone caller, then stand back and potently suggest that Griffin—and not Bright—was in fact the bomber. The problem with that strategy (with trying to rip out the piece of knitting at a later stitch rather than at the first) was that Griffin was such an unknowable commodity: it was impossible to know what he really knew, whom he would take down with him; he was a jiggling bowl of instability, offering no steady foundation upon which the defense attorney could erect a theory of guilt in order to exculpate Bright.

Better, Garland thought, to demolish the evidence about Griffin. Rip it out at the beginning, unravel the state's story before the prosecutor got it started properly, do it so thoroughly that no one would even *think* of suggesting Griffin again as the first knot in a string leading to the NSRP and to Bright.

At any rate, the case the state was beginning to weave was not flawless. Knit one, purl two: take Griffin and we'll give you Bright, too. The state's case relied on one of the oldest forms of injustice: guilt by association, and Garland was right to attack.

——◆——

Entirely innocent of the extent to which her tiny corner of the case had become a major building block slated for demolition by Garland, Janice Rothschild, feeling blissfully accomplished in the art of testimony after her experience at the first trial, gracefully mounted the stand and was sworn in.

"The first thing that he said I remember quite clearly," Rothschild testified under direct examination by Luck, "and that was: 'I am one of them that bombed your Temple.' And then he went on to say, 'I am calling to tell you there's five sticks of dynamite under your house at this time and they are lit. I am giving you time for your life.' I forget the exact wording of the end of the conversation because by then I was so frightened I just wanted to get out and get my children out. But that was the gist of it. . . .

"I noticed that there were great grammatical errors in it, and it was not—it was a southern voice, but it was not a cultured southern voice. . . . I wouldn't say it was completely illiterate by any means, it was of a medium high pitch. . . . I observed the same characteristics in that voice on the [tape] recorder . . . it was a medium high voice and had a certain lack of culture in tone and speaking qualities and that it was a southern voice, grammatically incorrect, but not completely illiterate. . . . I formed the opinion that this was the voice I had heard on the telephone.

"I enjoy acting," she ran on insouciantly, mildly perplexed but pleased at the court's interest. She was then like a bird smoothing its feathers on a green stretch of lawn, unaware that a cat is slinking toward her through the bushes. Garland stared at

Mrs. Rothschild with wide eyes and parted lips. She went on, "I have enjoyed identifying voices all my life. . . . I like to tell what part of the country a person is from, from hearing his speech."

She sat nodding her assent to the prosecutor's polite questions, the dark clutch of banded hair at the nape of her neck gently tossing, her white-gloved hands resting in her lap; meanwhile, Garland, across the room, looked to be in the grip of an apoplectic fit; there seemed inadequate cubits of air in the room for him to draw into his lungs and expel in damp gales of rage. He had whirled himself into a feverish state by this point in the witness's sincere and earnest testimony. He was so shocked, offended, stunned, and mortally wounded that the judge could permit such biased testimony that objections erupted from him in confused torrents of legalese.

"I make the objection that this evidence is hearsay, that it is hearsay of the rankest kind, that it is an effort on the part of the State to identify an unidentified voice, the witness having testified that she didn't know the voice, didn't know whose lips uttered the words over the wire, that she didn't know who he was, his age, but she knew that the voice was uncultured, an uncultured voice and a southern voice and made grammatical errors and had a tone to it and a pitch to it."

Tanksley compelled him to desist and allowed Mrs. Rothschild to continue.

"If she doesn't know Chester Griffin," Garland cried, on his feet again, aggravating the judge, "then she couldn't identify his voice over the telephone; if she couldn't identify his voice when she heard it, there is no way on earth for her to hear a voice on a tape recorder and identify that voice as the voice she didn't know over the telephone because a tape recording and telephone voice had a different sound altogether. I can get a recording and that is a recorded tone of voice." He was, at this moment, deliriously filibustering; whatever logic there was in his objection was less important than the fact that he was making an infuriated commotion, as if somebody were now trying to *pluck* the rooster. "But a telephone voice is a person who speaks to you directly over the wire without having to be transcribed to a record or tape, and that is known. Now she says that it was not a cultured southern voice and that is the reason why she says she identifies him now."

The judge managed to shut him up and encouraged Rothschild to continue.

"This is the most rank opinionated conclusive evidence that I ever heard in Court," shouted Garland, "and the rankest hearsay evidence that I ever heard in my life and I object to it and move to exclude it."

The beleaguered testifier continued.

"Of course, we move to rule that out on the ground that it is a conclusion of the witness, [the term *southern*] encompasses probably many *hundreds* of thousands of persons from the Tennessee River, Mississippi River Valley to the Atlantic—[his voice grows awestruck; strains of "This Land Is My Land" are heard in background]—on then from the *tip* of Florida to the *Appalachian* Mountains running up through and into Pennsylvania! . . . "

"I rule the question out, sir," said the judge.

The testimony limped on.

"Of course, we object to that," yelled Garland, who suddenly had figured out how to get some mileage for the defense out of the whole situation, "on the ground that a telephone call, a threat, would be irrelevant, immaterial and incompetent unless she could prove some connection as to who it was, if she knows the voice of Rogers and can identify the Rogers whom we contend bombed the Temple—and we expect to show that he went up there to Tennessee and tried to buy dynamite without a permit—"

"Mr. Garland!" said the judge, putting an end to that particular tack.

Then it was Garland's turn to examine the witness. He went after the genteel lady like a tomcat after a sparrow. But he was not out to make friends with Janice Rothschild, nor please her friends in the courtroom, nor behave with the obedient courtroom demeanor Tanksley required of him. This was about demolishing the state's key evidence; this was the work his client had hired him to do.

GARLAND [gently, curiously]: How many people do you know in the South who have the same tone, the same uncultured, same ungrammatical diction of the same kind that this man had, how many do you know?

WITNESS: I don't know two people that speak alike, and I

don't know anyone that speaks exactly like the voice that I heard, but I know that I heard it.

GARLAND: You don't know that class of people?

WITNESS: No, sir, I know all classes of people. . . . I am a drama graduate of the University of Georgia and for many years I had it as a sort of hobby to listen to voices and try to identify where the people came from. . . .

GARLAND: You mean by that you listened to voices and you could tell a western voice from a northern voice, you could tell a southern voice from a northern voice, is that what you mean?

WITNESS: Well, yes, there was a time when I could tell what part of Georgia they came from.

GARLAND: You could? But now, that time has passed and you can't do that anymore?

WITNESS: I could tell some parts of Georgia, I believe.

GARLAND: You are an actress?

WITNESS: I like to act, yes, not professional.

GARLAND: Would you mind imitating the voice of a New Englander for the jury, so they can hear you, imitate a New Englander, a Bostonian, we will say—

THE COURT: I rule out the last question as not being relevant or material.

GARLAND: Now you swore that you could imitate voices when Mr. Luck asked you, didn't you?

WITNESS: I didn't say that.

GARLAND: You didn't say that?

WITNESS: No, sir, I said that I enjoyed acting as a hobby.

COPELAND [Assistant Solicitor Carl Copeland]: I don't like to rise, but I don't like to see . . . questions asked in the form that tend more or less to be like it is insulting what the witness said. . . . We are certainly not up here to have this good lady made fun of and I want to object. I don't think it is proper and I want to object to his method of examining this lady. . . .

GARLAND: I state in my place I examine this witness as I

have every other witness in the history of my professional life. It is impossible for me to change my personality consistent with the desires of the Prosecutor. . . .

GARLAND: How many different types of voices are there of southern accents?

WITNESS: Innumerable ones.

GARLAND: Give the jury all the types of which you have knowledge, start off with number one and I would like for you to imitate them if you could. . . . Give me the various types of southern voices that you have sworn existed in my southland.

(Suddenly it is *his* southland. Janice Rothschild was born in Atlanta; her people had been in Georgia since the 1840s. But, since she was a Jew, Garland tried to out-southern her.)

WITNESS: I can't do that, I am an amateur. I didn't study it in school and therefore I don't know the names of these different voices, I just know that you can tell if people come from different parts of the South by their different accents. . . .

GARLAND: How many did you say?

WITNESS: I said there were innumerable ones because I didn't know how many.

GARLAND: Would you say there are as many as 20?

WITNESS: I feel sure there are.

GARLAND: Or more?

WITNESS: Probably more.

GARLAND: You are familiar with 20 because you swore—

WITNESS: No, I didn't say I was familiar with 20. . . .

GARLAND: Name the 20.

WITNESS: I didn't say I knew of 20 different ones that I could name, I simply said that there were undoubtedly that many, I thought. I said I was not a student of it and I didn't know the proper terms. I can just tell when I hear voices that they are from different parts of the South.

GARLAND: Well, name those that you know, are there 10 that you can name?

WITNESS: Well, Savannah, Atlanta, Middle Georgia, North Atlanta.

GARLAND: Where does the line end?

WITNESS: I couldn't tell you geographically but I know people north of Atlanta sound different from people south of Atlanta.

GARLAND: Go to Savannah, describe the Savannah voice.

WITNESS: Well, some of the words with "oa" in them are split, the syllable with "a."

GARLAND: Emulate one.

THE COURT: You need not do that.

GARLAND: You couldn't do it if the Court would let you, could you?

WITNESS: I could do it, but I would consider it highly undignified and would prefer not to.

GARLAND: Are you more concerned with your dignity than you are in telling the truth?

WITNESS: No, sir, but I am concerned with the dignity of the Court.

"He . . . pelted me with lengthy questions fraught with false statements, misleading implications, and deprecating asides," Janice Rothschild later recalled. "I was determined that he would not trap me and that I would show no doubt about the identity of the voice I had heard. By this time I was convinced that the government knew what it was talking about, that the FBI and GBI [Georgia Bureau of Investigation] had been watching these people for a long time, and that they knew they might not be able to prove the case because they couldn't place the defendant at the actual scene of the crime, but that they knew they had the right people. So therefore I was convinced that without perjuring myself I was going to be as stonewalling as possible and not give an inch. And I don't think I did give an inch. The more he deviled me the more determined I was that I wasn't going to tell him anything.

"He kept saying, 'But you are an actress, aren't you?' In fact, I was appearing in a play with the Theatre Atlanta which had just opened. He was trying to discredit me based upon the fact that I was an actress and therefore a wicked woman. All these ridiculously old-fashioned notions, but ones I could recognize. I didn't grow up here for nothing. I knew what he was aiming at."

In fact, Garland's dwelling on Janice Rothschild's acting abilities probably had less to do with stirring up puritan prejudices against actresses, and more to do with implying that her entire testimony and presentation were simply part of a role she was playing. And that this plum role—star prosecution witness!—should be given to the chief victim—the rabbi's wife!—to perform, was, he implied, scandalous.

GARLAND: How long ago was it that you emulated, imitated the voice of some character that you were portraying on the stage?

WITNESS: Last night.

GARLAND: Was that practice for this trial?

◆◆

GARLAND: You were downstairs, I assume, in your living room [when you received the phone call]?

WITNESS: A one-story house. [Mrs. Rothschild gently but consistently corrected all Garland's allusions to her vast imaginary wealth. With an elegant Jewess on the stand and a briefcase full of NSRP circulars, he could hardly be expected to restrain himself entirely. Later he would ask her a question beginning, "When you quietly rode down in your limousine (to) the FBI headquarters . . ." And he kept accidentally referring to Rabbi Rothschild as "Baron Rothschild."]

GARLAND: And how many words, now you count them without repeating them, how many words was said to you over the telephone by the voice? . . . How many words were spoken by this unknown voice to you at 6:30?

WITNESS: Do you want me to answer that without recalling the conversation to myself?

GARLAND: I want you to count them. . . . You have already said the words once. Now tell the jury how many words were used.

WITNESS: I just can't do it, sir, I am sorry. I can sit down and count them all out but I can't tell you offhand.

GARLAND: Well, sit down and count them all out, then. You are sitting down, count them all out.

WITNESS: I would say approximately 30.

GARLAND: I want to know exactly, just take this pencil and write out the conversation and count, if you want to be certain, I want to know.

WITNESS: 31.

GARLAND: Now, as I understand it, there were 31 words spoken, that is your testimony, isn't it?

WITNESS: Yes.

GARLAND: And these are the words that were spoken.

Garland then performed a small shenanigan, a quick sleight of hand: the penciled strokes of the thirty-one ominous words—"I am one of them that bombed . . ."—on the scrap of yellow legal paper disappeared. One moment Garland held it, read it to himself; the next, it was gone. Solicitor Luck, starting up from his chair, wanted it, the captured sentence fragments, the pale silvery lead of the persecuted Janice Rothschild's agitated handwriting. It seemed, at the moment, like a fingernail clipping stolen from an innocent for a witch's brew. Luck had an inchoate misgiving about what brew Garland was concocting. But then, with surprising abruptness, Garland lost interest in the rabbi's wife and let her step down, and the solicitor sat back down.

"She left the witness stand weeping," reported the *Atlanta Journal*, "following stinging cross-examination from Defense Atty. Reuben Garland."

"After ninety minutes of questioning me, Garland accomplished at least a part of his purpose," recalled Janice. "He had wound me to the breaking point and knew exactly which string to pull. With a seemingly innocuous question that caused me to think of the way the threatening call had affected our children, tears began to roll down my cheeks and I choked with emotion. Judge Tanksley excused me and asked his clerk to take me to chambers to recuperate."

Rabbi Rothschild had accompanied Janice to the courthouse, but in his own car. "Because I was no longer fearful after testifying in the first trial," said Janice, "Jack saw no reason to remain at the courthouse. It was Wednesday, his golf afternoon. If he hurried he could make it to the club by tee-off time." When she descended from the witness stand in tatters many hours later, she was heartbroken not to find him waiting for her. "As we passed the reporters in the hall outside, one told me that Jack had left—which did little toward helping me regain my composure. As soon as I could get to a telephone without being overheard I called the club, caught him before he left the locker room, and delivered such a hysterical tirade that he was dressed and back at the courthouse by the time I regained my composure and came downstairs. He had no idea what had happened, of course, and I was too angry to tell him. I got into my car and went home. He had one of the reporters fill him in and then followed me home to make amends."

"The afternoon paper . . . reported that I had left the witness stand in tears. When my mother saw it, she spilled a pot of freshly brewed coffee on her arm and spent a painful evening applying baking soda to it."

Unfortunately, Rothschild—lacking a true gift for commiseration—had no better a bedside manner with his wife than he did with his congregants. Rather than bestow the sympathy she desired, he spent the evening questioning her with fascination about Garland's technique. Always interested in the law, he regretted most of all having missed what appeared to be a most stimulating courtroom lesson.

That night an anonymous caller phoned the Rothschild's house and told the housekeeper: "You tell Mrs. Rothschild that she identified the wrong man—and she'll pay for it."

The trial continued.

At the courthouse the next day, Luck asked Garland for the piece of yellow paper, but the stout little defense attorney, tapping helpfully at all his suit pockets, seemed to have mislaid it.

On Thursday of the following week, January 22, Garland recalled Janice Rothschild to the stand and circled closer.

GARLAND: [I am talking about] the day you got the call, when the man said to you, and you swore to this jury, I am one of them that bombed the Temple, there are five sticks of dynamite under your house. If you are not out in five minutes you will die. Isn't that true, what you wrote down here?

WITNESS: That is approximately what I wrote down.

GARLAND: Approximately?

WITNESS: Yes.

GARLAND: You said that the voice uttered 31 words, didn't you?

WITNESS: Yes.

GARLAND: You wrote it on a piece of paper and carried the piece of paper out of the room with you.

WITNESS: I did not carry it out, you took that piece of paper.

GARLAND: And gave it to Tom Luck and you took it from him, is that right?

WITNESS: I have never seen that piece of paper since you took it from me, so I don't know where it is.

GARLAND: What did you do when the voice said, I am one of those that bombed your Temple?

WITNESS: He didn't say, I am one of 'those.' He said, I am one of 'them.'

GARLAND: You wrote it down on the yellow sheet, though, didn't you?

WITNESS: No sir, I wrote 'them,' I distinctly remember that.

GARLAND: You do?

WITNESS: Yes.

GARLAND: You swear you wrote down t-h-e-m and didn't write t-h-o-s-e up there on the stand, you swear that positively. . . .

WITNESS: I don't see how I could have written it, I really don't.

GARLAND: Do you positively swear you wrote t-h-e-m up there on that stand on the yellow paper with a pencil?

WITNESS: I swear I think I wrote it.

GARLAND: You just don't know, do you, you couldn't have written 'those'?

WITNESS: I don't think so, Mr. Garland, but you had me so upset by that time, it is possible.

Ah, ephemeral memory! Here lay the crux of all his badgering. A memory is not, after all, quite the same thing in evidence as a bullet, a fingerprint, or even an all-but-invisible strand of DNA. For even the DNA, though it operates in a domain beyond human perception, still participates in the physical world, while memory is of the province of the mind, where fantasy and dream coexist.

His point? It appeared that Mrs. Rothschild's memory was fallible, like everyone else's. Her ironclad recollection of the voice she had heard over the telephone (O untrustworthy medium!) on that fateful evening (an evening already well imagined by Garland for the jurors' benefit, the chaotic and frightening evening of the very day her beloved Church of the Jews had been bombed) had not itself been impeached, yet. But now her ability to recall a more recent event—the prior week's testimony—had a chink in it. Stress, it now appeared, could impair even the flawless memory of that great successor to Sarah Bernhardt, Mrs. Jacob Rothschild, just a tiny bit. And the jury knew, too, thanks to Garland's verbiage, that the fate of five innocent and trusting men lay in the perfect accuracy claimed by this stage actress for her so-called memory.

GARLAND: Don't you know you have a distinct recollection of writing 'those' and not writing 'them'?

WITNESS: No.

GARLAND: And you told your husband, My Lord, I made a mistake, after you came off the stand.

WITNESS: No, I didn't, I didn't say a word to him.

GARLAND: I wish I had that paper.

LUCK: He had the paper and I have been trying to get it back from him.

GARLAND: If you don't remember and you have a doubt, as you have expressed to this jury what you wrote with your own hand, how do you expect to remember what you heard with your ears when you were distraught and upset and listening to words of consolation and solace?

WITNESS: I could remember a lot more distinctly that night than I could here on the witness stand because with all that had gone on, I was not as distraught as I was when you cross-examined me.

GARLAND: But you are an actress and you are on the stage, and it is hard for me to ask you a question because you are an actress. . . .

Sitting erect, her ebony hair drawn severely back, her smooth skin and high cheekbones flawless, chin lifted, maroon lips neatly gathered, Rothschild retained, under siege, her dignity. She was extraordinarily aware that she stood for something, was representing not only herself and her husband, but the congregation, perhaps the Jewish people, in the stateliness of her demeanor, the gravity of her replies. She performed, in public, the Christian virtue of turning the other cheek: as he feinted and verbally struck at her, tugging at the strings of her temper, she responded with civility and modesty. It was a contest of verbal logrolling: he was a pro, but she was determined not to be dunked.

Exhausted, Garland now pleaded with the judge to adjourn for the night. His sleep at home, he told Tanksley and tried repeatedly to tell the jury, was being interrupted night after night due to mysterious harassment. Phone calls, honking cars, falsely summoned firetrucks and taxis, city tree-clearing equipment, and firecrackers tormented his sleep night after night, he explained. "Reuben would get home from the trial about midnight," said Fauntleroy Garland. "He'd sit in his den, trying to make notes on points for the next day's session. Almost exactly at midnight our telephone would start ringing. I'd answer, while I was trying to prepare something for him to eat. Most of the time there'd be voices with a foreign accent on the line: 'Ve gonna get all you Commie Garlands, all of you!' a voice would say and then the phone at the other end would be banged up in my face. 'You want tickets to a Russian concentration camp—you Commies, you?' "

In search of greater sympathy than he was receiving from Tanksley, who recommended he check in anonymously to a hotel for the duration of the trial, Garland wrote to Russell Maguire, the editor of the *American Mercury*: "The Jews and their allies sent taxies and ambulances to my home on West Paces Ferry Road on the hour every hour after one P.M. [*sic*] for four (4) nights. I only had about one hour and forty minutes sleep per night, and had I not been a very strong man and had not believed implicitly in my client's innocence, this imposition would have killed me!"

Whoever was behind the cruel mischief, they left the stout little defense attorney almost beside himself with fatigue. In court one day, hammering Janice Rothschild about her knack with southern accents, he suddenly felt that he could not go on.

GARLAND: . . . I am in an awful fix and I appeal in the sense of justice—give me time where I can cross this woman. . . . I know I am defending an innocent man and I ask your Honor for an adjournment until 9:30 in the morning. . . . Your Honor can observe my appearance. . . .

THE COURT: Can't you complete the examination tonight?

GARLAND: No, I just cannot. I have given my life to my profession and nobody has been more sincere than me, I don't care who he is, and I don't believe anybody ever lived that tried any more cases than me, and I want to give my client the best that I have got, because I believe in him and not to put me through this—

THE COURT: Mr. Garland, you have not been through any more than the rest of us.

GARLAND: I have been through more than any man because the responsibility of mine is greater and almost as great as your Honor, but you can sit in peace up there when here I recognize and understand is a woman who smiles and snickers now, and swearing anything—

THE COURT: That statement is highly improper, Mr. Garland.

"And of course, Reuben Garland, you could tell he was worn out," said alternate juror Morrison, "and he did tell the judge in front of the group that they had been calling him all night. And they'd grab us up and take us out of the room. He was all the time trying to tell us things he wasn't supposed to. But anyhow, Reuben Garland let it out to the jury and everybody that he'd been up all night because they had been calling him all night long. His telephone was ringing and he hadn't gotten no sleep and did not want to have trial that night. I assumed it was this guy's outfit—the States' Rights—I assumed it was that. He didn't particularly say—it could have been crackpots or something. Lots of them get into these things, see."

"Finally," recalls Janice Rothschild, "when all else failed, the florid-faced, white-haired attorney went into an act worthy of a Barrymore; someone in the audience was heard to say that there was some doubt as to where the best show in town was playing—at Theatre Atlanta or the courtroom. He clutched his throat, tore open his already loosened collar and tie, and gagged several times, giving—for all its melodrama—such a convincing imitation of a person having a heart attack that Judge Tanksley evidently felt he couldn't risk ignoring it.

"He recessed court until nine o'clock the next morning, whereupon Garland, having thus recovered his good health, proclaimed that he didn't believe a word of my testimony and intended to keep me on the stand all day long the following day to prove it."

On January 23, Garland completed his cross-examination of Janice Rothschild. He reminded her almost mischievously of the yellow page on which she'd written the telephone threat.

GARLAND: You remember the yellow paper?

WITNESS: I remember the yellow paper.

GARLAND: And I believe you said you didn't know where it was.

WITNESS: No, I knew the last time I had seen it was when you took it from me.

GARLAND: I had it? . . .

LUCK: May I ask Mr. Garland to produce the paper, he took it and I have been trying to get it back and Mr. Garland is concealing it. I specifically asked for it, it was in his possession and I asked after Mrs. Rothschild was off the stand, he couldn't find it at that point.

THE COURT: Mr. Luck, he stated he lost it.

GARLAND: I said I couldn't find it at the time.

Sidestepping Luck's desire to retrieve the yellow paper, Garland once again asked Mrs. Rothschild to recite the words as she swore she remembered them.

WITNESS: To the best of my recollection I wrote, "I am one of them that bombed your Temple. There are five sticks of dynamite under your house and they are lit and you have five minutes to save your life" . . .

GARLAND: Now, when I show you this paper and you find out you have written the word "those"—

THE COURT: Just a minute. Show her the paper.

GARLAND: May I present to you, madam, and show you D-35 and ask you to look at it and tell this jury if the words on that paper were not written by you in their presence.

(The rabbit is out of the hat! The nickel is in the boy's ear! The beautiful assistant is in one piece again! The yellow paper returns!)

WITNESS: I think that this was, I am not sure.

GARLAND: I move to strike that answer and I say that is a plan on the part of the witness to evade my questions.

THE COURT: Mrs. Rothschild, answer the question just as he asked it, to the best of your ability.

WITNESS: Will you repeat the question?

GARLAND: You have forgotten?

THE COURT: Read the question.

LAST QUESTION READ BY REPORTER.

WITNESS: I think so.

GARLAND: You don't know whether it is or not, you don't even recognize your own handwriting now?

WITNESS: Mr. Garland, I wrote this under great stress.

THE COURT: Don't go into that, just answer whether or not you wrote it, please, and let's go on.

WITNESS: I think I did but the handwriting was so rapid, I can't be absolutely certain it is mine. It is not my normal handwriting. I think it is.

GARLAND: You don't recognize your own handwriting, do you?

WITNESS: Not absolutely.

GARLAND: Now I want you to read this. . . .

WITNESS: "I am one of those that bombed your Temple. . . ."

Garland tortured Rothschild for another hour, in the course of which she offered: "I don't claim to be a memory expert and I am not certain." But his work with her was at this point complete. She was in the water; he was tap-dancing on the log. He had ridiculed any claim she might feebly have made as to expertise in accents; he had forced her to confess that she did not remember exactly what she herself had written down less than a week earlier; she had sat in the witness box and admitted to not recognizing her own handwriting; and when compelled to read the paper aloud, she had unwittingly revealed that she had gotten the most important word in her famous sentence wrong. Her memory, in short, was as full of holes as a sieve. "TEARFUL RABBI'S WIFE WINDS UP TESTIMONY," reported the *Journal*. This time Janice phoned ahead to her mother to avert the spilling of another pot of coffee.

Some later wondered whether the scrap had been tampered with. Had Garland or one of his assistants created a lifelike replica of Rothschild's scribbled transcript? The copy was accurate in all but two particulars: the handwriting, though painstakingly close, perhaps was not truly hers—thus her reluctance to claim it as her own—and the ungrammatical *them* had been transmogrified into the very proper *those*.

Tampering with evidence is a crime and one that Garland, like any other defense attorney, painstakingly avoided. One cannot positively assert that the yellow paper twinkling in Garland's fist on January 23 was not the same one that had been hidden on his person on January 14. But some found it possible that it was not, that it was, instead, the first yellow paper's evil twin. And the jury was left with the sad spectacle of the lovely, lovely lady who did not know her own handwriting.

The audio link of Griffin to the bombing conspiracy and to Bright was ripped away.

Five years later, Jacob and Janice Rothschild were returning home from Washington, D.C., seated in the bulkhead of the plane. Across the aisle sat two men who leaned over to introduce themselves. "They were the brothers Burdine," said Janice. "One was a lawyer and one was a doctor. And obviously, when they found out who we were, the lawyer wanted to talk.

"He told us that he was the associate to Venable in the first trial, and he said that he had been so upset at the anti-Semitism of the senior attorney, of Venable, that that was one of the determining reasons why he left the firm. And later on in the trip, he said to me: 'You know you did identify the right man.' "

Having dispensed with the state's chief witness, Garland presented the star defense witness, who gave an alibi for Bright: a rival scenario for the early morning hours of October 12, 1958. It was Marilyn Craig, furloughed from Milledgeville State Hospital, to which her husband had committed her, so that she could testify for Bright. A psychiatrist and a licensed practical nurse from the hospital waited nearby as Tanksley determined her competency to take the stand. He permitted her to proceed. "MENTAL PATIENT CALLED IN TO GIVE BRIGHT AN ALIBI," reported the *Constitution*. And the *Journal* explained: "She was injected into the ever-surprising Bright trial under a Georgia law which permits a lunatic to testify during a 'lucid interval.' "

Described by the *Constitution* as "chic with a Bavarian

braided hairdo, and wearing a salmon-pink coat-suit," she began in her smoky voice, with her "I am a lady and I damn well better be treated like one" stance.

"George Bright and I were at the Plaza Pharmacy, roughly two o'clock," she testified. "I had known George, oh, about two weeks, a little more. . . . We drove out on Peachtree Industrial Boulevard to an all-night little grocery store and I do not know the name of it, but I do know the location. . . .

"Anybody in there to wait on me?" she repeated Luck's question incredulously, engaging in the snappy-answers-to-stupid-questions parley at which she seemed to feel herself a pro. "Yes. The place is open all night. That's the reason I went out there.

We went out there to buy some things for breakfast because George and I, our intention was to go and on that evening was when they had one of these guided missiles, those satellite things. That was our intention was to watch it and it was to have been visible over Atlanta roughly about four a.m. Our intention was, when we left the pharmacy, was to go to some point of observation, which there were many around Atlanta. Just find a high hill some place where you would not have too much of the city lights behind you. Since, if you were observing with the naked eye and it was, after all, it was something to see if you could see it, and to just observe and then to go back to my home and to make breakfast. So we bought breakfast materials. On several times before when we had done the same thing, we had eaten breakfast in a public place and I said, "What the heck? Why don't we just go out to the house and have breakfast instead, since I have that home?"

We bought sausage. We bought coffee. We bought syrup and, oh, one thing he was going to do for me was spray for roaches. . . . Frankly, if I had had any idea that it would be so important perhaps I would have made a list of it or just not gone at all. . . .

I didn't speed, but I didn't particularly drive leisurely. In a sense I was, maybe, in a hurry to get out because we were going to get these things and then go by the house and get a blanket because—get each of us a blanket—because it was on the chilly side. And also, we thought at one time about making coffee and taking it in a thermos. . . . We also bought cigarettes. I bought mine and he bought his. Mine was Chesterfields and frankly I don't even remember the brand that he smokes but he smoked his brand and I smoked mine. Who paid for the groceries? That particular evening, we split that one up too. I think he paid for some part of it and I paid for the roach spray and in fact we had quite an argument there as to the relative merits of Brookfield sausage and Redfern, and I would have been there till yet, saying that Redfern was better.

These were the crucial half-hours and minutes; at this time a perpetrator was driving toward the Temple with a nitroglycerine bomb. According to Craig, she and Bright at those moments were weaving back along Atlanta thoroughfares toward her house to get a blanket and catch that glimpse of the *Pioneer* satellite. They made it as far as her driveway and had to change their plans.

"We turned on the radio and discovered that Pioneer I, I think that was the name—well, it was our answer to Sputnik, Pioneer I, it is one of the satellites, one of our attempts to build a satellite; I think it went out 68,000 and something and so forth and so on—and we turned on the radio to see how it was getting along. All the radios, several of the radio stations, did carry those accounts if you recall, or if you were at all interested in that sort of thing. Many people were. You would be surprised how many more people other than George Bright and me were out at that hour."

(Indeed.)

"We discovered that the blooming thing had blown a fuse or something and there was no point in going anywhere, so we sat there—in my home—and played records for a while, listened to the radio for a while. It was roughly about 4:00."

The side wall of the Temple had blown out twenty-three minutes earlier.

"I said, 'Well, there, we have got everything here for breakfast, there is no dad-blamed point in me going back down there, taking you all the way to the Plaza to get your automobile so that you can come back out here in about an hour's time. We will sit here instead.' We talked for a while and after a while, he began to yawn in my face and I yawned in his face, and I said, 'Look. The boys' bedroom is right out there. Go out and sleep for a while and I am going to sleep on the couch. . . . ' "

LUCK: On the same couch? Did he go to bed on the same couch with you?

WITNESS: Did he go to bed on the same couch with me?

LUCK: Yes.

WITNESS: Matter of fact, he didn't.

LUCK: Where did he go to bed?

WITNESS: And by going to bed, I mean lying down and going to sleep. Or, did you never sleep with your clothes on?

THE COURT: You just answer the questions, ma'am. . . .

WITNESS: Anybody would get a little riled. . . .

She appeared an experienced practitioner of relying on generic ideals of womanhood, though her own particular practice of the conventions had slid a bit.

LUCK: Did you become—did you engage in acts as man and wife?

WITNESS: No. We did not.

LUCK: During that entire time when you stayed together?

WITNESS: It's quite possible to spend a good bit of time with someone of the opposite sex without getting too interested in, in sex. It *has* been done, you know. . . . I am a little bit provoked at being asked that, I think most anyone would understand. . . . You would be surprised how many people have spent a good bit of time together and did not. Now I don't know what you might do, sir, I was not with you.

LUCK: Your Honor! . . . And where did he sleep?

WITNESS: For a very short period of time only, out on the—it is a porch-bedroom. It has open windows all the way around. It's glassed in all the way around. It was my boys' room. . . .

LUCK: Could you see him while you were there on that couch?

WITNESS: When I was there on the couch, I could have seen him and heard him. After I went to sleep, I couldn't. I don't pretend to be psychic or something.

Her expectation, as it usually was when she reached for her Chesterfields and kept herself from smiling at her own retorts by poking one between her lips and inhaling with a frown, was that she would be found, in some quarters at least, witty. She gave the impression that—given the choice all her life of being a dummy or being too smart for her own britches—she had gone for the depiction that at least had the word *smart* in it.

At any rate, she had done what she had come for—verified old George Bright's alibi. And she had done so out of the goodness of her heart and not with any secret motive, for they no longer saw each other. It was a good and forceful alibi, too, in that it was rich in detail, event, and location. But it had the flaw common to alibis of this type: it was not anchored in time.

It was a free-floating narrative. There was nothing she told about their night together that could not have happened on October 11 or October 10 or on January 23. The bit she tossed in about hoping to catch a glimpse of a satellite then in orbit and passing over Atlanta simply was not the same as if the two of them had had their photograph taken in Cape Canaveral in front of the launching pad at the moment of lift-off. "Mrs. Craig, what time was this so-called satellite, regardless of name, supposed to have left the Earth en route to the Moon?" asked Luck.

WITNESS: Earlier. But it was published in the paper and announced over the radio that it would be visible in the Atlanta area roughly around 4 o'clock in the morning. Four or 5 o'clock in the morning . . .

LUCK: Mrs. Craig, would you be surprised to know that there were no news releases as to the satellite on Sunday?

WITNESS: On Sunday?

LUCK: Sunday.

WITNESS: You know, they usually announce that a little bit previous to that so that people that are just like me, foolish to stay up late and go out and scan the Heavens because they realize history was being made, and who had a particular interest—and that is no interest of the Court—in the particular progress of that particular one, would go out and watch with the naked eye and if you didn't mind straining your eyes a little bit, you could see it.

LUCK: Now my question is, Mrs. Craig, that you testified a while ago that the news releases real early in the morning told you that the Pioneer satellite had failed. Would you be surprised to know that there were no news releases on Sunday morning about the status of the satellite?

WITNESS: On Sunday morning?

LUCK: Yes.

WITNESS: That was late Saturday night, was it not? And actually was early Sunday morning.

LUCK: Is it your testimony that you and George Michael Bright, sitting there in your house, fully clad, heard a broadcast to the effect, early Sunday morning, when you were about to go out and watch for it, that it had gone off course? Was that your testimony?

WITNESS: Oh, let's see, now. That has been some time ago. I had no idea that it would ever be quite so important. I do recall that it did go off course, anyhow, but I recall that was the reason we did not leave the house.

A USAF Pioneer satellite designed to orbit the moon was launched from Cape Canaveral on October 11, 1958. It reached a height of 70,200 miles but failed to break free of the earth's gravitational pull and burned up in the atmosphere forty-three miles into its flight. Still aloft at the hour when the Temple was bombed, it was failing to achieve the speed required to reach the moon. The prosecution in *State v. Bright* found no evidence that information of imminent failure was relayed by the Air Force to the media, and none was introduced by the defense. Still, whether or not Craig and Bright knew the space mission was about to abort, they apparently aborted their mission to go gaze at it.

The defense attorney asked the court if Craig might be excused to return to the hospital. Luck agreed that it might be better if she went on back. "Mrs. Craig left the stand glaring at the prosecutor," wrote John Pennington for the *Journal*. "Glaring steadily at the prosecutor, Mrs. Craig said: 'Maybe I'll see you there someday.'"

The alibi, in summary: Bright could not have bombed the Temple because he was sitting in Marilyn Craig's driveway at the time, receiving a world-exclusive report that *Pioneer II* had just blown a fuse.

At 9:35 P.M. on Friday, January 24, 1959, eleven days into the trial, the jury of twelve white males began their deliberations. At 11:45 P.M., they returned to the courtroom with their verdict. They had voted unanimously on the first ballot, after thirty-five minutes of discussion, to acquit the defendant. Said the jury foreman, Henry D. Furniss: "We felt the state did not present sufficient evidence for us to feel in any way that we could convict Bright for the crime with which he was charged."

"He was a likely suspect, you know," said Morrison. "He really didn't strike me as being too bright. But you can't condemn a man unless they prove it, and they never even did place him at the scene, or whatever. This is at night, you know. I don't think they've ever found out yet what happened. But it could have been some of his group. As far as I know, this is a group that *would* do such a thing, I think. A lot of people on the witness stand didn't seem too bright to me. The FBI did not impress me. I guess they're just trained not to give out information, but you'd think they would know more than what they are telling or admitting to. I personally got the impression they were holding back some things. Now what they were, I couldn't tell you. But you know, you expect them to be more knowledgeable. In my own mind, they did not bring out sufficient evidence to place him anywhere near the scene of the crime."

"Possibly we went to trial too quickly," said Luck, "before enough evidence could be gathered. There was incredible pressure in the press, from the city, from the community, to find the guilty men and get convictions as soon as possible. We simply proceeded before we had enough evidence. I feel certain that these were the guilty parties, but we had a very weak, circumstantial case."

The conclusion of the jurors and of court watchers was that the state had proved two things: Bright was an anti-Semite, and the Temple had been bombed.

Ultimately, charges against all five original defendants were dropped. Bright, Allen, Griffin, Richard Bowling, and Robert Bowling went home and attempted to resume the lives they had led three months earlier.

Garland, meanwhile, went to jail.

As soon as the jury returned their "not guilty" verdict, Tanksley turned his attention to Garland's conduct during the trial. He had been disrespectful on so many occasions, ignoring the judge's instructions, that the tally Tanksley had been keeping more than added up to contempt of court.

"Mr. Garland, for some years, had done sort of as he pleased in court," said Tanksley years later. "He had run over most of the judges. And he started out with me and I told him to conduct himself in a proper, dignified manner like a lawyer should. But I felt like he didn't do that—he would spit on the floor and say things to me I didn't figure he ought to say. So during the whole trial I felt he was disrespectful of the process of court—not of me personally. I didn't care about that. But I just felt like he had shown such little respect for the procedure that he should be punished for it.

"So at the end of the trial when the jury went out, I went to my office and started writing an order to punish Mr. Garland. Two contempt citations of twenty days each, one to follow the other. I always really felt that Mr. Garland should have been an actor instead of a lawyer."

Garland exclaimed: "Your Honor! You've bankrupted me! You've ruined me."

"Mr. Garland," said Tanksley, "I don't believe there's any reason for the court to hear further from you at this time, sir."

"Your honor!" cried seventeen-year-old Ed Garland from behind the bar. "Can I go to jail instead of my father?"

"Would you take a supersedeas order?" asked Reuben Garland—this would have suspended immediate enforcement of the contempt order.

"No, sir."

Bright left the Fulton County Jail for the first time since he had been incarcerated without bond on October 13, and a few minutes later, Garland replaced his client there to begin serving a forty-day sentence for contempt of court. The *Atlanta Journal* headline that night read: "BRIGHT RELEASED, HIS LAWYER JAILED."

Garland was placed in a cell at the top of Fulton Tower (the same jail in which Leo Frank had been held). But Garland's penal suffering did not equal that of most other prisoners there. "Daddy had represented the chief jailer, Chief Hugh Cromer, for twenty years," said Ed Garland. "He sealed in the turret—where condemned men once were hung—with glass windows and turned it into a suite for Daddy. The elevator got right off in this private section and the air-conditioning came blasting in, and he installed a phone and a TV and made it a private room for my father.

"Mother would prepare the food, and we would go down three times a day to deliver it. The black Cadillac would arrive in front of the jail, and the news media would be there. Charlie would get out with great formality and go around and open the trunk, and there would be the silver tray with a silver coffeepot. Pick up the tray and hold it aloft on one hand and walk into the jail."

"Garland's stay in Fulton Tower attracted a number of visitors during [his first] weekend," reported James Sheppard for the *Constitution*:

Dressed in baby blue silk-satin pajamas, a yellow chenille bathrobe and fur-lined slippers, Garland appeared relaxed as he talked with them. The door to his room was unlocked and he was free to stroll about the cellblock corridors and talk with prisoners and jailhouse officers.

In addition to greeting his visitors and receiving gifts, Garland dictated a few letters to his secretary. One of the presents was a lemon cheese cake. Garland gave it to a Negro prisoner, telling him to divide it with his cell-block mates.

Garland has a 20-by-20 foot sitting-sleeping room and a private bath. . . . Carnations and tulips adorn the room. He has perfumed soap. The sheets and blankets look clean. There's a tablecloth on the table. It is laden with telegrams, a Bible, candy, cake, nuts, cigarettes, soft drinks, etc.

There's a captain's chair in the room and a long bench to seat his visitors.

"Do I want to get out?" Garland repeated a reporter's question. "Wouldn't any man want to get out of jail?"

"Dad wrote poetry while in jail," said Ed. "He wrote one called 'The View from the Prison Bars.' "

While incarcerated, Garland decided to use his time productively and challenge Paul Webb in the upcoming election for state solicitor.

He launched his campaign from the jail. Early in the campaign, he phoned Janice Rothschild to ask for her help in rallying the Jewish community behind his candidacy and in dispelling rumors that he was anti-Semitic. She recalls it as the most amazing phone call she had received since the one in which a man had said "them."

"He was dripping with honey and feigned innocence," she recalled. " 'You know, Mrs. Rothschild,' he said, 'I don't have anything at all against the Jewish people. I was just trying to save the life of my poor, innocent client, and I'd appreciate it if you'd tell your folks over at the Temple so they'll vote for me.'

"I was so flabbergasted I could only say, 'Mr. Garland, your lack of respect for the American system of jurisprudence is so appalling that whether or not you are anti-Semitic is totally irrelevant.' Then I hung up. Jack, who overheard my side of the conversation, told me I should have said, 'Mr. Garland, I wouldn't vote for you even if you were *Jewish.*' "

Denied vital campaign assistance by the Rothschilds (the rabbi, not the baron), Garland appealed to Fulton County Jewish voters directly. On his campaign leaflets, he promised: "Reuben A. Garland will indict, prosecute and convict the guilty dynamiters of the Jewish Temple! Webb, possessed of this evidence, prosecuted the innocent and refused even to indict the guilty! Vote for fearless, courageous and impartial law enforcement. Elect Reuben A. Garland."

He meanwhile served thirty-seven days of his forty-day contempt citation. But by that point he would have liked to go ahead and serve the whole forty days, since he and his family and staff had organized a campaign event, media phenomenon, and public fete around his release date. Tanksley, however, was well aware that his famous prisoner had big plans.

"Well, he stayed in jail until about the thirty-seventh day," said Tanksley, "and during that time he was of course running for solicitor against Mr. Paul Webb. He was going to make a big show and parade when he finished his forty days. So I called in the sheriff and told him that just to quietly go down to the jail and take Mr. Garland on home and let him serve his last two days at home. And when the sheriff got down there, Mr. Garland said, 'Oh no! I'm not going home, I'm going to have a big picture-taking ceremony out here when I am released.' And the sheriff told him, 'Mr. Garland, get your things together, you are going home. We're going to take you home.' And the sheriff took him home to serve his last two days in confinement at home. So we didn't hear so much about it."

Garland lost that election for state solicitor, but he continued to enjoy a long and brilliant career as a trial lawyer.

15

"Oratory Is Not Enough"

1

The Temple congregation and the Atlanta Jewish community—so recently reassured of their place in the heart of Atlanta—were dismayed, confused, and intimidated by George Bright's "not guilty" verdict. There were those who lamented, "It's Leo Frank all over again!" and those who thought it.

On February 6, 1959, Rothschild broke his long silence and spoke to his own congregation about the recent events, and about fear. He had spent the last decade trying to lure them out of hiding, to encourage them to speak out on public issues like the first-class citizens they were. Now he faced a congregation again peering at him from inside psychological bomb shelters. "You *see* now?" he felt them thinking. "You see where all your fine talk has gotten us?" His immediate task was to allay the fear. Fear, for him, was one of the minor external emotional facts, like loneliness, or hurt feelings, of which he was supposed to be cognizant, but was not particularly. Fear, for him, was not a motivator. He had made it thus, he had placed it there, outside his core operations, assigned lowest priority. Like empathy, like tact, it did not come easily to him. But he tried, for their benefit, to consider and address it.

That Friday night, in a sermon entitled "Ordeal by Trial," he said:

> The bombing was a traumatic experience. We looked to the trial with desperate hope. Emotionally, we needed conviction. But let us not be misled by the acquittal. This represented democracy at work. How else would we want it to be? . . .
>
> As all of us unhappily are aware, our ordeal did not cease when the bombing was no longer news. Within the past few weeks, we found ourselves once more uncomfortably in the public eye. The trial that ended recently was front-page news for two solid weeks. When that trial ended in a quick acquittal of the accused, I sensed a disturbing and disquieting mood in our Jewish community. An undercurrent of fear, a mood of despair, a feeling of insecurity and uncertainty followed in the wake of the trial. The drama of the courtroom did not engender the same magnificent courage, the same deeply-rooted faith in the soundness of our fellow-citizens as did the bombing. . . .
>
> Many of us were dismayed by the conduct of the trial itself. Instead of an orderly progression of logic and evidence, there was a circus atmosphere and a beclouding of the issues. Sometimes it seemed that everyone but the accused was on trial. Particularly those unfamiliar with courtroom procedure were more than a little appalled by the seeming helplessness of the court to control and keep order. Yet this was democracy in action—and democracy is always in trouble defending itself against being used by forces that seek to destroy it. Yet we believe in democracy and in its eventual strength and success.

Why should we be afraid? he asked them. The fact that the Atlanta police and the FBI had apprehended suspects and had brought them to trial should be a source of consolation.

> This was no Frank case with all its attendant prejudice against the "JEW" and the "outsider." Whatever threats were made came not from a citizenry roused to

mob violence but from a bigoted few who themselves drew the wrath and scorn of the community. . . .

Another very real source of concern was the testimony that the defense elicited from its witnesses—with the help of cross-examination by the Solicitor's office. A picture was drawn of virulent and violent anti-Semitism. It was a shocking and distressing revelation—more so because most of us were blissfully unaware of this extreme sort of hate. The discovery that it existed battered at the foundations of our picture of America and undermined our confidence and faith.

[But] we cannot allow ourselves to be dismayed or misled. This is a small and relatively ineffectual group, almost alone in their bigotry, sending out reams of hate-literature. Whom do they convince? Only themselves.

But now their program and beliefs had a wider platform. The public press and an open courtroom became the soap-box for their animosity. And we were fearful. Of what? Have we so little confidence in the essential decency of our fellow-Americans that we believe they will be taken in by such lies? Have we so little faith in ourselves and what we stand for that we think people will believe them and not know us as we are? Granted that there are many non-Jews who harbor a sort of latent anti-Semitism, who have the natural suspicion of all men directed against the "out-group," the "different," the minority. Now, for the first time, they saw where their prejudices would lead them. The trial made them face themselves. Do you believe that they accept the National States' Rights Party as their spokesman? I don't. They recoiled in horror. Why should we be afraid?

Much of our insecurity stems from a lack of confidence in our status in the community. We are fearful lest the acquittal bespoke an attitude of indifference or of the inability of the community to see the seriousness of what is involved here. Not at all. It meant an absence of sufficient proof to make a case for conviction—nothing more. It did not signalize a permission for open season on houses of worship. . . . The community was as distressed and upset as we were with the outcome. Not because justice was not done. That is not for us to say. But because a stronger case could not have been made. They saw this as the first time that any of the alleged culprits had been brought to trial. They saw it as the first chance during all these bombings to use the law to stamp out such violence and put an end to lawlessness. . . .

When it ended, no mobs descended on us as a defenseless minority, no violence was unleashed. Quite the contrary. Everyone shared our feeling of frustration. What, then, is there to fear?

And he ended with his usual coda: that they should proceed with courage as Americans, with the words of the Jewish prophets in their hearts: " 'Justice, Justice, shall ye pursue.' "

Over time the community was calmed by the voices of Jewish people who had attended the trial, who had observed firsthand that the jury truly had lacked sufficient evidence on which to convict.

The congregants had to carry on, to trust in the expressions of goodwill pouring forth from the white and black Christian churches. The lack of a convicted perpetrator meant that any number of anti-Semitic segregationists and their confederates of malcontents could have been behind the act, anonymously sanctioning it or actively planning it. Without closure, without identification of a single assailant, the congregants were left almost with the impression that large anonymous social forces had zeroed in on them. It was as if the era's social dislocation had broken open the Temple, as if the expanding racial earthquake had shaken its pillars. The Temple members, therefore, had to address themselves to the general righting of wrongs, to the restoring of the landscape, to the improvement of southern civilization. They rebuilt, and they did so on firmer ethical and religious foundations.

In the coming years, Jack Rothschild continued to travel and preach on behalf of "the Negro's demand for self-fulfillment"—which was coming to be called "the direct-action movement," and soon would be known as the civil rights movement. Rothschild noted:

Somehow, the Negro's demand for self-fulfillment brings unhappiness to the white man. He resists with all the power at his command. He perverts the law for his own purpose. He intimidates those who seek the full measure of their citizenship. He puts a woman's stocking over his face and shoots into a House of God. . . . He burns a cross crowned by a Negro's hat—a modern golden calf about which he cavorts with religious frenzy. . . . His female counterpart takes up her role as protector of 'the cherished Southern way of life' by spitting once again on little children on their way to school.

"Mississippi has some *real* atoning to do," Rothschild muttered to the congregation when the Jewish Day of Atonement fell during the 1962 riots at the University of Mississippi (Ole Miss) over the enrollment of James Meredith, the first black student on that campus.

The bombing had launched him briefly into national prominence, and he would continue, until the end of his life—growing year by year a little heftier, a little balder, a little more acerbic—to be a strong, clear voice for social justice within the Jewish world, in high demand as a speaker, sought after as an author of articles and resolutions, and a role model for a new generation at Hebrew Union College. If he had seemed unflappable before the bombing, deaf to the threats ricocheting in his general direction from across the South, then after the bombing he was positively a marvel. He simply never flinched. He did not change his ways. He was as pushy, demanding, and unsympathetic to the moral plight of his congregants after the bombing as before it. In this he defied the main course of human nature, for a great many souls act publicly in support of an ideal; far fewer return after the first spray of gunfire or clubbing by the opposition. Bill Bremen made a motion to the board that he be named rabbi for life. Effectively, he was. And he remained careful—as he had been immaculately careful right after the bombing—not to capitalize upon, not to exploit the moment. He thought deeply—albeit while lounging in front of a televised baseball game, or while playing golf with three friends, to all appearances at his most relaxed, but then that was the sort of front he had always thrown up—he meditated on the issues of the day as they came within his line of vision. He navigated still by his reliable North star—the Prophets—so that what he said and did would contribute to the repairing of the world, and not rebound in some way to his own personal credit.

His talk circuit extended far beyond the South in the years following the bombing, as he accepted guest pulpits in Baltimore, Cleveland, Pittsburgh, Boston, Toronto, Minneapolis, and Westchester County, New York. The northern Jewish audiences were curious about the condition of southern blacks, but absolutely riveted by accounts of southern Jews. Rothschild defended the Lost Tribe that had become his own. "Just not to join a White Citizens Council is an act of heroism in some communities," he told the northern liberals. Back home, on the other hand, he continued to berate his southern landsmen:

> Every major religious organization has clearly stated its moral commitment [to full citizenship and equality for blacks]. How the Southern Jew wishes that Judaism didn't really say that. Or, since it does, that his national body or his own rabbi would stop reminding non-Jews of the fact. . . .
>
> The Southern Jew . . . more than all the other decent, God-fearing "moderates," equivocates and rationalizes. Above all, he joins his Christian friends (whose religion has also compromised them with uncompromising statements on the subject) in seeking to separate religion from life itself.

He was elected to the board of governors of Hebrew Union College and as the vice-president of the Atlanta Council on Human Relations. He interceded with judges on behalf of students and faculty arrested during restaurant sit-ins, and he hosted northern friends and acquaintances who were passing through Atlanta on their way to direct-action skirmishes in the deeper South.

In 1962, Dr. David Marx, the rabbi emeritus of the Temple, died at his home. "David Marx would have been ninety years old in March," Rothschild said in eulogy. "His life spanned almost the entire life span of our Temple. Such continuity of dedicated service is almost without parallel in the history of our Reform movement."

The majority of his congregation grew accustomed to the Temple's position in the spotlight on racial matters. Nudged repeatedly by their rabbi, the congregation began moving toward social responsibility and racial harmony in myriad ways. In the coming years it was the Temple, more than any other Jewish institution in Atlanta—more than most in the country— that was perceived by many Jews and blacks as straddling the fault line between the white and black worlds. Temple congregants were in the forefront of Atlanta citizens who devised innovative social programs transcending race and class.

In later years, as leadership of the Temple passed from Rothschild to his former student, assistant, and friend, Rabbi Alvin Sugarman, a host of interracial programs were instituted. These included the Martin Luther King Shabbat, an annual Friday night dinner and worship service hosted by Temple members for members of Ben Hill United Methodist Church, and the reciprocal Sunday morning prayer service at Ben Hill for Temple members. Also, the pulpit was periodically opened to local black ministers and to famous black speakers like the social activist Jesse Jackson, the congressman John Lewis, and the theologian and author Cornel West. The Temple congregants founded and housed the Zaban Shelter for Homeless Couples, as well as the Genesis Shelter for newborns and their families, now run in conjunction with nearby Christian churches. And they founded Exodus, an alternative high school for troubled teenagers, housed in the Temple and serving a student body that is 80 percent black. The possibility of interracial contact and friendship became practically a part of the Temple membership package.

In 1960, Martin Luther King Jr. moved home to Atlanta, prompting Governor Ernest Vandiver to observe: "Wherever M. L. King, Jr., has been, there has followed in his wake a wave of crimes including stabbings, bombings, and inciting of riots, barratry, destruction of property and many others. For these reasons, he is not welcome in Georgia."

Jack and Janice Rothschild, on the other hand, invited him and his wife to dinner.

Sitting down to a meal together was the great racial experiment of the era, and only the most intrepid of both races were willing to try. Frances Pauley, the great white housewife of the civil rights movement in Georgia (who drove alone across the South to meetings in rural black churches, worked on voter registration drives, and walked in the front lines of demonstrations), remembers her first integrated dinner party. Going blind now, living in an old-folks home, wearing housedresses, she shuffles papers on her coffee table, gropes through the drawers in her file cabinet. She can lay her hands on so much evidence of times gone by, but can no longer interpret it. "Now *everyone* remembers they were in favor of civil rights. But, then they were not. In fact, it was just about the worst thing that you could do. You'd lose your friends, you'd lose— I remember one of my very best friends was having a cocktail party, and she hadn't had a party since her husband had died and this was very difficult for her. So my husband and I said, 'We'll help you.' And my husband said, 'I'll be the bartender,' and this and that. So we helped her get ready for the party and all this because she really wanted to have the party. Then she says to me right before the party, 'Now, Frances, if you'll do me a favor, please don't talk about civil rights.' Well!

"One night I had some people in for dinner. We were all friends. We were working together. We all knew each other. It was summer, because I remember we were on the terrace. We had an absolutely great time. And somebody across the street called me the next day and told me if I had any more niggers coming to my house like I had last night, that I was going to be bombed. And I told her, 'Oh, I'm *so* sorry you feel that way. Did something happen down on the street? Was somebody ugly or did somebody misbehave?'

" 'Oh no, oh no, but we're not going to have that in this neighborhood.'

"And I said, 'I'm so sorry you feel the way you do, because you really are missing so much. We had a wonderful time last night, and I think you're just missing so *much* when you cut all this out of your life.'

"So then one of the houses across the street came on sale. My father was living with me—he was ninety-six when he died—and he had trouble walking up and down the hill. And my husband was getting to have this paralysis that got worse and worse. So I decided if I could move across the street there where it was flat, Bill and Papa could get out and walk more. So the For Sale sign went up, and I called and said I was interested in buying the house." The fine, thick-boned old woman, with a head full of cotton-white hair, chortled. "And the next thing I knew, the house was sold to somebody else. The neighbors had gone together and bought the house because they thought I was going to put a black family into it!

"I mean I *tried* to be a good neighbor. . . . "

Rothschild already knew Martin Luther King Sr. through their membership in an interracial group. The Rothschilds and the younger Kings first sat down to dinner together in the home of Janice's mother, who hosted a small dinner party for Martin and Coretta. "It was to be my first experience with a purely social biracial function," Janice recalls. "I wanted to tell people, to brag about it. When I could resist the urge no longer, I did mention it to a few carefully selected friends, only to discover that some of them had already entertained guests of both races in their homes together. . . . They appeared to be as relieved as I was to have broken the silence about it. . . .

"You know it was all very strange and new, how to act. I mean, when you had black guests, did you introduce them to your maid? So we did, and I remember the maid was so impressed that we introduced her, because these were people she wanted to meet.

"I remember a joke going around during the early days of the civil rights movement: The lady of the house and her maid sat down together in the kitchen and had lunch. And the lady says to the maid, 'I bet where you worked before you didn't sit down and have lunch with your employer, did you?' And the maid said, 'No, ma'am. I always worked for high-class people before.' "

A dinner party at the Rothschild's home was arranged: the Rothschilds invited Martin and Coretta King, Joe and Betty Haas, Cecil and Hermie Alexander, and Hermie's mother, Rosetta Weil, visiting from New Orleans.

"Our housekeeper . . . was more excited about it than I at first realized," said Janice. "When I discussed the menu with her and designated, for the entree, coquille St. Jacques, which I always prepared myself, she contradicted me: 'Ms. Rothschild, *you* may know very well what your fancy friends likes to eat, but

I know what colored preachers like to eat—we are having barbe-cued chicken.' " Janice served both.

"The Kings arrived . . . much later than the others," Janice recalled. "No explanation was necessary, but Martin apologized anyhow and explained that they had been delayed trying to find our house. (The street was poorly lighted and the numbers hard to read.) They finally had to drive up to one of the other houses to inquire. As Martin told us this, he quickly added, 'But we were careful not to embarrass you with your neighbors. I let Coretta go to the door so they'd think we were just coming to serve a party.'

"I still get a lump in my throat when I think of it."

In the 1960s, Rothschild was ever more frequently the recipient of requests, from his congregants and fellow rabbis, for introductions "to your friend, that nice young man who led the bus boycott." And it was increasingly the northern liberals who no longer had a handle on what exactly was going on in the Jewish South. At a 1963 banquet of a Union of American Hebrew Congregations (UAHC) board meeting in Washington, D.C., Dr. King—also in town and coincidentally visiting the same hotel—was invited to stop by and greet the rabbinic assembly. On his way through the dining hall, King spotted Janice Rothschild, detoured to her table, greeted her with a hug and kiss, and proceeded toward the dais. Delegates from across the room violently rubbernecked; those nearer to her peered in closer to see and to understand. "Our friends from the North," reported Janice lightly, "gathered around."

2

Meanwhile, in the larger world of Atlanta, the integration battles continued.

As the aged black hierarchy in Atlanta proceeded calmly from accomplishment to accomplishment, and the bespectacled, rather beefy-looking white men in city hall responded judiciously to the prodding of the black elders; and a few raw white voices tried to tame the malevolent white majority; and Atlanta thus half limped, half back-stepped into the glare of the modern era, toward some kind of partial racial accommodation, a fourth group weighed in.

The black student revolt against segregation began on February 1, 1960. Four black freshmen from North Carolina Agricultural and Technical College in Greensboro deliberately sat down at a Woolworth's lunch counter, ordered cups of coffee, were refused—"We don't serve colored here"—and sat there politely until the store closed. Then they came back the next day and tried again. The tactic spread by word of mouth across black college campuses where groups of students had been bracing themselves physically, philosophically, and spiritually to face the wrath of the defenders of Jim Crow. They leapt to follow the actions in Greensboro. Nashville, a center of black student political organization, was among the first; within two weeks there were sit-ins in eleven southern cities, most at Woolworth's and Kress's lunch counters. The students were heckled by spitting crowds; ammonia was thrown on them, as well as itching powder, hot coffee, and insecticide; they were arrested for trespassing. Students in northern cities—black and white—began picketing the same chain stores in solidarity.

But in Atlanta, home of Daddy King, birthplace of Martin, site of "Sweet Auburn Avenue," "intellectual capital of black America," where a few elderly black folks used the front door when visiting the mayor, the students were caught unawares. Their thoughts on books and the opposite sex, they were still traversing their green quadrangles in the peace and safety of segregation, reserving their adolescent shenanigans for the weekend social mixers, the drunken hoopla of Saturday afternoon football games, and the grown-up floor shows of the Auburn Avenue nightclubs. Their hopes on serious careers for themselves, their concerns on the younger siblings back home on the farm waiting to be sent for and educated, they had ignored, by and large, the political struggles of the 1950s.

Julian Bond remembers precisely when the news got to them. "It was about the third or fourth day of February 1960, I was sitting in the Yates and Milton Drug Store. This is a black-owned drugstore chain in Atlanta, and it was the place students went between classes—or even during classes. And this student came up to me with a copy of the *Atlanta Daily World* and he holds it up and it says 'GREENSBORO STUDENTS SIT IN FOR THIRD DAY.' And he says, 'Have you seen this?' and I said, 'Sure.' I was put out because I thought he meant, 'Do you read the newspaper?' You know, 'Are you an educated person, or not?'

"And he said, 'Well, what do you think about it?'

"And I said, 'Well, I think it's great!'

"And he said, 'Don't you think it ought to happen here?'

"And I said, 'I'm sure it'll happen here.'

"And he said, 'Don't you think *we* ought to make it happen here?'

"And I said, 'Whaddaya mean, *we*?'

"And this was Lonnie C. King. [No relation to Martin, he became the leader of the black student movement in Atlanta.]

"And he said, 'You take this side of the drugstore, I'll take this side, we'll call a meeting,' and over the next few days we expanded our circle larger and larger. He and I were both students at Morehouse, and we knew we didn't want this to be a Morehouse movement. It had to be all the colleges.

"That was the third or fourth of February. We sat in on the 15th of March. A rather long time. One reason it took so long is that Dr. Rufus Clement, who was president of AU, heard about our plans. And he calls us in and he says, 'Atlanta students are different. You can't do what the people have done at NC A&T or these other places. You have to do something different. You have to tell people why you are sitting in.'

"I think if we had thought about it we would have said, 'They *know* why we're sitting in. We're sitting in because we want to eat at these lunch counters.' But he said we should prepare a statement of purpose. And a woman named Herschelle Sullivan, who's now Herschelle Challenor, who has just come back to Clark-Atlanta University as a dean, and I and another woman named Rosalyn Pope wrote this statement called 'An Appeal for Human Rights.' And we took a little booklet called 'A Second Look at Atlanta' that had been written by Whitney Young and M. Carl Holman, and it detailed the disparities between black and white life in Atlanta. We took their book and stole from it—just stole from it—and wrote this long statement, 'An Appeal for Human Rights.'

"And it was eloquent, if I don't mind saying so. It opens by saying, 'We the students of the six affiliate institutions of the Atlanta University Center (Clark, Morehouse, Spelman, Morris

Brown, Atlanta University, and the Interdenominational Theological Center) have joined our hearts, minds, and bodies in achieving those rights which are inherently ours as members of the human race,' or something like that.

"So we take it to Dr. Clement. Dr. Clement goes to Lillian Smith. Lillian Smith gives him the money to have it published as a full-page ad in the morning *Constitution* and the afternoon *Journal* and the *Atlanta Daily World*—these three papers on March 9, 1960.

"When it comes out, Governor Vandiver says, 'This is not written by college students. This sounds as if it had been written in Moscow, if not Peking. This is a statement calculated to breed division and disgust.'

"Mayor Hartsfield is a much smarter guy, and of course has a much different constituency. He says: 'This is not written in Moscow or Peking. These are the aspirations of our own young people.' More than that, but just a very temperate, clever, and correct thing to say. Six days later, *bam*, we hit these lunch counters and we were on our way.

"We didn't go to any private places that first time. We went to publicly supported places: the city hall cafeteria, the cafeteria at the Trailways' bus station. We knew they were covered by federal law. We went to cafeterias in state office buildings and a cafeteria in a federal office building.

"Seventy-seven of us were arrested and taken to jail," said Bond. "We were not treated roughly. Chief Jenkins was a very decent guy. A really very decent guy for his time and place. Though he had some vicious people in his departments.

"We were in jail for a day. We'd called a lawyer in advance and asked if he would represent us, and he said, 'Sure, it'll be about $350 each.' Well, we knew we were going to have about seventy people arrested. You know, no way we could afford that. So we go to Donald Hollowell as an NAACP lawyer, and we know the NAACP pays for that.

"Instead of trying all of us, they take one person from each group because the circumstances are the same. And I'm the guy from my group; I was the leader of that group. So they bring me into the courtroom. It's in city court. And really this is a committal hearing. We're going to be bound over to a higher court. So just a few questions before the judge, and the key question is:

'How do you plead?' Well, I'd never been arrested before. I'd seen courtrooms on TV and in the movies and so forth, but I had never been in one before. So I have two lawyers. One is Colonel A. T. Walden, who is the dean of black lawyers. He's asleep. He's there. He's asleep. He was quite old by then. So I turn to Colonel Hollowell, and Hollowell says, 'Not guilty, you fool.' And so I say, 'Not guilty,' and just had the presence of mind not to say, 'Not guilty, you fool.' And then they bound us over and then we're bailed out and then we go home.

"And, of course, for years afterward the NAACP is complaining about, 'You get the headlines—we do the work. You get the headlines—we pay the bills.' It was like going to your parents, you know: 'You're having all the fun—we're paying the bills.' "

The old-time Negro leaders in Atlanta were walking a tightrope, strung between the white power structure on one side (whose policy of racial moderation and step-by-step progress through court decree had been adopted by the Negro seniors), and, on the other side, the restless black students (with whose far-reaching goals the elder blacks also agreed). Martin Luther King Sr. observed: "Our warnings to Hartsfield and the others that it was increasingly difficult to convince younger people to wait any longer for the rights their Constitution guaranteed them just weren't being heard. The storm kept brewing."

The older African American generation supported the students, by and large: "Black lawyers defended students," wrote Clarence N. Stone in *Regime Politics: Governing Atlanta 1946–1988*, "the Empire Real Estate board provided bail, ministers made their churches available for mass meetings, black physicians and their spouses picketed, and the presidents in the Atlanta University system made no effort to stop students from demonstrating—though they did urge caution and insist that academic work proceed." Chief Jenkins also intervened helpfully, telling the Morehouse president, Benjamin Mays, "Go back and tell your students that when they are going to demonstrate, sit-in, or picket, let me know in advance so that I will be able to dispatch the right officers to the scene." But as black students and their freely chosen leaders poured into the streets, the Negro power structure knew that in offering helpful cautions and suggestions to the students, they, no less than the white power structure, were trying to saddle a tornado. "It is hard to over-estimate," said Howard Zinn, then of Spelman College, "the electrical effect of the first sit-in in Greensboro."

3

Like passengers on a cruise ship, the daily lunch crowd in Rich's Magnolia Room—with much clinking of silver against china, and chiming of ice cubes in brimming glasses, and chitchat between ladies tilted toward one another across little tables in the acute angles of intimacy—attended to their own wants. Like passengers on a cruise ship ignoring the fact that the ocean floor is twenty thousand feet below them and that, outside the small windows, roars an elemental, dark wildness and a cold, indifferent vastness, the Magnolia Room lunchers ignored the fact—for who wanted their noses rubbed in it all the time?—that outside the store windows a life-or-death battle raged: that some people clamored to be called human, and others conspired to deny them that.

The ocean grew rougher; a storm threw waves higher and higher against the cheery, lit-up cruise ship, from out of whose small windows the notes of a Dixieland band flew. The waves of the storm lapped as high as the arched doorway into the Magnolia Room.

In deference to the older black generation (some of whose friends-in-high-places were the white owners of downtown eating and clothing establishments), the black students agreed to concentrate on integrating facilities in public buildings and in those related to interstate commerce—city hall, the county courthouse, the state capitol, the bus station, the train station. But as they saw their efforts yielding few results, they threw off the constraints, anxieties, and—they believed—misplaced loyalties of their elders and targeted Rich's Department Store for boycotts, sit-ins, and mass picketing.

On Wednesday, October 19, 1960, they sat in at Rich's little outdoor café, on a pedestrian bridge between two buildings; refused service, they moved en masse to the sixth floor and decamped outside the Magnolia Room, demanding entrance and service.

Now the Magnolia Room was not a center of power, a war room, a boardroom. Far-reaching decisions on city development and the allocation of public resources and the funding of Negro education did not take place here, between bites of chef's salad. The men who held the reigns of power and controlled the coin of the realm of Atlanta, Georgia, may never even have eaten here. But it became the target. Why?

Rich's was Atlanta. Rich's stood for Atlanta. It was the "store with a heart." It was the heart that was appealed to, when well-dressed young black men and women, Martin Luther King Jr. among them, turned up outside the doorway into the restaurant and asked to be seated, causing a godalmighty tumult and panic, causing salesclerks to jog through the aisles of kitchenware and linen, and alarms to ring in police headquarters.

And it was targeted because it was *there*, because it was visible, because ordering from a menu and sipping from a soup spoon while a thick, soft, white tablecloth cloaked one's lap was a thing the students knew how to do, and wanted to do more of. Storming the true seats of power was not possible: the students could not have known where they were; the owners of the banks, corporations, and utilities did not have street-level glass storefronts. And even if the students could have identified them, located them, and won entrance, what then?

Finally, it was not coincidental that a Jewish-owned store was the target of the sit-in movement in Atlanta. Yes, there was the store's "heart," a Jewish heart, and the students' hope of a residual decency and sympathy there that could be awakened. But, historically, it was the Jewish *role* to be at street level— not among the masses throwing rocks at shop windows, nor secluded anonymously behind windowless walls of power, but at street level. Historically, the Jew is the guy who owns the shop windows that, in a revolution, are going to have to be smashed.

Rich's leadership was paralyzed by the sit-in. Business sense, possessed in abundance by Rich's board of directors, is not the same as moral instinct. Business, and the fear of losing business, guided Dick Rich and Frank Neely: Would white customers stay away if the Magnolia Room seated blacks?

"Of course, not everyone *liked* the food," remembers Aline Uhry, who loved the food. "My friend who was an executive at

Rich's who ate there every day said he had a solution to the integration crisis, when there were sit-ins at Rich's. He said, 'Let all of them come in and eat one meal. It's so bad they'll never want to come back.' "

Meanwhile, long-time black customers, generations of black customers, mailed their Rich's credit cards back by the hundreds, in vast, silent support of the students. Was the store going to lose *black* customers if they did not seat black people in the Magnolia Room? Thus the paralysis. The police came and at the request of Rich's chairman, at the threshold of the Magnolia Room, arrested fifty black people for trespassing. Inside, the diners laid down their forks and watched, in silence, the struggle on the polished linoleum a few feet away.

Martin Luther King Jr. was the first grabbed and arrested. He was there at the personal request of Lonnie King: "You are the spiritual leader of the movement, and you were born in Atlanta, Georgia, and I think it might add tremendous impetus if you would go." Martin Luther King had consented and for the first time had made himself deliberately available for arrest.

And so the ivory-tower, air-conditioned, softly lit Magnolia Room became a battleground in the civil rights movement. In his office, Rich wept in aggravation and shame when told that King and the demonstrators had been removed from his store in handcuffs and jailed for trespassing.

"Those of us who wanted to see segregation ended," said Janice Rothschild, "bitterly resented what seemed to us to be [Dick Rich's] stubborn refusal to move ahead. I didn't go as far as to advocate boycott or tear up my credit card, as many did, but I stayed away from the store for the duration of the impasse. . . . Jack . . . was besieged on all sides to 'talk to Dick,' who was a member of the congregation and, prior to this time, a good friend. Jack hesitated. He believed that it was a matter in which he was not qualified to advise and that it would do no good." Rothschild later wrote to Rich that he had refrained from offering unsolicited counsel, explaining: "I knew there was no more decent and liberal member of our community than you and I couldn't see how my voice could do anything but add to the problems with which you were faced and the struggle to find a solution to them." Even so temperate a statement coming after the fact somehow angered Rich. "Dick made it clear," said Janice, "that our friendship had ended."

——— ≍✦≍ ———

King and the students refused to be bailed out of jail. "I cannot accept bond," said King. "I will stay in jail one year, or ten years," until the trespassing charges were dropped. "Chanting 'Jail not Bail' and singing 'We Shall Overcome' they made no effort to be released and remained behind bars for week after week," wrote Harold H. Martin. Outside, thousands of black students were sitting in all over Atlanta and hundreds more were arrested, and the Ku Klux Klan began marching.

Mayor Hartsfield, wrote the historian Taylor Branch in *Parting the Waters: America in the King Years, 1954–63,* "was in the center of a maelstrom at city hall. Telegrams for and against King were arriving hourly in stacks from all over the country. Police officials were rushing in with reports about the growing threat of violence between white and Negro picketers. Hartsfield, negotiating in the city council chamber with many of the city's most influential Negro leaders, was offering to begin intensive negotiations toward the desegregation of all downtown stores, and to say so publicly," if the students would come out of jail, declare a truce, and cease demonstrating while new downtown arrangements were instituted.

The 1960 presidential campaign between Senator John F. Kennedy and Vice-president Richard M. Nixon was then building toward election day. Within the Kennedy campaign, Harris Wofford, "a white Alabama aristocrat by birth," a Yale-educated attorney and author who had joined the campaign to head its civil rights division, tried to interest the senator in King's imprisonment in Atlanta. But the Kennedy campaign, no less than the Nixon campaign, was loath to support King, for fear of losing the South.

Hartsfield, the business elite, and the black leaders, as was their wont, reached a compromise without outside intervention. With white business leaders committing themselves to work toward desegregating downtown, the students agreed to be bailed out and were bailed out, and here is where more trouble began. In the face of all Hartsfield's negotiations to have King and the students released from jail, Judge J. Oscar Mitchell, of adjacent De Kalb County, issued a bench warrant ordering jail officials *not* to release King, but to transfer him to the De Kalb County jail. A few months earlier, in May 1959, King had been driving Lillian Smith, the novelist, through Atlanta to Emory University when a De Kalb County policeman—alerted by the presence of a black man and a white woman in the car—stopped them for questioning. "Lillian Smith had had dinner at their home, and Martin was driving her back to where she was staying at the Emory campus," said Janice Rothschild. "As Coretta told it to me, if she had been with them, it might not have attracted the police." King was still driving on his Alabama license, and he was charged with a misdemeanor and sentenced by Mitchell to a twelve-month suspended sentence for driving without a proper permit.

"The students were let go on Monday morning, October 24," wrote the historian Cliff Kuhn. "However, Judge J. Oscar Mitchell ... issued a warrant denying King's release on the grounds that the Rich's arrest violated the terms of a suspended sentence King had received in September for a May traffic offense."

King himself, from within the jail, urged the students to go home, and they regretfully left him. But, accompanied by a group of white theology students, they returned the next day to the Fulton County Jail to watch King's transfer from Fulton County to De Kalb County for his hearing before Mitchell. They were stunned at the sight of him: flanked by police and clanking with handcuffs, arm shackles, and foot shackles, King was marched to a squad car and put into the backseat next to a police dog. In court, Mitchell revoked King's probation and ordered him to serve four months at hard labor on a state road gang, to begin immediately.

"The segregationist mentality knows no subtlety," Chief Jenkins later wrote. "It was believed that Dr. King could be placed on a chain gang and all problems would evaporate."

Harris Wofford, Morris Abram, Sargent Shriver, Stanley Levison, Harry Belafonte, and Jackie Robinson were among those spreading the alarm that King's life now was in danger: "The state road gang meant cutthroat inmates and casually dismissed murders. King had to be freed or he would be dead," wrote Branch. His treaty unraveling, his phone ringing off the hook, Hartsfield was most concerned that the nation not confuse Atlanta, once again, with the rest of Georgia. De Kalb County, one of five counties across which the city of Atlanta had begun to sprawl, was outside the mayor's authority. He scurried to exempt Atlanta from blame for the mess. "I have made requests of all the news agencies that in their stories they make it clear that this hearing did not take place in Atlanta, Georgia," he announced.

But Governor Vandiver praised Mitchell's decision: "I think the maximum sentence for Martin Luther King might do him good, might make a law-abiding citizen out of him and teach him to respect the law of Georgia."

Out of this chaos the first of two historic phone calls was placed. Harried on all sides by aides with a thousand requests, Senator Kennedy was ambushed in a quiet moment by Sargent Shriver, who described King's plight and urged the candidate to call Coretta King in sympathy. "What the hell," said Kennedy finally. "That's a decent thing to do. Why not? Get her on the phone."

"I know this must be very hard for you," he said over the phone from the Chicago airport. "I understand you are expecting a baby, and I just wanted you to know that I was thinking about you and Dr. King. If there is anything I can do to help, please feel free to call on me."

Meanwhile, in the middle of the night, King was awakened and hustled out of the De Kalb County Jail. He was driven to the Reidsville state prison, given striped prison garb, and placed in solitary confinement.

The second call came from campaign manager Robert Kennedy. He had been tongue-lashing an aide, Branch reported, for his part in John Kennedy's call to Coretta. "You bomb-throwers have lost the whole campaign," he said to Shriver, then turned on aide Louis Martin. Defending himself, Martin stammered: "Well, one reason we did it was that they took Dr. King out of Atlanta on an old traffic charge of driving without a license. Then they sentenced him to four months on the chain gang, denied bail, and took him off in the middle of the night to the state prison. All in one day."

"How could they do that?" Kennedy asked doubtfully. "Who's the judge? You can't deny bail on a misdemeanor."

(Branch remarked: "Martin decided that Kennedy may have lost sight of the essential fact that King was a Negro.")

"Oh goddamit," said Kennedy.

The next morning, Mitchell changed his mind and signed an order to release King on two thousand dollars bail.

As King flew by private plane out of Reidsville, wire services carried the story that "a brother of Senator Kennedy" had called Mitchell personally to secure King's release. Wofford denied the story, saying that it was so implausible as to defy belief.

That night, reports Branch, John Seigenthaler told Robert Kennedy about the press rumor: "Guess what that crazy judge says in Georgia! He says you called him about King not getting bail."

"There was a long pause on Kennedy's end of the line. 'Did he say that?'

" 'Yes,' replied Seigenthaler. 'But don't worry. I . . . put out a denial.'

"After another long pause, Kennedy said, 'Well, you better . . . retract it.' "

Kennedy lore has it that Bobby's phone call to Judge Mitchell secured King's release, but that call appears to have been one within an intricate web of behind-the-scenes phone calls recently brought to light by the historian Cliff Kuhn. "Oscar Mitchell was an arch-segregationist who had first thrown the book at King for a minor traffic violation," wrote Kuhn, "then had taken the lead in keeping him in jail after the Atlanta charges had been dropped. Despite the growing furor over the case, he had already publicly refused to release King despite the issue of denying bail on a misdemeanor pending appeal being raised, reiterated in private his commitment to keep King locked up, and ultimately ordered him sent to Reidsville. Given such a background, it seems highly unlikely that Mitchell would have reversed himself simply in response to an irate, impromptu call by Bobby Kennedy."

Robert Kennedy's call to Mitchell in fact came at the suggestion of the Georgia governor, Ernest Vandiver, a segregationist in state politics, but a Democrat who had publicly supported John Kennedy. And it seems that John F. Kennedy himself first phoned Vandiver, requesting help in the King situation. A close friend of the governor's contacted Judge Mitchell to request King's release. The judge assented, in deference to the governor, but wanted to confirm that the idea for King's release truly had been generated by the Kennedy campaign. Thus, Vandiver called Bobby Kennedy, and Bobby Kennedy called Mitchell (who was waiting for the call), and Vandiver's role in the affair was virtually lost to history for three decades. The omission of his name from a version of the story given in 1964 by Robert Kennedy came "out of consideration for the governor's political career." President Kennedy and the historian Theodore White also "went underground" about it, "out of political considera-tion for Vandiver." In short, until recent times, his political career over, Vandiver himself preferred that his role in the liberation of King from jail remain unexplored.

The two Kennedy phone calls, of scant interest to the white press, had a tremendous impact on black America. Polls of black registered voters indicated a major shift in their sympathies away from the "party of Lincoln." Although he declined to support one candidate over another, Martin Luther King Jr. did state on the record for the Kennedy campaign that he was "deeply indebted to Senator Kennedy, who served as a great force in making my release possible."

The presidential election of 1960, the closest in the nation's history, led scores of political analysts and historians to ponder the results. As Branch noted:

> Everyone seemed to have a private theory about what had been the decisive factor, whether stolen votes in Chicago or Nixon's makeup man for the first debate. As legions of analysts sifted the results, it did not take them long to discover that the most startling component of Kennedy's victory was his 40 percent margin among Ne-gro voters. In 1956, Negroes had voted Republican by roughly 60–40; in 1960, they voted Democratic by roughly 70–30. The 30 percent shift accounted for more votes than Kennedy's victory margins in a number of key states. . . . On the day after the election, [the] Republican National Chairman . . . declared that his party had taken the Negro vote too much for granted.

"One plain fact shined through everywhere," Branch concludes: "two little phone calls about the welfare of a Negro preacher were a necessary cause of Democratic victory."

The Magnolia Room, with its airy confections and seclusive gourmands, was thus torn from its safe perch high above the Deep South and pasted into the black-and-white collage of the epoch's life-changing events.

4

In the early sixties, Temple member Betty Haas personally oversaw the integration of the Biltmore Hotel in her capacity as founder of the Atlanta Committee for International Visitors. She escorted African diplomats to the registration desk, explained that they were guests of the State Department, and said she did not want any trouble—and she did not get any. Congregants Hermie Alexander and Helen Eisemann Harris went together to restaurants to reassure the owners that they and their friends would continue to frequent the establishments, *and* bring their friends, once the restaurants integrated.

"I remember the day some black people came in my building and sat at the soda fountain," said Miriam Freedman. "I left my job and went down so I could be in on that scene. It was Jacob's Drugstore, the corner of Peachtree and Marietta; it was one of the first sit-ins. I went in and sat at the counter to show it was fine with me. No other whites were at the counter. There were four black people there. I looked at them but they didn't look at me. I ordered a Coke. I was afraid they weren't going to get served. It was a little hesitant, but finally they were served. When I left, I told one of the girls in the office, and she said, 'You're crazy,' and I said, 'Maybe so.'"

Temple women created a speech clinic for black children, and worked with an improvisational theater for black and white children about to go into integrated schools. Cecil Alexander, among his other civil rights efforts, wrote a letter in 1964 to national Jewish organizations asking them to refrain from having meetings in hotels or restaurants that discriminated. Janice Rothschild served as a copanelist with Coretta Scott King on the

"Rearing Children of Good Will" seminar sponsored by the National Conference of Christians and Jews.

Over the next few years, hundreds of black students from the Atlanta University complex and dozens of white students from Emory and Agnes Scott continued to picket the downtown restaurants still denying service to blacks and the stores still refusing to hire them as clerks. Particularly nasty scuffles erupted day after day inside and outside Leb's Restaurant, a New York–style deli in the middle of downtown, owned by Charlie Lebedin. SNCC demonstrators were dragged from the scene by Atlanta police; some engaged in vandalism and public urination before their arrests. Lebedin—known to the community as "Leb"—bitterly dug in his heels and refused to integrate. "On Monday, June 17 fourteen Negro and white students were arrested and charged with trespass, offering only passive resistance," reported the papers. "The students fell to the pavement, locked arms, and blocked the entrance. When owner Charlie Leb asked them to move, they refused, and Leb employees tried to remove them by force. They punched and shoved the students, who continued to lie on the ground."

A Jewish demonstrator was violently evicted from the Jewish deli one day during the demonstrations. "Julius Samstein . . . reported when he had attempted to enter Leb's he had been 'manhandled' by a tall Bible-quoting white man who told Samstein he was being 'obedient to Communism rather than Christianity.' He grabbed Samstein by the throat and pushed him across the sidewalk in front of the restaurant, saying, 'I've got Jesus in my heart and you ain't coming in here.' "

In the summer of 1963, fifteen-year-old Marcia Rothschild joined a downtown lunch-counter sit-in. Her presence there did not go unremarked, provoking a fierce phone call to her parents, as reported by Janice:

> CONGREGANT: Mrs. Rothschild, I can't believe it, but one of my Christian friends told me she saw Rabbi Rothschild's daughter downtown having lunch with a Nigra.
>
> JANICE (after a long pause, during which I wondered if perhaps she thought that Marcia was not my daughter also): Yes?
>
> CONGREGANT: Well, that couldn't be true, could it?

JANICE: Why, yes. It could. Is there something wrong?

CONGREGANT: Well, I couldn't believe that Rabbi Rothschild would let his daughter be seen having lunch with a Nigra. I'm just so embarrassed for my Christian friends!

JANICE (dripping with honey): Oh, I wouldn't be too worried about my Christian friends if I were you. If they hadn't learned any more than that at church, they couldn't really be *very* Christian, could they?

Marcia Rothschild's sit-in inspired one Temple family to resign, with an angry letter to the board. "The letter received the usual treatment," Rabbi Rothschild later said. "Someone moved that it be accepted with regret. But someone else entered the breach. 'Why with regret?' he wanted to know. And the Board— bless them—wrote a letter which said they were sorry the member had failed to 'learn the lesson of Judaism taught by our rabbi in word and deed'—and agreed they would be happier elsewhere."

Atlanta's new mayor, Ivan Allen Jr.—who was about to be the only southern elected official to speak out in support of President Kennedy's civil rights bill, including a very strong public accommodations section—turned to Rothschild for help as downtown sit-in demonstrations became more vicious. The mayor called a meeting of unyielding restaurateurs and hotel owners, including Leb, to urge them to change their white-only policies voluntarily. He asked Rothschild to address them "from the moral point of view." Rothschild spoke:

You throw up your hands in horror at the prospect of either a Federal or local public accommodations law. We don't need it, you say. We'll do it ourselves. But you don't—and you have no intention of doing it. You're just buying time. How, then, can you avoid helping make the passage of just such a bill inevitable? You deplore direct action, picketing, selective buying and all the rest. You say: we will work it out at the conference table. So you confer and appoint committees—and nothing happens because you don't really intend for anything to happen. But you know that your dalliance will bring about the very direct action that you deplore. Then you'll capitulate. After your city has been torn apart by dissension.

Ultimately, the Atlanta restaurant owners capitulated and opened their doors to black diners. Leb himself scrawled a brief statement of surrender on a page torn from a notebook, crossed it out, and then rescratched it. The Atlanta Jewish Archives owns this scrap of paper—a bit of confetti blown across time from the ticker-tape parade of revolutionary social change—and displays it under glass. It is an artifact of a return of a prodigal son: "Henceforth," scribbled Leb, "my restaurant will be open to all citizens who come to eat and who conduct themselves as ladies and gentlemen."

On Rosh Hashannah in 1963 Rothschild spoke in support of the March on Washington, in which a quarter of a million people gathered on the mall. Rothschild deplored the fact that whites continued to feel abused by black demands, "as though what the Negro seeks would decrease the white man's share in America, as though his being 'for himself' means that he is 'against you.'" The following Sunday morning, four young girls died at Sunday school when a bomb exploded in the Sixteenth Street Baptist Church in Birmingham, and Rothschild thundered from his pulpit: "What repentance is there for us in the murder of four children in a church! . . . We must *do* something. Oratory is not enough." "Temple members responded," said Janice, "by opening their hearts and their checkbooks. Within two weeks Jack received a total of $3,500 from 279 families, and more contributions continued to come in for weeks and months afterward." Rothschild mailed the money with a note to the Reverend John Cross, the pastor of the Sixteenth Street Baptist Church: "I realize this cannot soften the grief nor allay the horror of the bombing, but I hope it will be of some use nevertheless." He wrote thank-you notes to each of the congregants who contributed, including a letter to the daughters of Bud Mantler—Marcy, Meg, and Sophie, the youngest of whom was then three.

> I think that this was the nicest gift that we have received for the Church in Birmingham, and I'm sure that they will think that . . . too. I have sent your letter along with your check and I have an idea that they may want to

read it to the boys and girls of their religious school to show them that there are white children whose hearts are filled with love and concern for everyone, no matter what color their skins happen to be.

I am proud of you and shall continue to be proud of you as you grow and take your place in the life of our Congregation and Community.

In November 1963, Rothschild was given the honor of introducing King at the UAHC biennial banquet in Chicago, and he was furious to learn that the southern delegates (not Atlanta's!) were planning a walkout. "Sometimes, I suppose, I am genuinely naive," he said later. "I honestly didn't know that I was agreeing to undertake a revolutionary assignment. . . . Members of my own congregation accepted it as an honor, too, and were almost annoyingly complacent about my part in the whole proceedings." He ascended the dais at 11:30 P.M., and a crowd of three thousand people under a vast dome fell quiet to hear him. Whatever indignant small walkouts occurred were swallowed up by the immenseness of the place and the moment.

Who of us, watching the historic Freedom March can ever forget the full-throated roar of love and respect that greeted one man as he took his place at the speakers' rostrum? Such a spontaneous emotion left no doubt that here stood the acknowledged leader of his people in their struggle for human dignity. . . . The wild thunder of sound assured him of his place in their hearts and in the hearts of great numbers of Americans whatever hue their skin might be.

But not in all. For this man has not been always and everywhere so enthusiastically received. Just as in Isaiah's day, so are there in our own those "who say to the seers, 'see Nothing,' and to the prophets, 'Never tell us what is right, Speak to us pleasant words. . . . Get out of our way. . . . Let us hear no more of the Holy One of Israel.' "

But he would not "get out of their way." Nor would he cease reminding them of the presence of the Living God. . . . He has earned his place as the moral leader of our social revolution.

16

The Rabbi's Wife Did It

1

Nu? So who bombed the Temple?

"Well, the old Jewish humor started in that my first husband, Bud Mantler, did it," laughed Nancy Thal, "because Aaron and I were supposed to get married at the Temple Sunday morning October 12 and everyone said Bud didn't want me to remarry!"

"Yeah, well that joke is ridiculous," said Mantler, "because I was paying alimony until that day. That was the day I got off the schneid. That's a term in gin for when you close somebody out. When Nancy got remarried, I was the happiest guy in town."

SCENARIO 1: Bud Mantler did it.

2

"Well, everybody always thought that Ms. Rothschild was part of it," said Fauntleroy Garland with quavering emphasis. She was quite ill by 1994, in and out of the hospital with cancer and heart disease. In a pink velour housecoat and flattened slippers, smelling of Mentholatum, her white legs swollen and bare, she was confined by her health to one room of her vast and aging mansion. A folding TV table held a dozen brown prescription tubes; soap operas played on a portable television balanced on a lace doily near the edge of the antique dresser.

Mrs. Garland looked out through French doors onto a weedy garden and overgrown fountain. She seemed to recall that Reuben and others had suspected Rabbi Rothschild's wife of the bombing, though she may have been simply filling in the blanks illness had left in her memory. "Well, Reuben never did mention *him* in it, but there was his wife, who was a different type of person from what you would expect in a church, you know. Everybody always thought that she was part of it with a few others that got up the bomb, and that he and a large portion of the Temple didn't know this thing was going to happen. I guess where it came from was she took their side so violently."

"I think Reuben felt like that someone in the Jewish community did it," the Lawrenceville lawyer Gene Reeves said, echoing Fauntleroy Garland's impressions. "To attract attention to their cause. Reuben thought George was not guilty. He felt like that the people at that time were trying to paint themselves as persecuted. I don't know why he felt that way, but he seemed to think that. And he got so many vicious calls, too. He got so many threats on his own life during that period of time. And people were very vicious toward him for it. I mean, he incurred the wrath of the Jewish community en masse, because all the Jewish community thought George Bright was guilty. He thought that because no one was injured that someone within the Jewish community did it to call attention to their cause. He thought they were portraying themselves as being persecuted by the Klan or some anti-Jewish group and that they were using Bright as a scapegoat."

SCENARIO 2: Janice Rothschild did it.

3

"Wallace Allen brought up the subject of dynamiting the Jewish synagogue on Peachtree Street," said Chester Griffin in his first statement to police, the one he had nervously told to the detectives Perry and Strickland while sitting on the tall metal swingset in the goose-bumpy shade at Grant Park and had repeated to a police stenographer an hour later. "He stated that J. B. Stoner could be counted on to go to Anniston, Alabama, to pick up the dynamite from the KKK there. And that Billy could be a watcher while Wallace was in the get away car and the two Bowling boys would plant the dynamite and one of Ace Carter's men from Birmingham, Alabama, would set the fuse to it. . . . George Bright was to draw the diagram to place the dynamite and Wallace would case the building for the job."

Of course, Griffin retracted that statement. In the presence of his lawyer, Venable, Griffin recanted, albeit with even slimmer credibility: he said no one had ever talked about any bombing and that he had, in fact, *dreamt* the facts as they appeared in his first statement.

Griffin was like a citizen of one of the two countries in the famous riddle in which the traveler comes to a fork in the road and must ask advice of a bystander: the bystander either comes from a land in which everyone always lies, or he comes from a land in which the inhabitants always tell the truth. Unless Griffin—whom others identified as "feeble-minded," as "almost retarded-like"—lied creatively on both occasions, then truth may have resided in one of the two statements.

Placing the two side by side, the "dream" statement is clearly the more absurd. Meanwhile, he unconsciously lent verification to the first by his own mad dash to find a lawyer the moment he learned of the bombing. It seems one might productively rummage through the first statement, searching for fragments of truth.

SCENARIO 3: It was Allen's idea. Bright made the drawings. The Bowling brothers and an Alabama Klansman did it. The others waited nearby.

━━◄═►━━

Wallace and Sammie Allen angrily discredit Griffin's accusation and have denounced, since the day of his arrest, all implications that Allen was involved. Sammie Allen wrote a personal letter to President Eisenhower after the arrest, asking the president to consider "the possibility that the bombing was done by someone wishing to throw disrepute on the people who favor segregation and at the same time create a smoke screen behind which they themselves can work. . . ."

"Wallace Allen is an outstanding, upright citizen," wrote Garland, "and although he has cussed Jews openly, let's write his faults upon the sand and his virtues upon tablets, recognizing his achievements as home-owner, taxpayer, and a good father and husband."

"You know what it was like?" said Allen years later. "It's like a totally innocent man asleep on a park bench in Florida. The police wake him up shouting, 'You killed Mrs. Smith!' 'No I didn't,' says the man. The next day every newspaper in the country has the headline, 'MURDERER DENIES KILLING MRS. SMITH.' "

"I have never been a member of any organization," wrote Wallace Allen in 1993, two years before his death. "This includes but is not limited to any N.S.R.P., any Klan or any Nazi Party. I have never been involved with or know what caused or who caused any bombing of any kind anywhere including the Jewish temple in 1958."

"He died January 14, 1995, of a tumor in his pancreas," said his wife. "He died within four days. My husband had nothing to do with the bombing of the Temple. He had strong ideas, but he was real gentle in his way. He had plenty of faults, but he didn't do anything like that. He had decided opinions about what was going wrong in our country. He just didn't believe we were all alike.

"He was at home with me the night of the bombing. We stayed up late that Saturday night and watched *King Kong* on the TV. We had small children—we had trouble getting them to bed—we were night owls anyway. We had had an argument. I was ironing and he wanted me to quit ironing and come to bed and I didn't want to. I believe it was a pediatrician in Decatur heard about the bombing the next morning and called my husband. He thought immediately that it was someone trying to hurt them and destroy them. My husband said he always felt Detective Little had something to do with the setup."

Who would *make up* an alibi like this—that having finished watching *King Kong* on the late movie, the husband yelled at the wife to come to bed and the wife wanted to keep ironing? On the other hand, as in Craig's account of her evening with Bright, the spat did not have to have happened *that* Saturday night—there was no external corroboration. And they could have picked up the information about the airing of *King Kong* from the newspaper.

In fact, Allen's strongest alibi comes not from his loving wife and her memory of watching late-night movies with him, but from a page in his own handwriting. In July 1958, three months before the bombing, he wrote a letter back to George Lincoln Rockwell regarding anti-Jewish picketing in Atlanta focusing on the Mideast question. He disagreed with Rockwell's suggestion to picket the Temple, and he wrote: "The Temple would be wrong since it relates to the religious rather than the political." He did not even want to picket the place that summer; it seems unlikely he would have bombed it that fall. He disdained Rockwell, in any case, and looked down on the Bowling brothers and Griffin; the lot of them were, to him, ignorant rednecks. Playing with dynamite was their style, not his. They and the bombing were beneath him. Whether or not Allen's Saturday night involved *King Kong* and ironing, it probably did not involve the Bowling brothers and a suitcase heavy with dynamite.

4

The jailhouse snitch, DeVore, told an interesting tale. In his version, Bright, who had previously made a diagram of the target, was picked up from an all-night diner on Ponce de Leon by Allen and others in the middle of the night on their way to the Temple neighborhood. Richard Bowling parked his car, a Pontiac, along the ramp going up to the nearby expressway with a jack under the rear wheel. He ran across backyards to the Temple, laid and set the bomb, ran back to his car, and drove away without the jack.

SCENARIO 4: Bright made the drawings. Richard Bowling did it, while the others waited nearby.

"[George Bright] said he was an architect or something," said Jimmy Dave DeVore, the jailhouse snitch, "drew mechanical drawings, I don't remember exactly what he said about it, and that he had drew it and marked it in red, drew the plans to the Temple in blue and the place to put the bomb for it in red, and X-ed it."

But DeVore, other than on the subject of the abandoned tire jack, was short on new information and incorrect about some of what he had gleaned from whatever sources. "He thought they had a letter that he had wrote to Rothschild, Rabbi Rothschild, threatening him, . . . " he said, probably getting such information out of the newspapers. In court, Reuben Garland introduced the threatening letter (removed from Bright's house by detectives) in its entirety, at which point it was revealed that the threat referred to Bright's intended heckling of Rothschild at First Baptist.

In truth, Bright may have known or anticipated or suspected or, at the very least, later surmised what occurred early in the morning on October 12, 1958—when he himself was at large, with or without Craig. He even may have—in his detached, scientific, just-the-facts-ma'am way—shared technical information, diagrams, and drawings with the Bowlings, if they asked. It is also possible that the twice-tried, never-convicted George Bright was not involved with the crime.

The radical right consisted, in general terms, of two basic types: the thinkers and what Bright himself designated "the hotheads"—"the lunatics," Rockwell called them. Bright was of the first type, bookish, cerebral, a purveyor of classified information, a composer of threatening letters and ominous picket signs. The bombing cast discredit on his organization, he averred, hurt his organization, because the intellectuals of the NSRP did not want to be associated with that kind of action. "The informed people did not want that," he said. The NSRP could not have been behind the Temple bombing, he believed, because it just was not their kind of tactic: "Accomplished nothing. It would be negative to do such a thing."

Bright's position is that the bombing was not the work of

the sort of thoughtful men with whom he would have chosen to affiliate. But, then, as he himself complained, his choice of comrades on the extreme right was limited.

If he truly believed that the bombing of churches and synagogues was not the sort of tactic to which members of the National States' Rights Party would stoop, he had joined the wrong organization.

5

"Well, one of the five indicted in 1958 may have taken part in that little dynamiting of that Temple," said Bright. "*May* have. But I didn't know. I had no information." Bright, who is ever clear on the subject of his own innocence, offers a variety of different conjectures as to who really bombed the Temple:

"It *may* have been Richard Bowling.... [He was], ah, a hothead."

He rethought that shortly afterwards, while considering the numerous bombings of churches occurring in those years across the South.

"Well now, there was the church dynamiting, and what's his name was convicted of that.

"Stoner, yeah, J. B. Stoner. Now he may be the one who dynamited the Temple. Who knows? Nobody knows. He was a hothead.... Among any population you have a very small percentage of hotheads, serial murderers, criminals, and people of the mentality who would retaliate with force against anything. And that's probably what happened. I think J. B. Stoner may have been one.

"We were so effective otherwise. All of the anti-Communist organizations were becoming extremely effective without having—staying strictly within the law and the moral law. We didn't need any of that; we didn't want any of that."

Later in the same conversation he shifted gears again, despite the appearance of inventing things on the spot: "No, I really think J. B. Stoner—no, L. E. Rogers could have done it. Yeah. Because, I'll tell you what." He triggered an old memory here, in mentioning Rogers, and the group's suspicion of Rogers came tumbling back to him. "Now it made sense to us after. We discussed this afterwards. It made sense to us that since there were some bombings prior to that, that if we could be undermined by a gratuitous bombing and be blamed for it, then that would be a way to destroy us. So L. E. Rogers very well could have done it. Or the Communists themselves. Or the Jews themselves. They could have bombed their own temple. They didn't want us around."

Did you ever come to have suspicions about any of your codefendants? he was asked.

"Not really, no," he said. "Well, the police found out that one of those arrested was familiar with dynamite. But my God, every other person is familiar with dynamite. That doesn't—that was Richard Bowling. But that hardly makes him a—" He laughed. "I just thought of the possibility and then there was no doubt."

SCENARIO 5. Richard Bowling did it (similar to Scenario 3 and same as Scenario 4).

SCENARIO 6. J. B. Stoner did it.

SCENARIO 7. L. E. Rogers did it.

SCENARIO 8. The Communists did it.

SCENARIO 9. The Jews did it. (See Scenario 2.)

6

"J. B. Stoner was in the background," said Detective Strickland. "That's where it all came from. J. B. Stoner, I was told by the FBI, was writing to Hitler before the war, and to the point that he thought he was such a great man that he could perform miracles in describing his deformity and was asking him to make him normal. The number two man was Dr. Ed Fields. It's my personal opinion that King's assassination in Memphis was strictly Stoner and his outfit. The U.S. House of Representatives Select Committee on Assassinations [on which Strickland served as an investigator] centered in on him in Marietta [Georgia]."

On May 14, 1980, Stoner was found guilty of conspiring to bomb Bethel Baptist Church—Reverend Shuttlesworth's church—on June 29, 1958. He was sentenced to ten years in prison. In April 1982, when his conviction was upheld, he went underground as a fugitive for more than a year. He turned himself in in May 1983, served three years, was paroled, and resumed his racist activities. He is the current leader of the "Crusade Against Corruption." From his home in Marietta, outside Atlanta, Stoner runs this new organization, whose credo is "Since Aids is a racial disease of jews and negroids that also eradicates sodomites, the Crusade Against Corruption advocates that all of those groups be segregated far away from the White race so as to protect innocent White people from Aids. That is another reason why we must have complete separation of the races." One motto of the new organization is

> Aids is a racial plague of minorities, but,
> Lie down with dogs & get up with Fleas.
>
> LIE DOWN WITH HAITIANS, NEGROIDS,
> SODOMITES OR JEWS & GET UP WITH AIDS.

"God's great racial blessing of Aids makes White Victory Certain!" is another of the group's mottos.

The state in 1980 did not contend that Stoner planted the bomb at Shuttlesworth's church, but that he conspired with other persons to have it done.

Stoner's defense maintained that the bombing was done by black activists to gain sympathy for their cause.

FINAL SCENARIO. J. B. Stoner did it (same as Scenario 6).

7

Whether or not George Bright's October Saturday night nearly four decades ago included watching with Marilyn Craig for a nonaccelerating Pioneer satellite grounded by a burnt-out fuse is impossible to know. Also impossible to know is whether his Saturday night included watching from down the street as someone lit a bomb at the Temple, or included simply listening in the distance for the far-off sound of detonation.

Bright may or may not have known the bombing was going to happen, or likely to happen. He is an extremely private man. He has his own point of view. No physical evidence tied him to the crime. He was an intellectual of the far right, working in intellectual modes. He saw Richard Bowling as a hothead, and the Temple bombing as the war-play of individuals for whom books and leaflets were inadequate weapons. He was perhaps amused by Richard's volatility, perhaps annoyed by it. Because of his affiliation in the NSRP with Richard Bowling and with J. B. Stoner, he got roped in as a suspect. It is impossible to know what he really knew, or when he knew it.

Hearing Bright's contemporary recollections of the events of 1958, and reading the transcript of his trial, one finds discrepancies. *Now* he recalls that he first learned of the bombing on Monday afternoon when police knocked at his door—"I didn't have a paper at that time," he said, "no, unfortunately I did not hear about it or read about it or wasn't aware of it until I was told that I was under arrest for it." But in 1958 he testified, "The first I knew of the bombing was a report on the radio at Mrs. Craig's house."

Oddly, most Atlanta citizens who recall the bombing remember it vividly and compare the clarity and detail of the memory—where they were, what they were doing when the news was received—to their memory of learning of President Kennedy's assassination, what cognitive scientists refer to as a "flashbulb memory." This is true across the board, men and women, Christians and Jews, blacks and whites. Atlantans *remember* the moment they learned of the bombing of the Jewish temple on Peachtree. It was the sort of shattering of the status quo that seemed to lay down richer chemicals in the brain's memory banks; consulted, revisited even after many years, bright colors and clear sounds are dislodged. For Bright to be confused on *this* point—when did you learn that the Temple had been bombed?—especially in light of what the crime came to mean in his life, is troubling. Perhaps it is simply a glitch in his memory system. Presumably, not every American above a certain age recalls hearing of the shooting of JFK in Dallas. Presumably, there are Atlantans for whom the Temple bombing did not ruffle the surface of everyday life in a memorable way. But it must also be considered that falsehoods are more difficult to remember than truths. To recall an event from one's life is to invoke one's mental representation of a three-dimensional reality, with full sound, color, and movement; while to recall a response once given in a contingency is to attempt to retrieve a spur-of-the-moment blurt of words. Any professional who works in the sifting of truth knows that lies are more difficult to repeat accurately over time, especially after the situation that prompted the lie has faded.

The latest research on memory, on the other hand, indicates that flashbulb memories are not infallibly accurate. Bright may truly be able to retrieve both moments: learning of the bombing from Marilyn Craig's radio, and learning of the bombing when he was arrested for it the next day. The intensity of the second image may be shadowing the first—what memory researchers call a "time-slice problem," but the second doesn't necessarily invalidate the first.

Or, finally, one might consider the possibility that Bright learned of the bombing neither on Craig's radio nor when police banged on his door, but earlier. Perhaps knowledge of the Temple bombing did not reach him in the form of a report from official sources. He may remember it vividly. When he revisits the memory, clear colors and precise sounds may swirl into consciousness. It may be a memory he opts not to share.

Chester Griffin, now deceased, surely knew something was afoot, probably *had* sat in on meetings at which bombing the Temple was mentioned, however wistfully or fantastically. Otherwise, why did he flee to Stone Mountain and Venable the moment he heard the news? Yet he probably was not involved with the bombing itself. If he had been, his panic would have been triggered the night before, and not by L. E. Rogers's phone call the morning after.

Wallace Allen, deceased, certainly attended meetings at which violence against Jews was discussed. He felt himself surrounded by idiots. He probably was not present at the bombing. It was the work of idiots. Besides, he had opposed even the proposed *picketing* of the Temple.

If all the accounts and recollections and surveillance reports could be laid down atop one another, like slippery transparencies in an anatomy book, what would shine through on page after page, the glowing white skeleton, the bone structure underlying the plastic pages of pastel organs and ruby-red muscles, are the names of Stoner and the Bowling brothers. "Even as kids, living in the Techwood area, the Bowlings experimented with dynamite," said Strickland. Richard and Robert Bowling were known, to the children who grew up in the apartment house where, as adults, they lived off and on with their mother, as "the bomber brothers." The Bowlings' names are linked, in everyone's memory of scores of occasions and in dozens of law enforcement reports, with that of Stoner.

William Hugh Morris was the former Klansman who became Police Commissioner Bull Connor's informer in 1958 and offered evidence again in 1977, when the unsolved bombing cases were reopened by Alabama Attorney General Bill Baxley. State investigators summarized their 1977 interview with Morris: "When questioned ... whether or not Stoner told him that he bombed the Jewish synagogue in Birmingham, he stated Stoner did tell him that was his job. When asked did Stoner in fact tell him that he did bomb the Bethel Baptist Church he stated that's what he wanted his money for. . . . Mr. Morris seemed to think Stoner not only bombed those places but other places throughout the southeast. . . . Mr. Morris said that he believed Stoner had the Bowling brothers and possibly one other person that did bombings for him and with him."

"George Bright's life was ruined," said a lifelong friend of Venable's in 1993. "George is a fine person. It ruined his life. The man that did it, they picked him up: Richard Bowling. Richard Bowling is the man who blew that Temple, dear, and the reason he didn't blow it to bits is he set the clock wrong. . . . Richard Bowling's the one that went into the Temple and set the bomb. . . . I don't know if George Bright knew about it or not."

"Everybody knows that Richard Bowling was involved," the friend said again two years later. "I've always—everybody knew that. There was no such thing as George Bright bombing the Temple."

The Bowling brothers cannot join the Crusade Against Corruption with their old friend and companion, for both are deceased. Richard died, by most accounts, drunk in a downtown alley, and Robert is rumored to have died of AIDS. Their long-suffering mother, who spent years after the bombing trial working for Garland as a secretary, also is deceased.

Neither of the Bowling brothers left confessions or admissions behind, but one is left with the feeling—especially when contemplating Richard, the red-faced drunkard, as compared to Robert, the dapper companion—that one has gotten very, very close to the source of the Temple blast. Whether Stoner also was involved never has been established.

No one other than George Bright ever was tried for the Temple bombing.

17

The Table of Brotherhood

On October 14, 1964, the news came from Oslo that the Nobel Peace Prize was awarded to Martin Luther King Jr.

"It was kind of like, 'There's good news and there's bad news,' " said Vice-mayor Sam Massell of the reaction in Atlanta city government. "The good news: an Atlantan won the Nobel Prize! The bad news: it's *King*." Massell, a longtime Temple member and the subsequent mayor of Atlanta, who himself had excellent relations with Atlanta's black leaders, recalls that the reaction of the white power structure was consternation: "You know: 'We're happy to have this outstanding recognition, but sorry it has to go to *him*.' "

"To most of the world he was being looked upon as a new Gandhi," wrote Ivan Allen Jr. in his book *Mayor: Notes on the Sixties*, "and his selection for the award was generally well received. . . . He had been on the front lines from the very beginning, making tremendous personal sacrifices—being spat upon, cursed, jailed, and threatened with his life—because of his belief in the equality of men and his dedication to nonviolence. . . . The reaction was different in much of the white South, of course. We had made great strides in civil rights in recent years, but we hadn't come *that* far."

A group of black leaders visited Ralph McGill to propose an interracial dinner in Atlanta to honor King and celebrate his award. They envisioned as cochairs of the event and cohosts of the dinner McGill himself, then the publisher of the *Atlanta Constitution*; Dr. Benjamin Mays, the president of Morehouse College; Paul J. Hallinan, the Roman Catholic archbishop of Atlanta (who was gravely ill and would lend what help he could, often from a hospital bed); and Rabbi Jacob Rothschild of the Temple.

McGill, Mays, Hallinan, and Rothschild called on Mayor Allen, who agreed with the idea of the dinner and sanctioned the mailing of letters to Atlanta's white business leaders, asking for their cooperation and commitment. "Many of Atlanta's leading citizens have expressed a desire to give proper recognition to Georgia's first Nobel Prize winner," said the excruciatingly carefully worded letter, an early example of political correctness, signed by the four culturally diverse cochairs. "Your deep concern for Atlanta prompts us to ask your participation." Helen Bullard, a public relations executive and the former campaign manager for Allen, and Don McEvoy, the regional director of the National Conference of Christians and Jews, immediately agreed to head the banquet committee.

But Allen privately was pessimistic about the dinner's reception by the white power structure:

> We still had more than our share of racists and bigots in Atlanta and the rest of the South, and not all of them were blue-collar Wallaceites living with their hatred and bitterness on the fringes of town. Many of these people made up the privileged Southern class: people who belong to the exclusive country clubs and work in air-conditioned sky-scrapers and go home every evening to expensive lily-white suburbs so they can carry on their tirade against the Negro in smug isolation.
>
> There was still great bitterness inside the Southern business community toward Dr. King's successful efforts at desegregating public facilities. And so the awarding of the Nobel Peace Prize to him brought the haters out of the woodwork once more.

As the mayor feared, many of the recipients of the tactful letter were not pleased.

"A proposed banquet by Atlanta community leaders to honor Dr. Martin Luther King, Jr., . . . was running into obstacles Tuesday," reported the *Atlanta Journal.* "Sources said some of the 125 community leaders who received letters asking them to sponsor the dinner were telephoning each other questioning whether they should have anything to do with it."

"I must confess I hadn't visualized opposition," Rothschild later said. "The Mayor went to certain people in the community and came back to us and said, 'They won't go along.' Both the Mayor and the power structure thought that was the end of the matter. We simply went ahead and continued to plan the meeting."

Robert W. Woodruff, the president of Coca-Cola, was then seventy-five years old and recuperating from a horseback-riding accident at his country house in Baker County, in the southwestern corner of the state. Allen visited Woodruff there, told him about the dinner, "and expressed concern that the city would be humiliated if the white community boycotted it." Woodruff shared his concern. He asked Mayor Allen and the new president of Coca-Cola, Paul Austin, to return to Atlanta, convene a meeting of the members of the power structure, and present the issue to them head-on.

"As was the custom in those days," wrote the Atlanta reporter, political commentator, and author Frederick Allen, "the businessmen held their gathering at the exclusive, all-white Piedmont Driving Club, entirely oblivious to the irony of the circumstances. [Austin] told the assembly of two dozen bankers, lawyers, and businessmen in forceful terms that he wanted them to buy tickets and support the dinner. In case anyone missed the point, he added that he was speaking on Woodruff's authority."

The grumbled response of the businessmen lacked excitement.

"I don't think you could say there was overwhelming, enthusiastic endorsement for the planned dinner," observed Mayor Allen. "They were for it primarily on pragmatic grounds: that it would look bad for Atlanta's image if we did *not* honor Dr. King. I was asked to close the meeting by summing up what had been discussed, and some of my bitterness came out. 'Well, gentlemen,' I said. 'I have listened to your reasons for support and I am sure I'll find that you will support it financially and that you will glory in the very fine national publicity that you will receive. But on the night of the banquet it's my guess that very few of you will be present. Most of you will be out of town or sick, and you'll send someone to represent you. Don't let it worry you, though. The mayor will be there.' "

"What happened next was a chain reaction worthy of Rube Goldberg," wrote Frederick Allen.

> One of the men at the meeting, a banker, responded angrily to the pressure and began making phone calls urging his colleagues not to buy tickets at all. Among the people he called was Lou Oliver, the head of Sears, Roebuck in the Southeast, a man of progressive sensibilities who was angered in turn by the banker's open racism. 'Who does he think he's talking to?' Oliver spluttered, and he recounted the conversation to his secretary. She went out to dinner that night with her husband and another couple and repeated the story, and as it happened the other man was a stringer for the *New York Times*.

"BANQUET TO HONOR DR. KING SETS OFF QUIET DISPUTE HERE," read the *Times* headline, making the dispute a public one. That very week the government of Haiti was negotiating a loan with the Citizens & Southern Bank of Atlanta, and François "Papa Doc" Duvalier personally phoned Mills Lane, the C&S Bank president, from Port-au-Prince, demanding to know whether Lane was the "banker" reported in the papers. The situation illustrated precisely the larger context implied by Woodruff: that the city's neglect of King would not be only morally reprehensible, but would be an international embarrassment, especially for those Atlanta companies attempting, like Coca-Cola, to make inroads in the Third World.

Eager to assure the Haitian president that he was not the banker reported in the *Times*, Lane bought a block of tickets to the dinner. Other business leaders followed. The tickets began to be seen as hot items.

Janice Rothschild had been placed in charge of the city's gift to King; suspecting that Coretta, with little time to attend to housework, would not appreciate a gift of silver requiring maintenance and polish, Janice phoned Steuben's in New York to special-order a crystal-glass bowl, engraved with her sketch of a dogwood blossom, the symbol of Atlanta, and with words composed by the rabbi: "Dr. Martin Luther King, Jr.,—Citizen of Atlanta, Recipient of the 1964 Nobel Peace Prize, with Respect and Admiration, January 27, 1965." "I couldn't believe that the two of us, 'ordinary people,' were sitting there in our own living room putting together something connected with the Nobel Prize for peace," said Janice. Although Steuben's was swamped with Christmas orders, the artists promised to work overtime on the project, and the company reduced the normal price in view of the recipient and promised to get it to Atlanta on time, even if they had to charter a plane to send it in. When it arrived, a week early, the splendid piece was stashed in Rothschild's study.

"At first Jack and the others had not set their hopes too high," recalled Janice Rothschild. "They had been confident of getting five hundred people to attend and were prepared to be content with that number. Later they raised their goal to one thousand. They were sold out the week before. At the last minute they were scrounging for more tickets. From executive suites all over the city, secretaries began to call members of the committee begging them to 'please find just two more tickets for Mr. ——'. . . . Dick Rich's secretary called to ask Jack if he knew of any more. Jack said he would try, and he called Daddy King to see if the family had any extra tickets. And Daddy King was out looking for more tickets himself for the family. The maximum number of persons the largest facility in town could accommodate, 1,250, had been reached."

"To have such a dinner in Atlanta, Georgia, in those days was not at all a simple, uncomplicated undertaking," Jack Rothschild later said. "He was becoming a more controversial figure; the power structure and the politicians were not about to leap for joy at the prospect of honoring him. There were a few of us, however, who were determined that the city of his birth and his adult ministry would do just that. . . . A handful of us met for weeks making plans and arrangements without any hope of fulfilling them. And after all the foot-dragging and outright opposition, exactly 1,463 people gathered to honor Dr. King in the largest room then available. Another thousand were turned away. It was the largest gathering of whites and blacks—roughly two hundred more whites than Negroes—in the history of our city. We had to turn away for lack of space many of the most prominent of our citizens who leaped too late on the band-wagon."

━━ ▰◆▰ ━━

"Jack had come home early that afternoon in order to rest," recalled Janice. "Since he was to chair the dinner itself, he wanted to be in peak condition. Marcia and Bill were to attend with my mother, who wouldn't have missed it for anything, so they had to get their homework done during the afternoon. I was just about to wrap up the day's work myself when the telephone rang. It was Coretta. She wanted to know what I was planning to wear, a long dress or a short one. . . . It was the first time I had ever heard her voice any concern about such trivial matters as clothes. I told her I planned to wear my 'uniform' for formal dinners: a long black skirt and whatever top seemed best at the moment. She continued to discuss the question, still undecided as to what to do. . . . I finally realized what was bothering her. She was afraid that if she wore an elegant long gown it would embarrass members of their congregation who couldn't afford to be dressed as nicely as she. In my opinion, they would *shep naches* (derive great pride and joy) from seeing her dressed that night more glamorously than anyone, and I told her so. At that point it was so late that both of us had to hang up and begin dressing."

Outside the Dinkler Hotel, a few Klansmen had shown up to picket, as had the not-yet-Reconstructed Lebedin of Leb's Restaurant, but they were jostled aside by the throngs of fashionable partygoers, the mob of reporters and cameramen, and two hundred plainclothes policemen. Leb had been unable to find anyone to join him in his private demonstration against King, so he fell back into the press of curiosity seekers and resentfully watched the arrival of dignitaries as at a movie premier.

For those with tickets—the little slips of paper that couldn't be given away by the gross a month earlier, but now twinkled in the bearers' hands like the diamonds on their rings and bracelets—the evening grew more and more intoxicating the closer they got to their seats at the elegantly prepared tables. The high-society ladies in ball gowns—balancing stiff, professionally prepared hairdos and smilingly entering the ballroom on the arms of their tuxedoed CEOs and bank presidents—found themselves seated beside a Negro minister with a gold front tooth or a domestic in a wool suit or an astonishingly articulate young professor from Morehouse or a staid gray-haired black physician and his attractively coiffed and soft-spoken wife. It was miscegenation at the banquet table. And, for the moment, stature—lineage—derived from an entirely new, an unforeseen direction: "Oh?" the white women politely inquired, and responded with vivacious curiosity, "you go to his church? You were with him in Birmingham? You've practiced medicine in Atlanta for thirty years? You teach romanticism?"

It was unheard of. It was outlandish. It was titillating. Simply spearing and munching a curl of one's lettuce or cucumber side by side with black people munching on theirs was a singular experience for the white upper echelon, although since it did fall within the realm of the known—dining out with well-dressed friends—they assessed it as a skill that possibly could be mastered. "There was the natural uneasiness that would come at a first biracial gathering such as this," said Mayor Allen.

That night it was as if the African American people were from another country; since they were, abruptly, to be treated with respect and the appearance of equality, it was as if each were the ambassador to the United States from some exotic, far-off kingdom, from Niger or Ethiopia, as if each were an individual not 100 percent familiar with our ways, but one whom it would be an honor to teach. By the time the main course was served, whites and blacks were babbling at each other animatedly and passing the rolls hand to hand. The conversations took place on a plane that simply had not existed the night before and did not exist on this night anywhere else in the South.

The black guests were splendidly entertained that night— served by black waiters, their ice-water glasses resolutely refilled—in the ballroom of a hotel that, until recently, had barred them. They comported themselves magnificently with all the etiquette and perfect grammar and quiet wit at their command; they deftly wielded and wove their heavy-handled cutlery across the china dishes like cowboy heroes juggling and twirling their six-shooters in the air before holstering them. They knew that everything they did fascinated the whites, who kept tabs on all of them all over the room from the corners of their eyes. It was a night of tremendous satisfaction and silent hilarity for the African Americans, who displayed, to their bewildered white dinner partners, every one of the refined arts of dining and conversation.

"When we arrived at the hotel that night we beheld a beautiful sight," wrote Coretta Scott King. "The big ballroom was filled . . . [with] Negroes and whites from all levels. Judges and top-ranking industrialists were sitting at the same tables with cooks and porters, all mixed up deliberately. The audience was about sixty-five percent white and thirty-five percent black. It seemed as though everybody in Atlanta was there— completely integrated. Ten years, five years, even one year before, such a sight would have been unthinkable in a southern city."

"Everyone inside . . . was bubbling like champagne, sparkling and beautiful," said Janice. "Even Archbishop Hallinan, who had left his hospital bed just long enough to attend the dinner, looked buoyant, despite his mortal illness. When Martin and Coretta arrived, we felt as if we should be throwing rice, so joyful was the mood. I noticed she was wearing a long gown, but it wouldn't have mattered. The expression on her face that night made her more beautiful than anything she could have worn.

"We knew to expect a crowded ballroom and we knew to expect a barrage of reporters and cameramen, but we never could have imagined the crowds, the lights, and the cameras that we actually encountered as we made the long walk to our places at the head table. The vast room was so tightly packed that we had to squeeze sideways between the tables to reach our destination. Friends reached out to touch us as we passed, just to let us know they were there. . . . I was seated directly above the table reserved for the King family, so I had the pleasure of conversing with them from time to time. I knew Mrs. King Sr. from her visits to the Temple for our Sisterhood's annual interfaith programs, and knew her to be normally exuberant, but never as she was that night. She kept repeating, . . . 'To think that this could happen in our lifetime! The grandson of a sharecropper!' "

"It was a wonderful occasion," said Allen. "The King children were in the peak of their youth, climbing on top of the table and under the table. . . . The evening was also another chance for me to get to know Martin Luther King Jr. a little better. Here he was, winner of the Nobel Prize, giving him every reason in the world to be somewhat bitter or pompous toward people who had spent much of their past lives fighting what he had dedicated his life to do. But he was a big man, a great man. He had arrived late for dinner, and I remember his leaning over and apologizing to me.

" 'I forgot what time we were on,' he said with a grin.

" 'How's that?' I said.

" 'Eastern Standard Time, CST, or CPT.'

" 'CPT?'

" 'Colored People's Time,' he said. 'It always takes us longer to get where we're going.' "

The Nobel Prize winner, served dinner for the first time in his life in the Dinkler Hotel, surely referred to a great deal more by his remark than the fact of running a few minutes behind schedule.

Rabbi Rothschild opened the festivities. He praised the assembly for being there:

> You attest the truth that goodness and righteousness do reside in the human heart. You give the lie to the canard that prejudice is always stronger than decency, that hate is more powerful than love. . . .
>
> You—rich and poor, Jew and Christian, black and white, professional and lay, men and women from every walk of life—you represent the true heart of a great city. You are Atlanta. You—and not the noisy rabble with their sheets and signs now slogging sullenly the sidewalks beyond these doors. Here is a truth we must resolve never to forget. Let none of us ever again fear to summon this truth so simply, so eloquently and so forcefully brought home to us tonight by our presence here.

After other speakers honoring King, Rothschild had the floor again, since the presentation of the city's gift fell to him. He told a story from Jewish tradition, the legend of Adam terrified by darkness at the end of his first day of life. God tells him to grab two stones, the rock of Despair and the rock of Death, and to rub them together. As Adam does so, the friction sends up sparks and the first fire is lit.

> We are coming to understand that our hands, too, must seize the cold stones of Darkness and Despair and from them strike the flame that will guide mankind from the gloom of despair to the radiance of hope. We pray that together you and we—and all decent men everywhere—may bring dignity of soul, nobility of heart, and tranquility of spirit to every child of God—and thus ensure brotherhood and peace in all the world.

King accepted the bowl from Rothschild with expressions of deep gratitude. It was a moment of unspeakable fulfillment and satisfaction, he said, and he should treasure until the end of his days the sight of the warm and beautifully integrated audience before him in his hometown, in the heart of the segregated South. His voice flowing musically toward its high notes, King warned once again that if the South failed to move forward, history would record as the greatest tragedy of the era not the cruelty of the wicked, but the acquiescence of the good.

When he finished speaking, the audience gave him a standing ovation, then launched into song. "At [the] end," said Rothschild, "almost fifteen hundred people—white and black, Jew and Christian, rich and poor, humble workers and great ladies—rose, joined hands and sang 'We Shall Overcome.' " The whites, rather remarkably (perhaps it was from having seen TV footage) knew the melody and verses. Coretta Scott King would remember that moment as "the most surprising of all the tributes" connected with the Nobel Prize. "It was tremendously moving," she wrote, "the spirit of it. We *had* overcome a major barrier for a southern city. We felt, for that night at least, it was really 'black and white together' in Atlanta."

"That dinner proved to be an indescribably magnificent event," Rothschild later said. "I remember this occasion vividly and speak of it with pride and warmth because even though it may seem a small thing, . . . it was for us the climactic event of triumph and hope after years of struggle and heartache."

Shortly after the banquet, King wrote Rothschild formally to thank him, warmly adding in a handwritten postscript: "I will never forget the great role you played in making the testimonial the great success it was."

Archbishop Hallinan, back in his hospital bed, also wrote Rothschild, but his letter deplored the fact that the press had ignored completely the role played by the two clergymen and their religious communities. He complimented Rothschild on "the magnificent program" and offered his "admiration at [Rothschild's] handling of the whole affair," but continued, regarding the media coverage: "You were ignored, in fact the whole Catholic-Jewish contribution was passed over. . . . It is not a question of credit; it is a matter of factual record. This affair would not have come off at all had it not been for you, the Negro religious and academic leaders, & the Catholic cooperation."

Years later, after King and Rothschild were gone, Coretta Scott King wrote:

> Rabbi Rothschild shared in Martin's Dream as a basic tenet of his own religious teaching. He had the courage to proclaim his belief publicly long before it became expedient or even physically safe to do so in a Southern city. Through his wisdom and dedication, he was able to influence significant numbers of others to pursue the course of racial justice. He was in great measure responsible for the Atlanta dinner honoring Martin as recipient of the 1964 Nobel Peace prize, an occasion that heralded a new era in race relations in our city.

King spun a great many glorious metaphors and similes in the course of his oratory. In his voice people heard about the yoke of oppression, the beacon light of hope, the locomotive of history, the highway of justice, the ringing of freedom, the oceans of history, the ever-rising tides of hate, "the thunder of disinherited masses rising from the dungeons of oppression to the bright hills of freedom." But it was the words he had cried out eighteen months earlier, standing before the Lincoln Memorial above a dark sea of people, that stirred in the minds of the people that night as they stepped, for an enchanted hour, into the dreamt-of world: "I have a dream that one day on the red hills of Georgia," he had sung out, "the sons of former slaves and the sons of former slaveowners will be able to sit down together at the table of brotherhood." That night they turned up at the door, found their tables, pulled out their chairs, sat down, and ate. They ate at the table of brotherhood. And in a great many ways that night altered Atlanta, and thereby the South, forever.

18

"I Don't Like Being Told It's Not My Fight"

The last decade of Jack Rothschild's life did not involve so many happy endings as the King dinner. Suffering kidney stones, back pains, and slipped discs, he reluctantly became a frequent caller to the family doctor. "Tell me, Jim," he said once to his physician, James Weinberg, "do I have 'Learn-to-live-with-it' or 'It's-going-around'?" Hair loss was a given now, no longer worth a joke; what more deeply concerned him were what he felt to be lapses in his mental acuity and verbal suppleness. In the heat of controversial discussion or at a sermon's denouement, the telling word or phrase eluded him. Even more bewildering, his position on the ramparts of the race question was no longer clear. He had been a nearly solitary voice for justice for so long, that—as the civil rights movement grew and attracted thousands of new supporters from all regions, races, and religions—Rothschild felt lost in the crowd. Suddenly his own colleagues were dashing past him toward front lines well beyond the position he had staked out, and bravely held, for so many years. By staying in one place, he was slipping toward the rear.

On March 7, 1965, when hundreds of protest marchers were clubbed and tear-gassed and hospitalized by mounted police on the Edmund Pettus Bridge over the Alabama River at the edge of Selma, and, two weeks later, when thousands of marchers finally staged and completed the fifty-mile walk to Montgomery, Rabbi Rothschild was not among them. "He seemed somewhat regretful that he had not joined the Selma march," Janice later said. "So many of his colleagues from the Northeast had participated and stopped off in Atlanta between flights, that for a while I thought Jack was running a shuttle service between our house and the airport. Each time he visited with one of them, he came home looking slightly wistful. One especially scholarly friend stayed overnight with us on his way back to New England. I thought I knew him fairly well, but I had never seen him as exuberant as he was then. Jack, who knew him far better than I did, was astounded. 'I thought he never left his ivory tower!' he remarked in amazement."

Rothschild was like a sentry who has been assigned a position, who has held it steadfastly, whose orders have never been rescinded, and who therefore sticks to his post, despite the fact that the rules of the war have changed all around him and men are leaping pell-mell over his fortification toward distant engagements. The sentry has grown a bit stiff; and he begins to dream about home and dinner; and he feels too old, at any rate, to fly willy-nilly after all the others; and his post, after all, has not been without its flavor and rewards; and, besides, his orders have not changed. Coming a trifle too late, when the good man was just on the far side of flexibility and spontaneity, the great linked-arms interdenominational, interracial antiwar and civil rights marches of the 1960s passed Rothschild by. He felt, at this point in his life, that it required integrity to see his old position through to the end, that to rush into the streets was to leap on a bandwagon he had not made and did not completely grasp.

The attractions of racial intermarriage also were lost on him, yet another unexpected aspect of a young generation coming to maturity under a different set of rules. Opposed to religious intermarriage, Rothschild felt no more inclined to bless a marriage between the races. "One night at dinner, which had suddenly become a tête-à-tête for us on most evenings," said Janice, "I insisted upon discussing the subject with Jack, who did not really enjoy introspective conversation. . . . We did believe that both Marcia and Bill were so deeply committed to Judaism that regardless of who they married, they would insist upon their children being Jewish. That was all that mattered to us. At least, so we had always believed. Now, however, there was a new factor to be considered. How would we react if one of them decided to marry someone of another race? . . .

" 'We'd have to realize,' I said, 'that the problem would be ours, not theirs. They would have faced it already and resolved it for themselves before deciding to get married. It would be up to us to make the adjustment.'

"Jack stared at me long and hard. Finally—and with absolute finality—he replied, 'I guess you're just more liberal than I am,' and went back to eating his dinner. I never brought up the subject again."

Shortly after the Selma march, Rothschild wrote about it for the *CCAR Journal*, the periodical of the Reform rabbinate. In his article, he struggled to articulate his own position.

The presence of hundreds of priests, rabbis, ministers and nuns who poured into Selma during those hectic days spoke to the world in one voice. . . . I welcome my colleagues of whatever denominational bent to the battlefield. I trust that they will not see this single, dramatic, heroic act as the climax of their involvement. I hope that they will not now withdraw in the mistaken belief that the war is won. Above all, I pray that they will not confuse their own need for fulfillment—which I well understand and in no way deprecate—with the continuing need for the less dangerous, less dramatic acts . . . : to teach [men] to live by the moral law of God. . . .

There are those who will read into my words the need for self-justification and see in them merely self-exoneration and apology. "Why wasn't he in Selma?" they will want to know. There are some who will find in the self-same sentences only boasting and arrogance. "What's so great about all that?" they will ask.

So he humbly outlined his mission, the orders he had followed, that he had derived from the Prophets, the orders that had not changed. "[A rabbi] must himself have a deep dedication and a pervading commitment to the ideal of equality and dignity for all men. And he must be prepared to involve himself in every facet of community and congregational life that will translate his commitment into the minds and hearts of those whom he would lead. He must do so with patience and forbearance and tact—but there must never be the slightest doubt about what he believes or where he stands."

Rothschild, then 57, was one of the first to see Coretta Scott King after news of the assassination of her husband reached Atlanta. She was sitting alone in her living room, and embraced him and thanked him for coming. He was asked to deliver the eulogy at the citywide memorial service conducted by the combined clergy of Atlanta and held at the Episcopal Cathedral of St. Philip. "Now, at long last, we must set about changing not the laws of America but the hearts of Americans," he said. "Do we reject the potential Apartheid that threatens to take over our land? Then we must be willing to admit the Negro into the structure of our white society. Do we deplore violence? Then we must be willing to remove the cause of violence.... For the America that we create shall be his lasting memorial."

Rothschild continued to try to help integrate the public schools through work on committees, to upgrade city services in black neighborhoods, and to integrate residential neighborhoods and stem "white flight." He was therefore stunned when, in November 1968, in the middle of a speech at the Hungry Club to black business and professional leaders, he was booed and hissed. "Many of the members were Jack's friends, men with whom he had worked harmoniously for years in the civil rights struggle," said Janice, "men for whom he had great respect and whom he thought had equal respect for him. Nevertheless, he must have realized that he would be treading on thin ice with his remarks that day."

He challenged black separatism and the black power movement, arguing for the continued necessity for black and white to work together: "I am of a people, small in number and weak in power, whose only claim to greatness has been its willingness to be the conscience of mankind. Reviled and persecuted, decimated by pogrom and holocaust, we have still maintained our visibility and sought to obey the rabbinic dictum: 'Separate not thyself from the community.' I would urge upon the Negro a similar commitment." And they hissed. He had lived long enough to see the rise of "identity politics" and to feel the role of the "white liberal" challenged and derided.

"I don't like being told it's not my fight. It is," he responded. "As a Jew, I have a commitment to justice and dignity and equality. And as a Jew, I am not going to forgo my religious commitment in the face of black separatism any more than we Jews withdrew from the battle in the face of white segregationism."

And they booed. Integration, which he stood for, was now being toppled as an ideal in many black circles, and his right as a white man even to speak on the race question was challenged. He jotted a note to a white friend who had been in the audience that day, showing a touch of the old wryness: "This may well indicate that it is too late for us any longer to convince the Negro community of our determination and sincerity."

"The worst consequence of the speech," said Janice, "was the apparent ostracism placed upon us by our black friends. When Jack was honored with the Abe Goldstein Man of the Year Award from the Anti-Defamation League, not one of them showed up for the dinner. . . .

"Our cup of personal sorrow continued to fill that winter as our friend Ralph McGill died suddenly, on 3 February, of a heart seizure. Again the city mourned."

In 1970, Rothschild started his twenty-fifth year as rabbi of the Temple. He was uncharacteristically nostalgic in his sermon on September 30. When he described the uproar in 1955 over the Sisterhood's luncheon invitation to Dr. and Mrs. Benjamin Mays, many in the crowded sanctuary laughed. "You laugh—now," he said. "It wasn't funny then. I tell you this because it epitomizes a long journey we have made together . . . because after twenty-five years you deserve to be complimented for your patience and your courage.

"I am not unaware of the discomfiture and uncertainty that I may have caused you. . . . Yet you never once denied me the right to speak. . . . You never threatened me with dismissal for my stand. And much more than that, large numbers of you accepted my interpretation of Judaism as your own and stood with me in those early days when to be in the forefront of the fight was neither comfortable nor safe." He thanked God for allowing him to spend so large a portion of his life as rabbi of that congregation, and he pledged his strength and devotion in the years ahead.

"Although he had not yet begun to admit it to me," said Janice, "and perhaps not even to himself, he had little strength left to give. The pain of repeated bouts with kidney stones and slipped discs over the past fifteen years, though not life-threatening in themselves, had taken their toll in terms of energy and now began to interrupt his work more frequently and with increasing severity. More and more he mentioned retirement." The grief of the loss of old friends—to death, and to changed philosophies—weakened his lifelong cockiness and wit.

In May 1973, Rothschild—a heavy smoker for many years—suffered a "medium" coronary and was hospitalized. Restricted to living within doctor's orders, he gave up smoking, had few visitors, took walks. He resumed his duties that fall, but was compelled to remain temperate during the Yom Kippur War and to refrain from throwing himself into the thick of emergency fund-raising for Israel.

In December, Eloise Shurgin, the executive director of the Temple, died suddenly, causing Rothschild terrible grief. "Under those circumstances we were hardly surprised, though terribly upset, when Jack developed angina pains," said Janice. On New Year's Eve, he was hospitalized with the pain; he made phone calls to find a substitute rabbi for a wedding he was to perform the following day, got into a hospital gown, turned on the football game on TV, persuaded Janice to go home, and settled himself in bed. He suffered a massive coronary a few hours later. He was sixty-two years old. When Janice and Bill Rothschild returned to the hospital, the doctor met them at the elevator with tears falling from his eyes.

The old wit surfaced once more in the person of Bill Rothschild, who clearly had inherited more than his looks from his father. As close friends quickly gathered around, some offered the observation that Jack "would have wanted it that way, if he could have chosen—to go quickly."

"No. He wouldn't," said Bill, aware that his father had died while watching a football game. "He would have wanted to see who won."

⊶ ⊷

Janice wrote: "45 minutes before the scheduled time for Jack's funeral, Marcia, Bill, and I were held up by traffic at Brookwood Station, half a mile from the Temple. We couldn't understand why that part of Peachtree Street was so busy in the early afternoon of an icy, wet Wednesday, 2 January. Most of our close friends were still away on winter vacations. . . . We soon learned that the Temple was . . . their destination. It took us another fifteen minutes to reach the entrance ourselves, and then we had difficulty getting up the driveway even though police were facilitating our entry by turning the other cars away. Television crews blocked pedestrians crossing from the parking lot into the building. I couldn't believe what I was seeing. 'If only I could tell him,' I thought. 'He wouldn't believe it either.'

"Inside, the pews were packed as if it had been Yom Kippur . . . except that many of the faces were not Jewish. . . . Among them were then Governor of Georgia Jimmy Carter and First Lady Rosalynn. We were told that the entire executive staff of Coca-Cola attended also. Dr. and Mrs. Martin Luther King, Sr., were seated alongside the Carters in places of honor just behind us. As I sat down, Daddy King patted me comfortingly on the shoulder and whispered, 'Coretta will be along soon.' She had gone to the airport to pick up Congressman Andrew Young, who had flown in from Washington to attend the funeral."

At the end of the day, they stood beside him again. All the old friends and allies, all the old war-horses still among the living, stood up to say Kaddish—the mourner's prayer—over a man who had attempted to live justly in evil times.

⊶ ⊷

In the South at midcentury, a great number of people longed for whole, complete, well-rounded lives and felt bitterly cheated of them. As if from overpopulation—though hundreds of miles of dark forests and quiet fields surrounded the towns— the citizens chafed irritatingly against each other, and felt diminished and inhibited by the outsized, outrageous demands of their neighbors. The African Americans, who were truly deprived, felt this. And hundreds of thousands of average white people—farmers, housewives, salesmen, mechanics—also strangely felt this. They took the *Brown* decision, or were led to understand it, as a document depriving them of rights and property, as a dispossessory warrant with their names on it. It was as if uniformed agents of the federal government were now going to drive into their white neighborhoods, enter their houses, and select, say, Grandma Fanny's sideboard or the upright piano and then circle it and, breathing hard, and without permission, lift it and carry it out the screen door and across the front porch and onto their pickup. "Constitutional rights" seemed a finite thing—not like air or water, but more like each family's property, like the sideboard or the piano or a favorite set of water glasses or a rope hammock, which the federal government was now personally going to take away and drive over to the dirt roads and sandy yards of the Negro side, and hand out. They were inspired by their elected leaders to see civil equality as a small pie, so that if new folks got slices, the original folks would have less. It was why those who violently resisted the loss of Jim Crow are seen as right-wingers, as fascists, for the thrust of their ideology is profoundly antidemocratic: there simply are not enough citizens' rights for everybody to have some. Some of us have to be more equal than others.

There was a psychological corollary to this: it seemed there was not quite enough humanity to go around either. God smiled on some (white, Protestant, Anglo-Saxon) and kept others in the shade; and for those who felt themselves smiled upon, it seemed that the brightness of their divine favoritism would dim if others came out from the shadows. And for those denied, by prevalent ideology, their full humanity, there were some peculiar inner gymnastics to be engaged in before venturing onto public ground. If one was a Jew, for example, one might aspire to the position of vice-president of the States' Rights Council of Georgia, or one might drag black would-be customers out the door of one's deli feet first.

The true leaders promised those who would listen that democracy was a stable commodity, a renewable resource, that if blacks became full citizens it did not mean that whites were no longer full citizens, nor that American citizenship was not worth having.

A few prophetic leaders like Jacob Rothschild promised something more. For Jews who clung tightly to the popular, southern, midcentury definition of humanity—those who deplored the public use of Yiddish, those who discarded traditional Judaism in favor of splendiferous Christmas and Easter celebrations—he offered an enlargement, an enhancement of their inner lives. They were entitled to come out from the shadows, he told them in effect, and they were entitled to do so not by pretending to be Christians, or Christian-like, but by stepping forth as Jews. What Joe Jacobs possessed instinctively—the human dignity of self-acceptance—Rothschild offered his congregation. But there was a kind of twelve-step program to get there.

They could not come out from the shadows alone.

If they were going to stand forth as Jews, they needed first to accept the principle that all humans were equal in God's sight. And Rothschild's congregation knew all too well whom *that* meant including.

If the congregants had once pictured Rothschild as a sort of security guard at the threshold of a mansion in which a splendid society ball was under way, and had seen themselves as laden with menorahs and smelling of garlic and potatoes, with him blocking their entrance and pointing their way home, then they had had it wrong. He had *wanted* them to enter the sparkling ballroom; he had posted himself at the door not to turn them back but to make sure they did not pitch the menorahs and Sabbath candles and kiddush cups into the azaleas on their way in.

The path to that door, for Rothschild, lay through the realm of justice. He wanted to see black people in that metaphorical ballroom, too—a metaphorical ballroom that became briefly real on the night of the King dinner. The doorway had to be widened, the threshold lowered, the roof beams raised. If it was not justice for all, it was not justice and it was not worth having.

He required his friends to do as he had done—loosen their grip on the world of the senses, on the material and social southern world—and allow a higher truth to operate. By working for the rights of African Americans, by believing in human rights, his Jews would unfetter themselves as well.

" 'The ultimate measure of a man is not where he stands in moments of comfort and convenience, but where he stands in times of challenge and controversy,' " said Coretta Scott King, quoting from her husband's sermon "On Being a Good Neighbor." " 'The true neighbor will risk his position, his prestige and even his life for the welfare of others.' These words . . . could be applied as a fitting tribute to my husband's good friend, Rabbi Jacob M. Rothschild. Like Martin, Rabbi Rothschild was deeply committed to justice, equality, and brotherhood."

"Rothschild was a gift to this city, I'll tell you," said Frances Pauley. "It would have been so much easier for him to tend to his knitting and look after his congregation. It wasn't easy for people to speak out. You knew you had to be prepared for the knives you were going to get from every direction. And when you didn't have anybody with you . . . " She looked cloudily toward her window. "I have felt mighty alone myself. Something that has been very difficult for me: In recent years, now that I'm too old to do anything and I really can't (I'm just physically not able to), why then all these groups that would never help me and would never work and that were always sitting on the fence, they ask me to come to their annual dinner or their fund-raising dinner or something and give me a plaque. I've got a steamer trunk full of plaques in the basement. They give me a plaque and say all these nice things. It's all I can do to go. It's all I can do to be decent and go and not just get up and say, 'Where *were* you when we *needed* you?' For Rothschild to be highly respected by the total community and a leader in his religion and openly take the stands that he did, it was very brave."

The civil rights years can be seen as a bucking bronco, and Jack Rothschild as a man who chose to mount it. His name and the names of his allies in the white community, like Archbishop Paul Hallinan, Frances Pauley, Ralph McGill, and Robert Woodruff, are not household words in America. They are not even household words—other than as street names or building names—in modern-day Atlanta, which evolved from "The City Too Busy to Hate" to "Site of the 1996 Olympics."

But stories of integrity and courage ought to be rescued,

now and then, from the collective historical amnesia. African American equality under the law was not installed in the South at a nod from the Supreme Court, at a tip of the hat from Earl Warren. It did not come to pass without many bitter and violent confrontations. And not all the confrontations were white against black, black against white. Some of the most venomous fights were white against white. Angry white supremacists fought against white men and women of conscience. These liberal white leaders reached out to their peers in the black community and stood with them as a united front, in the face of threats and explosions.

"As I think of Jack Rothschild, I think of the civil rights movement, and I think of the prophets," said Rabbi Alvin Sugarman. "His was an absolute prophetic course. When he walked on that pulpit and he opened his mouth, it was as if Amos, Isaiah, Jeremiah, they were all right there. It was hands-on: here's a society that's corrupt, it's unjust; we call it like it is and do what we can to make it right. So his source—his rabbinic authority—and his human authority merged. And that had an incredible impact on the congregation and on my life, notwithstanding that for many, many years, walking out after services you heard, 'He's talking about civil rights *again.*' So there was this subtext of murmurs, and some of it probably wasn't so quiet. After his death, you heard: 'Our rabbi, he had the courage to stand out and fight, speak up and do the right thing. He was a force in the civil rights movement.' It was like an artist whose works, after his death, become masterpieces. For me there was an incredible blending: when you heard him speak, it was Jack Rothschild, it was Amos."

"For these many years I have labored to bring about the fulfillment of the prophetic ideal: one God in Heaven, one humanity on earth," said Rothschild in his last guest sermon at Hebrew Union College in Cincinnati. "Some of my colleagues—especially in the South—will maintain that it was all too easy in Atlanta, a more progressive and enlightened community than many others, and that given such circumstances they would have been able to accomplish more than I here, and I less than they there. Perhaps all of them are right. I only know what I have done. I wish it had been more."

NOTES

ABBREVIATIONS USED IN NOTES

AC	*Atlanta Constitution*
AJ	*Atlanta Journal*
AJC	*Atlanta Journal-Constitution*
BDAM	Birmingham Department of Archives and Manuscripts
BPD	Birmingham Police Department surveillance files
ESC	Emory Special Collections
FBI	Federal Bureau of Investigation bombing investigation files
Int.	Interview by author
JMR	Jacob M. Rothschild papers
NYT	*New York Times*
RAG	Reuben A. Garland papers

PROLOGUE

2 work of a "crackpot": "Underground Warned News Office before Blast," *AC*, October 13, 1958, p. 1.

2 "last empty building": Arnold Shankman, "A Temple Is Bombed—Atlanta, 1958," *American Jewish Archives* 23, no. 2 (1971): 131.

2 "The City Too Busy to Hate": H. Martin, *William Berry Hartsfield: Mayor of Atlanta*, p. 49.

3 "two types of people": Int. George Goodwin.

5 The *Thunderbolt* originally was the newspaper of the neo-Nazi, Atlanta-based Columbians, an organization founded in 1946. After the group's demise, the name was adopted by the National States' Rights Party, organized in 1958. Dr. Edward R.

437

Fields edited the paper in Marietta, Georgia. By 1963, the *Thunderbolt* had 15,000 subscribers, making it the most widely read periodical of the extreme right. (See Newton and Newton, *KKK Encyclopedia*, p. 421.) As of 1995, the paper still is in circulation, under the new name *The Truth at Last*, with the subheadings "News Suppressed by the Daily Press" and "America's Oldest Patriot's Newspaper." It still is published in Marietta. The issues carry no date, giving them longer shelf-life. Headlines in recent years have included the following: "REPEAL THE MARTIN LUTHER KING HOLIDAY," "4 MILLION JEWS IN RUSSIA MAY ALL MOVE TO U.S.," and "SHADOW GOVERNMENT WHICH RULES AMERICA," which accompanied an article focused on Henry Kissinger, Yitzhak Rabin, and Saul Bellow.

5   "people . . . are lunatics": George Lincoln Rockwell, quoted in "Got Ideas from Hitler, Author Says," *AJ*, October 17, 1958, p. 1 (copyrighted quote from *Northern Virginia Sun*).

7   "great plague": Branch, *Parting the Waters: America in the King Years 1954–63*, p. 268.

8   "Always able to shake off sleep . . . bombed' ": Blumberg, *One Voice: Rabbi Jacob M. Rothschild and the Troubled South*, pp. 79–80.

10   "if we talk about it": Sermon, "Can This Be America?" May 9, 1958, JMR, ESC.

10   "Horror": Jack Nelson, "Thousands of Spectators Stream by but See Little of Debris and Drama," *AC*, October 13, 1958, p. 6.

11   "Godless men": "Godless Bombing Aimed at All Atlantans, a 'Sick at Heart' Rabbi Rothschild Asserts," *AC*, October 13, 1958, p. 6.

I: A CRACKER CAMELOT

15   "A Cracker Camelot": Dana White and Tim Crimmins, "Looking for Atlanta," *The New Georgia Guide*. Athens: University of Georgia Press, in press.

15   "could be cutting": Int. Jean Levinson.

16   "Jack's mother's funeral": Int. Janice Rothschild Blumberg.

16   "hated his sermons": Int. Bill Rothschild.

16   "one of the *last* people": Int. Nancy Thal.

17   "a very *bright* person": Int. Aline Uhry.

17   "personal God": Int. Rabbi Emanuel Feldman.

18   "rabbi falls off a horse": Blumberg, *One Voice: Rabbi Jacob M. Rothschild and the Troubled South*, p. 49.

18   "fruit plate was set down": Int. Emanuel Feldman.

19   "Jack, you're very young": Int. Jean Levinson.
19   "I was not scholarly": Blumberg, *One Voice*, p. 12.
19   "sought mutual consolation": Rabbi Sidney Berkowitz, sermon delivered at the celebration of JMR's twenty-fifth anniversary as rabbi of the Temple, Atlanta, April 23, 1971, JMR, ESC.
20   "more Talmud than Rothschild": Blumberg, *One Voice*, p. 14.
20   "AM RABBI FREEHOF'S ASSISTANT": Ibid., p. 15.
21   "duties are extremely arduous": JMR to his mother and sister, August 28, 1942, JMR, ESC.
21   "Sorry to hear": Ibid., October 6, 1942, JMR, ESC.
21   "Sonny Fleishman": Ibid., November 4, 1942, JMR, ESC.
21   "on cavalry horse": Ibid., November 10, 1942, JMR, ESC.
21   sent home a joke: Ibid., December 20, 1942, JMR, ESC.
22   "I finally remembered": Ibid., November 11, 1942, JMR, ESC.
22   "I have a hunch": Ibid., December 18, 1942, JMR, ESC.
22   "3rd funeral today": Ibid., January 2, 1943, JMR, ESC.
22   "old home week": Ibid., January 2, 1943, JMR, ESC.
22   "to wit: Spam": Ibid., January 15, 1943, JMR, ESC.
22   "From living in hate": Blumberg, *One Voice*, p. 21.
23   "cool in the evenings": JMR to his mother and sister, July 12, 1946, JMR, ESC.
26   "Now, don't you niggers": Kuhn, Joye, and West, *Living Atlanta: An Oral History of the City, 1914–1948*, p. 359.
27   "Of the twenty-five . . . promotion": Int. George Goodwin.
28   "After Lee's surrender": Ibid.
28   "Atlanta *welcomed* the carpetbaggers": Ibid.
29   "If Atlanta could suck as hard": Kuhn, Joye, and West, *Living Atlanta*, p. 87.
29   "The city was saying": Int. George Goodwin.
30   "It was not a particularly colorful": I. Allen, *Mayor: Notes on the Sixties*, pp. 30–31.
31   "a kind of Cracker Camelot": Crimmins and White, "Looking for Atlanta," in press.
31   "nature of our upbringing": Allen, *Mayor*, p. 35.

2: THE WHITE MAN'S WAR

33   "central motivation was hatred": H. Martin, *Ralph McGill: Reporter*, p. 128.
34   "generally troublesome Negroes": McWilliams, *A Mask for Privilege: Anti-Semitism in America*, p. 213.

34 "cut-rate war . . . small favors": H. Martin, *Ralph McGill*, p. 128.

34 predicted Columbian control: Ibid., p. 212.

34 "American nationalist state": Newton and Newton, *KKK Encyclopedia*.

34 opened chapters in Philadelphia: Ibid., p. 128.

35 "show white people": McWilliams, *A Mask for Privilege*, p. 208.

35 "a lot of inferior races": Ibid., p. 209.

35 Emory Burke: Cook, *The Segregationists*, p. 155.

35 a former staff member: Ibid.

35 "lynch list": Newton and Newton, *KKK Encyclopedia*, p. 128.

36 "The JEWS": McWilliams, *A Mask for Privilege,* p. 214.

36 "Everybody in America": Ibid., p. 217.

36 "age-old inclination": Lipstadt, *Denying the Holocaust*, p. 135.

36 "dispossessed farmers": Wertheimer, "Antisemitism in the United States: A Historical Perspective," p. 40.

37 "stereotyped, involved in finance": Ibid.

37 "Cotton is a speculator's crop": Faulkner, *The Sound and the Fury,* pp. 149–50.

37 "Seeking to ferret out": Wertheimer, "Antisemitism in the United States," p. 42.

37 "detective agency": Ibid.

38 "mentally indolent": Valentin, *Antisemitism Historically and Critically Examined*, p. 168.

38 "The Scope of Jewish Dictatorship": Lipset, *The Politics of Unreason: Right Wing Extremism in America 1790–1970,* p. 136.

39 "Hitler's slaughter": Dinnerstein, *Anti-Semitism in America*, p.152.

39 Cold War unfolded: Wayne A. Clark, "An Analysis of the Relationship between Anti-Communism and Segregationist Thought in the Deep South, 1948–1964," p. 1.

40 powerful weapons at his disposal: Brandt Aymar and Edward Sagarin, *A Pictorial History of the World's Great Trials*. New York: Bonanza Books, 1985, p. 272.

41 "When Morgan County Solicitor": Dan T. Carter, *Scottsboro: A Tragedy of the American South*, p. 146.

41 " 'Show them' ": Ibid., p. 236.

41 "others looked electrified": Ibid.

41 "Reporters at the trial": Ibid., p. 240.

41 "chant of 'Jew money' ": Ibid., p. 241.

41 "Leibowitz's appearance": Dinnerstein, *Anti-Semitism*, p. 186.

42 "note the rise": Sermon, "The Greater Sin," Yom Kippur 5709, October 13, 1948, JMR, ESC.

43 "takes two to marry": Int. George Bright.
44 "this young man": Int. Richard Wasser.
45 "difficult political situation": Int. George Bright.
46 "Race mixing is the downfall": Ibid.
48 "segregationist lunacy": Int. Harvey Klehr.
49 "People of a temperate climate": Int. George Bright.
50 "blacks and whites to amalgamate": Ibid.
51 "GOLD of the Nations": *Protocols of the Learned Elders of Zion*, p. 25.

3: THE MOST BELOVED JEW NEXT TO JESUS

54 "gift of gab": Int. Rabbi Harry Epstein.
54 "theological problems": Int. Cecil Alexander.
55 "happiest childhood memories": Ellen Marx Rappaport, letter to *Reform Judaism*, Fall 1995.
56 "This resolution says": Janice Rothschild Blumberg, *One Voice: Rabbi Jacob M. Rothschild and the Troubled South*, p. 24.
56 "everlasting light": Int. Aline Uhry.
57 "high plane of sanity": In Steven Hertzberg, *Strangers within the Gate City: The Jews of Atlanta 1845–1915*, p. 70.
57 "inexpedient": Ibid., p. 69.
58 "beautiful music": Int. Janice Rothschild Blumberg.
58 "Last Sleep of the Virgin": Hertzberg, *Strangers*, p. 70.
59 "only the moral laws": The Pittsburgh Platform, 1885.
59 "only kind of Jewish religion": Lipson-Walker, " 'Shalom Y'all': The Folklore and Culture of Southern Jews," p. 124.
60 "members of the business community": Int. Herbert Elsas.
61 " 'got to read the prayers' ": Int. Cecil Alexander.
61 " 'Are we glad to see you!' ": Ibid.
61 "went to a bar mitzvah": Int. Bill Bremen.
62 "It is not uncommon": Lipson-Walker, " 'Shalom Y'all'," p. 128.
62 "pork chops with okra": Ibid., p. 293.
62 "oyster stew, steaks": Evans, *The Provincials: A Personal History of Jews in the South*, p. 92.
62 "proof of their participation": Lipson-Walker, " 'Shalom Y'all'," p. 130.
62 glazed bagel: Ibid., p. 276.
62 sprigs of holly: Ibid., p. 277.
62 "didn't want to be different": Ibid., p. 178.
63 "knew we were Jewish": Int. Jane Axelrod.

63 "Jewish leopard": Int. Herbert Elsas.
64 "My great-grandparents": Int. Caroline Haas Kahn.
64 "I was fifteen": Int. Cecil Alexander.
65 "Long-resident Jews": Lindemann, *Jew Accused*, p. 231.
66 "shockingly impious": Hertzberg, *Strangers*, p. 86.
66 Two congregations of Sephardim: Ibid. p. 96; Beton, *Sephardim & A History of Congregation Or Ve Shalom*.
66 "so exclusive it failed": Int. Aline Uhry.
66 "For a German Jew to marry": Int. Fred Beerman.
69 "born in 1909": Int. Aline Uhry.
70 "very high-class, studious": Int. Caroline Haas Kahn.
70 archetypal southern crime: Hertzberg, *Strangers*, p. 204.
70 "extraordinary favors": Quoted in ibid., p. 208.
71 "anybody except a Jew": Quoted in ibid., p. 209.
71 "Crack that Jew's neck": Hertzberg, *Strangers*, p. 205.
71 "little bitty guy": Int. Caroline Haas Kahn.
72 "Trolley car conductors": Dinnerstein, *The Leo Frank Case*, p. 56.
72 "Two thousand years ago": Quoted in ibid., p. 129.
73 dummy bore a sign: Ibid., p. 130.
73 Judge Lynch: Ibid., pp. 134–35.
73 "full of men": Ibid., p. 133.
73 "I am going to live": Ibid., p. 138.
73 "Frank got out of bed": Ibid., p. 139.
74 "If the prison": Ibid., p. 145.
75 "line was drawn," Int. Caroline Haas Kahn.
75 "likelihood of being attacked": Int. Tony Montag.
75 "worked with the Montags": Int. Rabbi Alvin Sugarman.
75 "way I became aware": Int. Janice Rothschild Blumberg.
76 "The older people": Int. Jackie Montag.
76 "Honey?": Int. Jane Axelrod.
76 "congregation welcomed": Int. Janice Rothschild Blumberg.
77 "Since when do Reform Jews": Ibid.

4: THE INVISIBLE CHECKERBOARD

78 "middle-dogs": Speech at the Temple in Atlanta, Georgia, April 25, 1995.
80 "stunned by the signs": Int. Jean Levinson.
80 "newcomers could not understand": In Kuhn, Joye, and West, *Living Atlanta: An Oral History of the City, 1914–1948*, p. 351.
80 "horrified to come": Int. Emanuel Feldman.
80 "grew up in Pennsylvania": Int. Julian Bond.

81 "she was quite fair-skinned": Int. Alice Washington.
81 "a 'damn Yankee' ": Int. Frances Pauley.
82 "The Negro child": Bartley, *The Creation of Modern Georgia*, pp. 151–52.
83 "buildings downtown": Kuhn, Joye, and West, *Living Atlanta*, p. 10.
83 "one of the first black doctors": Int. Alice Washington.
83 "Ph.D.'s took jobs as redcaps": Int. Donald Hollowell.
85 "Nothing looked the same": Int. Clifford Kuhn.
85 "Negroes weren't in politics": Kuhn, Joye, and West, *Living Atlanta*, p. 346.
86 "Going door to door": Ibid., pp. 336–37.
86 "effort lasted": Ibid., p. 337.
86 only candidate to woo: Spritzer, *The Belle of Ashby Street: Helen Douglas Mankin and Georgia Politics*.
86 "arrival of black political strength": Kuhn, "Two Small Windows of Opportunity: Black Politics in Georgia during the 1940s, and the Pertinent Oral History Sources," paper delivered at the joint meeting of the Georgia Association of Historians and the Georgia Political Science Association, Savannah, Georgia, February 29, 1992, p. 6.
86 "What made Atlanta great": Int. Harmon Perry.
86 "first winds of change": Int. Clifford Kuhn.
87 "epidemic of random murder": Egerton, *Speak Now Against the Day*, p. 365.
87 "legal lynchings": Bartley, *The Creation of Modern Georgia*, p. 139.
87 "going to a barbecue": Int. Edward T. M. Garland.
89 "equivalent to Apollo Club": Int. Harmon Perry.
89 "this was heaven": Int. Julian Bond.
90 "richest Negro street": Kuhn, Joye, and West, *Living Atlanta*, p. 39
90 "You had not been to Atlanta": Ibid., p. 10.
90 "WERD": Int. Harmon Perry.
91 already well-established street: Kuhn, Joye, and West, *Living Atlanta*, p. 37.
91 " 'The Avenue' ": Ibid., pp. 37–39.
91 "those little boys": Ibid., p. 55.
91 "black man's pride and joy": Ibid., p. 39.
91 "where we dressed up": Ibid.
92 "beautiful street": Int. Alice Washington.
93 "first time I saw Atlanta": Int. Donald Hollowell.
94 "a revelation to me": Ibid.

94 "to see a dentist": Int. Julian Bond.
94 "lots of restaurants": Int. Alice Washington.
96 "Southern born men": W. E. B. DuBois, "From Servitude to Service: Being the Old South Lectures on the History and Work of Southern Institutions for the Education of the Negro (Boston: American Unitarian Association, 1905), in Lewis, ed., *W. E. B. DuBois: A Reader*, pp. 248–50.
96 "an oasis": Kuhn, Joye, and West, *Living Atlanta*, p. 158.
97 "to the 'buzzard's roost' ": Ibid.
97 "cultural activities": Int. Alice Washington.
97 "very interested in what I saw": Int. Donald Hollowell.
98 "very insular world": Int. Julian Bond.
99 "white citizens of Atlanta": Ibid.
100 "Greetings and Salutations": Letter to Rabbi Louis Youngerman, March 12, 1947, JMR, ESC.

5: "Dear Rabbi: My Son Melvin . . ."

102 "Jewish sensitivities . . . sycophantic reaction": Blumberg, *One Voice: Rabbi Jacob M. Rothschild and the Troubled South*, p. 47.
102 "Far more important": Sermon, "The Greater Sin," Atlanta, Georgia, October 13, 1948, JMR, ESC.
102 "Why can't we have Christmas? . . . *the truth*": Sermon, "What Can We Tell Our Children?" Atlanta, Georgia, December 15, 1950, JMR, ESC.
104 Rothschild! What a lovely name: June Reisner Stevens, lyrics for JMR anniversary celebration, April 1966, quoted in Blumberg, *One Voice*, p. 28.
105 shout from the housetops: Letter to JMR, June 13, 1952, JMR, ESC.
105 "gentlemen have turned their backs": Letter to JMR, October 4, 1951, JMR, ESC.
106 "continue to have Hebrew": Letter to JMR, June 13, 1952, JMR, ESC.
106 "turned the clock backward": Letter to JMR, September 26, 1957, JMR, ESC.
106 "Line up all the travelers": Ibid.
107 "president of the congregation in 1895": Letter to JMR, October 4, 1951, JMR, ESC.
108 "combat the growing tendency": JMR to Rabbi Herbert Waller, January 19, 1953, JMR, ESC.

108   "organized a youth group": JMR to Rabbi Milton Grafman, March 12, 1947, JMR, ESC.

109   "Marvin Klein": Rabbi James A. Wax to JMR, January 3, 1952, JMR, ESC.

109   "Oi! Are you confused!": JMR to Rabbi James A. Wax, January 7, 1952, JMR, ESC.

109   "I am a Gentile": W. C. Byington to JMR, February 18, 1954.

109   "informant has badly misled you": JMR to W. C. Byington, February 16, 1954.

110   My son, Melvin,: May 17, 1957, JMR, ESC.(Names have been changed to protect privacy.)

110   "without prior conversion": Ibid.

112   "How to Be Happy though Jewish": March 15, 1947, Macon, Georgia, JMR, ESC.

114   "never knew what anti-Semitism was": Int. Nancy Thal.

114   "owned a little cabin": Int. Sam Massell.

115   "end up at the Standard Club": Int. William Schwartz.

115   "grounds were beautiful": Int. Nancy Thal.

116   "converted to Judaism": Int. Janice Rothschild Blumberg.

116   downpour . . . when necessary: Sibley, *Dear Store: An Affectionate Portrait of Rich's*, p. 27.

116   "an emporium of fashion": Ibid., pp. 40–41.

117   pay the teachers in scrip: Ibid., pp. 15–16.

117   handsome gifts to the city: Ibid., p. 16.

117   "a derisive competitor": Ibid., p. 12.

117   "Dick Rich was an attractive man": Int. Jackie Montag.

118   "headed millinery department": Int. Aline Uhry.

118   "like a family store": Ibid.

119   "Our social life was Jewish . . . couldn't get in": Ibid.

120   "a rule of thumb": Int. Jackie Montag.

120   "Reform Jews diversified": Int. Tony Montag.

121   "had a Christmas tree": Int. Nancy Thal.

121   "went Friday nights": Int. Herb Axelrod.

121   "I'm a Reform rabbi": Int. Janice Rothschild Blumberg.

122   "Who is that?": Ibid.

122   "booked up absolutely solid": Ibid.

122   took a deep breath: JMR to Dr. Jacob Marcus, November 6, 1946, JMR, ESC.

123   "He exaggerated": Blumberg, *One Voice*, p. 22.

123   "misguided splendor": Ibid., p. 27.

123   "rear end of a garage": JMR to Nina Friedman, March 7, 1947, JMR, ESC.

124 "because it is a girl": JMR to Rabbi Ely E. Pilchik, October 22, 1947, JMR, ESC.

124 how very, very sorry: Letter to JMR, April 27, 1948, JMR, ESC.

125 "de facto restrictions": Blumberg, *One Voice*, p. 41.

6: THE YIDDISH CAPITAL OF THE SOUTH

126 "they were Germans": Int. anonymous.

126 "weren't worth a goddam": Int. anonymous.

126 "Let me tell you": Int. anonymous.

126 "The Jewish elite": Int. anonymous.

128 "noxious emanations": Hertzberg, *Strangers within the Gate City: The Jews of Atlanta, 1845–1915*, p. 112.

129 "The Merlins were eight brothers": Int. Joe Jacobs.

129 "My uncles would come": Int. Sonny Epstein.

129 "more hospitable": Hertzberg, *Strangers*, p. 122.

131 "Where my people came from": Int. Joe Jacobs.

132 "On Sundays we used to go": Ibid.

134 "When immigrants arrived": Ibid.

134 "set up a school": Ibid.

135 "two types of Jews in the South": Ibid.

135 "the Klan in some places": Ibid.

136 "hatters came along and had a strike": Ibid.

138 A 1904 graduate . . . Jew in the 1930s: Joel Lyons, "Jewish Georgians and Coke in Perfect Harmony," *Jewish Georgian* 5, no. 1 (1994): 1–17.

138 "I get a call from Harold Hirsch": Int. Joe Jacobs.

141 "Yeah, I had a rep": Int. Max Kuniansky.

142 "I flew out of Italy": Ibid.

143 "The JEWS are taking all the wealth": McWilliams, *A Mask for Privilege: Anti-Semitism in America*, p. 214.

143 "I went down and talked": Int. Max Kuniansky.

144 " 'I hate the Jews because' ": McWilliams, *Mask for Privilege*, p. 214.

144 "We didn't want any police": Int. Max Kuniansky.

144 The Columbians faltered and faded: Newton and Newton, *KKK Encyclopedia*, p. 128.

145 "I happened to be at the station": Int. Fred Beerman.

145 "my fair-skinned brothers": McWilliams, *Mask for Privilege*, p. 220.

7: BLACK MONDAY

147 "seccession by armed force": Quoted in H. Martin, *Ralph McGill: Reporter*, p. 152.

148 "biggest damn-fool mistake": Williams, *Eyes on the Prize: America's Civil Rights Years, 1954–1965*, p. 38.

148 "I've not yet met": Int. George Bright.

148 "declaration of socialistic doctrine": Williams, *Eyes on the Prize*, p. 83.

148 "open the bedroom doors": Ibid.

149 "resist mixing races . . . stampede": *AC*, May 18, 1954.

149 inferior beings lacking in morality: Bartley, *The Rise of Massive Resistance: Race and Politics in the South during the 1950's*, p. 13.

149 90 percent of white southerners: Ibid., pp. 13–14.

149 "reformers were making progress": Int. Charles Wittenstein.

150 "lead pellets found": Johnston, *Mississippi's Defiant Years, 1953–1973: An Interpretive Documentary with Personal Experiences*, p. 34.

150 "What else could we do . . . my folks stand' ": Halberstam, *The Fifties*, p. 435.

151 "failed to prove the identity": Williams, *Eyes on the Prize*, p. 52.

151 "army of one hundred million": Cook, *The Segregationists*, p. 15.

151 "can dress a chimpanzee": Ibid., p. 17.

151 "blue-eyed, golden-haired little girls": Ibid., p. 18.

152 "respectable citizens of the community": David Halberstam, "The White Citizens Councils: Respectable Means for Unrespectable Ends, *Commentary* 22 (1956): 294.

152 "advent of the Councils": Ibid., p. 301.

152 "The real conflict": Int. Rothschild.

152 "Integration represents darkness": Cook, *The Segregationists*, p. 65.

153 " 'This thing will be solved' ": Ibid., p. 32.

153 Jew-hating organizations: Dinnerstein, *Anti-Semitism in America*, p. 162.

153 "unlike previous decades": Ibid., p. 164.

153 "assault mounted by the white South": Cook, *The Segregationists*, p. 151.

153 "Anti-Semitic forces": Ralph McGill, "Race and Anti-Semiticism," *AC*, October 15, 1958, p. 1.

154 "my informants agreed": Joshua Fishman, "Southern City," *Midstream* 7 (1961): 43–44.

154 " 'paradise lost' ": Ibid., p. 46.

155 Of all the nations: Cook, *The Segregationists*, p. 30.

155 "The NAACP is the worst": Halberstam, "White Citizens Councils," p. 294.

156 "just common ordinary citizens": Int. George Bright.

156 "ideal merger of Klan and Nazi": Newton and Newton, *KKK Encyclopedia*, p. 420.

156 "I went to find out": Int. George Bright.

156 "We were enthused . . . America be saved": Cook, *The Segregationists*, pp. 179–80.

157 "the life blood of our race": Ibid., pp. 180–81.

157 U.S. Naval Air Force: Army Medical Report, received by Chief of Police, Birmingham, Alabama, October 1963, FBI, BDAM.

157 "not in the U.N. police": November 4, 1951, letter for registration, FBI, BDAM.

157 "Abnormal Psychiatric": Dr. F. M. Geiser, December 15, 1952, Report of Medical Examiner by Receiving Main Station, Chamblee, Georgia, FBI, BDAM.

157 "quite anxious that someone": Ibid.

158 "This store is owned by Jews": Newton and Newton, *KKK Encyclopedia*, p. 197.

158 "Obsessive anti-Semitism": Ibid., 543.

158 "creepy little wild-eyed man": Cobbs and Smith, *Long Time Coming*, pp. 59–60.

158 " 'What about Jonas Salk?' ": Int. Harvey Klehr.

158 "children of the Devil . . . punishable by death": Newton and Newton, *KKK Encyclopedia*, p. 543.

158 "Hitler was too moderate": Unattributed article, FBI, BDAM.

158 via gas chambers: Newton and Newton, *KKK Encyclopedia*, p. 543.

159 "Defend the White Race": FBI, BDAM.

160 "Rally!": Ibid.

161 "SCIENTISTS SAY NEGRO": Ibid.

161 "super-organization": Watters, "How to Be a Hate Fanatic," p. 1.

161 thirty-six-point NSRP platform: Jim Bishop, "The Haters: Publications, Parties and Persons" *Pittsburgh Sun-Telegraph*, November 12, 1958, p. 21.

162 Headlines and stories: Cook, *The Segregationists*, pp. 169–72.

162 "Fire Your Nigger . . . niggers, too": Newton and Newton, *KKK Encyclopedia*, p. 543.

163 Annapolis-trained aviator . . . record: Cook, *The Segregationists*, pp. 155–56.

163 "smiling, good-natured man": Bishop, "The Haters," p. 21.

163 The ultimate objective: Cook, *The Segregationists*, p. 162.

164   "nothing against Jews": Faulkner, *The Sound and the Fury*, pp. 237–38.

164   "during their Egyptian sojourn": Cook, *The Segregationists*, pp. 163–64.

164   "biggest lie of all": Ibid.

8: NO MIDDLE GROUND

166   "The years do fly": JMR to H. Glenn McNair, August 1, 1951.

166   Your new moons: Isaiah 1:14–17.

170   "You might call it": Egerton, *Speak Now Against the Day*, p. 387.

170   "But the secret strategy": Ibid.

170   "Milling about freely": Ibid.

171   "They *rose* from the *dead*": Bartley, *The Creation of Modern Georgia*, p. 204; and conversation with David Walbert.

171   "a political science perspective": Bartley, *Creation*, p. 204.

171   "Accounts differ": Egerton, *Speak Now*, p. 388.

172   " 'Herman, you have no claim' ": Ibid.

172   "who set up": Bartley, *Creation*, p. 204.

173   "He . . . endlessly": Ibid., pp. 205–206.

173   How comforting: Sermon, "The Greater Sin," Yom Kippur 5709, October 13, 1948, JMR, ESC.

174   "Jack grew up in Pittsburgh": Int. Fred Beerman.

175   "I think the majority of them": Int. Herbert Elsas.

175   "ultraliberal social worker": Int. Richard Wasser.

176   a new sort of world opened: H. Martin, *Ralph McGill: Reporter*, p. 15.

176   "years of his loneliness": H. Martin, *Ralph McGill*, p. 15.

176   "proud and pleased to see you": Reb Gershon to JMR, October 7, 1957, JMR, ESC.

176   "I appreciate your sentiment": JMR to Reb Gershon, October 9, 1957, JMR, ESC.

176   "all the phrases": Reb Gershon to JMR, November 17, 1957, JMR, ESC.

177   "particularly helpful to me": JMR to Reb Gershon, November 19, 1957, JMR, ESC.

177   "a little older than me": Int. Miriam Freedman.

177   "Southern Regional Council": Sermon, "The Greater Sin."

177   King urged President Kennedy: Branch, *Parting the Waters: America in the King Years, 1954–63*, p. 380.

178   black man as a salesman: Bill Calloway, "Daring Spirit of

Modern Pioneers Made Atlanta the Great City It Is," *AC*, January 5, 1983, p. 13A.

178 "Isolated in their local communities": Hero, *The Southerner and World Affairs*, p. 482.

179 The majority of the rabbinate: Krause, *The Southern Rabbi and Civil Rights*.

179 "Jew is quiet": Ibid., p. 43.

179 "Somewhat ambivalent": P. Allen Krause, "Rabbis and Negro Rights in the South, 1954–1967," *American Jewish Archives* 21, no. 1 (1969): 23.

179 "Southern Jewish party-line": Int. Charles Wittenstein.

179 "I think it is true": Int. Rothschild.

180 "the majority of their congregations": Krause, *Southern Rabbi*, p. 45.

180 "The image of the Jew": Ibid., p. 46.

180 "Leadership has been silent": Quoted in William S. Malev, "The Jew of the South in the Conflict on Segregation," *Conservative Judaism* 13, no. 1 (1958): 45.

181 Supreme Court . . . rural southern schools: Howard M. Sachar, *A History of the Jews in America*, p. 803.

182 "90 percent of the civil rights lawyers": Ibid.

182 "30 percent of the white volunteers": Ibid., pp. 803–4.

182 "It made little difference": Krause, *Southern Rabbi*, p. 237.

182 kept a card file: Ibid., p. 15.

182 "The following people attended": Ibid., p. 56.

182 "Dear White American": Ibid., p. 237.

183 sent delegations to the north: Lipson-Walker, " 'Shalom Y'all': The Folklore and Culture of Southern Jews," p. 88.

183 "Every time one of you": Ibid.

183 "your long noses": Ibid.

183 "gripped by an overwhelming fear": Krause, *Southern Rabbi*, p. 238.

183 "Jew is panic-stricken": Jacob Rothschild, "The Southern Rabbi Faces Desegregation," *Central Conference of American Rabbis Journal*, June 1956, JMR, ESC.

183 "martyrdom is perhaps": Malev, "The Jew of the South," p. 35.

183 "risk the hair": Blumberg, *One Voice: Rabbi Jacob M. Rothschild and the Troubled South*, p. 68.

184 "relating to the word 'fear' ": Krause, *Southern Rabbi*, p. 37.

184 very few black Episcopalians: Reimers, *White Protestantism and the Negro*, p. 186.

184 "They were confronted": Int. Rothschild.

184 "clergymen who were committed": Int. Dow Kirkpatrick.

184   "looked to the religious community": Int. Allison Williams.

185   "Freedom of Speech": "Text of Ministers' Racial Statement," *AJC*, November 3, 1957.

185   "Inevitably ministers who confront": JMR, sermon, "Eighty Who Dared—A Salute to My Christian Colleagues," November 8, 1957, JMR, ESC.

186   "Our experience here meeting with blacks": Int. Sam Massell.

187   "plow up all those golf courses": Jenkins, *Keeping the Peace: A Police Chief Looks at His Job*, p. 34.

187   "iron curtain of segregation": Ibid.

187   "Christmas Eve of 1955": Ibid.

187   "It was a fine golfing day": Ibid., pp. 35–37.

187   "On January 9, 1957": Ibid., p. 38.

188   "the Rev. William Holmes Borders": Ibid., p. 39.

188   "segregated seating law": Ibid., p. 40.

188   "listening to the radio": Int. Bill Rothschild.

189   "What man of intelligence": Sermon, "The Challenge of a Dream," October 7, 1954, JMR, ESC.

189   "unless decent people take up the burden": Sermon, "The Greater Sin," October 13, 1948, JMR, ESC.

189   "hysteria prevails": JMR, "The Southern Rabbi Faces Desegregation."

189   "kicking and screaming": Int. Joe Haas.

189   "difficult for him": Int. Aline Uhry.

190   "bombarded with protests": Blumberg, *One Voice*, p. 56.

190   "not incumbent upon thee": *Pirket Avot: Sayings of the Fathers*, chap. 2, v. 21.

9: Brotherhood Night

194   "What Is the Christ-Killer": Transcript of testimony of Leslie E. Rogers, *The State vs. George Michael Bright*, No. 76,891, Fulton Superior Court, January 12–23, 1959, p. 294 (hereafter cited as Rogers transcript).

194   sinister Communist program: "Poisoning These United States: You Are the Target!" *American Mercury*, Russell Maguire, editor, undated newsletter, original in RAG.

195   "string one of them up": John Neel, "Heckle Rabbi Help Asked, Witness Says," *AJ*, December 3, 1958, pp. 1, 8.

196   "folks who have private convictions": Pat Watters, "Who Are These of Unholy Rage against a Faith?" *AJ*, October 23, 1958, p. 58.

196 "Dear Rabbi": C. T. Cooper Jr. to JMR, February 16, 1951, JMR, ESC.

197 "ancient hope for the world": Sermon, "Questions I Am Asked—What Christians Ask about Judaism," November 19, 1954, JMR, ESC.

197 "engaged in a small tug-of-war": John Pennington, "Bright Tugged Sign—Deacon," *AJ*, January 15, 1959, p. 1.

197 "preaching on brotherhood": Sermon, "Good Will Towards Whom?" February 13, 1958, JMR, ESC.

198 "talk to our Lions Club": W. C. Henson to JMR, April 9, 1951, JMR, ESC.

199 "Jews taught . . . to gather gold": Int. George Bright.

199 "How many Jews": Ashworth, "Bright Admitted Threat"; Ashworth, "State Says Bright Was at Bombing," *AC*, December 3, 1958, pp. 1, 14; Rogers transcript.

201 "Rothschild was the big chief": Int. George Bright.

201 typewritten, third-person account: "The Dark Trial of George M. Bright," undated, original in RAG.

204 "Neighborhood kids": William Attwood, "The Position of the Jews in America Today," *Look* 19 (November 1955), p. 32.

204 "an explosive laugh": Ibid., p. 35.

10: AGAINST THE CHOSEN AND CIRCUMCISED ELITE

206 "Let's go kill . . . Jewish conspiracy": Rogers transcript, p. 307.

207 "FBI is completely affiliated": Ibid., p. 310.

207 "If local conditions": Ibid., pp. 283–84.

207 notorious segregationist: Bartley, *The Rise of Massive Resistance: Race and Politics in the South during the 1950's*, pp. 148, 204.

207 "dirty rat": John Pennington, "Cellmate Names Bright as Leader," *AJ*, December 5, 1958, p. 1.

207 Japanese range-finder: Rogers transcript, p. 298.

207 book by a Russian author: Ibid.

207 "We met to discuss": Int. George Bright.

208 "The primary objective": Rogers transcript, pp. 304–5.

208 "I first became interested": Sworn statement of Chester Griffin, taken in the Fulton County Jail, Atlanta, Fulton County, Georgia, Wednesday, October 29, 1958, original in Reuben A. Garland's files (hereafter cited as Griffin statement).

208 "just a loner": Int. Bobbie Kinard.

208 "During the Clinton controversy": Griffin statement.

209   "Matt Koehl was engaged in political activity": Rogers transcript, p. 298.
209   "round-robin discussion": Ibid., pp. 277–78.
210   The group elected officers: Ibid., p. 299.
210   "best to be secret": Ibid., p. 290.
211   "cleaned the office": Ibid., p. 300.
211   to purchase seven chairs: Ibid., p. 308.
211   The next meeting we held was: Griffin statement, p. 2.
212   We carried the desk up: Ibid., p. 3.
212   Then our next meeting: Ibid.
212   portable folding cross: Rogers transcript, pp. 301–2.
213   a grass-killing chemical: Ibid., p. 306.
213   "The National Committee to Free America": Pat Watters, "How to Be a Hate Fanatic," *AJ*, October 21, 1958, p. 1.
214   "When Richard was sober": Int. Bobbie Kinard.
214   "small as a porcelain doll": Jim Bishop, "A Talk with the Suspects in Atlanta Blast Case," *Pittsburgh Sun-Telegraph*, November 11, 1958, p. 19.
215   crutches had been stolen: Ibid.
215   "right of slavery": Ibid.
215   "just for conversational reasons": "Information from Mrs. Wallace Hugh Allen," original in RAG.
216   "Very intelligent, loquacious": "Abstract of a Discussion with Allen Taken in Fulton County Jail," November 1958, original in RAG.
216   "had strong ideas": Int. Sammie Allen.
216   I went to the Plaza Drug Store: Hand-printed statement by Wallace Allen in jail, original in RAG.
217   "They *happen* to be open": Transcript of testimony of Mrs. Marilyn Craig, *The State of Georgia vs. George Michael Bright*, in the Superior Court in and for Fulton County, Georgia, Atlanta Judicial Circuit, p. 49 (hereafter cited as M. Craig transcript).
217   "On this particular night": Ibid., pp. 53–54.
218   "George followed me out": Ibid., pp. 56–57.
218   "We found we had a mutual interest . . . two weeks": Ibid., p. 57.
218   "Our Heavenly Father": Richard Ashworth, "Bright Admitted Threat, Jury Told," *AC*, December 4, 1958, pp. 1–17.
219   the best-known anti-Semite: Dinnerstein, *Anti-Semitism*, p. 164.
219   "the young führer": Pearson, *Diaries: 1949–1959*, p. 516.
219   opposed to "Jews as a group": "Got Ideas from Hitler, Author Says," *AJ*, October 17, 1958, p. 1.
219   "died happily and richly": Lipstadt, *Denying the Holocaust: The Growing Assault on Truth and Memory*, p. 66.

219 *Eskimo* meant "Jew": Pearson, *Diaries*, p. 516.

219 shot to death: Dinnerstein, *Anti-Semitism*, p. 164.

220 "heavily in debt": Summary of Sammie Allen's statement to police, p. 1 (hereafter cited as S. Allen statement), original in RAG.

220 "husband remarked": S. Allen statement, p. 1.

220 At the University of Mainz . . . conspiracy: Drew Pearson, "Son of Famous Comedian Heads Hate-Nest Close by the Capital," *AJ*, February 17, 1959, p. 18.

220 It was wonderful to talk: John Pennington, "Five Indicted in Temple Blast; 'Fat Cat' Letter Disclosed," *AJ*, October 17, 1958, pp. 1–8.

222 Dear Linc: Wallace Allen to George Lincoln Rockwell, original in RAG.

222 Identical signs: S. Allen statement, p. 5.

223 that Nasser repaid the attention: Author's conversations with Anti-Defamation League officials in New York and Washington.

223 "husband refused to have anything": S. Allen statement, p. 5.

223 "Nasser outlawed the Communists": Robert J. Murphy, "The South Fights Bombing," *Look*, January 6, 1959, p. 17; and Rogers transcript, p. 354.

223 "Jews Control Press": S. Allen statement, p. 2.

223 "Jewish-Controlled Press Lies": Rogers transcript, p. 356.

223 Arrowsmith sent two hundred-fifty: S. Allen statement, p. 2.

224 Griffin very nearly lost his job: Orville Gaines, "Blast Probers Press for Dynamite Source," *AJ*, October 20, 1958, p. 1.

224 "Atlanta's Jews": Arnold Shankman, "A Temple Is Bombed— Atlanta, 1958," *American Jewish Archives* 23, no. 2 (1971): 130.

224 "O Lord": "Rabbi Rothschild Speaks. Moses, Prophets, Jesus Fought to Erase Inequality," *AJC*, November 17, 1957.

224 "not mentally competent": Int. Sammie Allen.

225 A social gathering: Handwritten memo, original in RAG.

225 "Mr. Rogers asked me": Billy Branham to Reuben A. Garland, undated, original in RAG.

226 In the summer of 1958: J. D. Chapman to Reuben A. Garland, undated, original in RAG.

226 "too late for prayer": J. D. Felmut to Reuben A. Garland, undated, original in RAG.

227 synagogue in Gastonia, North Carolina: Dictated statement of Detective T. E. Linsey, May 5, 1958, BPD, BDAM.

227 "nigger-loving people": Shankman, "A Temple Is Bombed," p. 127.

227 "except Miami Beach": Ibid., p. 128.

227 Temple Beth-El in Birmingham: Jamie Moore, Birmingham Chief of Police, to J. Edgar Hoover, April 30, 1958, BPD, BDAM.

228 "Mr. Connor, I believe": "Statement of Eugene 'Bull' Connor, Commissioner of Public Safety, Made at 2:00 P.M., July 16, 1958, in Room 315, City Hall Building," Birmingham, Alabama, BPD, BDAM.

228 "On June 16, 1958": Ibid., p. 4.

228 I opened the conversation: Capt. G. L. Pattie, Birmingham Police Department, "Interview on Saturday, June 21, 1958, with Mr. 'S,' " BPD, BDAM, pp. 3, 5.

230 "As pastor of Bethel Baptist Church": Rev. Fred Shuttlesworth, introduction to Cobbs and Smith, *Long Time Coming*, p. 16.

230 detective observed Stoner and Bowling: Detective T. E. Lindsey, "Memorandum Re: Bethel Baptist Church ... bombing and the attempt [*sic*] bombing of the Temple Beth-El," July 14, 1958, BPD, BDAM, p. 1.

230 "called our informer long distance": "Statement of Eugene Connor," July 16, 1958, p. 5, BPD, BDAM.

231 "no question in my mind": Ibid.

232 "neither famous nor black," Blumberg, *One Voice*, p. 70.

232 "Bombings have shocked": Sermon, "Can This Be America?" May 9, 1958, JMR, ESC.

233 "lead the red-hot boys": Letter to JMR, March 1958, JMR, ESC.

233 "lunatic fringe ... so be it": JMR letter, March 27, 1958, JMR, ESC.

II: WHEN THE WOLVES OF HATE ARE LOOSED

237 "huge shockwave": Int. Richard Wasser.

238 "I was sheltered": Int. Marcia Rothschild.

239 "National television wanted me": Int. Rothschild.

240 "Atlanta has prided itself": "Rabble Rousers Share the Blame, Mayor Says," *AC*, October 13, 1958, p. 6.

241 "JEWISH TEMPLE ON PEACHTREE": Keeler McCarney and James Sheppard, "Jewish Temple on Peachtree Wrecked by Dynamite Blast," *AC*, October 13, 1958, p. 1.

241 "choice of education by democracy": "Integrated High School in Clinton Wrecked by Pre-Dawn Explosions," *AC*, October 6, 1958, p. 1.

242 "moral zeroes": *How Am I to Be Heard: Letters of Lillian Smith*; L. Smith to Lawrence Kubie, June 29, 1959, p. 227.

243 "Is Janice upset?": Blumberg, *One Voice: Rabbi Jacob M. Rothschild and the Troubled South*, pp. 89–90.

244 "Welcome to the club": Ibid., p. 90.

244 "a blow directed at us all": Edward Krick to JMR, October 13, 1958, JMR, ESC.

246 "To Bible Belt southerners": Blumberg, *One Voice*, p. 83.

246 "bunch of Al Capone gangsters": "Ike Brands Blasters as 'Capone Hoodlums,' " *AJ*, October 15, 1958, p. 1.

246 first time that agency: Robert J. Murphy, "The South Fights Bombing," *Look*, January 6, 1959, p. 17.

246 "Even as the thundering echo": Pat Watters, "Moderates' Voice Heard Amid Fury" *AJ*, October 24, 1958, p. 4.

247 "involving a Negro 'suspect' ": "Let This Bombing Come to a Swift Solution," *Atlanta Daily World*, October 15, 1958.

247 "accept our small gift": James Billops to JMR, March 2, 1959, JMR, ESC.

247 "proxy attack": Int. Julian Bond.

247 "Men free in mind": N. B. Herndon to JMR, January 30, 1959, JMR, ESC.

248 "now thirty and getting married": Int. Nancy Thal.

250 "tired and numb . . . received same type of call": Blumberg, *One Voice*, pp. 85–86.

251 "wonderful hamburgers": Int. Janice Rothschild Blumberg.

252 " 'Does this one hate me?' ": Ibid.

252 "they were having similar thoughts": Ibid., and Blumberg, *One Voice*, p. 87.

253 "Jack taking a drink": Blumberg, *One Voice*, p. 88.

254 "bring national discredit": William Bates, "State Political Factions' Leaders Join in Deploring Temple Blast," *AC*, October 13, 1958, p. 1.

254 "the slightest connection": Ibid.

254 "who believe in constitutional government": Watters, "Moderates' Voice," p. 4.

254 "Jewish church": Blumberg, *One Voice*, pp. 91–92.

254 "hell of a lot of Jew members": Bates, "Political Factions' Leaders," p. 1.

254 fondness for the Confederacy: "Gray Vets Aided by Temple," *AC*, October 13, 1958, p. 6.

254 protégé of the Talmadge faction: Clifford M. Kuhn, " 'There's a Footnote to History!' Memory and the History of Martin Luther King's October 1960 Arrest and Its Aftermath," paper presented at the 1994 Annual Meeting of the Organization of American Historians, p. 8.

255 "attempt to violate the Constitution": Bates, "Political Factions' Leaders," p. 1.

255 "Desecrated Temple": "Desecrated Temple Cries Out to Heaven," *AJ*, October 13, 1958, p. 1.

255 "furious, uninterrupted writing": H. Martin, *Ralph McGill: Reporter*, p. 157.

255 A Church, a School: Ralph McGill, "A Church, a School," *AC*, October 13, 1958, p. 1.

257 Pulitzer Prize: H. Martin, *Ralph McGill*, p. 159.

257 " 'Here's a reward, Ralph' ": Int. George Bright.

258 "Fret not thyself": October 12, 1958, JMR, ESC.

258 "YOUR FRIENDS AT TRINITY": October 12, 1958, JMR, ESC.

259 "WE ARE GRIEVED FOR YOU": Ibid.

259 "WE LAMENT THE TRAGIC": Ibid.

259 "OUR HEARTS BLEED": Ibid.

259 "MAY THE GOD OF ISRAEL": Ibid.

259 "Those of us who have come": Ibid.

259 "I am filled with shame": Ibid.

259 "words have yet been coined": Ibid.

259 "deep concern as well as great alarm": "Four Groups of Ministers Rip Bombing," *AC*, October 14, 1958, p. 5.

259 "as a gentile, Protestant": October 13, 1958, JMR, ESC.

259 "Christian friends": Ibid.

260 "temporary financing": Ibid.

260 "narrow-minded bigots": Ibid.

260 "Long proud of my lineage": Ibid.

260 "HEARTFELT SYMPATHY": October 12, 1958, JMR, ESC.

261 "HEARTFELT FRATERNAL SYMPATHIES": October 13, 1958, JMR, ESC.

261 "Your handling of yourself": Philip M. Klutznick to JMR, October 29, 1958, JMR, ESC.

261 "Dave Grundfest": T. H. Barton to JMR, January 23, 1959, JMR, ESC.

261 couple who ran a deli: Int. Babette Ferst Herzfeld by Jon Herzfeld.

261 "bumptious way . . . beautifully written letter": Ibid.

262 "reminded us bitterly": Blumberg, *One Voice*, p. 92.

262 "segregationist answer": October 12, 1958, JMR, ESC.

263 "stronger than ever": Int. Fred Beerman.

263 "Temple was overflowing": Int. William Schwartz.

263 "tiny ember of fear": Int. Janice Rothschild Blumberg.

263 "never heard anybody say": Int. Joseph Haas.

266 What message was the explosion: Sermon, "And None Shall Make Them Afraid," October 17, 1958, JMR, ESC.

267 "look back upon that hectic time": Sermon, "Faith vs. Fear— An Answer to Violence," May 26, 1959, JMR, ESC.

268   four-tier strategy: Int. David Berman, independent investigator.

12: "IF IT'S THE BOMBING YOU'RE INTERESTED IN, I DON'T KNOW ANYTHING ABOUT IT"

270   "wrapping dynamite": "Police Raiders Seize Threatening Note, Jail Fifth Bombing Suspect" *AC*, October 15, 1958, p. 1.

271   police detectives could say: Keeler McCartney, "Five Indicted in Bombing," October 18, 1958, *AC*, p. 1.

271   "definitely done by somebody": Pat Watters and Dick Link, "Tip on Bombing Hints Crack of Terror Ring," *AJ*, October 14, 1958, p. 1.

273   police recovered a transcript: Keeler McCartney, "Bombing Was Planned," *AC*, October 14, 1958, p. 1.

274   "Did you just hear the news": Sworn statement of Chester Griffin, taken in the Fulton County Jail, Atlanta, Fulton County, Georgia, Wednesday, October 29, 1958, original in RAG, p. 5.

274   "Knowing the warped minds": Ibid., p. 5.

274   "was to lay low": Ibid.

275   "we had a warrant to go up there": Int. W. K. "Jack" Perry.

276   "if it's the bombing": Ibid.

276   "use up the napkin dispenser": Int. C. J. Strickland.

276   covered with swastikas: Albert Riley, "Ike Brands Dynamiters 'Al Capone Hoods Who Insult the Confederacy,' " *AC*, October 16, 1958 , p. 1.

276   "Jew is the sworn enemy": Riley, "Ike Brands Dynamiters," p. 1.

276   "She doesn't like Jews": Jim Bishop, "Case History of Five in Temple Blast," *Detroit Times*, November 12, 1958, p. 28.

277   "I didn't have a paper": Int. George Bright.

279   "I really think J. B. Stoner": Ibid.

280   "You are going to witness": Richard Ashworth, "Bright Admitted Threat, Jury Told," *AC*, December 4, 1958, pp. 1–17.

280   "hardened fanatics": Int. C. J. Strickland.

280   "Only thing Griffin had": Int. W. K. "Jack" Perry.

281   "I was working with Strickland . . . the weakest, Griffin was": Ibid.

283   "would kill him": Ibid.

283   "he was in deep trouble . . . belonged to that outfit": Int. C. J. Strickland.

283   "came back to the station": Int. W. K. "Jack" Perry.

283 "I was present at a meeting": Statement of Kenneth Chester Griffin, October 13, 1958, signed, witnessed by Perry and Strickland, photocopy in RAG.

286 "The bomb was a very shrewd thing": Int. W. K. "Jack" Perry.

287 "trying to act like professionals": Int. C. J. Strickland.

13: "THE JEWISH RACE IS NOT ON TRIAL IN THIS CASE"

288 "Terrible food": Int. George Bright.

289 "longed for good old days": Tom Bennett, "James R. Venable, 90, Lawyer, Klan Group's Imperial Wizard," obituary, *AJC*, January 20, 1993, p. 6C.

289 "Let me get this straight": Ibid.

289 "Half of America": Int. Bobbie Kinard.

289 two black Muslims: "James R. Venable, 92, Leader of Klan Group," obituary, *NYT*, January 20, 1993, p. 32.

289 "Negroes don't have any trouble": Int. Bobbie Kinard.

289 "I'd represent Martin Luther King": Bennett, "Venable," p. 6.

290 "Saint Pope Gregory": Venable, *Choose Your Side*, pp. vi–viii.

290 Jews "resolved" themselves: Ibid., pp. 399–400.

291 When we got to the Station: Griffin statement of October 29, 1958, p. 5, in RAG.

292 I kept repeating: Ibid., pp. 5–6.

293 I had had this wild dream: Ibid., p. 6.

293 "made it too tight": Ibid., p. 7.

293 "wild goose chase": Ibid., p. 11.

295 "five men have been tried": Dick Link, "Fifth Man Faces Bomb Quiz by FBI," *AJ*, October 18, 1958, p. 1.

295 "pretended charges of vagrancy": Keeler McCartney, "Five Indicted in Bombing of Temple; Death Penalty Possible on Charge," *AC*, October 18, 1958, p. 1.

295 "I don't know anything about bombings": "Full Text of Statements to Press by Bomb Suspects," *AJC*, October 19, 1958, p. 21A.

295 "I have never taken part": Ibid.

296 "I am not guilty of the charge": Ibid.

296 "They have to have a scapegoat": Ibid.

296 Gentlemen, I deeply appreciate: Ibid.

297 "You're going to pay for it": "Missing 5th Suspect Is Seized," *AC*, October 18, 1958, p. 3.

298 house would be blown up: Link, "Fifth Man," p. 1.

298 "Confederate army": Ibid.

298 "Jew-loving" newspapers: Orville Gaines, "Blast Probers Press for Dynamite Source," *AJ*, October 20, 1958, p. 1.

298 "What recourse do we have": Dick Link, "Fifth Bomb Call Empties Two Emory Buildings," *AJ*, October 24, 1958, p. 1.

298 In New York City: "Race-Hatred Bomb Calls Plague N.Y.," *AJ*, October 18, 1958, p. 1.

298 "an affront to public intelligence": "Let's Give Thanks for Those Who Will Never Surrender," *North Side News*, November 25, 1958, original in RAG.

298 This is an effort to give the nation: Ibid.

299 "SYNAGOGUE BOMBING A FRAUD": *American Nationalist* 7, no. 59 (1959): 1–2.

300 offered its own reward: Ibid.

302 Venable began the voir dire: Handwritten notes, in RAG file.

303 "Jewish race is not on trial": Richard Ashworth, "Six Jurors Selected in Bombing Trial," *AC*, December 2, 1958, p. 1.

303 "two hundred years ago": Int. anonymous, April 1992.

303 *snot* in the punchline: Int. W. Whittier Wright.

304 "couldn't help being revolted": Blumberg, *One Voice: Rabbi Jacob Rothschild and the Troubled South*, pp. 99–100.

304 Eldon L. Edwards: John Pennington, "Five Indicted in Temple Blast," October 17, 1958, *AJ*, p. 1.

306 "For a criminal defense attorney": Int. Donald F. Samuel.

306 "I will tell you, dear": Int. anonymous.

307 "My husband knew of him": Int. Sammie Allen.

307 "I have this day employed": Original in RAG.

307 The opening minutes: Pat Watters, "Bright 1st to Face Bomb Trial Here," *AJ*, December 1, 1958, pp. 1–4.

308 the mother of the two defendants: Ibid.

308 "high-class redneck": Int. W. Whittier Wright.

309 While the [examination] was: John Pennington, "Expert Says Bright 'Lied,' " *AJ*, December 4, 1958, p. 1.

309 "We will show that George Bright": Richard Ashworth, "State Says Bright Was at Bombing," *AC*, December 3, 1958, pp. 1–14.

309 "I had gotten out of bed": Handwritten notes on trial in RAG.

310 "It invalidates any other": Ashworth, "State Says," pp. 1–14.

310 "We're not trying any religion": Richard Ashworth, "Bright a Plotter, State Says," *AC*, December 3, 1958, p. 4.

310 "Has it ever . . . been contended": *Donkle vs. Kohn*, 44 GA. 266, 271.

310 "Bright asked a question": *AC*, December 3, 1958, p. 4.

310 "very much of Adolf Hitler": Ibid.

311 "exciting being called by FBI agents": Blumberg, *One Voice*, p. 98.

311   "told myself to stop playing": Ibid., p. 101.

312   "My first experience": Int. Janice Rothschild Blumberg, and Pennington, "Expert Says," p. 101.

312   "big witness who points a finger": Jim Bishop, "Should the Bombers Die?" *Pittsburgh Sun-Telegraph*, November 13, 1958, p. 10.

312   "I was disturbed about the publicity": Rogers transcript, p. 357.

313   "They called and said": Int. Janice Rothschild Blumberg.

313   "He told me he planned": John Pennington, "Cellmate Names Bright as Leader," *AJ*, December 5, 1958, p. 1.

314   Well, sir . . . X'ed it: Transcript of testimony of Jimmy D. DeVore, *The State vs. George Michael Bright*, No. 76,891, Fulton Superior Court, Thursday, January 16, 1959, pp. 422–39 (hereafter cited as DeVore transcript).

315   "had ironclad alibis": Pennington, "Cellmate Names," p. 1.

315   "made a trip to Decatur . . . heard all this": Richard Ashworth, "Bright Told of Bombing, Witness Says," *AC*, December 6, 1958, pp. 1–5.

315   "some of that reward money": Pennington, "Cellmate Names," p. 1.

316   "George was at home . . . after that": John Pennington, "Ex-Prison Pal Quotes Bright as Saying He Led Bombing Plot," *AJ*, December 5, 1958, p. 1.

316   "left the store in company": Ashworth, "Bright Told," p. 5.

316   Edwards . . . Felmet . . . Morgan . . . Cole: John Neel, "Bright Says Character Is 'Spotless,' " *AJ*, December 6, 1958, pp. 1–4.

317   next few impeached: John Neel, "Bright's Case Goes to Jury," *AJC*, December 7, 1958, p. 7.

317   shoes removed . . . "I am George Bright": Ibid., pp. 1–7.

317   "I have a spotless character": Neel, "Bright Says," p. 1.

318   "first I knew of the bombing": Neel, "Bright's Case," pp. 1–18.

318   "L. E. Rogers planned . . . rendered in this case": Neel, "Bright's Case," p. 18.

318   polygraph test: Pennington, "Expert Says," p. 1.

319   "dangerous man smart enough": John Neel, "Jury Still out in Bright Case after 6 Hours of Deliberation," *AJ*, December 8, 1958, p. 1.

319   "This man is on trial": Ibid.

319   "hopelessly deadlocked": Richard Ashworth, "Bolling Freed on Bond as Jury Trying Bright Is Locked Up for Night," *AC*, December 9, 1958, p. 1.

320   "We'll get you": Ibid.

320   released on bond: Richard Ashworth, "Bolling, Allen Free on Bond, Jury Deadlocked on Bright," *AC*, December 9, 1958, p. 1.

320   "Yeah, well, there weren't any . . . we could go home": Int. W. Whittier Wright.

322   "seem to be hopelessly deadlocked": John Neel, "Temple Bomb Case Ends in Mistrial," *AJ*, December 10, 1958, p. 1.

322   "What I thought?": Int. Judge Durwood T. Pye.

14: "I Am One of Them That Bombed Your Temple"

323   "very jocular guy": Int. Joseph Haas.

323   "rode in the car": Int. Gene Reeves.

324   "Whenever Reuben was on trial": Int. Earl Hickman.

324   "something always going to happen": Int. John Nuckolls.

324   "He had this entourage . . . would *insist* on it": Int. John Nuckolls.

325   "bigger-than-life": Ibid.

325   I have just purchased from you: RAG to Honorable "Doc" Austin at Muse's, September 23, 1959, RAG.

326   "some of the family came": Int. Fauntleroy Garland.

327   "Reuben would run a wire": Int. John Nuckolls.

328   "defending a man for murder": Int. Elliott Goldstein.

328   "some of the little nuances": Int. Gene Reeves.

328   "Schley Howard": Int. Judge Durwood T. Pye.

329   "half the morning about a color": Int. John Nuckolls.

329   "tried a case . . . got off for manslaughter": Ibid.

331   "not sure a black man was entitled": Ibid.

332   "mailed Jesus a bill": Int. anonymous.

332   "put him in today's setting": Int. Gene Reeves.

332   " 'What is *stare decisis*?' ": Int. Edward T. M. Garland.

333   He left the decision: Int. George Bright.

333   Dear Mr. Garland: Mr. Burdine: Original in RAG.

334   The defendant in the case approaching: Original in RAG.

334   To Mr. Ruby Garland: A. G. Bright to RAG, January 5, 1959, in RAG.

334   "At the prisoner's side . . . establish this fact' ": "Bright Again Faces Court on Monday," *AJC*, January 11, 1959, p. 18A.

335   Suggestions to STRIKE FROM JURY PANEL: Undated, original in RAG.

336   "Kill him!": Int. Edward T. M. Garland.

336   "Anytime he had a Jew": Int. Miles Alexander.

336   "lovely, sweet, Christian": William Osborne, "Orkin Charges Cruel Acts, Sues for Divorce in De Kalb," *AC*, July 13, 1962, in RAG.

337 "Rosenfeld is a Jew!": Arthur Mefford, "Don Juan—and the Georgia Peach," *Timely Detective Cases*, February 1953, Vol 6., No. 6, p. 76.

337 "There were barriers": Int. Robert Lipshutz.

337 Mr. Hambrick was with the police: Undated, original in RAG.

338 "THIS PICTURE DEFINITELY": Undated, original in RAG.

338 "It is indeed reassuring": William Stephenson to RAG, November 13, 1958, in RAG.

339 "Allen thinks he is Jewish": RAG to William Stephenson, November 25, 1958, in RAG.

339 "Jews have a deep-seated hatred": ERF to RAG, April 22, 1959, in RAG.

340 "standing room only": Int. Judge Jeptha Tanksley.

340 "Do you believe that the Communist movement" ... "his beliefs and opinions?" [Garland's questions]: Original in RAG.

341 "why I got caught on the thing": Int. Manley R. Morrison.

342 "has strong anti-Semitic tendencies": John Pennington, "Hartsfield, Jenkins Called in Bright Case," *AJ*, January 13, 1959, p. 1.

342 "an innocent man!": Ibid.

343 I overrule that objection ... interested in apologies: John Pennington, "Rabbi's Wife Ties Griffin to Threat," *AJ*, January 14, 1959, p. 1.

344 "We didn't laugh": Int. Manley R. Morrison.

345 "terrifying experience": Transcript of testimony of R. E. Little, Jr., *The State vs. George Michael Bright*, No. 76,891, Fulton Superior Court, Thursday, January 15, 1959, p. 185.

345 "first-rate, high-class person": Int. W. Whittier Wright.

347 "first thing he said ... heard on the telephone": J. Rothschild, *The State vs. George Michael Bright*, No. 76,891, Fulton Superior Court, Wednesday, January 14, 1959, p. 35 (hereafter cited as J. Rothschild transcript).

347 "I enjoy acting": Ibid., p. 7.

348 "this evidence is hearsay": Ibid., pp. 14–15.

348 "If she doesn't know Chester Griffin": Ibid., p. 15.

349 "most rank opinionated conclusive": Ibid.

349 "Of course, we object to that": Ibid., p. 3.

349 How many people do you know in the South: Ibid., pp. 13, 44, 77.

351 I can't do that: Ibid., p. 73.

352 "pelted me with lengthy questions": Blumberg, *One Voice: Rabbi Jacob Rothschild and the Troubled South*, p. 101.

353 "He kept saying": Int. Janice Rothschild Blumberg.

353 How long ago was it: J. Rothschild transcript, p. 46.

353 You were downstairs: Ibid., pp. 50–53.

354 "left the witness stand weeping": Pennington, "Rabbi's Wife," p. 1.

354 "After ninety minutes": Blumberg, *One Voice*, p. 103.

355 "Jack saw no reason": Ibid., pp. 101–3.

355 "afternoon paper reported": Ibid.

355 anonymous caller phoned: Ibid., p. 104.

356 the day you got the call: J. Rothschild transcript, pp. 61–62, 65–66.

357 Don't you know you have a distinct: Ibid., pp. 66–67.

359 "voices with a foreign accent": Lamar Q. Ball, "West Paces Ferry Nights of Terror Bared in Reub Garland's Ordeals," *North Side News*, January 29, 1959, p. 1.

359 "The Jews and their allies": RAG to Russell Maguire, March 16, 59, in RAG.

359 I am in an awful fix: J. Rothschild transcript, pp. 29 ff.

360 "you could tell he was worn out": Int. Michael Morrison.

360 "when all else failed": Blumberg, *One Voice*, p. 105.

360 You remember the yellow paper: J. Rothschild transcript, pp. 78–86.

362 "don't claim to be a memory expert": Ibid., p. 93.

362 "TEARFUL RABBI'S WIFE": John Pennington, "Tearful Rabbi's Wife Winds Up Testimony," *AJ*, January 23, 1959, quoted in Blumberg, *One Voice*, p. 106.

363 Five years later: Int. Janice Rothschild Blumberg.

363 "MENTAL PATIENT": James Sheppard, "Mental Patient Called in to Give Bright an Alibi," *AC*, January 20, 1959, p. 1.

363 "ever-surprising Bright trial": John Pennington, "Bright Trial Contradictory," *AJ*, January 20, 1959, p. 1.

363 "chic with a Bavarian hairdo": James Sheppard, "Woman Provides Alibi for Bright" *AC*, January 20, 1959, p. 1.

364 "George Bright and I were at": M. Craig transcript, p. 3.

364 "Anybody in there": Ibid., p. 12.

364 We went out there to buy: Ibid., pp. 13–15.

365 "We turned on the radio": Ibid., p. 22.

365 "blooming thing . . . on the couch": Ibid., p. 24.

366 On the same couch: Ibid., p. 25.

366 Did you become: Ibid., p. 27.

367 "this so-called satellite": Ibid., pp. 67–68.

368 USAF Pioneer satellite: Andrew Wilson, Curtis Peebles, and

H. J. P. Arnold, "First Steps into Space," in *Man in Space*, ed. H. J. P. Arnold (New York: Smithmark, 1993), p. 23.

369 "felt the state": John Pennington, "Bright Acquitted on First Ballot," *AJC*, January 25, 1959, p. 20A.

369 "He was a likely suspect": Int. Michael Morrison.

369 "went to trial too quickly": Int. Tom Luck.

370 "had done sort of as he pleased": Int. Judge Jeptha Tanksley.

370 "You've bankrupted me": John Pennington,"Bright Released, His Lawyer Jailed," *AJ*, January 24, 1959, p. 1; James Sheppard, "Bright Acquitted of Bombing," *AC*, January 24, 1959, p. 1.

371 The *Atlanta Journal* headline: Pennington, "Bright Released," p. 1.

371 "Daddy had represented": Int. Edward T. M. Garland.

371 "Garland's stay in Fulton Tower": James Sheppard, "Charges Stand for 3 in Blast," *AC*, January 26, 1959, p. 6.

372 the most amazing phone call: Blumberg, *One Voice*, p. 107.

372 his campaign leaflets: In RAG.

373 "about the thirty-seventh day": Int. Judge Jeptha Tanksley.

15: "ORATORY IS NOT ENOUGH"

375 The bombing was a traumatic experience. ... What, then, is there to fear?: Sermon, "Ordeal by Trial," February 6, 1959, JMR, ESC.

377 "Negro's demand for self-fulfillment": Sermon, "A Year of Happiness," September 28, 1962, JMR, ESC.

379 "Just not to join": "Social Upheaval and Personal Peace," a Joshua Loth Liebman Memorial Lecture, Temple Israel, Boston, April 6, 1962.

379 berate his southern landsmen: Rothschild, "No Place to Hide," *Southern Israelite*, August 1963.

380 "Wherever M. L. King, Jr., has been": Branch, *Parting the Waters: America in the King Years, 1954–63*, p. 267.

381 "Now *everyone* remembers ... *tried* to be a good neighbor": Int. Frances Pauley.

382 Rothschilds and the younger Kings: Blumberg, *One Voice: Rabbi Jacob M. Rothschild and the Troubled South*, pp. 144–45.

382 "purely social biracial function": Blumberg, *One Voice*, pp. 144–45.

383 "that nice young man": Ibid., p. 151.

383 "Our friends from the North": Ibid., pp. 164–65.

384   "third or fourth day of February . . . we're paying the bills' ": Int. Julian Bond.

387   "Our warnings to Hartsfield": Stone, *Regime Politics: Governing Atlanta 1946–1988*, p. 52.

387   "Black lawyers defended students": Ibid., p. 53.

387   "Go back and tell your students": Ibid., p. 55.

388   "It is hard to overestimate": Ibid., p. 52.

388   black students agreed to concentrate: Ibid., p. 54.

389   "not everyone *liked* the food": Int. Aline Uhry.

390   "You are the spiritual leader": Branch, *Parting the Waters*, p. 350.

390   Rich wept in aggravation: Ibid., p. 354.

390   "Those of us who wanted": Blumberg, *One Voice*, p. 142.

390   "I knew there was no more decent": JMR to Richard R. Rich, March 9, 1961, JMR, ESC.

391   "Dick made it clear": Blumberg, *One Voice*, p. 143.

391   "I cannot accept bond": Ibid., p. 351.

391   "Chanting 'Jail not Bail' ": H. Martin, *Atlanta and Environs: A Chronicle of Its People and Events*, p. 319.

391   "a maelstrom at City Hall": Branch, *Parting the Waters*, p. 353.

391   "white Alabama aristocrat": Ibid., p. 207.

392   "Lillian Smith had had dinner": Int. Janice Rothschild Blumberg.

392   "students were let go": Clifford M. Kuhn, " 'There's a Footnote to History!' Memory and the History of Martin Luther King's October 1960 Arrest and Its Aftermath," paper prepared for delivery at the 1994 Annual Meeting of the Organization of American Historians, p. 1.

392   stunned at the sight of him: Branch, *Parting the Waters*, p. 358.

392   "segregationist mentality": Jenkins, *Keeping the Peace: A Police Chief Looks at His Job*, p. 27.

392   "road gang meant cutthroat": Branch, *Parting the Waters*, p. 359.

393   "this hearing did not take place": Ibid.

393   "maximum sentence for Martin Luther King": Ibid.

393   "What the hell . . . feel free to call on me": Ibid., p. 362.

393   "You bomb-throwers . . . Oh goddamit": Ibid., pp. 364–65.

394   Wofford denied the story . . . "better retract it": Ibid., p. 367.

394   "Mitchell was an arch-segregationist": Kuhn, "Footnote to History," p. 6.

395   "out of consideration for the governor's . . . for Vandiver": Ibid., p. 10.

395   "deeply indebted": Ibid., p. 367.

395 Everyone seemed to have: Branch, *Parting the Waters*, pp. 374–75.

396 "One plain fact": Ibid., p. 378.

396 "black people came in": Int. Miriam Freedman.

397 "Negro and white students were arrested": H. Martin, *Atlanta and Environs*, vol. 3, p. 368.

397 "tall Bible-quoting white man": Ibid., p. 369.

398 Marcia Rothschild's sit-in: Blumberg, *One Voice*, p. 156.

398 "letter received usual treatment": Rothschild, "One Man's Meat—A Personal Chronicle," *CCAR Journal*, 1965, original in JMR, ESC.

398 "moral point of view": Blumberg, *One Voice*, p. 159.

398 You throw up your hands in horror: Notes on address to hotel and restaurant proprietors, 1964, JMR, ESC.

399 "what the Negro seeks": Sermon, "The Journey through Time," September 18, 1963, JMR, ESC.

399 "What repentance is there for us": Sermon, untitled, September 20, 1963, JMR, ESC.

399 "I realize this cannot soften": JMR to Rev. John H. Cross, September 27, 1963, JMR, ESC.

399 I think this was the nicest gift: JMR to Meg and Sophie Mantler, October 25, 1963.

400 "a revolutionary assignment": Rothschild, "One Man's Meat."

400 Who of us, watching: "Introduction of Martin Luther King, Jr., UAHC Biennial, November 20, 1963.

16: THE RABBI'S WIFE DID IT

401 "old Jewish humor": Int. Nancy Thal.

401 "that joke is ridiculous": Int. Bud Mantler.

401 "everybody always thought": Int. Fauntleroy Garland.

402 "I think Reuben felt like": Int. Gene Reeves.

402 "Wallace Allen brought up subject": Statement of Kenneth Chester Griffin, October 13, 1958.

403 personal letter to President Eisenhower: "Wife of Temple Bombing Suspect Asks Ike to Aid in Investigation," *AJC*, November 23, 1958, p. 1C.

404 "outstanding, upright citizen": RAG to Honorable Carl B. Copeland, February 7, 1961, in RAG.

404 "You know what it was like": Conversation with author.

404 "I have never been a member": WA letter to author, February 19, 1993.

404 "He died January 14": Int. Sammie Allen.

404 "He was at home with me": Ibid.

405 "The Temple would be wrong": Wallace Allen to George Lincoln Rockwell, original in RAG.

406 "said he was an architect": DeVore transcript, pp. 422–39.

406 "He thought they had a letter": Ibid.

407 "one of the five indicted ... he was a hot-head": Int. George Bright, January 22, 1992.

407 "we were so effective": Int. George Bright.

407 "really think J. B. Stoner": Int. Bright, January 15, 1992.

408 "that was Richard Bowling": Ibid., January 22, 1992.

408 "J. B. Stoner was in the background": Int. Clifford J. Strickland.

409 Aids is a racial plague: Crusade Against Corruption Application for Membership. Received from ADL by author.

410 "I didn't have a paper": Int. George Bright; John Neel, "Bright's Case Goes to Jury," *AJC*, December 7, 1958, pp. 1, 18.

410 cognitive scientists: Conversation with Eugene Winograd.

412 "living in the Techwood area": Int. Clifford J. Strickland.

412 "bomber brothers": Conversation with Mary Patton.

412 "When questioned ...": Int. with William Hugh Morris by Bob Eddy and John East, June 29, 1977, BPD, BDAM.

412 "George Bright's life was ruined": Int. anonymous.

17: THE TABLE OF BROTHERHOOD

414 " 'There's good news' ": Int. Sam Massell.

414 "as a new Gandhi": I. Allen, *Mayor: Notes on the Sixties*, p. 95.

415 "Many of Atlanta's leading citizens": "Banquet for Dr. King Meets Obstacles Here," *AJ*, December 29, 1964.

415 Allen privately was pessimistic: I. Allen, *Mayor*, pp. 95–96.

416 "A proposed banquet": "Banquet for Dr. King."

416 "I must confess": Int. Rothschild.

416 "expressed concern that the city": Frederick Allen, *Secret Formula*, p. 337.

416 "As was the custom": Ibid.

416 "I don't think you could say": I. Allen, *Mayor*, p. 98.

417 "Rube Goldberg": F. Allen, *Secret Formula*, p. 338.

417 "BANQUET TO HONOR" ... Lane was the "banker": Ibid.

417 Eager to assure: Ibid., p. 339.

418 "the two of us, 'ordinary people,' ": Blumberg, *One Voice: Rabbi Jacob M. Rothschild and the Troubled South*, pp. 168–69.

418 "not set their hopes too high": Int. Janice Rothschild Blumberg, and Blumberg, *One Voice*, p. 171.

418 "not a simple, uncomplicated": Sermon, "A Rabbi in the South," at Hebrew Union College-Jewish Institute of Religion, January 9, 1970, JMR, ESC.

419 "Jack had come home early": Blumberg, *One Voice*, p. 172.

420 "the natural uneasiness": I. Allen, *Mayor*, p. 98.

421 "When we arrived at the hotel": C. S. King, *My Life with Martin Luther King, Jr.* (New York: Avon Books, 1970), p. 16.

421 "bubbling like champagne ... grandson of a sharecropper": Blumberg, *One Voice*, p. 172.

422 "a wonderful occasion ... get where we're going": I. Allen, *Mayor*, pp. 98–99.

422 You attest the truth: Opening remarks, Recognition Dinner, Dinkler Plaza Hotel, Atlanta, Georgia, January 27, 1965, JMR, ESC.

423 We are coming to understand: Presentation of bowl to MLK, January 27, 1965.

423 "joined hands and sang ... struggle and heartache": "A Rabbi in the South," January 9, 1970.

424 King wrote Rothschild: MLK to JMR, March 8, 1965, JMR, ESC.

424 "You were ignored": Archibishop Paul J. Hallinan to JMR, February 9, 1965, JMR, ESC.

424 Rabbi Rothschild shared: C. S. King, foreword to Blumberg, *One Voice*, pp. vii–viii.

424 "sons of former slaves": MLK, speech at Civil Rights March on Washington, August 28, 1963, quoted in Williams, *Eyes on the Prize: America's Civil Rights Years, 1954–1965*, p. 204.

18: "I Don't Like Being Told It's Not My Fight"

426 " 'Learn-to-live-with-it' ": Blumberg, *One Voice: Rabbi Jacob M. Rothschild and the Troubled South*, p. 188.

427 "seemed somewhat regretful": Ibid., p. 181.

427 "One night at dinner": Ibid., p. 187.

428 The presence of hundreds: Jacob M. Rothschild, "One Man's Meat—A Personal Chronicle," *Central Conference of American Rabbis Journal*, 1965, JMR, ESC.

429 "Now, at long last, we must set": "Memorial Address for Martin Luther King, Jr., 'Martin Luther King, Jr.—A Memorial,' " April 5, 1968, JMR, ESC.

429 "members were Jack's friends": Blumberg, *One Voice*, p. 207.

429 "I am of a people": Address to the Hungry Club, "Promise Denied and Hope Fulfilled," November 13, 1968, JMR, ESC.

430 "This may well indicate": JMR to Howard Hurtig, November 18, 1968, JMR, ESC.

430 "worst consequence . . . city mourned": Blumberg, *One Voice*, pp. 209–10.

430 "You laugh—now": Sermon, "Past, Present and Future," September 30, 1970, JMR, ESC.

431 "little strength left": Blumberg, *One Voice*, p. 215.

431 "Under those circumstances": Ibid.

432 "see who won": Int. Janice Rothschild Blumberg.

432 "45 minutes before . . . attend the funeral": Blumberg, *One Voice*, pp. 1–2.

435 "The ultimate measure of a man": C. S. King, foreword to Blumberg, *One Voice*, p. vii.

435 "Rothschild was a gift": Int. Frances Pauley.

436 "As I think of Jack Rothschild": Int. Rabbi Alvin Sugarman.

436 "For these many years": "A Rabbi in the South," January 9, 1970, JMR, ESC.

BIBLIOGRAPHY

Archival Materials

Ida Pearle and Joseph Cuba Community Archives and Genealogy Center of the William Breman Jewish Heritage Museum, Atlanta, Georgia:
Atlanta Jewish Federation Records
Leo Frank Papers, 1913–1915
The Temple Records, 1870–1988
Special Collections, Robert W. Woodruff Library, Emory University, Atlanta, Georgia:
Floyd Hunter Papers
Frances Pauley Papers
Jacob M. Rothschild Papers
Ralph McGill Papers
Birmingham Police Department Surveillance Files, Department of Archives and Manuscripts, Birmingham Public Library, Birmingham, Alabama.

"Creating Community: The Jews of Atlanta from 1845 to the Present," Atlanta History Center exhibition, October 24, 1994, to December 11, 1995; a project of the Atlanta Jewish Federation in collaboration with the Atlanta History Center, Jane Leavey, projects director.

Interviews by Allen Krause in connection with his rabbinic thesis, "The Southern Rabbi and Civil Rights," conducted between June 22, 1966, and December 20, 1966, American Jewish Archives, Cincinnati, Ohio.

Reuben A. Garland Sr. Papers, Edward T. M. Garland, Atlanta, Georgia.

U.S. Federal Bureau of Investigation 16th Street Baptist Church bombing investigation files, 1963–1965, Department of Archives and Manuscripts, Birmingham Public Library, Birmingham, Alabama.

INTERVIEWS

Alexander, Cecil. October 24, 1992.

Alexander, Henry. June 26, 1994.

Alexander, Miles. September 28, 1993.

Alverson, Judge Luther. November 2, 1993.

Allen, Sammie. January 14, 1995 (telephone); May 14, 1995 (telephone).

Allen, Wallace. January 1992 (telephone).

Ashendorf, Dorothy. October 11, 1993 (telephone).

Axelrod, Jane and Herb. January 22, 1992.

Beerman, Fred. August 10, 1993.

Berman, David. February 5, 1995; May 5, 1995

Bond, Julia. September 3, 1993.

Bond, Julian. November 26, 1993.

Bloom, Rabbi Irving. April 9, 1993.

Blumberg, Janice Rothschild. December 24 & 26, 1991; October 4, 1993.

Brayboy, Ella Mae. February 23, 1993.

Breman, Bill. May 12, 1993.

Bright, George. January 15, 21, & 22, 1992; February 3, 1992.

Curry, Connie. September 8, 1993.

Ellis, Elmo. September 27, 1993.

Elsas, Herbert. October 19, 1993.

Epstein, Rabbi Harry. February 16, 1993.

Epstein, Sonny. November 30, 1993.

Feldman, Rabbi Emmanuel. November 3, 1992.

Freedman, Miriam. November 1993.

Garland, Edward T. M. July 28, 1993.

Garland, Fauntleroy Moon. September 14 & 15, 1992.

Garland, J. Richmond. June 15, 1993.

Garrett, Franklin. January 25, 1993.

Goldstein, Elliott. March 9, 1993.

Goodwin, George. October 14, 1993.

Griffin, John. October 25, 1993.

Haas, Be. February 4, 1993.

Haas, Joseph. November 2, 1992.

Hallowell, Donald. February 3, 1992.

Herzfeld, Babette Ferst. Interviewed by Jon Herzfeld, January 1995.

Hesmer, John. September 15, 1993.

Hickman, Earl. March 16, 1993.

Jacobs, Joe. October 15, 1993; December 7, 1993.

Jelks, Ed. March 18, 1993.

Jenkins, James. August 25, 1993.

Kinard, Bobbie. April 22, 1993 (telephone); May 15, 1995 (telephone).

Kirkpatrick, Rev. Dow. November 1, 1993.

Klehr, Harvey. September 1995 (telephone).

Kuhn, Clifford. February 22, 1994.

Kuniansky, Max. November 3, 1993.

Levinson, Jean Rothschild. December 5, 1993.

Lipshutz, Robert J. July 27, 1993.

Little, Victoria D. July 1995 (telephone).

Lockerman, Doris. August 12, 1993.

Luck, Tom. February 25, 1993; March 20, 1995 (telephone).

Mantler, Marshall "Bud." July 29, 1995 (telephone).

Massell, Sam. December 18, 1991.

Merlin, Jerome. November 30, 1993.

Montag, Jackie and Tony. November 12, 1993.

Morrison, Michael. July 20, 1995.

Nuckolls, John. September 20, 1993.

Pauley, Frances. August 30, 1993; October 10 & 21, 1993.

Pendergrast, Nan. October 27, 1992.

Perry, Harmon. October 18, 1993.

Perry, W. K. "Jack." February 16, 1995.

Pye, Judge Durwood T. May 10, 1993.

Reeves, Gene. October 8, 1993.

Rothschild, Bill. April 25, 1993.

Rothschild, Jacob. Interviewed by P. Allen Krause, June 23, 1966.

Rothschild, Marcia. April 28, 1993.

Samuel, Donald F. Author's husband.

Schwartz, William. September 30, 1993.

Scott, Lucille. October 27, 1993.

Sherman, Mary Louise. November 10, 1993.

Strickland, Clifford J. March 1995 (telephone); interviewed by David
    Berman, March 1995.

Sugarman, Rabbi Alvin. October 3, 1993.

Tanksley, Judge Jeptha. October 5, 1992.

Thal, Nancy. July 10, 1993; September 10, 1993.

Uhry, Aline. June 15, 1993; July 25, 1993.

Washington, Alice. October 6, 1993.

Wasser, Richard. June 22, 1993.

Williams, Rev. Allison. March 30, 1993.

Winograd, Dr. Eugene. October 22, 1995 (telephone).

Wittenstein, Charles. December 10, 1991; September 7, 1993.
Wright, W. Whittier. April 22, 1993; March 29, 1995.
Zaban, Erwin. May 5, 1993.

MAJOR WORKS CITED IN NOTES

Allen, Frederick. *Secret Formula*. New York: HarperBusiness, 1994.

Allen, Ivan, Jr., with Paul Hemphill. *Mayor: Notes on the Sixties*. New York: Simon & Schuster, 1971.

Anti-Defamation League of B'nai B'rith. *Extremism on the Right*. New York: Anti-Defamation League of B'nai B'rith, 1988.

———. *Hate Groups in America: A Record of Bigotry and Violence*. New York: Anti-Defamation League of B'nai B'rith, 1988.

———. *The Protocols of the Prague Trial*. New York: Anti-Defamation League of B'nai B'rith, 1953.

Aymar, Brandt, and Edward Sagarin. *A Pictorial History of the World's Great Trials*. New York: Bonanza Books, 1985.

Bartley, Numan V. *The Rise of Massive Resistance: Race and Politics in the South during the 1950's*. Baton Rouge: Louisiana State University Press, 1969.

———. *The Creation of Modern Georgia*. Athens: University of Georgia Press, 1990.

Bauman, Mark K. *Harry H. Epstein and the Rabbinate as Conduit for Change*. Cranbury, N.J.: Associated University Presses, 1994.

Berman, Paul, ed. *Blacks and Jews: Alliances and Arguments*. New York: Delacorte, 1994.

Beton, Sol, ed. *Sephardim & A History of Congregation Or Ve Shalom*. Atlanta: Congregation Or Ve Shalom, 1981.

Birmingham, Stephen. *"Our Crowd": The Great Jewish Families of New York*. New York: Dell, 1968.

Blumberg, Janice Rothschild. *One Voice: Rabbi Jacob M. Rothschild and the Troubled South*. Macon, Ga.: Mercer University Press, 1985.

Branch, Taylor. *Parting the Waters: America in the King Years 1954–63*. New York: Simon & Schuster, 1988.

Cantor, Norman F. *The Sacred Chain: The History of the Jews*. New York: HarperCollins, 1994.

Carson, Clayborne, David J. Garrow, Gerald Gill, Vincent Harding, and Darlene Clark Hine, eds. *The Eyes on the Prize Civil Rights Reader: Documents, Speeches and Firsthand Accounts from the Black Freedom Struggle, 1954–90*. New York: Penguin, 1991.

Carter, Dan T. *Scottsboro: A Tragedy of the American South*. Baton Rouge: Louisiana State University Press, 1992.

Cash, W. J. *The Mind of the South.* New York: Vintage Books, 1991.

Chanes, Jerome R., ed. *Antisemitism in America Today: Outspoken Experts Explode the Myth.* New York: Birch Lane, 1995.

Clark, Wayne A. "An Analysis of the Relationship between Anti-Communism and Segregationist Thought in the Deep South, 1948–1964." Ph.D. dissertation, University of North Carolina, Chapel Hill, 1976.

Cobbs, Elizabeth H./Petric J. Smith. *Long Time Coming.* Birmingham, Ala.: Crane Hill, 1994.

Coleman, Kenneth, ed. *A History of Georgia.* Athens: University of Georgia Press, 1991.

Cook, James Graham. *The Segregationists.* New York: Appleton-Century-Crofts, 1962.

Dinnerstein, Leonard. *The Leo Frank Case.* Athens: University of Georgia Press, 1987.

———. *Anti-Semitism in America.* New York: Oxford University Press, 1994.

Du Bois, W. E. B. *The Souls of Black Folk.* New York: Bantam Books, 1989.

Egerton, John. *Speak Now Against the Day.* New York: Knopf, 1994.

Evans, Eli N. *The Provincials: A Personal History of Jews in the South.* New York: Macmillan, 1976.

———. *The Lonely Days Were Sundays: Reflections of a Jewish Southerner.* Jackson: University Press of Mississippi, 1993.

Faulkner, William. *The Sound and the Fury.* New York: Random House, 1956.

Garrison, Webb. *The Legacy of Atlanta: A Short History.* Atlanta: Peachtree, 1987.

Gerber, David A., ed. *Anti-Semitism in American History.* Champaign: University of Illinois Press, 1987.

Gladney, Margaret Rose, ed. *How Am I to Be Heard: Letters of Lillian Smith.* Chapel Hill: University of North Carolina Press, 1993.

Golden, Harry. *Mr. Kennedy and the Negroes.* New York: World, 1964.

———. *Only in America.* New York: World, 1958.

Goldfield, David R. *Black, White and Southern: Race Relations and Southern Culture 1940 to the Present.* Baton Rouge: Louisiana State University Press, 1990.

Halberstam, David. *The Fifties.* New York: Villard Books, 1993.

Hall, Jacquelyn Dowd. *Revolt against Chivalry: Jessie Daniel Ames and the Women's Campaign against Lynching.* New York: Columbia University Press, 1993.

Henderson, Harold P., and Gary L. Roberts, eds. *Georgia Governors in an Age of Change: From Ellis Arnell to George Busbee.* Athens: University of Georgia Press, 1988.

Hero, Alfred O., Jr. *The Southerner and World Affairs*. Baton Rouge: Louisiana State University Press, 1965.

Hertzberg, Steven. *Strangers within the Gate City: The Jews of Atlanta, 1845–1915*. Philadelphia, Pa.: Jewish Publication Society of America, 1978.

Hunter, Floyd. *Community Power Structure: A Study of Decision Makers*. Chapel Hill: University of North Carolina Press, 1953.

Jenkins, Herbert. *Keeping the Peace: A Police Chief Looks at His Job*. New York: Harper & Row, 1970.

Johnston, Erle. *Mississippi's Defiant Years, 1953–1973: An Interpretive Documentary with Personal Experiences*. Forest, Miss.: Lake Harbor Publishers, 1990.

Kaufman, Jonathan. *Broken Alliance: The Turbulent Times between Blacks and Jews in America*. New York: Touchstone, 1995.

Killian, Lewis M. *White Southerners*. Amherst: University of Massachusetts Press, 1985.

King, Coretta Scott. *My Life with Martin Luther King, Jr.* New York: Avon Books, 1970.

Krause, Allen. "The Southern Rabbi and Civil Rights." Master's and ordination dissertation, Hebrew Union College and Jewish Institute of Religion, 1967.

Kuhn, Clifford M., Harlon E. Joye, and E. Bernard West. *Living Atlanta: An Oral History of the City, 1914–1948*. Athens: University of Georgia Press, 1990.

Lewis, David Levering, ed. *W. E. B. DuBois: A Reader*. New York: Holt, 1995.

Lindemann, Albert S. *The Jew Accused: Three Anti-Semitic Affairs— Dreyfus, Beilis, Frank, 1894–1915*. New York: Cambridge University Press, 1991.

Lipset, Seymour Martin. *The Politics of Unreason: Right Wing Extremism in America, 1790–1970*. New York: Harper & Row, 1970.

Lipson-Walker, Carolyn. " 'Shalom Y'all': The Folklore and Culture of Southern Jews." Ph.D. dissertation, Indiana University, 1986.

Lipstadt, Deborah. *Denying the Holocaust: The Growing Assault on Truth and Memory*. New York: Plume, 1994.

Martin, John B. *The Deep South Says Never*. New York: Ballantine Books, 1957.

Martin, Harold H. *Atlanta and Environs: A Chronicle of Its People and Events*. Athens: University of Georgia Press, 1987.

———. *Ralph McGill: Reporter*. New York: Little, Brown, 1973.

———. *William Berry Hartsfield: Mayor of Atlanta*. Athens: University of Georgia Press, 1978.

McWilliams, Carey. *A Mask for Privilege: Anti-Semitism in America.* New York: Little, Brown, 1948.

Newton, Michael, and Judy Ann Newton. *KKK Encyclopedia.* New York: Garland, 1991.

Pearson, Drew. *Diaries: 1949–1959.* Edited by Tyler Abell. New York: Holt, Rinehart & Winston, 1974.

Pendergrast, Mark. *For God, Country and Coca-Cola: The Unauthorized History of the Great American Soft Drink and the Company That Makes It.* New York: Scribner's, 1993.

Protocols of the Learned Elders of Zion. Translated from the Russian of Nilus by Victor E. Marsden, reprinted from English edition of Briton Publishing Society, London, England; distributed by The Realm of Ohio, Lodi, Ohio.

Reimers, David M. *White Protestantism and the Negro.* New York: Oxford University Press, 1965.

Raphael, Marc Lee. *Profiles in American Judaism: The Reform, Conservative, Orthodox and Reconstructionist Traditions in Historical Perspective.* New York: Harper & Row, 1988.

Rosten, Leo. *The Joys of Yiddish.* New York: Pocket Books, 1970.

Sachar, Howard M. *A History of the Jews in America.* New York: Knopf, 1992.

Sibley, Celestine. *Dear Store: An Affectionate Portrait of Rich's.* Atlanta: Peachtree, 1990.

Spritzer, Lorraine Nelson. *The Belle of Ashby Street: Helen Douglas Mankin and Georgia Politics.* Athens: University of Georgia Press, 1982.

Stone, Clarence. *Regime Politics: Governing Atlanta, 1946–1988.* Manhattan: University Press of Kansas, 1989.

TANAKH: The Holy Scriptures. Philadelphia, Pa.: Jewish Publication Society, 1988.

Valentin, Hugo. *Antisemitism Historically and Critically Examined.* Translated from the Swedish by A. G. Chater. Books for Libraries Press, 1971.

Venable, James R. *Choose Your Side.* James R. Venable, 1971.

Warren, Robert Penn. *Segregation: The Inner Conflict in the South.* New York: Random House, 1956.

Watters, Pat. "How to Be a Hate Fanatic." *Atlanta Journal,* October 10, 1958, p. 1.

Wertheimer, Jack. "Antisemitism in the United States: A Historical Perspective," in *Antisemitism in America Today: Outspoken Experts Explode the Myth,* edited by Jerome R. Chanes. New York: Birch Lane Press, 1995.

Williams, Juan. *Eyes on the Prize: America's Civil Rights Years, 1954–1965.* New York: Penguin Books, 1987.

Wistrich, Robert S. *Antisemitism: The Longest Hatred.* New York: Schocken Books, 1991.

Woodward, C. Vann. *The Strange Career of Jim Crow.* New York: Oxford University Press, 1974.

INDEX

ACKNOWLEDGMENTS

I must thank first those citizens of the Atlanta of 1958 who opened their stores of memories to me, especially those closest to the events described here: Janice Rothschild Blumberg, George Michael Bright, Judge Jeptha Tanksley, and C. J. Strickland, and the late Judge Durwood T. Pye, Fauntleroy Moon Garland, and W. K. "Jack" Perry. And to the children of the participants—Bill Rothschild, Marcia Rothschild, James Jenkins, and especially Edward T. M. Garland—my thanks for allowing me to construct this version of your families' histories.

Thank you to my editors at Addison-Wesley, Nancy Miller and William Patrick, for editing with a kind touch and sense of humor, and to production editor Beth Burleigh Fuller and copy editor Sharon A. Sharp for wrestling the unwieldy thing into print. Thanks to Dan Franklin, of Jonathan Cape Publishers in Britain, for your enthusiasm.

My profound gratitude to those who read and commented on earlier drafts of the manuscript: Samuel Freedman, Irena Grudzińska-Gross, John Baskin, Mark Silk, Rabbi Mark Kunis, Jane Isay, Cliff Kuhn, Judith Alexander Augustine, Jill Harris Brown, Jane Axelrod, Andrea Servady, Howard Samuel, Rosalyn P. Greene; it changed for the better after contact with each of you.

Everlasting gratitude to David Black, my great reader, booster, and ally; my once and future agent.

Thank you to the Lyndhurst Foundation for your generous support during the writing of this book.

Thank you, again, to Marty Hagen of Word Wizards for

501

your skillful transcriptions and your keen ear for the way personality shines through sentence structure and word choice.

Thank you to Ellen Glaser Rafshoon for intelligent, prompt, and always excellent research, and to independent investigator David Berman for sharing your insight and findings. Thank you to Kathleen Bailey, research assistant and office assistant—you gracefully took on as many roles as I could throw at you and beautifully performed them all.

Thank you to Kathy Knox and Beverly Allen of the Special Collections Department of Robert W. Woodruff Library, Emory University; to Jim Baggett of the Department of Archives and Manuscripts, Birmingham Public Library; and to Sandy Berman of the Ida Pearle and Joseph Cuba Community Archives and Genealogy Center, Atlanta, for placing before us, time and again, precisely the artifact we'd hoped might still exist.

Special thanks to Ruth Manning, Kathryn Legan, Tema Silk, Estee Kunis, Debbie Schneider, Victoria Greenhood, Rise Morgenstern-Arkin, Dr. Andrea Casher, Donna Boxer, Phyllis Holmen, Sue Kaufman, Sheri Katz, the Bells, the Raikhels, Ruth Samuel, and Garry Greene.

Donny I've thanked at the beginning of the book by offering the whole thing to him, a partial trade-off for burnt meals, absent Sundays, and abrupt middle-of-the-night inquiries like "Is the crime complete when an overt act to effect the object of a conspiracy is done by at least one of the conspirators?"

Molly, Seth, Lee, and Lily Samuel, bright, sweet, gorgeous children: I'm finished. You can use the computer now.

Edward Zeltsen

About the Author

MELISSA FAY GREENE's first book, *Praying for Sheetrock*, was a finalist for the National Book Award as well as the National Book Critics Circle Award, and winner of the 1991 Robert F. Kennedy Book Award. Ms. Greene's second book, *The Temple Bombing*, is the 1996 winner of The Southern Book Critics Circle Award, a 1996 *New York Times* Notable Book, and a finalist for the National Book Award. The author is a native of Macon, Georgia, and lives in Atlanta with her husband and four children.